New Image
of Religious Film

New Image
of Religious Film

John R. May, editor

Sheed & Ward
Kansas City

Sheed & Ward™ is a service of The National Catholic Reporter Publishing Company.

Library of Congress Cataloguing-in-Publication Data

New image of religious film / [edited by] John R. May.
     p.   cm.
  Essays by participants of an international symposium held in 1993 at Villa Cavalletti in the Alban Hills south of Rome.
  Includes bibliographical references and index.
  ISBN: 1-55612-761-8 (alk. paper)
  1. Religious films--History and criticism--Congresses. 2. Motion pictures--Religious aspects--Congresses.   I. May, John R.
  PN1995.9.R4N48   1997
  791.43'682--dc21
                                 97-5897
                                   CIP

Published by: Sheed & Ward
               115 E. Armour Blvd.
               P.O. Box 419492
               Kansas City, MO 64141-6492

To order, call: (800) 333-7373

www.natcath.com/sheedward

Cover design by James F. Brisson.

Cover photograph of *The Mission* (Roland Joffé, 1986).

Contents

For
Don and Leona

"We are members one of another."
– Ephesians 4:25

Acknowledgments

This volume owes its remote debt of gratitude to the principal organizers of the 1993 Cavalletti Conference on "The New Image of Religious Film" – Robert A. White, director of the Gregorian University's Center for the Interdisciplinary Study of Social Communication, and Henk Hoekstra, president of the International Catholic Organization for Cinema and Audiovisuals (OCIC) – and to Marta Giorgi, whose gracious managerial skills kept the conference running smoothly.

As editor of the volume, facing at times seemingly insurmountable challenges to my computer literacy, I am profoundly grateful to everyone at Louisiana State University who patiently and regularly listened to my woes *du jour* and unfailingly provided me with the help or knowledge that I needed at the time to recover from the setback that I was experiencing – Susan Kohler, my former secretary who continues to serve the Department of English as Secretary to the Chair and Office Manager; Claudia Scott, Wanda Hughes, and Jennifer Whalen, all members of the department's secretarial staff; my colleague and friend Kevin Cope for help, both in person and over the phone, with early and persistent problems with formatting on the disks I'd received from my far-flung international contributors; Diane Lenoir of the College of Arts and Sciences Text Processing Center; and lastly, but no less importantly, members of the college's Cumputing Services, especially Terry Newgard and most recently Jason Chambers, who, at a time when despair had taken me by the hand, retrieved five of seven essays from the technological black hole that my tired editorial disk had released them into. Special thanks to two students of mine, both friends, who helped in different ways with the editorial process – Bob Robinson for translating with efficiency and precision one of the foreign language submissions, and Jeff Dupuis for assistance with another.

As a contributor to the volume, I am grateful to the students in my undergraduate classes on religious and film, and in a graduate seminar on contemporary film theory, who offered their reactions to my essay. To the other contributors to the volume, who met the various deadlines and who remained patient during the prolonged period in which family problems and personal commitments necessarily impeded my progress with the editorial work, beyond the extra time that my limited computer talents demanded, I say simply, "Grazie milione."

The film stills, thanks to Brother Alexis Gonzales, F.S.C., are reproduced courtesy of the Film Buffs Institute, Loyola University, New Orleans, with the exception of those for *The Seventh Seal* (Film Stills Archive, Museum of Modern Art); *A Short Film about Killing* and *The*

Sacrifice (ZOOM Film-dokumentation); *A Short Film about Love* (Zentralstelle Medien); *Jesus of Montreal* (Concorde-Film); *Blue and Thérèse* (OCIC/Brussels), and *Dues e o diabo na terra do sol* (OCIC/Latin America).

As always I marvel at the enduring support and love of my wife, Janet, especially when it seems as if I'm really wedded to the computer. Finally, I must elaborate on my special gratitude to my brother and sister-in-law, Donald and Leona May, to whom I have dedicated my work on this volume – for their fidelity, generosity, companionship and love through the years.

1

Introduction

In the early fall of 1993, an international symposium on the changes in the religious imagery in film and on interactions between religious film, theology, and religious culture was held at Villa Cavalletti in the Alban Hills south of Rome. Jointly sponsored by the Center for the Interdisciplinary Study of Social Communication (CICS) at the Pontifical Gregorian University, the International Catholic Organization for Cinema and Audiovisuals (OCIC), the Center for the Study of Communication and Culture (CSCC), and Italy's National Council on Research, the conference attracted over fifty participants, representing six continents and sixteen different countries, including several third-world nations. It was by far the most diverse group of critics, scholars, filmmakers, and students of film that had ever, in the knowledge of the participants, been brought together in one place. This collection of essays is the direct result of the dynamic exchange and provocative interaction of that conference. It reflects both the diversity and unanimity of opinion that the conference yielded.

Since the emphasis of the conference was on the *new* image of religious films, the essays in this volume – all by participants in the conference – concentrate on developments in the members' areas of expertise related to film, theology, and culture within the last fifteen to twenty years, not however without reference to the history that preceded this period. Readers will find here judicious reflection on a rich range of concerns: the language of religious film, film criticism and interpretation of religious film, theological reflection on the nature of the religious film, changes in religious consciousness and developments in the sociological analysis of film culture, the relation between film and mass media studies, and the religious film in church, society, and education.

There is general agreement that the worldwide distribution of films by directors such as Bergman, Fellini, Bresson, Buñuel, Ray, and Kurosawa in the late 1950s and early 1960s marked a turning point in the interpretation of religious film, from a fairly narrow evaluation of the morality of films or recognition of their explicit religious subject matter (e.g., biblical epics) to a consideration of the specifically religious or theological issues raised in films. Yet another significant change is noted in the last decade and a half, in which efforts have been made to discern the theological or religious implications of films that do not deal explicitly with religious issues, events, or even symbols. The acts of "seeing" and "hearing," fundamental to the film experience, are also essential to the experience of faith and therefore to the theological enterprise. Recurring mythological references in contemporary films are explored – cinematic analogues of both redemption and damnation, figures of "Christ" and "Satan."

Some contributors discern what could be called the new spirituality in cinema. Still others urge the (re)alignment of theology and anthropology as a basis for linking religion and film, culture and faith. Even the presentation of alienation, isolation, or fragmentation as reflections of human experience would seem to be a fertile ground for the initiation of theological discussion, if not of deepened religious consciousness. While not denying the presence of both direct and indirect religious references in films, some rightly insist that in the final analysis the perception of the viewer is the principal factor in discerning whether films have religious significance or not.

Since the conference engaged film scholars from diverse backgrounds (literature, art history, sociology, anthropology, philosophy, theology), it is inevitable that a major source of the collection's stimulation of new ideas is precisely through the clash of divergent perspectives, as in the recurring (often implied) debate over "high" and "low" culture. Although film theory has from its beginnings considered cinema as art, there is, once again, strong sentiment here for not relegating "entertainment" films to a level unworthy of theological consideration, as if only so-called high film art deserved the attention of church and critics. Moreover, theologians' general "discomfort" with films, even distrust of them, is acknowledged and regretted, though explanations for the phenomenon may be hard to come by – except perhaps as a reflection of earlier ecclesiastical disputes over the seductive potential of images, or as a recurring but fortunately minority tendency these days to consider "popular" culture as an unworthy ally in the process of evangelization.

New Image of Religious Film is divided into six sections, roughly conforming to the areas of dialogue at the Cavalletti Conference. Part 1, entitled "Developments in Criticism and Interpretation," sets the stage for the rest of the volume first by sketching a broad history of the interaction of film and theory and then by surveying and classifying the principal English-language works on the relationship between religion and film. In "Approaches to Film Criticism," Ambros Eichenberger takes us through a century of theoretical and critical approaches to the appreciation of film, including his appraisal of the current status of the engagement of religion and film, which sets the stage for his insightful recommendations for a more fruitful dialogue between theology and cinema. My essay, "Contemporary Theories Regarding the Interpretation of Religious Film," begins with a distinction that continues as a focus of debate throughout the volume; namely, whether one ought not to speak of the "religious interpretation of film" rather than of "religious film" as such. It also delineates what I perceive to be the five stages in the developing dialogue about the religious dimension of film (in the English-speaking world, at any rate), all of which nonetheless currently coexist – religious discrimination, visibility, dialogue, humanism, and aesthetics.

Part 2 focuses on "The Changing Language of Religious Film," offering both an overview of the subject as well as two essays on the treatment of specific religious subjects – changes in the representation of the image of Jesus on our screens and the cinema's more recent approaches to the treatment of the demon or, generally speaking, of the problem of evil. As Peter Hasenberg's subtitle to "The 'Religious' in Film" announces, he takes us from Nicholas Ray's *King of Kings* (1960) to Terry Gilliam's *The Fisher King* (1991), showing in succession how traditional religious themes have been adapted to changing audiences (and thus to changing cultural demands), how religious themes have been integrated into more popular genres, and, finally, how aesthetically innovative directors have devised new ways of dealing with religious ideas. Peter Malone in "Jesus on Our Screens," making an important distinction between Jesus-figures (representations of the historical Jesus) and the traditional Christ-figure borrowed from literature (fictional characters resembling Jesus), emphasizes recent developments in the cinematic presentations of Jesus, ranging from variations on the gospel narratives to other more limited appeals to Jesus – satiric and verbal appeals, similarities to marginalized characters, and uses of the crucifix, even in horror films. In "The Problem of Evil in Contemporary Film," Reinhold Zwick offers a challenging analysis of the representation of *malum morale* in recent cinema – from the predictable dualism of highly popular genres, through more sophisticated portrayals of evil *in* the human soul, to presentations of conversion and possible rebirth. Zwick, reasonably enough, demonstrates a decided preference for those more subtle films that yield their insights into the universal human problem, only after repeated viewings.

In Part 3, there are two essays on "Changes in Religious Consciousness" stimulated by film as the distinctive art of the twentieth century. Sylvain De Bleeckere's "The Religious Dimension of Cinematic Consciousness in Postmodern Culture" makes a provocative case for the postmodern sensibility of film as a welcome rupture with modernism's materialism, if not atheism, as exemplified by Eisenstein's early role in the development of a film theory that supported Soviet Communism's studied use of the medium in the service of worldwide revolution. Building on the biographical, apocalyptic, and iconophile bases of the postmodern union of film and religion, he moves persuasively from the relationship between "light" and the Creator in Jewish-Christian scriptures (especially Genesis 1) to the centrality of light for directorial creativity and the postmodern cinematic religious experience. In the essay entitled "From Eve to the Virgin and Back Again: The Image of Woman in Contemporary (Religious) Film," Diane Apostolos-Cappadona builds her demonstration of our contemporary consciousness of "gender" in film art, first, on Mircea Eliade's concept of the "sacred" (the theoretical basis for her placing the word *re-*

ligious in parentheses) and, then, on the best in feminist scholarship in art, theology, and film studies. Crucial to her proposal of a feminist religious aesthetic as well as a methodology for a (centrist) feminist religious reading of contemporary films is a heightened awareness of the power of images as culture's primary indicators of gender identification and theological values.

Although we would hope that theologians as well as film critics with a religious sensibility would find all of the essays in this volume illuminating and provocative, Part 4, "Theological Reflection on Religious Film," – will most obviously attract the attention of theologians and, we hope, challenge their understanding of the theological significance of film. As the very subtitle of the essay "Toward a Theological Interpretation and Reading of Film: Incarnation of the Word of God – Relation, Image, Word" suggests, Joseph Marty grounds his quest solidly in the mystery of the incarnation, which establishes through faith a relationship between the seen and the unseen. Films that open us up to mystery, however dimly, are liberating like the word (Word) of God; indeed, as Marty explains on his way to constructing his theology of film, image and word comprise both the aesthetics of film and the dynamics of revelation and the incarnation.

Michael Paul Gallagher in "Theology, Discernment and Cinema," emphasizing the effect that film-viewing has on the audience, suggests the use of St. Ignatius Loyola's rules for spiritual discernment as a specific way of assessing the long-term effect on the viewer of the "anonymous religiousness" of contemporary cinema. Building on Balthasar, Rahner and Lonergan, Gallagher implies that theologians especially should be familiar with film's capacity to evoke wonder as an apt tool of pre-evangelization. Working from her experiences in film education, Marjeet Verbeek provides in "Too Beautiful to Be Untrue: Toward a Theology of Film Aesthetics" an assessment of contemporary culture's emphasis on the aesthetic that blurs the distinction between high and low art – a situation that theologians can ill afford to disregard. Her proposal for a new harmony between theology and art seeks once again to link the classic triad of *verum, bonum* and *pulchrum*. Insofar as aesthetics integrates style and substance, film art is never separated from ethical appreciation. Thus, Verbeeck insists, films are capable of liberating the human spirit and possibly of evoking a viewer's faith in the beauty of creation.

Part 5 is concerned, as its title indicates, with "Developments in Mass Media Studies." Leaning more toward the practical than toward the theoretical side of the issue of film's interrelationship with religion, it offers essays on the place of film in religious education, on its role in the individual's religious growth, and finally on a methodology for discovering the religious worldview of a film. With his considerable experience in the field of film education, Henk Hoekstra in "Film Education in a Christian Perspective: Some Contemporary Approaches" provides us with an overview of the possibilities for designing a Christian approach to film education that capitalizes on the medium's language for expressing and experiencing the central phenomena of the spiritual life. For Hoekstra, the ideal Christian film educational program would be goal-oriented, systematic, and "dialogical," that is, grounded firmly in our ability to share with one another as we dialogue with the films in question.

Paralleling Michael Paul Gallagher's insights into the potential effect of films on their viewers' growth in spiritual awareness, Robert A. White in "The Role of Film in Personal Religious Growth" presents a thorough overview of recent approaches in mass media studies, settling on the effect of social context on our reception of film as a source of symbols for integrating our life experience and thus for spiritual growth. Whereas Gallagher bases his insights on rules of discernment from spiritual theology, White appeals to the sociopsychological dynamics of the media, and film in particular, as an essential dimension of popular culture in constructing a model for media involvement in our spiritual development.

"A Methodology for Finding the Filmmaker's *Weltanschauung* in Religious Film" is in a sense at the heart of this whole endeavor, for if it is universally assumed here that films can be "read" for their religious implications – and it is – Johan Hahn's essay confidently provides us with a methodology for interpreting films, sensitive to the subjective dimension of our perception of audio visual media. Hahn's outline of the appropriate dramatological, iconological, symbolic, narratological, and mythic modules that make up his phenomenological approach to film interpretation puts the process on a more scientific basis, yielding results that can be tested and discussed, ideally becoming the basis for some general agreement about the filmmaker's worldview. Although here as elsewhere in this volume our main concern was with developments related to film, it will be clear that each of these essays has broad implications for the whole area of the audiovisual media, and thus for television as well as film.

Finally, in Part 6, the collection focuses on three third-world cinemas – one national, two continental – and the recent developments there in the treatment of religion in film – India, Latin America, and Africa. In "India's Cinema: Home and World, the Foci of Religion," Ray Kancharla traces the evolution in representations *of* the family *for* the family – the social unit traditionally at the heart of Indian culture and society – within the context of both "popular" cinema and the so-called New Wave, acknowledging justifiably the centrality of Satyajit Ray's cinematic presentation of the tension between "home and world" for an understanding of shifting religious values in India. With more than a quarter of a century of experience as a film critic on Brazilian Catholic and international ecumenical juries, José Tavares de Barros in "The Religious Film in Latin America" observes that the treatment of religion in the best Latin American feature films tends normally to be implicit, thus highlighting universal human values, even though there continue to be many fine documentary films that treat directly issues affecting church and society, including the progressive tendencies of the Latin American church. Not surprisingly, Tavares de Barros notes, the quincentennial "celebration" of America's discovery resulted in a number of sharp exposés of the church's shameful involvement with the invading armies, and the sad, enduring loss of native autonomy.

Finally, François Vokouma's "Recent Developments in the Religious Film in Africa" follows the tentative steps in the past quarter century toward the independence of African filmmakers, paralleling the emergence of African nations from the colonial domination of the past, while admitting with regret that African cinema is still largely dependent upon foreign financing and technical assistance. Through his involvement with the Panafrican Festival of Film and Television of Ouagadougou (FESPACO), Vokouma provides an insider's view of the emerging indigenous cinema's often satirical view of the efficacy of religious rites and the hypocrisy of religious personalities, including those of native religions as well as of the colonizing faiths – Christianity and Islam.

In addition to these sixteen original essays by a richly divergent group of international commentators, *New Image of Religious Film* includes an international bibliography of works related to the subject of religion and film, as well as an exhaustive index of all the films open to a religious interpretation appealed to by the contributors. References to films in each essay will normally, on first mention, include the name of the director and the date of release. Foreign language films will be followed in parentheses by the title of the English release, when it is available. Where the English title of a foreign film is already better known internationally (as is the case, for example, with most of Ingmar Bergman's films), it alone will usually be referred to.

It should be clear from the start that none of these essays is imagined to be the final word on its subject. In fact, as I suggested above, they were both the stimulants of discussion and the results of it, inasmuch as they were presented in draft form at the conference and then revised afterwards. Let the discussion continue.

John R. May
Louisiana State University

Part 1

Developments in Criticism and Interpretation

1

Approaches to Film Criticism

Ambros Eichenberger

Generally speaking, it seems to be agreed that little thought and knowledge is required in order to know what is happening in a film or to make a judgment about whether the movie is worth seeing or not. Thus, everyone who buys a ticket is a potential critic, gifted with an immediate sense of a film's quality. That is why, for most viewers, film criticism is simply the expression of satisfaction or dissatisfaction with a current movie: "I liked it!" or "I didn't like it!" Popular magazines more often embrace this rather elementary kind of "criticism" and perception with their simplistic systems of ratings based on popularity.

I. Film Criticism and Film Reviewing

Serious filmgoers, who consider films something more than mere escapist entertainment for mass audiences, are understandably asking for more! A professional critic, more demanding than even the serious viewer of films, finds the movie experience to be as important and meaningful as literature, painting, dance and other more classical forms of art. Thus, he strives to go beyond mere viewing by initiating a process of reflection and inquiry that builds upon the basic emotions everyone experiences when seeing a film. The result of such a reflective discourse about films is usually to produce greater meaning, or even a new reading that is valuable not only to the critic's audience, but also, ultimately, to the culture at large.

II. Historical Approaches

Film reviewing and, later, film criticism became formalized after the turn of the century. The year 1913, in fact, seems to have been a decisive one for recognizing film as a factor of culture in serious publications, and not just as a matter of entertainment for the moviegoing market. In the German-speaking world, the first truly analytical film review appeared on April 18, 1913 in the *Neue Zürcher Zeitung*. It was written by Willi Bierbaum about

3

the Italian film *Quo vadis?* by Enrico Guazzoni. Eight days later a serious review of the same film was published by Kurt Pinthus in the *Leipziger Tagblatt*, which can be considered a "milestone" in the recognition of cinema as an element of culture genuinely characteristic of the twentieth century.

The first article about film in English was published in *The New York Times* in 1896, but it was nothing more than a report about a cinematographic exhibition. The real impetus to film criticism as a professional activity in the United States came almost twenty years later, in 1915, when D. W. Griffith's *Birth of a Nation* was attracting attention in intellectual as well as popular circles. A second major impetus was registered many years later, in the 1950s and early 1960s, when the first films of Ingmar Bergman (*The Seventh Seal*, 1956), Federico Fellini (*La Strada*, 1954) and the French New Wave appeared. These foreign films finally came to be considered in the United States as a mirror of trends in modern society and as an acceptable part of intellectual life that could not be ignored in contemporary discourse.

III. The Influence of Film Criticism

Questions about the influence of film criticism in the cultural life of a society produce controversial answers. Some are convinced that film critics have played, or are still playing, an important part. This observation is evident, for example, regarding the influence and the achievements of the *Cahiers du cinéma* group in France and by the work of its most famous critic, André Bazin. *Cahiers* was an enterprise that produced not only excellent film critics but also famous filmmakers such as François Truffaut.

A similar statement can also be made about the influence of German film criticism on the development of the new German film. In fact, it is no exaggeration to say that there would be no new German cinema with its worldwide recognition without the collaborative presence of the German film critic.

IV. The Formalist and the Realist "Schools"

The variety of critical approaches to cinema is connected, on a deeper level, with different conceptions of what cinema is or should be. Two "schools" could be identified from the very beginning – one called formalist, the other realist. The formalist position emphasized the ability of the cinema to restructure normal space and time, and to create through its formal techniques, such as editing and composition, a new, artificial locus of emotions, dreams, fantasies, and so forth. Famous directors like Sergei Eisenstein and Alexander Pudovkin stressed the fact that the medium was made to "manipulate" reality and to transform it into another poetic, political, fictional and "fantastic" universe.

In opposition to this formalist position, the realist school with its well-known spokesman Siegfried Kracauer considered film merely as a "window to reality." That does not mean that he favored only documentary films, but rather that he found certain subjects, such as costume dramas, less acceptable because they are too far away from the psychological experience of the spectator. This realist discourse was influenced by the wave of neorealist films after World War II, which came mainly from Italy as a new genre with themes and stories taken from street life, shot on location, and acted by nonprofessionals, in the midst of their suffering and joy.

V. A Wide Range of Theories

With the growth of cinema's apparatus and its transition to sound, color, larger screens, greater audiences and a more articulated presence in society, film criticism too became more complex, developing other positions and perspectives beyond formalism and realism. First of all, the need for theory was more consciously acknowledged, as well as the need to admit that some kind of theory underlies any critical response to the movies – even when the critic is not aware of it or pretends to have no theoretical or ideological assumptions at all.

The Seventh Seal, Ingmar Bergman, 1956

In this rich and complex context, well-known studies have sought to analyze more systematically the links between cinema, ideology and film criticism, such as Bill Nichols's recent work *Ideology and the Image*.[1] The editorial policy of *Cahiers du cinéma*, established after the death of André Bazin, is in fact another, though older, example. Both of these theoretical systems were inspired by Marxism, which was quite vigorous at that time.

VI. Contemporary Approaches

In addition to these Marxist-inspired ideologies, one can complete the list of more contemporary film theories with appeals to political, social, philosophical, historical, and even – sometimes – religious perspectives on the nature of film as art. Often these different approaches are related to a specific historical period, favoring a set of ideologies or disciplines that are "in" at the time. One can observe that a new social, political or spiritual movement usually initiates a new cultural discourse with specific interests – new methods, new ways of analysis and inquiry, and even a new language. A few decades ago, the influence of psychoanalysis was quite strong in film criticism. Later on, structuralism came into full flower. Today one often has to subscribe to a postmodernist philosophy and "jargon" in order to be taken seriously. In addition to these contemporary approaches, the rise of feminism ushered in a new era of interest in analyzing the particular ways women are portrayed in all kinds of moving images.

The views of cinema expressed through these different theories are conflicting and often controversial. While some of them emphasize the creative role of an individual artist, others pretend that every artist is so heavily determined – and sometimes so unconsciously – by the codes and the rules of a given society that the "culture" and not the artist himself creates the film and the film's language. In this regard, the French philosopher Christian Metz in *Film Language* offers instructive insights.[2]

1. The Humanist Approach

The credo of a humanist film critic is characterized by a few clear principles. His most fundamental is the conviction that films are not only a product of an industry, produced under financial pressure and sold worldwide with vast advertisement campaigns (as the Hollywood system did in the early 1990s with Steven Spielberg's *Jurassic Park*), but also, like other forms of art, expressions of a deliberate human activity by an individual artist, identifiable as Chaplin, Hitchcock, Tarkovsky, or Rohmer (just as Shakespeare, Dickens, and Tolstoy are identifiable for their plays and novels).

Value orientation is a second characteristic of the humanist's approach. He looks at films not only or merely as a source of entertainment or escapism, but also as a representation of universal human values, of the truths of human experience, of insights that will help us to understand better the complexity of human life and human society. With such criteria in mind, the critic tries to identify from the mass of ordinary films the exceptional ones that fit this process of dealing with the human condition, suggesting something to the spectator of what it means to be human.

To stress value and content in the humanistic approach to film criticism does not mean that aesthetic preoccupations can be neglected. The critic must also consider excellence in the development of aesthetic elements insofar as content and form work together to produce meaning and relevance. Aesthetic failures also affect the moral and spiritual qualities of a film. There will be no morally good films without accurate casting, pertinent camera angles, a soundtrack appropriately amplifying or minimizing the impact of the images and the dialogue, and so forth.

Humanist criticism can be applied to all genres of film, including westerns, melodramas, even horror films or slapstick comedies. Generally speaking, the humanist approach not only concentrates on the "text" and on the structure of a film, but also on its "context." Thus, film analysis is completed by extrafilmic considerations, which explains why this approach sometimes is blamed for being too general or for lacking analytical rigor.

Looking at the context of a film from a humanistic point of view also includes the examination of the relationship between the film, the audience and the society. More than critics with other orientations, the humanist is interested in knowing about the social or psychological effects movies have on the outside world. Such an approach tends toward being very "global," leaving more specific aspects of films unexplored. As a result, other complementary theories of film criticism arose involving their own distinctive discourses. Among these others, we will focus on those that are relevant to the investigation of the religious and theological dimensions of cinema.

2. The Auteurist Approach

The auteurist approach is based upon a theory of criticism developed by the editors of *Cahiers du cinéma*, most probably as a European critical reaction to the North American way of filmmaking that is dominated more by the producer than by the director or the scriptwriter. *Auteur* criticism is interested both in the individual films of a director as well as in all the films he has made, in order to determine whether a consistent body of artistic excellence, of personal visions, themes and motifs has been achieved. Describing and evaluating the work of an artist in terms of uniqueness, consistency of style, biography, and so forth can be extremely useful. This is especially so if the "author" is totally responsible for the films he has made, as happened with such outstanding film personalities as Griffith, Eisenstein, Murnau, and Stroheim in the past and with Tarkovsky, Bresson, Rohmer, Kurosawa, Kieslowski, and Wenders more recently. The analysis of formal cinematographic elements such as composition, camera movement, lighting, editing and the like in the major films of "one" director cannot be overlooked (if of course the analysis is not to be limited to technical aspects) when probing deeper into the fields of meaning and significance.

3. Social Science Film Criticism

The areas of concern in what has been called "social science criticism" are broad. This approach sees films primarily in their social and psychological contexts, inasmuch as film production and moviegoing, unlike other more private forms of art, have always been social phenomena, involving a large number of people at the stages of both production and consumption. Thus, the critics of this "school" are interested, more than others, in studying the effects of films on the viewers' behavior, emotions and attitudes. The critics want to know if and how a movie is affecting the conscious or the unconscious dimension of an individual moviegoer or of a collective audience.

Social science critics are also interested in knowing how far films and filmmakers are determined by the sociocultural ground they are rooted in. Films therefore are scrutinized for evidence of the collective dreams and myths of a society as well as its conscious or unconscious desires that they share or reveal. Movies are considered a mirror of the psyche of a particular society, for example, of China, Africa, or Indonesia.

The attempt at such a sociopsychological analysis is not new. The famous German critic Siegfried Kracauer tried in the late 1940s to find an explanation for Hitler's rise to power through his study of German films, *From Caligari to Hitler*,[3] because he was convinced that these films reveal elements of the psyche of his people. At the same time, Parker Tyler in *Magic and Myth of the Movies* followed a similar path.[4]

VII. A Theological Approach?

1. The Need for a Theory

Compared with this wide range of different approaches to film criticism, interpretations from a religious or theological point of view are still relatively exceptional. Some interesting and promising attempts have been made – for example, by John R. May and Michael Bird in *Religion in Film*.[5] More recently groups of Students at Theological faculties in Germany, Holland and Switzerland have examined theology, spirituality and film in collaboration with OCIC and have published (in German) the multivolume series *Hinter den Augen ein eigenes Bild*.[6]

Despite such honorable efforts, there is still no elaborated "theory" of a theological or religious approach to film interpretation as it has been attempted, if not achieved, for other disciplines. The gap between theological considerations, including pastoral ones, and contemporary art, culture and film is still formidable, although one can observe a growing awareness of the fact that both "worlds," however differently they function, can learn substantially from one another. Theological and spiritual traditions have something to offer the film world insofar as they are concerned with the quest for deeper meaning, truth, and wisdom about human life, history and destiny. On the other hand, there is no doubt that many films, past and present, can provide a stimulus and a challenge to theological disciplines and to theologians to learn more about "the human journey" and the individual or collective struggle for survival – phenomena that are mirrored in so many films.

2. The Case for a More Relevant Theology

For the time being, most film professionals and cultural devotees seem to consider theology or even Christianity as being quite removed from the major issues and concerns film directors are interested in – a discipline surviving somehow in an academic ghetto, striving still for control but losing it more and more. They project little hope for a dialogue apart from contributions concerning the theology of liberation in Latin America, which is considered by many intellectuals, filmmakers included, as useful and prophetic.

Regarding film criticism in particular, the negative image of theology as being irrelevant or functioning as an instrument of censorship and control instead of interpretation and "liberation" has been reinforced by some well-known, questionable past experiences with certain organs of the churches. Great filmmakers like Luis Buñuel have suffered from the "clerical" mentality that is ready to control and to condemn rather than to analyze, to engage, and to understand.

However, since the promulgation of the documents from Vatican Council II, which urged a much more positive and constructive approach to modern culture, we do not have to go back for guidance to the authoritative and even arrogant procedures of the past. This would seem to apply as well to the principles expressed by Pope Pius XI in his 1936 encyclical letter on film, *Vigilanti Cura*, because they take a one-sided view of cinema as a *"spectacle nuisible,"* a position that is more intelligible under the circumstances of those days.

In order to become more relevant and better prepared to interpret films and to follow the developments in the film industry, theology will have to rethink and reformulate some of its functions and positions (*"redeployer la théologie"*), with special attention to those elements, concerns, contents, perspectives, and questions implicit in the film stories and documentaries we see on screen. Among the elements that need to be reconsidered and reformulated in order to enrich the dialogue between theology and culture, I will first mention three rather general ones and then proceed to three other more specific, content-related considerations.

VIII. Attempts at a Renewal: General Conditions

The three general conditions for a theological renewal in the field of film criticism are expressed in an exhortative form:

> First, bring theology closer to anthropology! Learn the anthropological lesson beside the theological one!

> Second, develop a more systematic theology of the "image," specifically in the Western theological tradition!

> Third, become more sensitive in (and competent at) identifying possible religious dimensions in cinema! (This exhortation is directed to both film critic and film viewer.)

1. The Anthropological Lesson, or "a Theology from Below"

The most important and fundamental principle, which has to be considered as the heart of a Christian-oriented film-critical activity, is the need to learn the anthropological lesson. From a Christian point of view, the concept of anthropology is necessarily associated with the mystery of incarnation. God's coming into this world adds a new quality to the science and the destiny of human beings, distinguishable from what we called earlier the "humanist approach." Wolfram Pannenberg, a well-known German theologian, speaks *"von Anthropologie in theologischer Perspektive,"* an expression that is obviously very useful for our purpose and can be characterized simply as *"Christian* humanism."

This concept affirms a faith in God's presence in the world, not excluding the modern world, and in the midst of his creation. It must be a stimulus to the search for God and his Spirit, not so much in an abstract "heaven," but more concretely in events and films that deal with the secrets of human history and the human heart, even when the human heart feels that it is living in a godless, secularized society. The admonition to learn the anthropological lesson in addition to the theological one must lead to a new consideration of the link between the sacred and the secular, useful in order to analyze and perhaps to influence modernity and modern culture.

Numerous film productions clearly illustrate that a search for meaning along the lines of an *Anthropologie in theologischer Perspektive* is meeting a current need of society. Wim Wenders's *In weiter Ferne, so nah (Far Away, So Close,* 1993) can be cited as an example, as well as Kieslowski's *Blue* (1993), the first part of his *Three Colors* trilogy. This was aptly noted by the critic who wrote that *"le film représente la réussite d'un incroyable voyage intérieur qui va ramener Julie, la protagoniste, du silence à la musique, de la solitude au partage, de la mort à la vie."*[7]

2. The Need for a Theology of the Image

A second element concerns the need for a more systematic development and promotion of a visual culture in theology – in addition to the work that has already been done regarding a theology of the word. The vehemence of past arguments concerning "images" in the Jewish, Islamic and Christian traditions is an indication that the phenomenon is not a peripheral, but rather a central one. Hence, it needs greater attention than has usually been invested in it, at least in our western theologies and churches.

Film criticism that is sensitive to this dimension will take into account more seriously and more carefully the "aesthetic" structure and qualities of a movie, in addition to the attention customarily given to the content and the story of films in religious educational circles. Myths, symbols, metaphors, parables and other relevant aspects of the visual and literary arts have to be rediscovered and reevaluated insofar as they may reveal hidden pictures and "messages" about man and his search for God. Many painters from the past, like Caspar David Friederich and William Turner, tried to capture the "sublime" (*das Erhabene*) through the use of light in their landscape painting. Many filmmakers today try something similar in the design of their cinematic *mise en scène* and in the structure of their narrative. This is obviously the case with metaphors expressing the search for the father (*Vatersuche*) in the films, for example, of Pavel Lungin, Theodoros Angelopoulos, Sergei Bodrow and Fernando Solanas, or in the surprisingly frequent references to angels, both visible and invis-

Blue, Krzysztof Kieslowski, 1992

ible, in recent films by Wim Wenders and Jane Campion. Such works are full of interesting theological implications, so much so that they cannot be understood in depth without attention to this dimension.

Aesthetic values have always been considered a possible revelation of God's mystery in the world, from the great Russian writer Fëdor Dostoevski to contemporary authors like the German philosopher George Steiner, who in his book *Real Presences* insists that "everything that we recognize as great in literature, music and art has been inspired by religion and has religious significance."[8] That is surely true also of the twentieth century's distinctive art – the cinema – wherever and whenever it can be identified as art and not simply as a commercial product, and thus worthy of being interpreted and evaluated from a theological point of view.

3. The Subjective Factor of Perception

Finally, discerning religious or theological dimensions in works of cinematic art depends to a great extent on the personal interest of the critic and the spectator. The subjective factor cannot be neglected inasmuch as film is aimed ultimately at the heart and the mind of the viewer himself. The dispositions, expectations, and (often selective) perceptions of the viewer seem to be so important that French philosophers and historians of art have even claimed that *"ce sont les regards qui font les tableaux."*

The lack of interest in religious matters experienced by many critics, both the fear of not being competent theologically as well as the growing ignorance in such concerns, recently affected their reception of Kieslowski's *Decalogue* (1988-89), not only the quality of their interpretations of it, but also their very willingness to review it. Yet, if the antennae of critical perception were wide open to a theologically-oriented anthropology, critical awareness of possible religious significance would be extended also to secular films in trying to find implicit evangelical (as well as other religious and human) values.

In other words, this approach is not restricted to a category of films that explicitly articulate religious traditions, persons or institutions, like the so-called "Jesus films," but to many other genres as well. From a theological or a religious approach to film and film criticism, efforts can and must be made to discover and to explicate the mysterious presence of God and of his Spirit also in works that depict daily life situations or everyday life stories (*Lebensgeschichten*) as we find them, especially in the tradition of neorealism, which has continued into the present.

Religious and Christian-inspired film criticism will deepen our "social" or "political" experiences related to the Gospel message about the presence of Christ in the poor and the suffering. Such a perspective can sometimes change the whole "paradigm" for the interpretation of a film. Because our religious imagination and our understanding of "holy images" are too restricted, God and his Spirit may actually be present where we assume their total absence.

IX. Special "Content" Conditions

1. The Search for Identity

The search for an identity, as well as the loss of it, seems to be a major concern of the so-called postmodern societies in the West. The topic has been heavily explored in the field of philosophy by Martin Heidegger and Theodor W. Adorno, in the field of literature with considerable depth in the works of the famous Austrian writer Robert Musil and, last but not least, in the field of cinema by a significant number of directors from different countries.

If the filmmakers are from developing countries, the search for national, regional, ethnic or cultural identities is predominant, as illustrated by productions from Latin America, Africa and Asia. The main trend in the new Chinese cinema from the so-called "fifth generation," for example, is to expose the search for a new identity, relating problems between individuals and groups to conflicts between ancient Confucian culture and modern transformations in society. Similar trends can be observed in post-communist Russia, where Marlen Chuziew, in his outstanding autobiographical film *Infinitas* (1993), searches for a new personal identity and for the pre-communist values of his country and his culture.

A common denominator related to identity in western movies can be found in the discovery of the "subject." In a postmodern approach, the subject is open to the realization of many different possibilities, since it is not yet what it is or can be! Very often these possibilities of another life and another identity are the result of a (painful) break with social and religious conventions, with other constraints. They can be imposed also by the working conditions in an industrialized and rationalized society, as the French director André Techiné shows in his film *Ma Saison préférée* (1993), where two professionally successful people pay for their success with alienation from their inner selves and from deeper human and family values. A similar process related to efforts at starting a new life is presented in another French film, *Un Coeur en hiver* by Claude Sautet, and in an excellent Turkish movie, *Le Visage secret* by Ömer Kavur.

The theological implications of such quests for new and deeper meanings to life have to be reformulated and reanimated, with reference of course to the fact that, according to our Jewish-Christian traditions, man is created in the "image of God" (*"ad imaginem Dei"*) with all the potential included in such a definition. The aging French actor Alain Cuny, who became a director in 1991 adapting Paul Claudel's *L'Annonce faite à Marie* to film (*The Annunciation of Mary*) and died in May 1994, was following this line of reflection, reminding us in a discreet way that we human beings are not yet what we are called to be, although we can discover *les traces* of a future fulfillment that is the goal of our life.

2. A Need for Redemption?

A growing number of films portray a universe of human sufferings from various points of view, including the cynical and purely commercial. These films are presenting another challenge to a theological approach to contemporary cinema because the question of suffering and whether it can be meaningful is still a major concern of Christian faith and continues to be addressed in a special theological discipline called soteriology.

In terms of setting, plot, dialogue, style, attitudes, messages, and so forth, this new category of *Katastrophenfilme* offers, as already mentioned, a variety of insights and situations. Many of these films focus on urban hells, where social unrest, violence, drugs, prostitution, and decadence are dominating elements. In his 1993 film *Short Cuts*, Robert Altman gives a long and almost hopeless picture of urban life in Los Angeles: a paradigm of a godless world without solidarity, communication, love or hope.

But some films contain elements and proposals, which may be hidden or outspoken, to transform such violence and cruelty into a more human universe. Feeling the danger of a possible nuclear catastrophe, Andrei Tarkovsky proposed in his last film *Offret* (*The Sacrifice*, 1986) to come back to the classical concept of "sacrifice" as a contribution to a possible salvation and liberation. At the end of *Blue*, Kieslowski makes a pointed reference to the concept of love as it is presented by Saint Paul in his letter to the Corinthians, in order to suggest a way out for humankind. The American film *City of Hope* (1991), directed by John Sayles, ends with the cry, "We need help, we need help." It is articulated by somebody who looks like a clown, perceiving more than all the others the critical situation we are living in.

Even if the world is presented and reflected as godless in many products of modern art, a committed theologian will have to continue the quest for meaning, keeping in mind that theology is more than a teaching to nice, harmless children in Sunday school, knowing and feeling that very often the fundamental doubts and self-questionings about human lives, destinies, stories and histories cannot find easy answers. Thus, movies with no apparent moral or theological impact can also be "religious," as is suggested by what has been characterized in the past as *theologia negativa*.

3. The "Sacramental" Universe

A third "content topic," that would be potentially stimulating for a film criticism sensitive to religion and theology (especially from a Catholic or Orthodox point of view) could be called "sacramental" or holistic. This multidimensional concept of reality is related to the growing need in our fragmented societies to rediscover life as a whole (*Ganzheit*). A holistic approach is eager to bring into focus lost correlations between the outer and the inner worlds, the visible and the invisible, the immanent and the transcendent, the rational and the mystical, the secular and the sacred, *le palpa-*

ble et l'impalpable. The aesthetic language and style used in order to suggest such correlations is a meditative or contemplative one, employing elements taken from nature – a procedure that was familiar, for example, to Andrei Tarkovsky. This is true not only of his films but also of his writings about the philosophy of the image, inasmuch as he considered nature itself as an "icon," according to his own native Orthodox tradition.

Today a number of works belonging to this holistic category of films are coming from eastern-European countries and Asia, where human existence is not yet as fragmented and as rationalized as it is in the western world. The South Korean film *Why Bodhi Dharma Left for the Orient* (1989) by Yong-Kung Bae, based on Zen-Buddhist elements, is an especially apposite instance of this type of film. Recent films from China, like *Horse Thief* (1986) by Tian Zhuangzhuang or *Life on a String* (1991) by Chen Kaige, can also be mentioned in this context, because they present an atmosphere of harmony, not only between man and nature, but also between life and death, heaven and earth.

It must be noted that such holistic visions are also achieved by some western directors. The established German *auteur* Wim Wenders, for example, is trying to familiarize modern minds with angels, and the American Robert Redford has been successful in his beautiful film *A River Runs through It* (1992) in evoking the world of the sublime and the ineffable, reaching moments of unexpected grace by using fishermen, a river, trees and green landscapes as symbols. Even a wild film like Cyril Collard's *Les nuits fauves* (*Savage Nights*, 1993), exploring an AIDS victim's incredible will to live despite self-destructive urges occasioned by the disease, can be considered as holistic, because the statement made by the protagonist at the end of the film expresses the hope that there may be a final harmony, a final peace, and a final reconciliation between life and death, the creator and his creation, time and eternity – another cinematic passage with theological implications!

A religiously-oriented critic is invited to discover, even to "hunt" for, similar symbols and metaphors, not only the conventional but the nonconventional as well. Such an effort demands greater-than-average attention to the visual structure of a film, particularly in church-related circles, which tend to concentrate heavily on the content and the morality of a movie. These new or "New Age" religious images, which do not necessarily follow a traditional Christian iconography, demand appropriate reflections about the neglected cosmic dimensions emerging from the mystery of the incarnation. Myths, archetypes, even magic elements and "basic instincts" need to be integrated into such a holistic interpretive approach that depends so much on intellectual discipline, in order to reach, if possible, deeper zones of the human soul, connecting and unifying its conscious and unconscious dimensions, its rational and mystical urges.

Endnotes

1. Bill Nichols, *Ideology and the Image: Social Representation in the Cinema and Other Media* (Bloomington: Indiana University Press, 1981).

2. Christian Metz, *Film Language: A Semiotics of the Cinema* (New York: Oxford University Press, 1974).

3. Siegfried Kracauer, *From Caligari to Hitler* (Princeton: Princeton University Press, 1947).

4. Parker Tyler, *Magic and Myth of the Movies* (New York: Holt & Co., 1947).

5. John R. May and Michael Bird, *Religion in Film* (Knoxville: University of Tennessee Press, 1982).

6. Michael Kuhn, Johan G. Hahn and Henk H. Hoekstra, eds., *Hinter den Augen ein eigenes Bild* (Zurich: Benziger, 1991).

7. *Le Monde* (9 September 1993).

8. George Steiner, *Real Presences* (London/Boston: Faber, 1989).

2

Contemporary Theories Regarding the Interpretation of Religious Film

John R. May

Serious scholarly inquiries into the interpretation of religious film arose in the U.S. in response to the acknowledgment of film as art, generally coinciding with the worldwide popularity of certain European and Asian masters in the late 1950s and early 1960s, especially Bergman, Buñuel, Fellini, Truffaut, Ray, and Kurosawa. Their films, on limited distribution at art movie houses and on university campuses, introduced a small but highly influential audience to an artistic freedom in cinema that had not been enjoyed by American directors for over four decades, while the so-called Hays Office exercised control of film production and distribution. The freedom experienced by the immensely popular international directors was not to be experienced in the United States until the Motion Picture Association of America, under the direction of Jack Valenti, abolished the production code in 1966. The following year, Hollywood released two films – *The Graduate* and *Bonnie and Clyde* – that permanently altered the tone and content of America films. The combination of the demise of the production code and the universal popularity of foreign films signaled the need for broader approaches to the discernment of "religious" films among pastors, theologians, and church-related critics of cinema.

To facilitate my task in surveying the English-language works on the interpretation of religious film, I propose to offer in advance some important distinctions and clarifications of terminology as well as to acknowledge the critical assumptions that have informed my reading of the religious critics of film. Although I will review all of the pertinent works in the area, I will read works prior to 1978 with a view to the more contemporary approaches to the relationship between cinema and religion of the past fifteen or so years. As the title indicates, of this survey focuses on theories of interpretation, on general approaches to the discernment of religious film, as opposed to the practice of interpretation, i.e., to the actual analysis of specific films. There is a sense in which theory seems to imply a certain method of approach to practical criticism, and even though I shall have occasion to mention particular films and directors, such refer-

17

ences are by way of illustration of theory rather than exercises in film criticism.

The title of this essay also appeals to "the interpretation of religious film." It could, it seems to me, just as easily read "the religious interpretation of film." The latter phrase highlights the fact that films are properly designated religious not by the writer, director or distributor, but by the critic or viewer of the film. To the extent that I prefer the latter formulation – "the religious interpretation of film" – it is precisely because it both emphasizes the act of interpretation and, equivalently, preserves the secular origin of film as the technological century's art form. Either way it should be clear that this is a survey of works that are principally concerned with "film as text" as opposed to, but not excluding, the film as it reflects the artistry of the director, as it imitates external reality, as it affects its audience, or as it is historically or culturally situated. Having made these distinctions, I hasten to add that each of these "opposed but not excluded" aspects of film art will, from time to time, seem important to one or another theoretical school or representative of a school of interpretation.

As will be obvious too from the critical works surveyed, interpretation includes "evaluation" as well as "critical analysis." These distinct moments of the interpretive process need further specification. Evaluation can be either moral or aesthetic, or both, thus yielding judgments about whether a film is good or bad (morally) for the viewer, or whether it is art or not. Critical analysis is concerned with the meaning of the film as artistic communication, and even though critics rightly insist that film like any art cannot be reduced to propositions, they must necessarily write in discursive terms about the aesthetic impact of the film. Such discourse, though, is never a substitute for the total personal experience of the film itself.

"Religion" is used here as the general term that applies to the common ground held by all the major religions; to appeal to the language of logic, Christianity and Judaism are among the species for which religion is the genus. Religion or religious, therefore, will never be used as a synonym for a particular religious belief.

Insofar as film is still an active component of popular culture, we need to keep in mind too the distinction between "entertainment" and "art," such as formed the basis for the altered public acceptance of film in at least the U.S. in the late 1950s. Although art is necessarily entertaining in a root sense, not everything that passes for entertainment can be considered art. What is or is not art should be judged on aesthetic grounds. As we shall see even those who judge film from an ethical or moral point of view would agree with this norm.

"Ethics" and "morality" will be used interchangeably for those approaches to the discernment of religious films that give the evaluative nod to norms for conduct or behavior. The other source for religious discrimination is of course doctrine or creed, and I shall use "theology" as opposed to "morality" to designate the search for evidence of systems of belief in the fictional worldviews of films.

We will be concerned here with "feature films," which by definition fall between the extremes of documentary filmmaking and avant-garde or experimental films. "Realism" and "expressionism" or "formalism" are terms used to designate either the principal approaches of film theory or the divergent cinematic techniques used by film directors. Whether it is theory or technique that is being referred to should be clear from the context. The so-called classical style, used in all Hollywood feature films, is a mixture of realistic and expressionistic techniques.

I. The Interrelationship of Religion and Film

Simultaneous with the cultural developments referred to above, though not reflecting on the change in cinematic sensibility occasioned by the new freedom, William Lynch's *The Image Industries* (1959) offered a prophetic analysis of the peculiarly American problem created by the bigness, centralization, and pluralism in mass communication. In Lynch's words, the problem with "the image industries" – of which cinema is a major part – is "the increasingly centralized management of the imagination of a whole nation."[1] What seems so regrettable from our current vantage point is that his recommendations for cooperative dialogue among artists, theologians ("the moralist, the moral theologian, the religious thinker, the creative and speculative theologian" 11), critics and universities have never been heeded. Perhaps they were too idealistic for a culture mired in commercialism. At any rate, as we shall see, Micheal Medved's recent *Hollywood vs. America* is clear confirmation of our failure to heed Lynch's warning.

The four fundamental issues that Lynch described are still major concerns of most serious critics of our film industry: (1) the failure to distinguish between fantasy and reality, weakening our ability as a nation to distinguish between the two; (2) the general flatness of our cinematic imagination, sacrificing emotional sensibility to the representation of actions; (3) fixation on certain seductive and lucrative topics, like sex and violence, severely restricting our freedom of imagination; (4) and the preference for the "magnificent imagination," the spectacular instead of the everyday reality of human existence (20). A reflection today of what Lynch somewhat derisively called "magnificence" would be Hollywood's current obsession with the creation of spectacular special effects rather than with the epic screen.

II. Five Theoretical Approaches

If any dialogue developed in the ensuing decades, it was not the dynamic exchange among the principal cultural forces involved in the creation, production, interpretation and evaluation of the products of the entertainment industries, that Lynch projected the need for. It was instead a dialogue among theologians, moralists, pastors, and critics – the detached dialogue of academic and pastoral discourse. A survey of these critical texts reveals, it seems to me, at least five distinct theoretical approaches to the religious interpretation of film. I have chosen to call them, in order of emergence, religious discrimination, visibility, dialogue, humanism, and aesthetics. Each persists as a force in the continuing "written" dialogue, although "religious aesthetics," as we shall see, seems to have become the most challenging area of inquiry today.

In *Religion in Film*,[2] I proposed a more generic overview of the interrelationship of religion and film, based on the acknowledged schools of thought in the academic interdiscipline of religion and *literature* – heteronomy, theonomy, and autonomy. Heteronomy considers literature the handmaiden of faith, whereas autonomy insists that literature can be judged only according to its own norms, with theological implications sought in terms of their literary analogues. Theonomy, following Paul Tillich, sees both literature and religion grounded in ultimate reality, that is to say, God. I have noted these terms parenthetically in the headings where they seemed at least analogously related to this fuller system of classification.

1. Religious Discrimination (Heteronomy)

The classic text in religious discrimination is surely Frank Getlein and Harold C. Gardiner's *Movies, Morals and Art* (1961) – "classic" at least in the sense that it antedates by a decade the flood of books that responded to the new freedom in American film. It is also classic in the way it parallels T. S. Eliot's seminal essay "Literature and Religion," which is considered by many as heralding the founding of the academic discipline of religion and literature.[3] After Getlein's history of the emergence of film as art, Gardiner begins his theory of the moral evaluation of movies with words that ape Eliot's famous defense of Christian orthodoxy as the ultimate norm by which great literature would be judged: "I hold – and many agree with me – that the total artistic judgment, the complete critical evaluation of a piece of art, includes a moral dimension."[4] Insisting that only one act is involved, not two, Gardiner explains that "the 'artistically well done' includes the morally sound conception and the morally good effect" (104). Film, like any work of art, "gives pleasure," and pleasure's reasonableness "resides in the fact that art appeals to man as man," that is, to "those emotions that can legitimately (morally) be exercised" (106). Before he has finished his exposition, Gardiner reverts to the traditional Catholic moral norms for judging the appropriateness of films for audience viewing, discerning occasions of sin and using the principle of the twofold effect.

Regretting the moral indifferentism of most cinema, Gardiner borrows a marvelous phrase from Rene Ludmann, *"phénomène de sédimentation,"* to describe the baleful effect of cinema on its audience.[5] "Little by little the moral sense silts over" (161), Gardiner warns, because movies fail to take a moral stand, indeed too often suggest that there is no moral problem at all. In the final analysis, religious films for Gardiner, appealing to John Ford's *The Informer* (1935), are those that "do two things . . . they can bring home to the viewer a sense of his own combined majesty and frailty; and they can broaden the horizons of his natural charity so that the widened love can be transmuted into a supernatural charity" (174).

Anthony Schillaci's *Movies and Morals* (1968) was perhaps the most astute *apologia* for the revised approach to film classification adopted by the U.S. Bishops' National Catholic Office of Motion Pictures (NCOMP). Treating film as art, he acknowledges that art and morality are distinct but inseparable realities when he says "that Movies are truly Art, and that all true art must be moral."[6] For all the apparent sophistication of his argument in defense of the autonomy of art, Schillaci proves more timid even than Harold Gardiner when it comes to indicating what is or is not religious. Whereas Gardiner, at least implicitly, offered an affirmation, Schillaci never abandons the cautious negative. Films cannot be considered religious (because they are not artistic), he concludes, if they "[diminish] our humanity, and either [turn] us in on ourselves by a narcissistic fascination, or against others with a sadistic vengeance" (57).

In *Seen Any Good Dirty Movies Lately?* (1972), James W. Arnold sought a broader basis for "the social-moral analysis and evaluation of movies," one as he says "that is intellectually respectable."[7] Appealing to a 1970 essay by Andrew Greeley,[8] he agrees that for the Catholic "the really Real" is not only gracious but also accessible. Films are religious, Arnold concludes with Greeley, if they raise or consider important the following questions: "Is reality purposeful or absurd? What is the root of man's estrangement and suffering? Does good or evil triumph? Does death triumph over life, or life over death? Who is the good man? How ought he to live? And is the Real hidden or accessible?"(14). Arnold finds Fellini's films, for example, a perfect match for the sentiments of Langdon Gilkey's observation that "life seems, in a baffling and mysterious way, to share both creativity and sin, wonder and terror, joy and despair, and in the midst of its fateful tragedy, to reveal facets of hope, renewal and love."[9] Although there is an unmistakably moral context to Arnold's work, he seeks the moral in a solidly theological worldview and hence provides a transition to both "religious dialogue" and "religious humanism."

With the appearance of Michael Medved's *Hollywood vs. America: Popular Culture and the War on Traditional Values* in 1992, it became clear that the issue of morality as a norm for judging film has not faded away even if the alignment with a particular religious tradition has been traded for a cultural consensus of traditional values determined by polls. Medved, a practicing Jew, displays all of the strong ethical instincts so characteristic of the prophetic tradition. Three of the section headings indicate his outline of the problem: "The Attack on Religion," "The Assault on the Family," and "The Glorification of Ugliness."[10]

When confronted by religious and other critics of culture, the leaders of the entertainment world, Medved says, deny its impact on society in two ways: (1) no one, they say, has conclusively proven that movies cause people to act destructively; (2) moreover, entertainment merely reflects the world we live in (240). Medved responds to the first argument by offering a distinction: they may not "cause" antisocial behavior, but they "encourage" it (242). He quotes a study by Dr. Jennings Bryant of the University of Alabama to the effect that influence comes in the form of "subtle, incremental, cumulative changes in the way we view the world" (245), a contemporary version of Ludmann's *phénomène de sédimentation.* The most devastating argument against the industry's denial that it influences viewers is hidden, Medved shows, in the very assumptions of advertising. As for the industry defense that it merely reflects the world around us, one can only conclude with Medved that entertainers are sadly isolated from the value judgments of their fellow countrymen.

By implication, therefore, religious films for Medved would be those that support the majority values of the American family. Appealing to surveys taken in 1990 and 1991, Medved finds that the vast majority of Americans (in the 70-90% consensus range) "never doubt the existence of God," consider "spousal sexual fidelity" a "key to a good marriage," are "very satisfied" with their families and communities, consider hard work the key to success, feel safe in their homes and think the police are doing a good job, and entertain strong patriotic sentiments (256-57). If Medved's survey of American opinions in support of a kind of "civil morality" seems banal (if not vapid), it is perhaps not surprising: polls have never been a particularly satisfying basis for moral judgment. Medved's significant contribution to the dialogue lies in his plea for media "responsibility" over protestations of "rights" (322).

2. Religious Visibility

Religious visibility as a theoretical approach limits the consideration of religious films to those that appeal to identifiable religious elements; and where recognizable religious elements are sought, there has been little genuine change over the past twenty-five years, though very recently a subtle shift in emphasis can be noted. The chapter titles in Ivan Butler's *Religion in the Cinema* (1969) run the gamut of possible explicit Jewish-Christian elements: Bible stories and biblical blockbusters, early Christians, crusades; Christ in cinema, priests, ministers, and the church; preachers, evangelists, missionaries; monks and nuns; churches; saints, visionaries, legends and miracles; and the like.[11] Although Butler's approach begins descriptively, implied norms of religious orthodoxy emerge when he offers a superficial reading of certain "anti-religious" films, including most of Buñuel and Pasolini.

The principal difference between Butler's *Religion in the Cinema* and Gerald E. Forshey's *American Religious and Biblical Spectaculars* (1992), published almost a quarter of a century later, lies in the latter book's focus on spectaculars and, more importantly from a theoretical perspective, on its detailed efforts to demonstrate the effects of the historical context on the presentation of religious material. "Americans regularly rewrite history," Forshey observes, adding that what is important in Hollywood's appropriation of the biblical *mythos* is "whether the presentation coincides with the current generally accepted view, for example, of race, native Americans, women, or labor."[12] The myth of the spectaculars, he adds, "demonstrates how the audience must act in history if they are to receive God's blessing for themselves and the nation" (11).

Paul Giles's *American Catholic Arts and Fiction*, published the same year as Forshey's book (1992), shifts the discussion of recognizable religious elements from the external and explicit to the implicit and ideological. His stated purpose is "to examine the continuing significance of religion, and specifically Roman Catholicism, as an ideological force within modern American literature, film, and photography."[13] Giles focuses on those cultural refractions or "demystified forms" of Catholic theology that can be discerned in the "density and indeterminacy" of the works of the greater American Catholic artists. Although he limits himself to born or converted Catholics, he rejects "that old fashioned kind of biographical approach that seeks to domesticate texts through relating them to the events of one author's individual life" in favor of analyzing texts "in terms of a wider cultural pattern, to indicate how cultural materials affect artistic composition in ways the author would probably not recognize, and hence to elaborate the *unconscious sediments* of artistic production" (30, my emphasis). The sedimentation that has bothered critics thus far was a reflection of cinematic effects upon the morality of the general audience; Giles searches as a critic for evidence of the cultural sedimentation of Catholic theology in the works themselves.

What makes his book so interesting in this context – however limited his appeal to filmmakers may be – are the implications for our analysis of the religious film. Religious films are those whose contours have been shaped by the religious influences on their creators. His specific focus is on certain "unorthodox and sophisticated" Catholic filmmakers – Ford, Altman, Hitchcock, Scorsese, and Coppola – because their works, he believes, "provide more insight into how Catholicism has operated in modern times as an implicit ideological aesthetic that continues to have psychological and cultural relevance" (27). Some of the sediments of Catholic theology that he discovers in the filmmakers he treats are burlesque (of old world pretense) and ritual in Ford and Altman, guilt and salvation in Hitchcock and Scorsese, and transubstantiation and hierarchy in Coppola.

Because, for Giles, cultural influences shape the artistic product, we can avoid neither the narrow assumption (which is his) that biography is crucial in the discernment of religious or Catholic films nor the broader implication that, insofar as religious cultures exceed the confines of formal belief, one ought conceivably to be able to perceive the sediments of Catholicism, for example, in the works of born Protestants or Jews, or even nonbelievers, though clearly the preference would be for those who are saturated with the particular religious culture.

3. Religious Dialogue

Within American Protestant churches, the obvious need for education to the emerging reality of film as art took the form of theological dialogue with film rather than of direct moral assessment as it had among Catholic theologians. *Celluloid and Symbols* (1970), a collection of essays edited by John Charles Cooper and Carl Skrade, supported the thesis "that theology needs to be in dialogue with the cinema but must never regress to a monologue which would seek to 'baptize' the film-maker or impose any kind of theology on him."[14] Skrade's "Theology and Films," the lead essay, insists that "films can help us regain, in contemporary form, the basic questions which we affirm Christianity can answer – or at least permit us to live with these questions as we honestly and openly await the answers" (3).

A year later, in *Church and Cinema*, James Wall, editor of *The Christian Century*, described the changing times as "a theological climate in which the reality of God came to be sought within secular structures as well as within conventional religious structures."[15] Insisting that "the film-maker is an artist who presents a vision of reality in his work, a vision that can enrich our own, whether or not we share it" (13), he saw three reasons for the church to be involved; namely, because it is a sustaining community, an agent of change, and a sensitizing community. Religious films, for Wall, would by implication be those that strengthen the church in these areas. Because many films today avoid the familiar principles of plot and logic, Wall concludes, we have to get away from asking "what it's about," presumably so that we can allow the suppositions that we bring to the viewing of the film to interact with the reality of the film's world ("what the film is").

In *Popcorn and Parables* (1971), Robert Kahle and Robert E. A. Lee, writing from and to an American Lutheran experience of cinema, proposed film as "a resource for our own faith and for our communication of religious truths to others."[16] "By learning how to understand and utilize movies," they write, "Christians can turn motion pictures into a helpful tool rather than a threatening weapon" (6). Contemporary cinema serves "a function similar to Christ's parables" (37) insofar as it uses "ordinary, mundane entities" as symbols to communicate their meaning or emotion. Thus religious films, for Kahle and Lee, are those "that may work to soften the hardened heart and may prepare the way for a future Christian witness" (40). Although Kahle and Lee anticipate later developments in theological film criticism through their insights into parable and symbol, ideas take precedence finally over cinematic elements related to story.

Another Lutheran response was *Marquee Ministry* (1972) by Robert Konzelman, whose central thesis was that the church has the power to help determine whether film will be a negative or positive force in our culture if it finds a more creative way than law and censorship to exert an influence on the content of secular films.[17] His stance, though, is decidedly less inclusive than Kahle's and Lee's, and his criteria for selecting films (such as relevance, integrity, and quality) have more of a moral than a theological ring to them. Defining feature films that we are dealing with as "secular films," Konzelman notes the inevitable effect upon "morals, beliefs, and values if the cultural wash is left to itself in the world, to sweep over it at random and unchecked" (4). "Dialogical film study," as he envisions it, "approaches motion pictures as a communication out of and to our culture" (25).

Although religious dialogue as an approach toward the evaluation of religious films is surely continuing today, the bases for film education have shifted in the ensuing two decades, as we shall see, from the implicitly defensive to the ecumenically inclusive ("religious humanism") and the explicitly aesthetic ("religious aesthetics").

4. Religious Humanism (Theonomy)

No theological critic of film to date can match Neil Hurley's comprehensive and prophetic grasp of worldwide film culture. Will the moving image confirm our prejudices, Hurley asked in *Theology Through Film* (1970), or will it "serve that reason which, after all, is the universal spark of the divine which the Stoic philosophers believed to bind all men together in some mysterious cosmic fraternity?"[18] Hurley readily admitted that his view "presupposes religious transcendence in some form as a constant of man, society, and culture" (8). "A religious principle" that he discovers at work in films assumes that "people will identify negatively with forms of evil and villainy and positively with sacrifice, suffering, and selfless forms of love" (6).

Eight years later (1978), when Hurley published *The Reel Revolution: A Film Primer on Liberation*, he actually began by asserting that "film is the new humanism and . . . in speaking to literates and illiterates alike it can tease out of us a sense of greater possibilities, alternative selves, and new horizons."[19] His contention is that "movies as 'the reel revolution' meet the requirements of true education – which is to aid in the escape of the best possible self among the many latent personalities in each of us" (xii). Whereas in his earlier work all films seemed at least potentially religious, not all films are genuinely liberating; this narrowing of possibility is perhaps to be expected since in Hurley's view "liberation films" are a species of the genus "religious."

Although generally acknowledged as a serious art form, movies have yet to be perceived "as a revolution," Hurley writes, because "critics and viewers of cinema have not looked for liberation techniques and themes in movies" (xiii). The "reel revolution" rests on three criteria, Hurley believes: (1) "a subtle but very real judgment on the larger society that supports film," (2) "enduring themes of conformity, acceptance, frustration, protest, rebellion, and the appetite for justice," and (3) "enduring statements of universal and profound significance on the human condition" (xiii). Although Hurley has a keen sense of film as an artistic medium, the emphasis here, as his second criterion makes perfectly clear, is still principally on *themes* reflected in movies.

Halfway around the world in Australia, Peter Malone, another Catholic commentator on film, published two works at practically the same interval as Hurley, that paralleled his achievement in exploring film as religious humanism – *The Film* (1971) and *Films and Values* (1978). In the first volume, Malone seeks in film "the harmony between Christian and basic human attitudes,"[20] by demonstrating film's appeal to our fundamental human drives. "Truth," he reminds us, "cannot be self-contradictory"(3). *Films and Values* is more obviously humanistic, based as it is on the assumption that "true entertainment equals true education."[21] Exploring ten films from the 1960s and 1970s in detail, Malone shows how cinema both reflects and shapes the changing mores and values of that turbulent period.

It is somewhat more difficult, though, to know precisely where to place Ronald Holloway's 1977 work, *Beyond the Image*. His exposition ranges from "discrimination" through "dialogue" to "humanism" as it strives to propose "a theology of cinema" and proceeds to outline the principles that a "religious cinema" would involve. His theology of cinema itself never seems to go much beyond variations on the tantalizing suggestion that "cinema, or the motion picture, is the outer expression of a philosophy [theology] of procession [i.e., process]."[22] "A theology of motion," he writes, "must have both a past and a future. A theology of cinema not only records and documents; it projects into the future" (14).

Humanism enters his guidelines for a religious cinema when he proposes that "in his depiction of truly human situations and characters, whether they be comic or tragic, the artist confirms his conviction as to whether Christian values and virtues are ultimately worthwhile." Moreover, Holloway insists, "the subject matter itself is not the first nor the primary consideration, but how it is interpreted by the artist." When he indicates that "the critical approach to interpreting the film's meaning *as a whole* is much safer, especially in praising or recommending a film" (my emphasis, 42), it is by no means clear whether his norm is ethical or aesthetic. What is clear, however, is that Holloway approaches his subject from the vantage point of a thorough knowledge of our century-long history of film.

The Run of the Country, Peter Yates, 1995

In a 1993 essay, "Religious Themes in Films of the Last Decade," Holloway clarifies some of the ambiguity of his earlier, longer work when he distinguishes between "spiritual" and "religious" cinema, where the latter refers, he admits, "more to subject matter on the surface than to depth of meaning in thematic treatment."[23] His examples then range, in our classification, between "religious visibility" and "religious humanism." In the same issue of *Media Development*, Alan Pavelin (whose 1990 work *Fifty Religious Films* has yet to be released in the U.S.) also enunciates a position that moves beyond "religious visibility" to "humanism." After listing films that would normally pass for religious "in most people's minds," such as biblical spectaculars and films about saints and nuns (or presumably other religious personages), he proposes "a fourth image" – "the ordinary unsaintly individual going through some kind of spiritual struggle or crisis."[24] Insisting that there are no hard and fast rules about the genre of "religious films," he defines his new category in terms that are unequivocally humanistic: "a film which deals substantially and seriously (but not necessarily humorlessly) with religious issues or, more generally, with the fundamental questions of the human condition to which religions address themselves." Even "agnostic and critical viewpoints," he admits, "could be included here" (25).

5. Religious Aesthetics (Autonomy)

General Theories

It was not until 1981 that an extensive study by an American theologian appeared that sought to move beyond morality, explicit religious elements, or humanistic themes to define religious significance in terms of cinema's specific art. Thomas M. Martin's *Images and the Imageless: A Study in Religious Consciousness and Film* is the sort of harmonization of concerns that Lynch had in mind in *The Image Industries*, except that Lynch sought active cooperation among the participants. Martin notes that although sophisticated interdisciplinary methodologies were emerging by mid-century in religion and literature, "the discipline [of religion and film] is young and the methodologies are at best in their formative stages."[25] In his brief survey of the earlier scholarship, he notes with justification that even where the emphasis was not on themes, but on film as a medium, "the focus [was] not broad enough" (ii-iii). "This small volume," he goes on to promise, "attempts to relate the film medium to religious studies by means of the spatial interpretation and orientation (the image, the sense of direction) that is common to both forms of reflection" (iii).

Martin contends with good reason that "the persistent experience of electronically transmitted stories has a profound impact on the basic notion of oneself as it relates to one's religious sense of reality" (3). Four terms are pivotal to the development of his thesis: "image, imaginative construct, story, and religious [consciousness]" (3). Martin explains: "Where images are generally in response to immediate situations, imaginative constructs are geared more toward absorbing direction as a whole" (17). Stories are the flesh and bones humans give to images and constructs, he goes on to say; they result from the individual's need to "work out the issues of the self in dramatic forms, not necessarily to fit some established order but to establish some emotional order or integration" (21). Finally, for Martin, "religious consciousness is the sense of relatedness that the human has with the others of the world as all are rooted in a common greater whole" (29).

Film as the art of moving pictures, Martin writes, "has a greater ability to produce a total environment than either painting or photography because it can include in its form more of the ingredients of a normal setting" (46). Taking examples from slow-motion, time-lapse, microscopic and satellite photography, he explores cinema's uniqueness as a source of images: "It is precisely this ability to awaken a sense of awe and wonder in the beholder that is necessary in laying the foundation for religious consciousness in a culture which tends to reduce experience to 'one damn thing after another'" (52). "Human consciousness cannot be the same today as it was prior to the extension of its vision through film. Neither can religious consciousness ever be the same" (55), he observes, while cautioning that "Awareness of the mystery and awesomeness of all existences, of all beings, of all the expressions of life forces does not necessarily lead to a sense of their radical interrelatedness but is a prerequisite for this extraordinary sense of reality [as part of a common greater whole]" (57).

"No story," Martin demonstrates, "can develop without some underlying construct" (63). Moreover, he adds, "all constructs, even in the most banal of stories, are seen as presenting one with a fundamental option about life. And, therefore, every story one encounters has some effect on or challenge to one's sense of reality" (63). Martin discovers five basic models affecting human consciousness – supernatural, process, romantic, secular and depth – and explains them in this way (the names in brackets are the principal figures in intellectual history he associates with each): "The supernatural model [Calvin, Aquinas] with its layered hierarchy to existence challenges the human life to make itself correspond to the higher governing forms if it wants fulfillment. The process model [Whitehead, de Chardin] places the human life in an ever fluctuating process that entails an intricate interplay in all facets of the process that is interacting with a whole which is dependent on but not reducible to the sum of its parts. The romantic model [Schleiermacher, Coleridge] is seen as the reverse of the process. One must go back to the pulsating source of nature if one wishes to attain an experience of fulfillment. The secular context [Bonhoeffer, Cox] offers a picture of more isolated entities set by their outward structure while the depth model [Freud, Jung, Campbell] insists on a unique inner space that must be probed if one wishes to have an authentic existence" (108).

"Human consciousness," Martin admits, "has reached sufficient sophistication to realize that it is not discovering the structure of reality as it is in itself. Rather, it is probing for insight through its systems of symbolic reflection" (114). Moreover, "stories are an important step forward in achieving a stability and texture for a people, for they have the ability to introduce a cohesive world view with a minimum of violence to the particulars of life. Such a cohesive force is necessary for a stable society" (119). Yet "the religious sense," Martin reminds us, "cannot exist if there is no identity with a greater whole" (130). Because the camera makes available radically new sources of consciousness and because "films present a dimension of beings not open to human experience prior to film, this new experience is bound to transform one's sense of oneself and the basic relationship to Being in general" (134). Finally, Martin concludes, "when one is living in a cultural juncture in which the public imagination is fractured, then art forms can supplement the images of one's private imagination by making available the creative integrations of artistic geniuses" (151).

Michael Bird, in his essay "Film as Hierophany," provides another general theory of the aesthetic interrelationship of religion and film, appealing to Paul Tillich's theology and the realist theories of André Bazin and Amédée Ayfre. Because of film's special affinity with reality, he explains, it must direct us to discern "the holy within the real. . . . While many films have portrayed ostensibly religious subjects, these films have too often erred precisely in their disregard for the medium's stylistic virtues."[26] "What is required in a cinematic theology is a consideration of how the style of film can enable an exploration of the sacred," insists Bird, appealing to Tillich's observation about religious art that it is style not subject matter that is of principal significance. The style that Bird, following Bazin's disciple Ayfre, finds conducive to hierophany is one that paradoxically transcends the everyday through the everyday. Its cinematography "does not exhaust reality but rather evokes in the viewer the sense of its ineffable mystery" (14). Bresson's *The Diary of a Country Priest* (1950) becomes for Bird the quintessential example of this kind of realism, in which humble objects reveal their striving for the sacred and actors apparently refrain from acting. Although Bird does not seem to have been aware of Paul Schrader's *Transcendental Style in Film* (1972), their approaches to the religious dimension of cinema are remarkably similar; in addition to Bresson, Schrader treats Dreyer and Ozu.[27]

Bird's indebtedness to Tillich is obvious when he states that the "continual discovery [of the fragility of existence] in the reality of the void, the silence, the boundary situation becomes the point at which we are brought face to face with the reality of negation, behind which lies its ground, the affirmation within which it resides (for Tillich, the experience of non-being enclosed within being)" (20). Thus, film becomes hierophanic insofar as it remains true to its realistic properties, "invested with the power for the disclosure of that continual striving within culture toward the holy, by bringing us into the presence of the real as it 'calls up' meaning from its inner depths" (21).

A third general approach to religious aesthetics can be found in Andrew Greeley's *God in Popular Culture* (1988), which offers a theology of popular culture rooted in sociological and theological theories of the religious imagination. Greeley's thesis is particularly helpful in this context insofar as it works on both the (generic) religious and (specific) Catholic levels. His sociological theory is based on an epistemological premise that he finds in both Lonergan and Whitehead; namely, "that 'out of the corner of our eye,' so to speak, in the act of knowing, we perceive purpose, design, even love binding together the cosmos."[28] Because religion finds its origin there, it is "primarily an activity of the creative imagination" (59). In support of his thesis, he provides the following sociological evidence: humans have a "built-in propensity to hope" and the capacity for hope-renewing experiences. Whereas any reality is potentially a trigger for hope, Greeley has discovered, some experiences are more obviously "sacramental" in that they more surely point to the source of our hopefulness: "fire, the sun, water, the moon, oil, love, sex, marriage, birth, death, community" (64). The imagination records the experience after its impact on the senses, and the recollection and sharing of these experiences leads to the formulation of stories designed "to stir up in the other person resonances of experiences similar to those which the religious storyteller himself or herself has had" (67).

Religion becomes communal, Greeley asserts, "when a person is able to link his own grace experience with the overarching experience of [his] religious tradition" (67). Thus, each person's religious story is one of relationships, and religious storytelling is "an attempt to communicate from imagination to imagination" (69).

Greeley's theology of the religious imagination depends heavily on his sociological observations. "Imagination," he begins, "is the source of religion because we are experiencing, ordering, and reflective beings" (89). Moreover, experience (shaped by the images and symbols of our religious tradition) and narrative (the stories of our faith) precede religious reflection or theological discourse as such. Insofar as Catholic theology sees human nature as deprived rather than depraved, Greeley explains, it has always – at its best – embraced the works of culture as an essential part of religion (91) because popular culture attempts to order experience through storytelling. Film is of course a part of popular culture, and it fits perfectly Greeley's definition of story as "any work of culture which attempts to organize experience." Greeley does not claim that every film is a possible source of the sacramental (as described above), but that some deserve to be so considered. And because his theology is thoroughly incarnational, Greeley insists that (unlike Protestant, Jewish and Islamic thought that sees radical discontinuity between God and world) "the Catholic religious sensibility sees the whole of creation as a metaphor: everything is grace" (94). It would seem to me more congruent with his line of argument if he had said that grace is everywhere, and everything is potentially grace.

Finally, Greeley distinguishes three levels of religious "story" and therefore of religious films. All films are religious in some sense, he says, "because all stories implicitly try to assign meaning even when they assert that there is no meaning or that meaning is a deception" (96). Secondly, implicitly religious films are "stories in which powerful religious symbols, lurking in the unconscious or preconscious and prevalent in the world religions, abound and create an implicit or preconscious ambience of meaning." Lastly, theological films are those "in which questions of meaning and grace are explicitly part of the narrative" (97).

Specific Approaches

The particular approaches to the religious interpretation of film that fall within the category of religious aesthetics can, I believe, be grouped conveniently under four headings: archetypal patterns, mythic orientations, the analogy of action, and visual story. At this point in our survey, it is clear that theory yields specific methodology, which readily lends itself to the practice of religious interpretation.[29]

1. Archetypal Patterns: In *Film Odyssey* (1976), Ernest Ferlita and I, applying the archetype of the quest, tried to isolate those "elements of the art of film [that] are parents and children of hope."[30] Aside from the obvious appeal to visual imagery related to journey – the celebration of the road as a metaphor for our human search for meaning – we attempted to show how composition of frame, movement of the camera and movement within the frame, types of visual continuity (i.e., narrative), and finally editing could contribute to cinema's celebration of hope. Religious films, in the best artistic tradition, we concluded, are "a celebration of life's promise that transcends the individual to reach out to and sustain the aspirations of others" (4).

2. Mythic Orientations: Neil Hurley, in his essay "Cinematic Transfigurations of Jesus" (1982), was the first theological critic of film to offer an overview of cinema's fictional appropriations of the Jesus story,[31] anticipating by almost a decade Peter Malone's more comprehensive treatment of the subject in *Movie Christs and Antichrists* (1990).[32] Following the distinctions proposed by Theodore Ziolkowski in *Fictional Transfigurations of Jesus*,[33] Hurley abandons the reference to Christ figures in favor of the terminology of Jesus transfigurations. Inasmuch as Christ is a title that faith applies to Jesus, Ziolkowski recommended reserving "Christ" for the context of faith and using the personal name "Jesus" for fictional variations of the evangelical narrative. Malone preserves the traditional literary terminology of the "Christ figure" for fictional characters in film, but uses "Jesus figure" for cinema's realistic presentations of the Gospel story. Christ figures, he proposes, are either redeemer figures (who suffer unjustly) or savior figures (who liberate others). Malone's mythic analysis of film is based on the assumptions that emotional response precedes our initial intellectual grasp of film's moving images, and that content draws response from the audience, while technique enhances response. Values, Malone says, are discovered in a film's content, especially in the treatment of the basic human drives to live, love, live socially, and transcend self.

3. The Analogy of Action: Ernest Ferlita's "The Analogy of Action in Film" (1982) demonstrates convincingly that the possibility of religious meaning in film like drama is often effectively realized through analogy of action, a dramatic device at least as old as the Greeks but perfected by Shakespeare. The unity of his plays is discovered, Ferlita claims, not in "that single plot line which Aristotle preferred and the neo-classicists canonized, but in the analogy of action, in the interdependence of several stories so juxtaposed one to another that each elucidates the central action, first by its similarity but finally by its difference."[34] Utilizing the insights so admirably expressed in William Lynch's *Christ and Apollo*,[35] Ferlita observes that "in its passage through the finite on its way to insight, [the analogy of action] makes everything radiate the same light and yet its own proper light" (55). *Wild Strawberries* (1957) and *Seven Beauties* (1976) in

Ferlita's exposition become excellent examples of the way in which screen-writer-directors have created plots that illumine the spirit through the analogy of action.

4. Visual Story: In my essay "Visual Story and the Religious Interpretation of Film" (1982), I attempted to connect film and religion through the theology of story. My principal assumption about film is the unassailable one, I think, that all feature films are stories. Story in cinema, however, is discerned in terms of film's unique formal elements – composition, movement, and editing – rather than simply in terms of those formal structures that film shares with literature; namely, setting, character, dialogue, dramatic tension, and plot.[36] Taking the extremes of story as explored by John Dominic Crossan – myth and parable – I tried with assistance also from the works of Huston Smith and Herbert Richardson to construct a paradigm for the interaction of the extremes of story and the fundamental religious questions.[37] Between myth and parable, as Sheldon Sacks demonstrates in *Fiction and the Shape of Belief*, there are three intermediate forms of story – apologue, action, and satire – that can profitably be analyzed as reflectors of religious concerns, although no one has done this yet, to my knowledge.[38] Since the publication of *Religion in Film*, which I edited with Michael Bird, I have continued to explore the shared cinematic and religious dynamics of story, with emphasis in the 1992 collection of essays, *Image and Likeness*, on the reflections of Jewish-Christian belief in classic American cinema.[39]

Resurrection, Daniel Petrie, 1980

III. Conclusions

It seems to me that this survey of the serious academic works on the religious interpretation of films has demonstrated, perhaps not surprisingly, that
early concern with the "morality" of films has not altogether faded, despite
a decade and a half of efforts to discover the cinematic equivalents of religious sensibility. Nor has the marked tendency to reserve the term "religious
film" for those films that exhibit explicit, recognizable religious elements;
in fact, outside of the United States, it may even be the dominant approach
to the identification of religious film.

There is, I think, an irony in this delineation of the discussion. Originally, when the basis for religious evaluation of films was morality, all
films were considered at least potentially religious insofar as morality
judges behavior and all feature films involve action of some sort. The tendency to limit the discussion, as we have seen, grew out of the developing
desire to avoid the narrow discrimination of morality as a norm for deciding what was or was not religious in favor of the greater intellectual
stimulation of theological issues. There were and still are, however, too
few directors who like Bergman or Fellini raise explicit theological questions.

There are, nonetheless, solid and convincing grounds for asserting
that any film, even those without explicit religious elements, can still be
considered as potentially religious, if not Jewish or Christian or Catholic.
Where this is defended with reason, the basis for religious interpretation is
sought in terms of cinema's analogues for religious insights. Just as the
advocates of morality as a norm for evaluating film from a religious perspective began with the assumption that cinema is an art form and that
morality was bound up with the aesthetic, so too the proponents of "religious aesthetics" necessarily root their discussion of the religious implications of film in the formal elements of cinema itself.

Endnotes

1. William Lynch, *The Image Industries* (New York: Sheed and Ward, 1959), 4.
   Subsequent page references to the works surveyed here will be noted in parentheses in the text, following the initial bibliographical citation.

2. John R. May, "Visual Story and the Religious Interpretation of Film," in *Religion in Film*, ed. John R. May and Michael Bird (Knoxville: University of
   Tennessee Press, 1982), 24-25.

3. T. S. Eliot, "Literature and Religion," in *Essays Ancient and Modern* (New
   York: Harcourt, Brace, 1936); reprinted in *The New Orpheus*, ed. Nathan A.
   Scott, Jr. (New York: Sheed and Ward, 1964), 223-35.

4. Frank Getlein and Harold C. Gardiner, *Movies, Morals and Art* (New York:
   Sheed and Ward, 1961), 103.

5. Rene Ludmann, *Cinéma: Foi et morale* (Paris: Cerf, 1956).

6. Anthony Schillaci, O.P., *Movies and Morals* (Notre Dame: Fides, 1968), 23.

7. James W. Arnold, *Seen Any Good Dirty Movies Lately? A Christian Critic Looks at Contemporary Films* (Cincinnati: St. Anthony Messenger Press, 1972), 3.

8. Andrew Greeley, "The Bread of Faith," *The Critic* (Sept./Oct. 1970). As Arnold notes, Greeley proposes a kind of Catholic humanistic profession of faith that aids in the discernment of religious sensibility in films: "I believe that Love is at the core of the universe; that man is estranged essentially because of his inability to respond to Love, since he is estranged from Love; this estrangement is ended by the intervention of Love in the Person of the Son of Man. Thus, life triumphs over death, though only by dying itself. Love and life are proclaimed by celebrating. The most appropriate human relationship is friendship, both because it mirrors Love and because it represents through trust, which is its essence, life's triumph over death by dying itself. The work of Loving Life in the world is moving toward completion. Man's role is to strive so that the world may be pervaded by friendship. Whenever men come together in friendship, the Spirit of Loving Life is present in their midst, inspiring them to break out of the bonds of hesitation, doubt and distrust in order that they might be for one another" (as quoted in Arnold, 14-15).

9. Langdon Gilkey, *Naming the Whirlwind* (Indianapolis: Bobbs-Merrill, 1969), 259.

10. Michael Medved, *Hollywood vs. America: Popular Culture and the War on Traditional Values* (New York: HarperCollins, 1992), ix.

11. Ivan Butler, *Religion in the Cinema* (New York: A. S. Barnes, 1969), 7.

12. Gerald E. Forshey, *American Religious and Biblical Spectaculars* (Westport, CT: Praeger, 1992), 10.

13. Paul Giles, *American Catholic Arts and Fiction: Culture, Ideology, Aesthetics* (New York: Cambridge University Press, 1992), 1. Three other works, appearing within the previous decade, focused principally on American cinema's explicit references to Jews and Catholics: Patricia Erens, *The Jew in American Cinema* (Bloomington: Indiana University Press, 1984); Lester Friedman, *The Jewish Image in American Film* (Secaucus: Citadel, 1987); and Les and Barbara Keyser, *Hollywood and the Catholic Church: The Image of Roman Catholicism in American Movies* (Chicago: Loyola University Press, 1984). Another fascinating work, Mark Le Fanu's *The Cinema of Andrei Tarkovsky* (London: British Film Institute, 1987), details the director's explicit appeals, despite censorship, to Russian Orthodox Christianity (as well as to eastern religions).

14. John Charles Cooper and Carl Skrade, *Celluloid and Symbols* (Philadelphia: Fortress, 1970), ix.

15. James M. Wall, *Church and Cinema: A Way of Viewing Film* (Grand Rapids, MI: Eerdmans, 1971), 8.

16. Robert Kahle and Robert E. A. Lee, *Popcorn and Parables: A New Look at the Movies* (Minneapolis: Augsburg, 1971), 6.

17. Robert G. Konzelman, *Marquee Ministry: The Movie Theater as Church and Community Forum* (New York: Harper and Row, 1972), 1.

18. Neil P. Hurley, *Theology Through Film* (New York: Harper and Row, 1970); republished as *Toward a Film Humanism* (New York: Delta Paperbacks, 1975).

19. Neil P. Hurley, *The Reel Revolution: A Film Primer on Liberation* (Maryknoll: Orbis, 1987), xii.

20. Peter Malone, *The Film* (Melbourne/Sydney: Chevalier, 1971), 3.

21. Peter Malone, *Films and Values* (Melbourne/Sydney: Chevalier, 1978), 3.

22. Ronald Holloway, *Beyond the Image: Approaches to the Religious Dimension in the Cinema* (Geneva: World Council of Churches, 1977), 11.

23. Ronald Holloway, "Religious Themes in Films of the Last Decade," *Media Development* 40:1 (1993), 12.

24. Alan Pavelin, "Films Evoking a Sense of Religion: The Classics and Their Successors," *Media Development* 40:1 (1993), 25.

25. Thomas M. Martin, *Images and the Imageless: A Study in Religious Consciousness and Film* (East Brunswick: Bucknell University Press, 1981), ii.

26. Michael Bird, "Film as Hierophany," in *Religion in Film*, ed. May and Bird, 13.

27. Paul Schrader, *Transcendental Style in Film: Ozu, Bresson, Dreyer* (Berkeley: University of California Press, 1972).

28. Andrew Greeley, *God in Popular Culture* (Chicago: Thomas More, 1988), 59.

29. Works on individual directors that are sensitive to film as a medium while exploring the religious dimension include two on Ingmar Bergman – Arthur Gibson, *The Silence of God: Creative Response to the Films of Ingmar Bergman* (New York: Harper and Row, 1969) and Charles B. Ketcham, *The Influence of Existentialism on Ingmar Bergman* (Lewiston, PA: E. Mellen Press, 1986) – and one on Lina Wertmuller – Ernest Ferlita and John R. May, *The Parables of Lina Wertmuller* (New York: Paulist, 1977).

30. Ernest Ferlita and John R. May, *Film Odyssey: The Art of Film as Search for Meaning* (New York: Paulist, 1976), 4.

31. Neil P. Hurley, "Cinematic Transfigurations of Jesus," in *Religion in Film*, ed. May and Bird, 61-78. For cinematic variations on the myth of the loosing of Satan, see John R. May, "The Demonic in American Cinema," ibid., 79-100.

32. Peter Malone, *Movie Christs and Antichrists* (New York: Crossroad, 1990).

33. Theodore Ziolkowski, *Fictional Transfigurations of Jesus* (Princeton, NJ: Princeton University Press, 1972).

34. Ernest Ferlita, "The Analogy of Action in Film," in *Religion in Film*, ed. May and Bird, 45.

35. William F. Lynch, *Christ and Apollo* (New York: Sheed and Ward, 1960).

36. John R. May, "Visual Story and the Religious Interpretation of Film," in *Religion in Film*, ed. May and Bird, 23-43.

37. John Dominic Crossan, *The Dark Interval: Towards a Theology of Story* (Niles: Argus Communications, 1975); Huston Smith, *The Religions of Man* (New York: Harper and Row, 1958); Herbert W. Richardson and Donald R. Cutler, eds., *Transcendence* (Boston: Beacon, 1969).

38. Sheldon Sacks, *Fiction and the Shape of Belief* (Berkeley: University of California Press, 1966).

39. John R. May, ed., *Image and Likeness: Religious Visions in American Film Classics* (New York/Mahwah: Paulist, 1992).

Part 2

The Changing Language
of Religious Film

3

The "Religious" in Film:
From *King of Kings* to *The Fisher King*

Peter Hasenberg

"I am the janitor of God," says the mad city tramp Brian Parry in Terry Gilliam's *The Fisher King* (1991), thus hinting clearly – though incidentally – at a religious dimension to the film, which is mixed from the beginning with other allusions, such as the Pinocchio fairy tale and the myth of the Holy Grail. *The Fisher King* is a serious comedy, above all a story of guilt and redemption, with comedian Robin Williams as the wise fool, the spiritual guide of the guilt-ridden hero. This is an unusual context for religious themes compared with traditional treatments of religion in cinema. Gilliam, once a member of the famous, though to some infamous, Monty Python group, has struck a fresh note for the Hollywood gospel. *The Fisher King* may well mark a new threshold in the history of religious cinema. We have come a long way since the 1960s, a decade that offered a number of "classical" religious films and, in fact, started with the most traditional treatment of a religious subject, the filming of the New Testament – Nicholas Ray's 1960 remake of Cecil B. De Mille's *The King of Kings* (1927).

The aim of this essay is to describe tendencies in the treatment of "the religious" in film since the 1960s, with special attention to the last fifteen years. My observations come from the point of view of a Catholic film critic, not a Catholic theologian, and I shall restrict my observations to those films that justify a religious interpretation by giving recognizable hints of such a reading.[1]

If we try to deal with "the religious" in film, we cannot judge movies within a framework of narrow, dogmatic evaluations. We are well advised to adopt the widest definition of "the religious." My suggestion is that we should define the term as the sum of all references to religion in the broadest sense. Thus, we should start with a description and classification of all the elements in the text that refer explicitly or implicitly either to religious texts, religious institutions, religious practices (visible) and experiences (visible or invisible), or to attitudes towards other people that are inspired by religious beliefs.

In this way, we can find references to religion on the following five levels of the organization of individual films:

1. character (representatives of religious institutions, personae defined by religious beliefs, and so forth),

2. plot (elements of action initiated by characters described above; plot outlines with references to – or by analogy with – structures of religious texts, stories of redemption, hagiographies, etc.),

3. theme (for example, sin, grace, redemption, suffering),

4. setting (synagogue, church, monastery, convent, vicarage, and the like),

5. audio-visual structures (references to religious iconography, to sacred music, etc.).

If we try to analyze historical developments, we must consider the social and cultural context, especially the economic and aesthetic developments in cinema itself. My thesis is this: the articulation of "the religious" in film is shaped, on one hand, by the influence or standing of religion in the contemporary social and cultural context and, on the other, by the significant economic and aesthetic trends of the film market that define the systems of communication that the director can use to convey his message.

I. Society, Culture, and Cinema

From the 1960s to the 1990s, the treatment of the religious in cinema has changed significantly. To begin a survey of recent trends in religious cinema with the 1960s is appropriate because this decade was characterized by significant changes on various levels in society. It marked the definitive end of the postwar era and the beginning of significant political and cultural changes. A reorganization of society began then as new political and social impulses arose out of the youth generation (the hippie movement, student revolts, and the like). Just as hope spread during the 1960s, frustration set in during the 1970s (Watergate, Vietnam, economic crises, etc.), followed by a period of dominant conservative values in most western states during the 1980s.

In eastern Europe, movements toward freedom from communist repression characterized the 1960s (e.g., the Prague spring of 1968), which, although defeated at the time, helped to prepare the breakdown of the communist system at the end of the 1980s.

The 1960s were also marked by a significant step toward a society dominated by the visual media, a postmodern society which, Jean Baudrillard argues, knows itself only through its reflection in the media.[2] Postmodern society on the whole does not rely on traditional values. N. K. Denzin defines its characteristics as a nostalgic, conservative longing for the past, coupled with an erasure of the boundaries between the past and the present; an intense preoccupation with the real and its representations; a pornography of the visible; the commodification of sexuality and desire; a consumer culture which objectifies a set of masculine cultural ideals; intense emotional experiences shaped by anxiety, alienation, *ressentiment*, and a detachment from others.[3]

In our postmodern society signalized by the loss of traditional values, individualization, and cultural pluralism, the institutionalized form of religious practice has come under a severe crisis, which became obvious in the 1960s. Sociologists of religion claim that Christianity in a modern industrial society features tendencies toward deinstitutionalization and toward the individualization and pluralism of religious practice, ranging all the way from a fundamentalist retreat to an opening out toward the integration of non-Christian religious beliefs and practices.[4] Although religion, in its institutionalized form, may seem to disappear, basic "religious" questions appear in the writings of postmodern deconstruction theorists[5] and in the claims of art historians that, far from disappearing, the holy or sacred remains a dominant (though often disguised) theme of modern art.[6]

In addition to radical change in society, the 1960s saw transformations of cinema. New economic structures as well as aesthetic innovations helped shape the commercial cinema of Hollywood and the art cinema of Europe,[7] where a new generation of filmmakers began to dominate the scene. The "nouvelle vague" in France was the most prominent among a number of "new waves" in other countries (e.g., Great Britain, Western Germany, Czechoslovakia). The concept of "auteurism," defended by French critics and filmmakers, stressed the overall significance of the director as the creative source of a film. The new filmmaking was noted for (1) a dominance of the subjective point of view, (2) a critical view of society, sometimes even with a strong political motive, and (3) a conscious and critical use of conventional narrative and genre structures.

The market for movie entertainment, however, was dominated by products of the U.S. film industry. Significant trends in the development of the Hollywood entertainment industry began to take shape in the 1960s and reached their height during the 1970s. This phenomenon has been called the "New Hollywood."[8] The studio system of the classical Hollywood period of the 1920s, 1930s, and early 1940s could not be revived. The market was more fragmented and competitive than before, which influenced the economic and aesthetic qualities of the films of the period. As historian Thomas Schatz observes:

> In one sense the mid-1970s ascent of the New Hollywood marks the studios' eventual coming-to-terms with an increasingly fragmented entertainment industry – with its demographics and target audiences, its diversified "multi-media" conglomerates, its global(ized) markets and new delivery systems. And equally fragmented, perhaps, are the movies

themselves, especially the high-cost, high-tech, high-stakes blockbusters, those multi-purpose entertainment machines that breed music videos and soundtrack albums, TV series and videocassettes, video games and theme park rides, novelizations and comic books.[9]

Important aesthetic trends in commercial Hollywood cinema since the 1960s include (1) the strong influence of youth culture (rock music, life-style, comic book heroes, etc.), (2) the growing importance of technology (sound systems, special effects, high-tech cinema, and the like), (3) a marked tendency towards a "multi-functional movie" that mixes various genre structures as its guiding aesthetic principle. Thus, a film like *Star Wars* (1977), a typical example of this trend, manifests an intentional marketing strategy in the "radical amalgamation of genre conventions," an "elaborate play of cinematic references," and "a purposeful incoherence which actually 'opens' the film to different readings (and readers), allowing for multiple interpretive strategies and thus broadening the potential audience appeal."[10]

The dominating genres and themes of Hollywood entertainment included the action film with the undefeatable hero, the "muscle man," or the "destroyer" (Stallone, Schwarzenegger, Van Damme, Hulk Hogan); the science-fiction film as an example of high-tech cinema; the horror movie, also dominated by the special effects of catastrophe and disaster (including animal horror stories of werewolves, sharks, and dinosaurs) and nightmarish visions of the destructive psychopath ("splatter" movies).

The popularity of these genres seems to reflect the dominant marks of the postmodern society described above; namely, the consumer culture that objectifies a set of masculine cultural ideals as well as emotional experiences of anxiety, alienation and detachment from others. Against this dominant trend of action, high-tech and horror films, traditional genres of the family comedy, the romantic comedy and the western were successfully placed on the market although these genres too showed influences of the dominant trends.

II. Changes in the "Language" of Religious Films

Changing social and cultural contexts, as well as developments in the film industry, also had an effect on the religious dimension of films. If we look at the 1960s, there was the "Hollywood type" of religious film – the grand-scale epic, that was both entertaining and educational. It combined the pleasures of the audio-visual spectacle with religious instruction, addressing principally an audience that was well-acquainted with the teachings of the Bible and the church. On the other hand, we find, especially in Europe, a number of individual directors offering discussion of theological questions. These filmmakers grew up in a milieu strongly determined by religious institutions and religious practice. Ingmar Bergman, Luis Buñuel, Federico

Fellini and Pier Paolo Pasolini often talked about the strong influences of religion during their childhood, and this is clearly reflected in their films.

Film directors active in the 1970s and 1980s had grown up in a completely different cultural context. In eastern countries that were dominated by Marxist ideology, religion had a different influence. In the case of Andrei Tarkovsky, for example, we see religious tradition serving as an instrument of revolt against the overall secularization of communist ideology. Tarkovsky's ambition as an artist depends, among other things, upon a decided interest in the spiritual sources of Russian Orthodoxy, combined with a strong sense of the values of nineteenth-century Russian philosophy and literature. Although Tarkovsky preferred to talk about art and philosophy rather than about religion, the spiritual dimension is evident in all his films and writings.[11] Directors of European and American countries, who grew up in a more secular culture, often are reluctant to admit a religious dimension (e.g., Wim Wenders) or prefer to discuss human problems in their films without any explicit references to religion in its traditional form.

Among modern directors, there are only a few, like Martin Scorsese, who talk about their religious education and about religious experiences in their films. Most modern filmmakers, such as Alain Cavalier, Denys Arcand, and Krzysztof Kieslowski, typically like to be thought of as nonbelievers or agnostics. It is futile to discuss whether they are not in one sense or another religious; they prefer the point of view of the observer of, not of the participant in, a religious culture. Their approach is more investigative, more distanced than the position of Bergman or Buñuel with their lifelong struggle to deal with the psychological and theological problems caused by the normative religious milieu into which they were born.

The generation of filmmakers who began to work during the 1960s grew up in a society in which religious institutions had begun to lose their influence. The fact that they grew up in a media society is evident in their work. Seeing classical Hollywood movies was an important part of their education.

Changes in the composition of the audience are of equal importance. The typical moviehouse audience today is made up of young people between the ages of fifteen and twenty-five. Because of the secularization process, filmmakers can no longer rely on a universal knowledge of facts about Christianity. With his *Decalogue* cycle (1988-89), the Polish director Krzysztof Kieslowski caused consternation among a number of critics and viewers who could not figure out which commandment each episode referred to. Denys Arcand's *Jesus of Montreal* (1989) was well received by an audience still familiar with the Bible, but created problems for those others who could not recognize the quotations and other references to the New Testament narrative.

The rest of this essay will be dedicated to a more detailed description of dominant trends in religious cinema. Given the cultural situation already described, a filmmaker has to choose his own way of expressing religious ideas. There are, I propose, three main ways of dealing with the problem: (1) traditional religious themes can be adapted to changing audiences; (2) religious themes can be integrated into genre formulas known to be popular with audiences; and (3) new ways of dealing thematically and aesthetically with religious ideas can be devised by directors.

III. New Variations on Traditional Themes

The most obvious changes in the "language" of religious films can be observed in films dealing with traditional religious themes, especially films based on the Bible. We have examples of film versions of the New Testament from each decade, but the approach is different in each case and reflects the changes I have described.[12]

The 1960s witnessed two principal examples of Hollywood's cinematic engagement with the New Testament, Nicholas Ray's *King of Kings* (1961) and George Stevens's *The Greatest Story Ever Told* (1965). Both films are typical of the standard Hollywood format insofar as they are spectacles for the big screen, offered as educational entertainment to an unspecified audience of people from eight to eighty. Nicholas Ray's film is a Hollywood reinterpretation of the Bible, combining passages from the New Testament with purely fictional elements. Within the context of Ray's work, *King of Kings* is a kind of "antique western" with a double plot structure juxtaposing two types of "revolutions" – Barrabas's violent attacks on the Roman invaders and Jesus' message of peace and forgiveness. The absence of action scenes in the Jesus story is counterbalanced by the excitement of the Barrabas subplot. Compared to this film, George Stevens' *The Greatest Story Ever Told* – although relying a bit too heavily on the star system – is a serious Hollywood film, with a significant appeal to European sensibility in the person of its main actor, Max von Sydow, Ingmar Bergman's man of suffering. Unusually faithful to the Bible, the film strives for dramatic effect by introducing Satan (Donald Pleasance) as an antagonist.

European cinema's answer to the Hollywood epics is one of the universally acknowledged masterpieces of religious cinema – Pier Paolo Pasolini's *The Gospel According to St. Matthew* (1966). It is a subjective interpretation by an artist, which does not aim at any kind of historical reconstruction, but tries to find the contemporary relevance of Jesus' message by seeing it from the perspective of a Marxist interpretation of society.

Changes in culture and in the aesthetics of cinema are demonstrated in the controversy generated by films about Jesus since the 1960s. The series of so-called scandals of the screen that began in the 1960s includes Pasolini's *La Ricotta* (1962), Monty Python's *The Life of Brian* (1979),

Herbert Achternbusch's *The Ghost* (1982), Jean-Luc Godard's *Hail Mary* (1984), and Martin Scorsese's *The Last Temptation of Christ* (1988). The controversies surrounding these films manifested a strong interest in the person of Jesus Christ, as well as questioning the authority of the church by advancing nonorthodox, individualistic interpretations of the New Testament.

In the 1970s, the changes in the Hollywood system were reflected in new biblical movies influenced by the shift in audience (described above). *Jesus Christ Superstar* (1972) and *Godspell* (1973) are the first versions of the New Testament for a specific youth audience – "hippies" and rock music fans. In *Jesus Christ Superstar*, we can detect a more distanced approach toward the subject, as the central point of view shifts. Author Tim Rice and composer Andrew Lloyd Webber make Judas their principal character, a man who is not an atheist but nonetheless wants to be convinced that Jesus is really the son of God. Furthermore, the film is a janus-faced product of the emerging new media-dominated culture. It is one of the first examples of multimedia marketing; it also includes a criticism of the media's capacity to make stars and of the viewer's appetite for the sensational, evident both in the characterization of King Herod, who urges Jesus to demonstrate his power for a show-business effect, and in the final vision of the show's apotheosis.[13]

Another example of the genre of biblical epics of the 1970s can be seen as a reaction against the opening up to new audiences and new theological trends. Such a "reactionary" trend is typified by the fundamentalist film *Jesus* (1979), directed by John Heyman, Peter Sykes and John Kirsh as part of the "Genesis" project for presenting the Bible in a literal visual translation of the text.

At the end of the 1970s, the problems of the genre are reflected in *The Life of Brian*, made by the Monty Python comedians and perhaps the only "religious" film with a cult following among young audiences. *The Life of Brian,* with its abundance of irreverent jokes, sometimes suffering from an obvious inclination towards the vulgar, the ridiculous or the blasphemous, is not a theological criticism of the Bible. Rather, it targets modern tendencies of religious pluralism (as in the scene of competing "messiahs" in the marketplace) and, above all, Hollywood's treatment of religion – the combination of educational intentions and spectacular effects, the mixing of genres (the flying saucer episode), and the "musicalization" of serious themes (the parody in the final song).

In the 1980s, the films of Scorsese and Arcand offer even different approaches to the evangelical material. If the insight of the 1970s was that biblical epics could no longer be made, at least not for the screen and the young cinema-going public, then both Scorsese and Arcand reflect these adjustments. Scorsese's *The Last Temptation of Christ*, based on the Kazantzakis novel, treats a theological issue: the human and the divine natures of Jesus. Many problems viewers had with the film can be resolved,

I think, if we begin with the assumption that Scorsese does not present a coherent character, but rather a series of images of Jesus – some realistic, others surreal or supernatural, still others from the final dream sequence, all images on various levels of a fictional construction. Scorsese's Jesus also resembles the director's typical heroes – men obsessed by visions whose range they cannot grasp. His is a Jesus of the "mean streets."[14] The film has been misunderstood as an attempt to undermine Christian faith, but it is better seen as a postmodern vision constructed from a variety of images and meant to invite us to see Jesus from a new point of view. The fact that Scorsese does not want to give a coherent illusion of reality is supported by his aesthetic strategy of introducing irritating elements within a texture of well-known and traditional iconographical references. The very end of the film – a simple strip of celluloid – is the final destruction of the illusion.

Denys Arcand's *Jesus of Montreal* is a film by a nonbeliever who is nevertheless fascinated by the character of a man fighting the hypocrisy and materialism of modern society. Arcand, whose work is noted for its acute social criticism, admits that he is not a practicing Christian, but that the message of Jesus had some memorable elements that he wished to relate to contemporary society.[15] The starting point of his project is the simple question: what can Jesus mean to us today? For Arcand, the message of the Bible is, one among others, from those of world literature (Dostoevski, Shakespeare) with serious reflections on the meaning of life, to those of modern advertising that uses Christian iconography (walking on the water) for selling perfume and offering messages of happiness and promises of success in life. The critical analysis of the media and the merchandizing of ideas only hinted at in *Jesus Christ Superstar* or *The Life of Brian* is made a dominant theme in Arcand's film.

The films of Scorsese and Arcand accentuate the problems of talking about religion in a secular context. They offer different approaches for different kinds of viewers. They are open to interpretations of nonbelievers who deny the dual nature of Jesus as God and man, yet they are also full of allusions that can be appreciated only by those who are well-informed about the Bible and the teachings of the church and that may give them a new perspective on belief.

Whereas Scorsese and Arcand are still using a number of elements of the traditional genre, filmmakers of the avant-garde have gone one step further. The best example in this area is Jean-Luc Godard's controversial film *Hail Mary*. His version of the biblical story of Mary, retold in a modern context, is by no means a traditional story. Godard's film reflects the diversity of language; it is a collage of various forms of discourse dealing with the mystery of birth and creation in juxtaposition to texts of various types. Vulgarisms contrast with quotations from the Bible, scientific language with pornographic language, rational utterances with emotional outbursts. Another example of avant-garde filmmaking is Derek Jarman's *The*

Garden (1989), a visual symphony reflecting the author's meditation upon his own imminent death and his apocalyptic view of contemporary British society.

These changes in the biblical epic have been discussed with reference to the cinema. Although the genre has lost favor with the cinema-going public, it nonetheless continues to attract audiences on the television screen, as for example Zeffirelli's *Jesus of Nazareth* (1976), the *Anno Domini* series, and the film versions of the Old Testament now in production.

IV. The Popularization of Religious Themes

Changes in the biblical epic resulted from the fact that new audiences were addressed, and filmmakers began to reflect the media context of the message. Another new tendency in the cinema of religious ideas may be called popularization. Popular genre structures are used as a vehicle for introducing religious ideas. This is less surprising when we look at the deep structures of popular genres and discover their special affinity with religious themes. My examples in the following discussion are drawn from three of the most popular movie genres – science fiction/fantasies, thrillers, and comedies.

The science fiction genre can be used simply to devise up-to-date or seemingly modern variations on traditional stories: fairy tales, westerns, detective stories, and so on. But the genre is also a vision of history, a depiction of a future society, often including a representation of the world's end.[16] This means that it has an eschatological perspective and that one of its main concerns therefore is to define what it means to be human against the background of other forms of existence, like aliens or artificial intelligences created by man.

Changes in Christian attitudes toward film criticism of the religious dimensions of popular cinema are marked by the discussions of Stanley Kubrick's *2001: A Space Odyssey* (1968). This film provided a summarized version of human history, with a Darwinian interpretation of our beginnings, yet also with a symbol of mystery – the monolith, a strange artificial construction with a powerful energy, perhaps the memory of stored wisdom. The principal storyline focuses on the human hubris of creating tools that eventually defeat us. The "godlike" computer HAL is given the power over life and death. The impressive concluding segment with its delirious combination of color, sound and movement can be read as a journey into eternity and as a vision of man's longing for paradise. This example of science fiction with a strong undercurrent of religious sensibility was open to vastly divergent interpretations, from a seemingly rational but hypothetical vision of man being manipulated by some extraterrestrial intelligence to an acknowledgment of a symbolic treatment of God's existence.

It became almost fashionable to use religious motifs in popular science fiction movies during the 1970s and 1980s. Noted examples are the *Star Wars* trilogy (*Star Wars*, 1977; *The Empire Strikes Back*, 1980; and *Return of the Jedi*, 1983), the *Star Trek* movies (1979, 1982, 1984, 1986, 1989, 1991) and Steven Spielberg's *E.T.: The Extra-Terrestrial* (1982). These were, for the most part, fairy tales or adventure stories. *Star Wars* combined the fairy tale and the mythological story of the conflict between good and evil with the religious motif of the "Force" as a transcendental power. The spiritual guides of the hero – Obi Wan Kenobi, Yoda, and Darth Vader, become a variation of the Christian concept of the Trinity. The mission of the spaceship *Enterprise* led Captain Kirk and his crew on a search for God in the fifth film of the series (*Star Trek V: The Final Frontier*, 1989). And *E.T.* was a Spielberg fantasy about a Christ-like extraterrestrial redeemer, a child's dream of God.

A cult movie of the 80s, Ridley Scott's *Blade Runner* (1982), is not as obvious an example of religious themes as the films cited above, but it is surely more interesting. On the surface, it seems to be above all a variation of the detective thriller with the future world introduced as a variation on the basic pattern, but hidden beneath this surface is a serious attempt to raise fundamental questions of existence. The tragic figure is the replicant Roy Batty, who is trying to find his "maker" to get from him an extended period of "life." Tyrell, the man who created the artificial being, is portrayed as someone trying to play God. He greets Batty, his creature, as the "prodigal son," one of the very few explicit references to religious motifs. A "religious" reading of the film reveals that the story is designed to raise fundamental queries about life. In fact, Deckard, the officer called to "terminate" the replicant, comments on Batty's "death" as follows: "He wanted to know what everybody wants to know. Where do I come from? Where am I going? How long have I got?"[17]

All types of crime fiction have always had a strong affinity with theological speculations about evil, the nature of guilt, and the necessity for redemption.[18] Religious dimensions in crime movies have taken various forms over the last two decades. An Amish community standing for love and peace confronts the world of urban violence in Peter Weir's *Witness* (1985). Ulu Grosbard's *True Confessions* (1981) combines the detective story with a meditation on ethics. Unlike Weir's film, however, Grosbard's shows that crime and corruption are present even in the Christian community. The paradox of a society relying on Christian rituals and values, yet depending upon violence as a means of controlling business, is depicted in *The Godfather* trilogy (1972, 1974, 1990) by Francis Ford Coppola.

Two recent examples of thrillers with a religious dimension are Martin Scorsese's *Cape Fear* (1991) and Abel Ferrara's *Bad Lieutenant* (1992). Scorsese's film is a remake of the J. Lee Thompson film of the same name (1962). One of the obvious additions to the original plot of a killer taking revenge on a family is the religious dimension. Scorsese's killer, played as an incarnation of the devil by Robert de Niro, has his body covered with tattoos, all symbols and quotations from the Old Testament. The devil incarnate seems to have come to earth to haunt a family for the evil they have done. Unlike the earlier version, Scorsese's film levels a sharp criticism at modern society. His protagonists are far from being close to the ideal happy family; in fact, they seem to have lost genuine values and traditional orientations.

Abel Ferrara's *Bad Lieutenant* is a most unusual example of a spiritual thriller. Ferrara, who made his reputation as an "underground" filmmaker, shows the darkest side of urban existence. His protagonist is a policeman close to a complete breakdown, a man who has lost control of his life. When he is confronted with a nun who has been raped by young drug addicts, he experiences the mystery of true forgiveness. He comes to see his own life in a new way. In his despair he cries out to Jesus for help and has a vision of Jesus approaching. Ferrara's film is almost unbearable in its naturalistic description of the ugliest sides of a policeman's life with all its moral depravity. On the other hand, he juxtaposes the ugly and the holy by offering a very concrete, though naive vision of Jesus intervening in man's life in a situation without hope.

The Godfather, Part II, Francis Ford Coppola, 1974

The third popular genre I am concerned with, by stark comparison, effectively shows the sunny side of life. Marked by its movement toward a better society (a "happy ending") and its deep mythical structures of rebirth, salvation, and forgiveness,[19] comedy has a natural penchant for religious subjects although there are very few examples of good comic inventions in "religious" cinema. The popularization of comedy seems to result more often in works of minor artistic quality, as the *Oh, God!* trilogy indicates: *Oh, God!* (1977), *Oh God! Book II* (1980), *Oh God, You Devil* (1984). God appears in these films as a visible character, but in diminutive perspective – as the friendly, well-meaning old grandpa, portrayed on the screen by comedian George Burns. Various attempts have been made to use a convent as an apt setting for comic purposes, most successfully in *Sister Act* (1992), a kind of musical comedy based on the traditional simple plot – Catholicism made popular in a pop setting.

Serious religious themes have been integrated most successfully in comedies that are situated on the boundaries of the genre where it merges into tragedy. The best examples are Woody Allen's urban comedies, mixing Bergman's existentialism with a Noel Coward battle of the sexes. Allen's philosophical and theological meditations upon existential problems have reached an admirable perfection with films like *Hannah and Her Sisters* (1986) and *Crimes and Misdemeanors* (1989).

Another outstanding example in the comedy genre is Terry Gilliam's *The Fisher King*, mentioned in the introduction to this essay, a serio-comic story about an "odd couple" that is perhaps the most typical example of a film using all conventions of modern commercial cinema, but with a depth of thought too.

The religious dimension in these and similar films must to be taken seriously. Religious ideas such as meditations upon guilt, redemption and the meaning of life are not used in a speculative way to make an otherwise unattractive story more sensational. These films constitute ways of talking to people about their existential problems at a level on which they can be easily addressed. Critics often tend to prefer the more intellectual efforts of modern filmmakers, but such a stance is unjustified. These examples show that directors as well as audiences are very much interested in religious questions.

V. New Spirituality, New Aesthetics

Whereas one might call the tendency described above as an attempt to adapt to the demands of the movie business and thus to conform to secular society by offering multi-perspective films with religious themes, another tendency might be described as a counter-movement to the classic *auteur* cinema. The principal proponents of art cinema have tried to find new aesthetic formulas to express their sense of spirituality. Three directors are presented below as representatives of tendencies that might be regarded more precisely as the "new religious cinema": Andrei Tarkovsky, Wim Wenders, and Krzysztof Kieslowski.

Tarkovsky is in a way the prophet of the most radical form of "auteurism," an artist of highest ambitions and a kind of modern-day martyr of the cinema, at the same time the prophet of a new revitalization of the rich spiritual sources of eastern Europe. Wenders, on the other hand, works within the secularized society of western Europe; he is the prophet of a "secular spirituality," and Kieslowski is somewhere in-between, a man who grew up in a society with a very strong religious tradition, but who exhibits a secular approach in his treatment of religion.

Andrei Tarkovsky is the most prominent figure in the European religious cinema of the 1980s.[20] His reception by western European filmmakers and critics was most unusual inasmuch as he seemed to be the incarnation of a radical noncommercial attitude as well as a radical aestheticism of cinematic style, the very opposite of the Hollywood format in its visual combination of meditation and overwhelming power.

His outstanding quality lay in his ability to revive the spiritual traditions of Russia. Tarkovsky's use of religion is a perfect example of a strategy designed to defend the richness of the eastern European spirituality not only against a communist ideology based on "scientific" principles but also against western materialism and decadence. Religion in Tarkovsky's films is closely related to literature, well acquainted as he was with the tradition of the great nineteenth-century Russian literary humanists like Tolstoi and Dostoevski, and the idealism of the German romanticists.

Tarkovsky's style is the complete opposite of the popularizing tendency described above, although he too uses the science fiction genre to articulate his message in *Solaris* (1972) and *Stalker* (1979). His films are hermetic, enigmatic, and full of private memories and literary references; nonetheless their power is also felt by people who do not understand all his allusions. His meditative style based on the logic of association invites people to bring in their own memories, made easier by the universal symbols he uses like water, fire, and home. Another tendency evident in Tarkovsky's work is a kind of sacralization of art. The artist in his search for the truth, the absolute, the ideal is endowed with an aura of spirituality. Tarkovsky becomes a kind of prophet, a high priest or spiritual guide, engaging people who do not see what he sees most clearly.

Wenders is a completely different type of personality and director. His works have never been regarded as religious on the surface, but research by theologians has uncovered a strong spiritual dimension to his films.[21] Almost all of his films are road movies. They tell stories of people who have lost their families or their *Heimat*; they are people alienated from their normal course in life and forced to find their own way because they cannot rely on traditions. Wenders's attitude toward the world is nonideological, believing as he does that German tradition – its political and cinematic history – has been cursed by the ideological use of images. Wenders's way of seeking the truth, therefore, cannot rely on memory, on reviving a spirituality of old. His approach to reality lies in the openness of "seeing." The "act of seeing," different from the act of reflecting, is a way of being open to reality, perhaps a way of seeing things anew.

There are very few explicit references to religion. In *Kings of the Road* (1975), the hope for redemption is reflected in an object found along the road: a crucifix with a Jesus figure that seems to be flying upward. When one of the protagonists raises his arms in imitation of the gesture of the Jesus figure, he implicitly relates to a religious context. In his recent works, however, Wenders has incorporated a more explicit religious dimension, as in his films about angels – *Wings of Desire* (1987) and, more so, *Far Away, So Close* (1992), which has a definite Christian message. The angels announce that they are messengers of the light and that they are trying to bring people closer to "Him."

Krzysztof Kieslowski was born to a culture deeply influenced by religious traditions, yet his approach to reality is perhaps the most radical position of an observer free from any ideological and theological positions. He started his career as a director of documentaries, as an acute observer of human life in its complexity and contradictions. His fictional work is a genuine continuation of his project "to see human life as it is." In his documentary work, he found out that he could not observe people in those moments when they were confronted with radical choices and thus realized

A Short Film About Love, (Long Version, *Decalogue VI*)
Krzysztof Kieslowski, 1989

that he could not get to the "inner life" through the documentary method. So he created his fictions as a kind of moral trial, moving his characters like chessmen into situations of complex ethical choices and observing how they react. He neither preaches nor tries to convince people that God exists. His characters seem to be under the influence of some power, but the films are open to divergent interpretations that see the workings of chance in human life as well as the possibility of God's intervention in it.

In his *Decalogue* cycle, the Ten Commandments are his frame of reference. The situations he invents with his coauthor Krzysztof Piesiewicz are always so complex that they do not offer easy answers. The commandments are not presented as a solution to the problem but as a means to sharpen our awareness of ethical problems in a world that has abandoned clear definitions.[22]

The examples discussed here prove that the religious is present in modern cinema as a dimension of far greater importance than one might suspect in a "secular" world. As I have tried to show, religious motifs and ideas are to be found in almost all genres and, to some extent, a study of these dimensions now raises greater problems of analysis than in times past when "religious films" could be identified more easily. The effort is well worth making.

Endnotes

1. See the position described in Peter Hasenberg et al., *Religion im Film: Lexikon mit Kurzkritiken und Stichworten zu 1200 Kinofilmen* (Cologne: Katholisches Institut für Medieninformation, 1992), 9-13.

2. Jean Baudrillard, *America* (London: Verso, 1988), 104.

3. Norman K. Denzin, *Images of Postmodern Society: Social Theory and Contemporary Cinema* (London: Sage, 1991), vii.

4. See Karl Gabriel, *Christentum zwischen Tradition und Postmoderne, Quaestiones Disputatae*, 141 (Freiburg: Herder, 1992).

5. See Philippa Berry and Andrew Wernick, *Shadow of Spirit: Postmodernism and Religion* (London: Routledge, 1992).

6. See Dietmar Kamper and Christoph Wulf, ed., *Das Heilige: Seine Spur in der Moderne* (Frankfort: Athenäum, 1987).

7. See Pierre Sorlin, *European Cinemas, European Societies, 1939-1990* (London: Routledge, 1991), 138ff.

8. See Thomas Schatz, "The New Hollywood," in *Film Theory Goes to the Movies*, ed. Jim Collins, Hilary Radner, and Ava Preacher Collins (London: Routledge, 1993), 8-36.

9. Ibid., 9ff.

10. Ibid., 23.

11. Tarkovsky's theory of art is developed in his book *Sculpting in Time* (Bodley Head, 1986).

12. For a more detailed discussion of the history of the genre, see the essay by Peter Malone in this volume, and *Jesus in der Hauptrolle: Zur Geschichte und Ästhetik der Jesus-Filme, film-dienst Extra* (Cologne: Katholisches Institut für Medieninformation, 1992).

13. See my *"Clown und Superstar,"* in *Jesus in der Hauptrolle*, 36-41.

14. See David Thompson and Ian Christie, eds., *Scorsese on Scorsese* (London: Faber and Faber, 1989), 116-45.

15. See the interview with Arcand quoted in the film's press book.

16. Consult theories of the genre such as Robert Scholes and Eric S. Rabkin, *Science Fiction: History-Science-Vision* (New York: Oxford University Press, 1977) or Ulrich Suerbaum, Ulrich Broich, and Raimund Borgmeier, *Science Fiction: Theorie und Geschichte, Themen und Typen, Form und Weltbild* (Stuttgart: Reclam, 1981).

17. The commentary given by Deckard was omitted in the director's cut of the film.

18. In crime fiction, the detective and the priest have been regarded as twins: G.K. Chesterton's Father Brown became as famous in literature as his "secular" counterpart in the movies, Sir Arthur Conan Doyle's Sherlock Holmes.

19. For example, see Northrop Frye, *Anatomy of Criticism: Four Essays* (Princeton NJ: Princeton University Press, 1957), esp. 163ff.

20. For further readings on the evaluation of Tarkovsky's work by Christian film critics and theologians, consult *Erinnerungen an die Wahrheit: Andrej Tarkowskij, Beiheft 3 der FILM-Korrespondenz* (Cologne: Katholisches Institut für Medieninformation, 1987).

21. See my essay and other contributions on Wenders in Michael Kuhn, Johan G. Hahn, and Henk Hoekstra, eds., *Hinter den Augen ein eigenes Bild: Film und Spiritualität* (Zürich: Benziger, 1991).

22. See Walter Lesch and Matthias Loretan, eds., *Das Gewicht der Gebote und die Möglichkeiten der Kunst: Krzysztof Kieslowskis "Dekalog" – Filme als ethische Modelle* (Freiburg: Herder, 1993).

4

Jesus on Our Screens

Peter Malone

The scene is a boardroom, up-to-date and flashy; the occasion, a marketing presentation. The board members, male executives, including some nattily-garbed clerics, discuss business in their assured way. Some nuns sit, demurely attentive. Onto the screen flashes an Identikit slide, a young man with curly hair, curly beard. You might momentarily mistake him for Jesus. But, no. It's not a mistake. The board's talk is of charism, media image and research for U.S. presidential election candidates: they are searching for a marketable Jesus. This is evangelization by media, a publication of the Gospels with live photography of Jesus – Jesus in action. The head cleric has a candidate who matches the Identikit, a hitchhiker he picked up on the autostrada, a man just released from an institution. This, of course, is only a movie. It is called *Cercasi Gesú* (*Looking for Jesus*, 1982). It is Luigi Comencini's offbeat presentation of a Jesus-figure for the 1980s.

I. A Century of Images of Jesus

To appreciate how Jesus Christ has been imaged on our screens, it will help to survey each decade of the century and note the changes or developments.[1] From the beginnings of cinema in the 1890s, Jesus stories have been a popular staple of movie entertainment and instruction.

Already by 1900, the Salvation Army in Australia had produced *Soldiers of the Cross*, an evening of film clips, slides and lecture on the Gospels and church history. However, it was not the art traditions of centuries that influenced the new medium, but rather the popular art of the times, the plaster statue and holy card style. This was to continue, reinforced by the popularity of such grandiose directors as Cecil B. De Mille. Within ten years, by 1910, national industries were in their infancies. The technology of cameras, projectors and film stocks contributed to the popularity of the "one-reeler," especially at American nickelodeons. Biblical stories, from commercial producers and religious groups, proliferated. Italy and France were prominent in making these films.

The next decade was significant. By 1920, Jesus had been seen in already established "full-length feature films." *From the Manger to the Cross*, filmed on location in Egypt, was a reverent attempt at high religious cinematic art. However, the British censors decided that it was not appropriate for the figure of Jesus to be seen fully on screen; suggestion of his presence (back of the head, shoulder, etc.) would be sufficient. The United States did not follow this lead, and D.W. Griffith included the Gospel story among those in his 1916 film *Intolerance*.

Cecil B. De Mille was the principal figure of the 1920s, combining evangelical fervor with showmanship. His 1927 *The King of Kings* set expectations of how the movies would handle the Bible: sex, sin and extreme reverence for Jesus. De Mille ordered his star H. B. Warner to stay, even to eat, alone in his trailer to preserve the atmosphere of a sacred, superhuman haloed Jesus. This reverence continued into the 1930s.

By 1940, however, there had scarcely been any significant images of Jesus on screen except in the French film *Golgotha* (1935). Jesus is glimpsed from the back or at a distance in *The Last Days of Pompeii* (1935). During the war years, there were even fewer images of Jesus. 1950 saw controversy and a sign of things to come with Roberto Rossellini's *The Miracle* (scripted by Fellini), a contemporary allegorical treatment of Mary's pregnancy.

The 1950s more than made up for the reticence of the preceding decades. Biblical stories seem to have been destined for wide-screen Cinemascope treatment. Indirect glimpses of Jesus were still in vogue, however, in such movies as *The Robe* (1953) and *Ben-Hur* (1959). Then a number of churches decided to make their own biblical and gospel films in the 50s, the Methodists with the 1953 *Prince of Peace* and the Catholics with Fr. Patrick Peyton's short star-studded dramas for his Rosary Crusade. These films did not feel the need to conceal Jesus.

The 1960s was the decade of the Gospel movies. Perhaps it was the freedom and changes of the era, but Jesus was no longer hidden: Jeffrey Hunter became the *King of Kings* (1962), and Max von Sydow portrayed a nordic Jesus in *The Greatest Story Ever Told* (1965). Passion sequences were included in *Pontius Pilate* and *Barabbas*, made in Italy in 1962. However, critics were more impressed with the starker, black-and-white Jesus of Pier Paolo Pasolini's 1964 *The Gospel According to St. Matthew*.

During the 1970s there were both developments and changes. Franco Zeffirelli's mini-series *Jesus of Nazareth* (1977) highlighted how literal in interpretation previous movies had been. Zeffirelli was reverent, but took pains to locate the Gospels as religious writings of their time. The changes came in the stylizing of the Gospel images, especially with contemporary music, in the rock styles of *Jesus Christ Superstar* and *Godspell*, both movies released in 1973. Other directors took to using images of Jesus to make points – for instance, Dalton Trumbo's having Donald Sutherland as Jesus drive a train through the dreams of a World War I amputee in

Johnny Got His Gun (1971). Presuppositions about biblical epics were given a satiric jolt by the Monty Python group's British humor in *The Life of Brian* (1979). Still, as late as 1979, Peter Sykes's very literal *Jesus*, starring Brian Deaon, was released.

After Zeffirelli and the rock operas, what next? The late 1980s saw two significant attempts to portray Jesus. Martin Scorsese's adaptation of Kazantzakis's *The Last Temptation of Christ* (1988) was a fictional interpretation of Jesus and his tormented sense of mission as well as of an imagined temptation to get down from the cross and live a decent, ordinary life. In 1989 came the adroit story of the Christ-like Daniel, and his staging of the passion, in Denys Arcand's *Jesus of Montreal*.

The trend of the 80s to use images of Jesus to make points and to illustrate characters and themes (as well as to critique them) has become more widespread, with frequent use of the crucifix, of verbal images (as in the debates of *The Name of the Rose* [1987]) and of Jesus as icon (as in Abel Ferrara's *Bad Lieutenant* [1992]). This trend needs further consideration, and is in fact the principal focus of this essay.

II. Terminology

Gospel stories and images are an intrinsic part of world culture, especially western culture. The metaphors of crucifixion, resurrection, son of God, and miracles are used by believer and nonbeliever alike. A distinction can be made between the "Christianity of Faith" and the "Christianity of Culture." The former is lived Christianity, commitment (however minimal), belief and an acknowledgment of Jesus as Lord and Savior, usually in a church community. The latter is an understanding and use of the tenets and stories of Christianity that does not necessarily involve any personal commitment. Filmmakers generally use aspects of the Christianity of culture.

Since the middle of the nineteenth century, there has been a terminology of biblical interpretation and theological study, associated with rationalist scholar Ernst Renan, that distinguishes between the "Jesus of history" and the "Christ of faith." In the name of historical accuracy, scholars attempted to establish the facts about Jesus of Nazareth, the "Jesus of history." In contrast, the believers in the Gospels were committed to the "Christ of faith." This distinction is still maintained, but it is less useful and helpful than it was in the wake of developments in biblical studies and the growth of a personalized spirituality centered on Jesus. This distinction is not at all useful in achieving an understanding of Jesus-figures.

Preference here is given to the distinction between "Jesus-figures" and "Christ-figures."[2] Malachi Martin, in his 1977 book *Jesus Now*, develops this distinction and uses it to appreciate how Jesus Christ has been presented and interpreted in the arts for 2000 years. "Jesus-figure" refers to any representation of Jesus himself. "Christ-figure" describes any figure in the arts who resembles Jesus. The personal name of Jesus (in line with contemporary spirituality, thought and practice) is used for the Jesus-figure. The title "Christ" – the "Messiah," or the "Anointed One" – is used for those who are seen to reflect his mission. In cinema, writers and directors present both Jesus-figures and Christ-figures.

One might ask how the distinction between faith and culture relates to these figures, to "Jesus-figures of faith" and "Jesus-figures of culture." (A suggestion has been made that the later might be represented in lower case type as jesus-figures.) However, it is difficult to assess faith and/or culture in popular cinema, since the director may be drawing on faith experience while asserting the portrait is cultural. A useful example is *The Last Temptation of Christ*, an amalgam of Greek Orthodox Nikos Kazantzakis's novel, Calvinist Paul Schrader's screenplay, and Catholic Martin Scorsese's direction. Is this "fictional" portrait a faith/Jesus or a culture/Jesus – or both?

It is necessary to note that Jesus-figures can be "realistic" or "stylized." Any representation of Jesus as a thirty-year-old, first-century, middle-eastern man might be realistic, but this is not how Jesus is generally represented. Nonetheless, most artists seem to be trying to represent Jesus "realistically." The work of the Renaissance painters and the movies of Cecil B. De Mille are all presumed attempts at realism, despite the Umbrian backgrounds or the special effects. Even the highly-praised *The Gospel According to St. Matthew* was an attempt to make Jesus more realistic and less a Hollywood concoction, and *Jesus of Nazareth* offered historical background and explanations to make Jesus more real.

The tradition of literal interpretation of the Scriptures has also reinforced the belief that artists are presenting a realistic Jesus-figure. Pasolini's infancy stories are no more realistic than those of *King of Kings* or *The Greatest Story Ever Told*. They just look starker in black and white and in simpler locations (which are Italian, especially the high mountain of the crucifixion, rather than Palestinian). Most of the popular screen Jesus-figures are based on literal, almost fundamentalist, readings of the Gospels.

And that of course means that almost all Jesus-figures are, in fact, stylized. It might be more obvious to western sensibilities regarding an Aboriginal Madonna and Child or an African Madonna and Child than in contemplating the work of Raphael, but these images are stylized. The coming of Jesus as Superstar at the end of the 60s and in the carnival and vaudeville atmosphere of *Godspell* shocked many devout people, believers or not, but it highlighted how much the Jesus-figure was in fact stylized – and freed artists of the 70s and 80s to be adventurous in the way they dared to portray Jesus. What would *Jesus of Montreal* be without *Jesus Christ Superstar*?

III. Jesus-figures in the 1980s and 1990s

The Jesus-figure, which is the dominant focus of this study, is any representation of Jesus himself: a crucifix, a statue of the Sacred Heart, a Rouault Jesus-clown, verbal references, a "Negro Spiritual," the music of Bach's *Passion* or Andrew Lloyd Webber's *Jesus Christ Superstar*. The range of Jesus-figures indicates how movie-makers have felt freer to use "sacred" images to dramatize, illustrate or critique their characters and values.[3] They are following the lead of directors like Dalton Trumbo, whose *Johnny Got His Gun* had a brief tongue-in-cheek glimpse of Jesus. Ken Russell, dubbed by journalists as the British *enfant terrible* of his day, appears on the dust jacket of John Baxter's biography of him, large as life in sloppy clothes, grinning from a cross, crowned with thorns. Arresting and bizarre images of Jesus recur in the fantasies of Russell's characters, in *Mahler* (1974), *Tommy* (1975) and *Lisztomania* (1975), and more explicitly in *The Devils* (1971), where Oliver Reed's Jesuit Father Grandier becomes Jesus walking on the water or coming down from the cross to embrace Mary Magdalene during the Rosary fantasy prayers of Vanessa Redgrave's Mother Superior in Richelieu's Loudon.

IV. Satiric Images

A striking play on Jesus-figures in a satirical context came in Peter Medak's 1973 *The Ruling Class*, starring Peter O'Toole. An insane member of the British aristocracy, he spends a great deal of his time on a mantelpiece, arms extended as in crucifixion. Obviously, he sees himself as Jesus on the cross. However, he is treated by a psychiatrist and is eventually proclaimed cured. Lest he appear normal, he switches from being Jesus to being Jack the Ripper.

In 1981, comedian Mel Brooks made *History of the World – Part I*, which poked fun at topics as diverse as Moses, the Ten Commandments (fifteen until Moses accidentally drops a tablet of five), and the Inquisition (with nuns becoming Esther Williams-like figure swimmers). It also included a Last Supper skit that parodied Leonardo da Vinci, with John Hurt as Jesus. It was a flip farce, potentially (and actually) offensive, yet Brooks is obviously a comic writer-director, mocking religious pretensions.

Brooks had a British precedent in *The Life of Brian* (1979), the Monty Python team's brilliant parody of biblical epics and factional Christianity. The film avoids leaving itself open to attack as being offensive to Christianity by showing Brian's birth and his harridan mother; nonetheless, North American Christians campaigned against the movie. The Magi, having delivered their gifts at Brian's house, notice the real crib up the street and hastily retrieve their offerings. Less defensible perhaps is the mass crucifixion sequence with its good-mannered distributor of crosses as well as the group of the crucified singing, "Always look on the bright side of life." These are images of the Jesus of culture, not the Jesus of faith. Because they may offend, sensitivity needs to be respected. At heart, though, they are images critical of religious hypocrisy.

The story opening this essay was from the Italian film *Cercasi Gesú,* whose central character is a genial man named Giovanni, who looks a bit like a contemporary Jesus, with his curly hair and beard. After being discharged from a mental institution, he gets a ride from a modern priest who happens to be in charge of the publication of a life of Jesus, illustrated with photos of a Jesus look-alike. Giovanni meets the computer's requirements for a Jesus face that the public would find attractive. When he agrees to do the job, he is scrubbed, coiffeured and groomed for maximum photogenic appeal.

The Ruling Class, Peter Medak, 1972

He upsets his mentors (except the simple priest assigned to look after him whom, Giovanni realizes, the others look down on) when he intervenes at a press conference. He is silenced, but finally bangs out an extemporaneous ballad on the piano about the deal made with him and about his being silenced for the benefit of the journalists.

Behind the scenes, he resembles Jesus in his caring for a drug-addict mother who squanders the money he gives her, a terrorist who has befriended him, and children whom he allows to play in forbidden places. The parallels are not particularly subtle, but they are done well with considerable humor and with some significant irony about the church and our living of the Gospels.

One may not expect to see Jesus on screen in a film titled *The Favor, the Watch and the Very Big Fish*, but Ben Lewin's 1991 film is central to a discussion of the 80s and 90s. Its plot is similar to *Cercasi Gesù*. Bob Hoskins plays a photographer commissioned by a religious dealer to illustrate the life of Jesus with photos of Gospel tableaux. Parallel to this plot is another concerning a young woman and her concern for a melancholy Jewish pianist, played by Jeff Goldblum, who is arrested and spends some time in jail. He emerges with long hair and a beard – the perfect candidate for the model of Jesus. He accepts. Although he is quite cantankerous on the set, he is a perfectionist about the photographs themselves. In a park, he is literally mistaken for Jesus and is asked for a miracle. When he agrees to pray for and lay hands on a blind boy, he closes his eyes devoutly, as do the women who request the healing, and the boy is accidentally hit on the head with a flying ball, recovering his sight. The film looks at the consequences for the pianist, who begins to believe in his healing gifts, and for people who think he is Jesus, as he finally walks on water. Thus, the movie pokes satiric fun at faith and religiosity.

The Jesus-figures in these movies are cultural vehicles for alerting audiences to authentic religion and genuine living out of Gospel principles as compared to the phoniness and hypocrisy of so many professed Christians and their practices.

V. The Marginalized

Jesus lived on the margins of the Jewish society of his day, identifying with lepers, attracting the prostitutes and the extortionate tax-collectors, and offering discipleship to women. Yet he is persecuted and finally executed. No wonder that minority groups identify with Jesus. Sidney Poitier's agreeable Homer, the builder in *Lilies of the Field* (his 1963 Oscar-winning performance), shows the American black, in the context of Homer's building a chapel for refugee German sisters, as more religious than his employers.

In the 70s and 80s, homosexuals emerged as a group demanding recognition and respect. With the strict stances taken by the Catholic Church on issues of sexual morality, it is not surprising that gay writers and movie directors have decided to use Christian icons and imagery to make points about their identity and their plea for just treatment by society. A visually daring treatment can be found in Paul Verhoeven's *The Fourth Man* (1979), a study of a Dutch Catholic homosexual writer played by Jeroen Krabbe. Already in the opening credits, tracking shots of the writer's bedroom reveal crucifixes and other statues. A tone is set. Later, he becomes infatuated with a young man glimpsed at a railway station.

A church sequence tests the limits on using images of the Jesus of culture: the writer enters a church to pray and glances toward a life-size crucifix high on a side wall. As he looks again, he imagines (and the audience sees) the young man, wearing a red loincloth, stretched on the cross. The man approaches, embracing the legs of the crucified, drawing down the loincloth. An editor's cut shows an elderly woman quizzically watching the writer, who looks embarrassed and glances at the crucifix, which is now the original figure of Jesus. Sexuality, religion, infatuation, prayer, even homosexuality: it is difficult to elaborate in words on the complexities of the images and the challenges to an audience's moral and religious presuppositions.

Designer turned movie-maker Derek Jarman has made many short films that are experimental both in technique and in content. His experimentation in feature films began with his homoerotic interpretation of the St. Sebastian story, *Sebastiane* (1975). Jarman, who has worked with Ken Russell (doing the production design for *The Devils*), uses flamboyant images similar to Russell's. His religious imagery and Christian symbolism reached something of a climax in his experimental feature *The Garden*, which won a mention from an OCIC jury at the Berlin Film Festival of 1990. In it the Jesus-figure is used to highlight the plight of homosexuals (and the HIV-infected) as well as to expose British intolerance.

A more reticent movie-maker with the same interest and a more autobiographical commitment to the theme is Terence Davies, the British writer-director of *Distant Voices, Still Lives* (1988). In his *The Long Day Closes* (1992), the central character is a prepubescent boy moving from primary to secondary school, beginning to be aware of his sexual orientation (with crucifixion overtones). He is devout (filmed praying in Davies' own Liverpool parish church), though starting a journey that will lead him out of the church.

VI. Horror

A standard confrontation in vampire movies is for the hero to grab a crucifix or a cross, or to try to make a cross with sticks or even his fingers in order to ward off the approach of the living dead. In origin, a representation of the power of the Jesus of faith, the crucifix, when used to ward off vampires, is obviously a well-known image of the Jesus of culture (at least to frequent moviegoers).

Francis Ford Coppola has given us the most lavish and intelligent recent vampire movie, *Bram Stoker's Dracula* (1992). It offers a 90s audience a range of Antichrist images in terms of vampires, associating them with the end of the Victorian era and the emergence of science and technology, confronting traditional religion and values. There is, however, a strong prologue taking the audience back to the 15th century to explain why Vlad, Count Dracula, became the avenging living dead.

Vlad, a Christian crusader, is betrayed, and his wife, deceived by Turkish misinformation, destroys herself. In powerful visual imagery, Vlad (Gary Oldman) turns against God, piercing the huge crucifix in his chapel. It gushes blood, the blood of Christ, in profound contrast with the vampire's desperate thirst for life-giving blood, which sets him on his course of death and destruction. The link with sexuality is strong, heterosexual love and lust being associated with the life-blood. This line of reflection can lead into age-old myths in which Christianity intermingles with pagan myths and practices.

VII. The Crucifix

Crucifixes have already been noted as key to so many movies with Jesus-figures. Because the sign of the cross is so central to Christian faith, it is appropriate and inevitable that the visual focus will be on the crucifix. There is no problem when the appeals are tasteful. Thus, in his novels of the 40s and 50s, Giovanni Guareschi found that the perfect place for Jesus to speak with Don Camillo was in the parish church and from the crucifix. In the 1953 film *Don Camillo*, the padre, played by French comedian Fernandel, berates Jesus on the cross about football matches, biased umpiring and cheating, then angrily drop-kicks the ball through the confessional opening. Jesus yells out cheerfully, "Goal." *Don Camillo*, received a 70s television series remake, starring Mario Adorf.

But the crucifix continues to constitute a serious confrontation with the wisdom of this world, as two examples will illustrate. In Cliff Osmond's *The Penitent* (1986), the audience is taken into the world of a remote Mexican village, where each year the passion of Jesus is reenacted, with the man chosen to portray Jesus staying on the cross for the same length of time as Jesus and running the risk of death. The main plot concerns a husband and wife, seduction and fidelity. The chosen candidate (Raul Julia), after walking the village path to Golgotha, concedes his place to his rival (Armand Assante). The amoral Assante is sure that he will not die. As the husband endures on the cross and the people raise a crucifix facing him, the camera cuts from one to the other, creating a moral crisis for him and confronting the audience with the two images. Who is the crucified Jesus and what does his crucifixion mean?

The other example is from a British production of 1987, Mike Hodges' adaptation of Jack Higgins's best-seller about the IRA and gangsters in London, *A Prayer for the Dying*. Mickey Rourke is a disillusioned gunman who has accidentally killed a busload of school children. He has also befriended a parish priest (Bob Hoskins) and fallen in love with the priest's blind niece (Sammi Davis). However, he has one last hit, a seemingly repectable funeral director who is actually a thug (Alan Bates). They confront one another in the loft of the church. As the suitcase-bomb explodes, Rourke is sent hurtling from the loft. A life-size crucifix breaks his fall. He grasps the figure of Jesus, clings to it, in fact embraces it. Not able to hold on for long, he falls to the church floor. But the crucifix, loosened from the wall, crashes down on top of him. When the priest and his niece return to the church, the IRA gunman has repented and is urged to make his act of contrition. He dies whispering, "God."

An example in the same vein comes from the author of *The Exorcist*, William Peter Blatty, in his movie *Twinkle, Twinkle, Killer Kane* (1980), also known as *The Ninth Configuration*. The setting is a rehabilitation center for disturbed soldiers returned from Vietnam, involves a strange psychiatrist and includes a great deal of religious symbolism, including the Eucharist and a crucifix.

Two recent cinematic characters converse with Jesus on the cross, first in prayer and then in denial. Early in Oliver Stone's *Born on the Fourth of July* (1989), Tom Cruise as Ron Kovic, the enthusiastic young athlete, prays for guidance in his decision to join the Marines and fight the communists in Vietnam. Wounded in body (he is a paraplegic) and in spirit (he has accidentally killed a comrade, though officials cover it up), he comes home desperate and drunk and rails against the crucifix and his mother's unyielding belief; his own loss of faith in absolutely everything he believed in is apparent. He is on his own cross.

Quite different in its entertainment approach is Brett Leonard's version of a Stephen King horror story, *The Lawnmower Man* (1992). A mentally disabled gardener, Jobe (Jeff Fahey), lives in a church attic where he is disciplined, literally beaten by the sadistic pastor. He talks to Jesus on the church's large cross as he cleans and dusts. He becomes involved in experiments in virtual reality, his intelligence evolving beyond expectations. However, he is also programmed as a war weapon by Washington. By now a neo-"Frankenstein" monster, he is confronted within the computer games by the doctor who "created" him. Diabolical, Jobe crucifies the doctor who has come to rescue him, the brightly-colored, stylized computer-image crucifix a symbol of the future.

One of the most striking of the crucified Jesus-figures is in Abel Ferrara's *Bad Lieutenant* (1992). Harvey Keitel portrays a corrupt New York police officer whose descent into drugs, sexual degradation and greed is grimly detailed. A nun is raped in the sanctuary of a church by youths high on drugs. During this rape sequence, joltingly rough, we glimpse the church's statuary in montage, but also see Jesus dying on the cross, a symbol of what the nun experiences.

Unmoved, the lieutenant investigates the case until he interrogates the nun in the sanctuary of the church. She refuses to name her assailants, forgiving them like Christ on the cross. This forgiveness disturbs him; he cannot fathom it. Desperate and high on drugs, he hallucinates, seeing the crucified Jesus standing in the aisle of the church gazing at him with compassion. As he crawls toward Jesus, he abuses him in gutter language, demanding to know where Jesus was when he was experiencing his moral collapse. As the lieutenant is momentarily graced, redemption seems possible. These images of Keitel and the statuary are reminiscent of his first film role in Martin Scorsese's first feature film, *Who's Knocking at My Door?* (1968), where he goes into the confessional, and we see the church icons and images in a three-minute montage.

Another *de profundis* film ("out of the depths" of human misery) is Rolf de Heer's *Bad Boy Bubby* (1993). Bubby is a 35-year-old man, isolated from the world, whose slatternly mother uses an old broken crucifix to supervise him when she is away. This leads to the exploration of explicit and implicit religious themes.

VIII. Verbal Figures

So far, the emphasis has been on visual Jesus-figures. The movie version of Umberto Eco's *The Name of the Rose* (1987), directed by Jean-Jacques Annaud, offers verbal figures. The occasion of the murders portrayed in the film is an assembly of Franciscan friars and Roman church authorities at a Benedictine monastery in northern Italy in the winter of 1327. The topic of dispute is whether or not Jesus owned his own clothes. (This, of course, is not as trivial as it may sound – the Franciscans urge that Jesus did not own his own clothes and, therefore, the church should not own property, a view that is vigorously, if not theologically, disputed by the bishops taking part in the assembly.) The verbal conflict dramatizes comically but effectively how the words of Jesus – appeals to his teachings – can be used and misused.

But the murders in the monastery are also theological in implication. It is alleged that a book of Aristotle's *Poetics* has been discovered that discusses laughter. Another seemingly trivial question is raised, yet one definitely related to the Jesus-figure: Did Jesus laugh? One's answer to the question has deadly practical consequences. If Jesus did laugh, then Christians would feel free to laugh. This would lead to frivolity, with the faithful not taking the church's power structures as seriously as they should, and authority would be undermined.

One of the difficulties with verbal references to Jesus is that the use of the name "Jesus" or "Jesus Christ" often provokes Christians to feel ultra-sensitive, to think that they are listening to blasphemy. It is probably better to consider this expletive use of Jesus' name as "profanity" rather than as "blasphemy," a use intended to be deliberately offensive. However, we should be quick to notice that, in this context, there can be effective figurative use of Jesus' name. For example, in *At Close Range* (1986), when Sean Penn is threatened, "I'll beat the Jesus out of you," he answers, "I haven't any Jesus in me."

IX. *The Last Temptation of Christ* and *Jesus of Montreal*

Martin Scorsese and Denys Arcand made the two major contributions of the 1980s to images of Jesus on screen. *The Last Temptation of Christ* (1988) is not a Gospel portrait as such. It is a speculative portrait, a "fiction," grounded in the Gospels. In fact, it is probably a more effective treatment of Gospel narratives than the popular spectaculars of the past. This Palestine is rough, gritty, dusty, trying to situate its characters in a more "realistic" past. The film draws on information about customs of the period (from dances and celebrations at wedding feasts to the appearance of prostitutes, like Mary Magdalene, and their brothels) and suggests an "authentic" atmosphere. The American accents of Jesus, the apostles, Paul and all figures except for Pontius Pilate, the foreigner (David Bowie with his English accent), posed difficulties for non-American audiences and reminded us that all portrayals of Jesus speaking English (or Italian) of any accent are stylized.

This movie was criticized as blasphemous because it presented Jesus as "human" and not "perfect." However, *The Last Temptation* might be seen as illustrating the saying from the Letter to the Hebrews that Jesus was like us in everything with the exception of turning away from God in sin. He is presented as tormented by the burden of his mission, struggling with accepting what God is asking of him. This comes to a head in the famous temptation scene, the temptation to ordinariness: that Jesus had done enough, that he could fittingly come down from the cross, recover from his passion, marry, settle down, have a family, live to a ripe old age and go to his reward. The setting for the "temptation" shows Jesus on the cross, mocked by onlookers, experiencing abandonment by God and imagining the possibility of not dying and living this alternate life. His hallucination, however, includes a dispute with Paul about the need for him to die on the cross for his followers to believe in his preaching. The apostles finally come to his bedside to tell him that his opting out was too easy and not what they expected. Then, still hallucinating, Jesus goes back on the cross. Such reflections on the implications of the Incarnation have greater depth than the usual biblical movies.

Members of the mainstream churches, accustomed to appreciating the Scriptures in their context and to applying the techniques of literary criticism, found this Jesus-figure arresting and thought-provoking. It was members of the fundamentalist churches who were stuck on their literal interpretation of the Gospels, which becomes a literal misreading of so much of the text, isolating it from its spiritual heritage in the Old Testament and from its emergence in the Greco-Roman world of the first century A.D. Kazantzakis wrote his novel in earthy and colloquial Greek, drawing on vivid imagery to dramatize his points. Paul Schrader, the scriptwriter, and Scorsese have followed this lead by incorporating earthy symbolism – for instance, the motif of blood, even to a literal "sacred heart" taken from Jesus' breast and Peter's eating the bread of the Last Supper with blood dripping from his mouth. Thus, *The Last Temptation* is a singularly personal movie from Scorsese, interpreting the Gospel figure of Jesus for the questioner and searcher of the twentieth century – believer and nonbeliever alike.

Denys Arcand's *Jesus of Montreal* received an Oscar nomination for Best Foreign Film of 1989. Arcand is as daring as Scorsese in his story of a troupe of actors putting on a passion play in Montreal. The enigmatic Daniel (Lothaire Bluteau) is made to parallel Jesus in significant ways, in his "hidden life," in his relationships with women, in his cleansing of the modern temple of the television studio and in his being tempted by the worldliness of the corporate lawyer, strolling high in a glass skyscraper. Arcand also has Daniel arrested, taken to a Jewish hospital after being rejected by authorities at the Catholic hospital, dying, but still living in the hearts of his disciples, who will make him present in their memories and perform his play. Daniel is one of the most striking of recent movie Christ-figures.

Moreover, the scenes of the passion play itself – the play within the play, as it were – offer some of the best Jesus-figure images seen on screen, a compassionate Jesus, quietly intense but able to relate well to all people. The sequence in which Jesus feeds the crowds (the play's audience in Montreal is offered pieces of bread to eat as they watch the enactment) is most moving. The crucifixion sequence is both stylized and realistic, culminating as it does with the police coming to arrest Daniel and taking him down from the cross. Writer-director Arcand grew up as a Catholic, but later rejected the church. Is his exploration of his Catholic upbringing in this movie really a faith/Jesus as well as a culture/Jesus? Arcand has given a creative lead to religious filmmakers.

X. Christ-Figures

The Christ-figure is any purely fictional character who resembles Jesus, significantly and substantially. This emphasis on significance and substance is necessary to avoid trivializing the Christ-figure. Thus, not every Mexican who is named Jesus is immediately a Christ-figure, or every Mafioso who desperately signs himself before being massacred. It almost goes without saying that reading meanings into works of art may be a commendable exercise of piety, *eisegesis*, but it is not the process for identifying Christ-figures. *Exegesis* is more appropriate, looking at the "text" and "texture" of the artwork in order to discern the Christ-figure in it.

The Christ-figure is a way of being led back to the Jesus of the Gospels, a way too of clarifying and enhancing our understanding of Jesus-figures. The Hebrew scriptural background of the Gospels portrays the ideal Israel (and thus, for Christians, Jesus himself) that as the Servant and as the Son of Man. Briefly, this indicates that Jesus suffers and dies for others and that he is raised from the dead to new life, thus empowering others to new life. Contemporary discussions on these roles of Jesus indicate (by allusion to the Exodus story) that Jesus is also a liberator. Christ-figures can be seen as redeemer-figures when they lay down their lives for others (Sidney Carton in *A Tale of Two Cities*), empower others (several of Clint Eastwood's western heroes, particularly *High Plains Drifter*, *The Outlaw Josey Wales*, and *Pale Rider*) and liberate others through suffering or engaged leadership (*Romero*, *The Mission*).

In cinema, spirituality tends to be implicit rather than explicit, a latent spirituality underlying the film and waiting for sensitive commentators to expose it. Paul Schrader says that it is the role of a critic to identify the religious motif, the role of the theologian to interpret it. A movie may be a product of the artistic sensibility of a writer or director, of deep personal

The Shawshank Redemption, Frank Darabont, 1994

religion and conviction, and of faith, but this is not generally known. The implicitly religious material, when it is "of culture," can be recognized more readily.

A popular Martin Ritt Western of 1967, with the immediately suggestive title of *Hombre* (Everyman?), was a variation on the *Stagecoach* genre. In this instance, the hero of native American descent (played by Paul Newman) is despised by the passengers. But, when they find themselves under attack and in danger of death, they must rely on him to save them. He, in fact, must decide whether he is prepared to die for such a selfish group. Put in Gospel language, it is clear that the movie plot dramatized, but did not make explicit, the basic passion myth.

XI. Antichrist-Figures

There have always been figures of evil in the cinema. Since the late 1960s and "the death of God" era, more images of the devil have appeared – *Rosemary's Baby* (1968), *The Exorcist* (1973), *The Omen* (1976), and so forth. We can also speak of antichrist-figures that are scripture-based and can illuminate the struggle between good and evil. The computer HAL of *2001: A Space Odyssey* (1968), the great white shark of *Jaws* (1975), *The Birds* (1963), the monsters of horror-lore, vampires, werewolves all dramatize dark human experience.

Christ-figures and antichrist-figures in the arts, literature, theater, television drama and cinema can be (whether they are derived from faith or from culture) key images in making the Gospels and the church credible, a contemporary means of apologetics. The new religious films offer fresh, challenging images of the Jesus of faith and the Jesus of culture, a range of characters who resemble Jesus – the Christ-figures – and a range of demonic characters – the antichrist-figures. As we move into the second century of cinema, it is clear that "Jesus" is still on our screens.

Endnotes

1. See also Gerald E. Forshey, *American Religious and Biblical Spectaculars* (New York: Praeger, 1992).

2. Neil Hurley offers a well-defined variation on the standard terminology related to Christ-figures in film in his "Cinematic Transfigurations of Jesus," in *Religion in Film*, ed. John R. May and Michael Bird (Knoxville: University of Tennessee Press, 1982), 61-78.

3. For a fuller view of some of this same material, see my *Movie Christs and Antichrists* (Sydney: Parish Ministry, 1988; New York: Crossroads, 1990.)

5

The Problem of Evil
in Contemporary Film

Reinhold Zwick
(Translated by Stephen Uppendahl)

Within only a few years the critical assessments of culture that lamented a
"deficit of evil" or even making evil a "taboo" have been reversed – not
only in academic study but also in society and the arts.[1] Presently we witness a "renaissance of evil,"[2] and this is one of the most significant symptoms of the crisis of a modern era that is based on the complete rule of
reason and therefore – within the scope of our subject – on patterns of interpretation that wanted to dissolve evil completely into social and psychological explanations. The crisis of the project of enlightenment is combined
with a "return of the Holy,"[3] a phenomenon that affects many facets of life.
In the process, art is emancipating itself ever more from its responsibility
for enlightenment and is again taking up the traditions of the "Black Romantic," with its pathos of transgression and its preference for the sinister.
Thus, it is not surprising that contemporary art bears witness to the omni-
presence of evil with a new intensity. Art does this not just in presenting us
disturbing, haunting accounts and fantasies of evil, or simply by attempting
to express the incomprehensible traits of evil through modern artistic de-
signs. It quite often attempts also to question evil as to its very roots, to
offer interpretations, and moreover at times to suggest a path for coping
with and overcoming evil.

   The preoccupation with evil is especially true of film art, which
since its very beginnings has been said to have a special affinity for the
dark, demonic and cryptic. In fact for some, who despised it, film was
even considered to be an "invention of the devil" himself.[4] Since film was
and is a significant reflector of those experiences, fears, and desires that
have moved men during their respective lifetimes, it also necessarily possesses an extraordinarily rich palette of forms for examining evil. In a narrative mode – therefore in a form that corresponds to biblical and, finally,
to any religious speech – film often thematizes evil by using elements
from the old mythological symbol languages, and often (consciously or un-

consciously) also within Christian coordinates, or, to be more precise, within coordinates that are familiar in the theological-philosophical tradition. In doing so, film keeps and updates the repository of structures, symbols and pictures of mythological and religious thought.

Regarding the proverbial "many faces of evil," one must of course ask which of its dimensions should be considered more closely here. It seems to make more sense to eliminate so-called "natural evil" which is crystallized paradigmatically in innocent suffering or natural catastrophes and always raises the classical question from theodicy about the "best of all possible worlds." Instead, we want mainly to concentrate on that area which has always been considered to be the true realm of evil by Christian philosophers and theologians – namely, evil in the moral sense or *malum morale* (Augustine). Representative of innumerable similar voices, Walter Kasper sums it up this way: "The dimension in which the problem of evil can be meaningfully negotiated is the dimension of human freedom."[5] This is because, as we can add with Paul Ricoeur, "evil would cease to be evil if it stopped being a type of freedom that derives itself from freedom."[6] The option of having the possibility of freedom, which culminates in the necessarily free, loving embrace of God and, at the same time, includes the freedom to refuse God, is an essential aspect of Christian belief.[7] In the face of a radical determinism or a completely relativized position "beyond good and evil" (Friedrich Nietzsche), the recognition of freedom and will accompanies the recognition of the possibility of experiencing guilt. Just as there is the freedom to be evil, there is the possibility to overcome or at least weaken the power of evil. Therefore, theologically speaking, the possibility of turning back (conversion), which has to do with free will and responsibility, is located in the soteriological context of forgiveness, mercy and salvation. In other words, there is a religious dimension to the discussion of evil when it is carried out with a view toward hope or the prospect of an end to evil.

I. The Manicheasm of Mainstream Cinema

It is amazing how little of the axis of "freedom," which is a fundamental coordinate of Christian-inspired western thought concerning evil, can be found in most of that "moral institution" called film and in the popular consciousness that it mirrors. Instead, especially in the case of blockbuster films (whether actual or only hoped for), the old explanations of evil recur; that is, the schemes that were thought to have been intellectually out of date for some time, if not considered to be incompatible with Christian monotheism from the start. All of the historical models are again suddenly present in film in a colorful simultaneity, as well as the history of their development, and this seems true of more than just the concept of evil.

There is still a strong presence of dualistic interpretations of evil in mainstream film, where a great deal of gnostic thought and symbolism is passed on – similar to the way it has reappeared on the surface of contemporary consciousness. What is still popular are the innumerable film stories which – often with a very simple manichaeism and following a rather worn aesthetic and dramatic path – show externalized powers of evil operating against the good hero. Whether western or Kung Fu, fantasy or science fiction, action adventure or spy thriller, what would the screen be without the eternal, archetypical-mythical fight between good and evil? These film depictions regularly take advantage of the rich reserves of a complex symbolic system. The narrative configurations and mythological structures of evil are very often primarily religious in origin, although presented in a secular light. In this way, popular film contradicts the attempt to reconstruct the "renaissance of evil" free of religious influence.

Within the broad repertoire of the externalized powers of evil against which, in the dualistic mode, the similarly externalized and personified (individual or collective) faction of good is fighting, the many forms and incarnations of the devil and the demonic have been losing ground since the heyday of the occult film in the late 1970s and the early 1980s. They are, however, in no danger of extinction. The dismissal of the devil by a theology that considers itself to be enlightened and that for some time now announced the "end of the demonic age" is today apparently not being adhered to by the popular religious attitudes represented in the narrative film, often hiding behind the mask of the profane. Especially because they have always been able to change their face, the devil and demons have been able to survive in the arts (though not only here). In the 80s, the cloven hoof changed into a horse's tail ("Lou Cypher" in Alan Parker's *Angel Heart*, 1987), and the serpent of the Garden of Eden became a lithe sado-masochistic man dressed in leather (in Derek Jarman's *The Garden*, 1990). In the apparently immortal *Omen* series, the antichrist disguised himself as a child, then finally as a girl – in *Omen IV* (1991) as well as in Martin Scorsese's *The Last Temptation of Christ* (1988). In his own perfidy, he even dresses up as a clown (Stephen King's *It*). By contrast, the classic devil/demon and his accompanying rites (adoration or exorcism) are rarely seen at this time. The fantasy genre, which – with its plunderings of the iconography of the Middle Ages – would have been fertile ground, quickly dried out. Only the burning red-horned devil in Ridley Scott's *Legend* (1985) will remain in our memory; he loses in the archetypal cosmological fight of good against the "powers of darkness" – still cited in the Second Vatican Council.[8] Of greater longevity, however, has been the attraction of the occult, where the *zeitgeist* pendulum has swung away from technological civilization, from the hyper-rationality of the computer age, toward the archaic and animistic (or to a similar paradoxical polarity). Among the films that deal with voodoo magic (e.g., *Angel Heart*), John Schlesinger's *The Believers* (1987) is an interesting example, in that it also deals with questions of multicultural and multireligious co-existence.

The devil himself seems once again to have found a niche in the comedy film, where he was given asylum in the earliest days of cinema in the films of Georges Méliès. As a poor gullible soul-hunter along *Highway 61* (by Bruce McDonald, 1991), he makes the viewer almost pity him. He has a difficult time as well in dealing with *The Witches of Eastwick* (1987), even without taking into account that in his role of the potent lecher he has, in a sense, already been disarmed. Also in his many varieties of arch-villains (e.g., as the "Joker" in *Batman*, 1989) – beasts, poltergeists and half-beings, like zombies, vampires and werewolves – the devil,

Angel Heart, Alan Parker, 1987

as the incarnation of evil, has lost a great deal of his horror. Of course, one must be careful in the face of his recent downfall and exile into the likes of these inferior followers not to be too quick in handing out the devil's death certificate. The devil has survived splendidly, despite the fact that Karl Rosenkranz declared him to be totally "superfluous for the arts" almost 150 years ago. Although the personification of evil may also be a case of "anachronistic symbolism" (Käte Hamburger)[9] and the recourse to the "conventional satanic paradigm" a contribution to conventional theodicy,[10] one will still have to live with the fact that the idea of the devil has shown itself to be resistant to any critical ideological dismantling.[11] A dualistic contemplation of evil will always be attractive because it frees the individual to a great extent from the claims of freedom, inasmuch as it puts guilt and responsibility into the hands of another, namely, the tempter.

II. Growing Ambivalences

The old dualism of good and evil and its accompanying symbolism – such as colors (light vs. dark), space (up vs. down), fighting (fair vs. dirty) or even eating (dining vs. feeding) – continue to control the popular genres. But the more evil distances itself from the person of the devil, the more threatening it becomes; and its fight against the forces of good, who want to destroy it, is carried out with ever so much more intensity. Whereas before, as in Don Coscarelli's typical B-movie *Phantasm* (1977), evil was easy to locate and could be clearly conquered in a fairly fought battle and then driven back into the dark depths from which it had crept. In what are now for many the "good old days" of mutual deterrence, the Americans clearly embodied the good and the Russians evil (*Rocky IV*, 1985), whereas today the grey area between good and evil is expanding.

The more the interferences and ambivalences grow, the more the desire for redemption – which has always remained in the background – falls into a crisis of orientation. For instance, in science fiction films, where evil is presented in a cosmic and technological mode especially suitable to the experiences and imagination of modern industrial societies, the clear fairy-tale-like good vs. bad distinction of the *Star Wars* era is over. The monstrosities lurking in the future since then have become more and more horrifying and destructive, as in the *Alien* trilogy. Ever more deceptive replicas and more perfect mechanized men are paralyzing the contours of the order of creation. The victory of good over evil has become increasingly inconsequential. Global misery changes less and less; despite brief rays of hope, the Los Angeles of *Blade Runner* (1982) is in the end still the apocalyptical Moloch it began as.

The *Terminator* films, on the other hand, show the viewers how good and evil can change sides and how violence under different circumstances

– and with its destructive capacity reduced to below-lethal levels – can suddenly become the tool of salvation. In the heavily religious substructure of *Terminator II* (1991), the fighting-machine "Schwarzenegger" has been transformed from the soulless and destructive incarnation of evil into a "Christopher"-transfiguration, who carries a new messianic child through the fires of hell seeking to devour it.[12] At least in this film, good and evil, guilt and innocence are still well differentiated – for the youths in the audience at least. This note of optimism concerning differentiation, however, is on the whole diminishing in the popular genres. New prototypes for this trend in the area of the Mafia-thriller and the western are Abel Ferrara's *King of New York* (1990) and Clint Eastwood's *Unforgiven* (1992). These two films are disturbing less for their violence than for their intertwining of guilt and innocence, making it impossible therefore for the viewer to avoid making the always difficult and thus uncomfortable moral judgment.

For example, in the character of Frank White, the "King of New York," whose road to the top of the Mafia drug ring is littered with corpses, Ferrara does not just give us an egomaniacal killer with simple contempt for mankind, but instead a man who, despite his brutality, is very sensitive and still possesses his moral judgment. Scarred by a long prison sentence and the constant fear of being killed – thus always confronted with his own mortality – the "king" suddenly directs all of his thoughts and deeds toward coming up with the millions of dollars necessary to save a children's hospital in Harlem. As Ferrara states, "Frank White is someone who strongly believes in the ability to change things. He, as an individual, has a vision and knows that he can turn his vision into reality. He still believes that life is worthwhile, although he himself is by no means a saint." Because "he spent half of his life in prison and grew up in such a brutal reality, he for once wants to do something good."[13] However, Frank's project is doomed from the beginning – not only because the good is to be a result of evil, but also because he isolates himself within his sphere through his humanitarian efforts. When he finally dies from a gunshot wound in a taxi surrounded by police, his death is a lonely and exhausted one, full of resignation. It is nonetheless more a death of liberation than of punishment, like the demise of Pier Paolo Pasolini's pimp *Accattone* (1961), who dies saying, "Now I'm fine." Frank White is liberated from the earthly "valley of tears," in which his feverish, tumultuous dance between sex, drugs and violence marked by a basic feeling of *carpe diem* was, in the end, only a desperate surrogate for real life. One doesn't want to see Frank completely fall from God's grace, despite all of his guilt.

With the advent of ambivalent protagonists like Frank White or Eastwood's gunslinger Bill Munny, the old dualistic patterns of these popular genres have been abandoned. Although there are still characters in the films of Ferrara and Eastwood who clearly embody evil especially, at least the heroes combine the traits of both good and evil in such a way that the viewer becomes uncertain in his search for identification. Disgust, rejection and sympathy all fight for a place in the viewer's heart and mind. Which of these feelings wins depends on how much room for play the "mixed-trait" characters have to change evil into good, and how much strength and freedom the characters themselves possess.

The work of Martin Scorsese has, in a special way, dealt with this precise problematic of trying to avoid the simplistic dualism of good vs. evil. His films provide some of the most penetrating examples in popular cinema of religious transparency in the representation of violence and mercy, revenge and forgiveness, guilt and salvation. The same characteristics that Scorsese once applied to the boxer Jake La Motta, respectfully portrayed in the film *Raging Bull* (1980), link him with many of the characters in his films – "the Catholic inheritance, the feeling of guilt, the hope for salvation."[14] Especially in the different configurations of the "dark angel" in Scorsese's films, the unavoidable "simultaneity of good and evil" takes shape – "good doesn't exclude evil and evil doesn't exclude good."[15] This tension perseveres especially in Christian belief and forms the foundation for the need for salvation in man insofar as it cannot be resolved through human strength alone.

Scorsese's defense of ambivalence toward the moralistic black-and-white type of portrayal can be seen easily in his remake of *Cape Fear* (1991). He abandons the earlier version's simplistic contrast of "innocent victim" and "evil pursuer" by introducing an act of dishonesty, a moment of guilt, from the past of the otherwise honest lawyer Sam Bowden – his withholding of a report that would have been grounds for a more lenient sentence for his former client Max Cady. This revelation, of course, makes Cady's desire for revenge more understandable and thus gives the story a complex subtext that pits eternal moral law against human justice and supports the relevance of acting according to one's conscience. While Bowden's omission opens him to the possibility of prosecution by the judicial system and violates the code of ethics for lawyers, he is obviously obeying the voice of his own conscience, which forbids him from helping Cady obtain a not-guilty verdict due to the obvious seriousness of his crime. Although Bowden remains true to basic Christian morality, which recognizes the finality of the individual's conscience, he is nonetheless guilty of wrongdoing even within these coordinates – and this is the exact ambivalence here – because he does not recuse himself from the case. Instead, he indirectly assumes the role of judge as well as advocate, in his determination to make sure that the justice of God triumphs. This is what he has in common with Max Cady, except that in Max's case guilt and innocence are weighted differently.

In the beginning as Max starts to seek "justice," the viewer can find some reason for his actions. Max claims that God made his revengeful campaign for justice legitimate, not just by orally quoting the Bible, mostly the Old Testament, but also by having its maxims etched permanently on his body and an image of the Bible itself, balanced on the scales of justice, tattooed on his back. Of course, he purposefully forgets everything that Scripture says about forgiveness, loving one's enemy, and nonviolence. Instead, he arrogantly identifies himself with Nietzsche's *Übermensch*, who stands above morality of any sort; then he claims to be an angel of revenge chosen by God, and finally to be God himself. The story of the first "fall of man" is repeated not only in his "wanting to be like God," but also in his assuming the role of a Mephistophelian seducer of Sam's daughter. Through these increasingly diabolic actions, Max becomes more and more like Lucifer, whose fall is repeated in Max's descent. And the life into which Sam and his family are reborn – covered with mud they remind us of the first humans in the Yahwistic story of creation (Genesis 2:4bff) – is a life that will remain marked forever by the loss of innocence.

III. Evil in the Abyss of the Soul

If one accepts the interpretation of Max Cady as the personification of the darker aspects of Sam's soul, then *Cape Fear* already belongs to those films that prefer to uncover evil in the depths of the unconscious, as the abyss that lurks in everyone. Such journeys into the sinister regions of the psyche have long been part of film. One needs only to recall Georg Wilhelm Pabst's *Geheimnisse einer Seele* (*Secrets of a Soul*, 1925), the classic Bette Davis thrillers, and, of course, Orson Welles's *Lady from Shanghai* (1946), who dies programmatically with the words: "Evil is in me." Besides some dark comedies like *Barton Fink* (1991), it seems, however, that the journeys to the darker regions have greatly increased in hopelessness and fright in the last few years, as well as in popularity. Film, then, has apparently reacted to our growing *neue Unübersichtlichkeit* or "new lack of clarity" (Jürgen Habermas) about reality and the increasing feeling of elementary insecurity that it leaves behind.

This new cinema of horror, according to its apologists, binds numinous uneasiness with aids to overcome everyday bad experiences, in that it cathartically liberates built-up fears. In the situation where the viewer, in his own reality, finds himself more frequently losing his footing and where it becomes more and more difficult to differentiate between right and wrong, good and evil, the old simplistic dualisms begin to appear to be nothing more than nostalgic relics of what was once thought to be neatly ordered reality. One likes to seek safety in them for a while – that is the reason for their continual success – but at the same time one is aware of their deficiencies, and that the real threat comes from the evil within every single one of us. By trying to visualize this, films are, of course, asking questions (at least implicitly) about the freedom to do/be evil and about the possibility of resisting it. It remains to be seen whether evil will be explained away within the controlled circles of inner mechanisms and thus whether film has become the heir to that psychoanalysis long in distress with its claims to a complete explanation, or whether there remains enough freedom of will in us so that the possibility of escaping the power of evil does not completely fade.

In many cases it certainly seems that the dimension of evil should only be measured with the help of psychological and environmental optics. Taken out of a religious context of freedom, guilt and redemption, this evil turns into a simple "defect" in the end. What is depressing about this can be seen in the dialogue between the young philosopher Otto Weininger and Sigmund Freud, imagined by the Austrian director Paulus Manker, in which Weininger complains that, through the psychological abolition of responsibility and guilt, the possibility of repentance and the changing of ways becomes untenable, and thus hope is taken away (*Weiningers Nacht*).

The fact that looking into the depths of the soul is a result of the spirit of the modern criticism of religion is often hidden. Even if their focus is secular, films like to play with the thoughts and image arsenals of religious denominations and thereby achieve – at least on the surface – the (pseudo-)religious, (pseudo-)mythical touch that is so commercially successful today. Of course, one can also use other classical motifs to give numinous evil a concrete form. One type that is especially well-liked is the motif (mentioned above as a possible interpretation of Scorsese's *Cape Fear*) where the "dark side" of an individual is personified in the outside world in the form of an opposing *oder Doppelgänger* character (as is the case too in *Angel Heart*). *Cape Fear* is a clever new variant of the old motif of the split personality that has been used often in both film and literature to try to capture the dialectics of good and evil.

Jonathan Demme, like Alan Parker, uses a number of religious motifs and allusions in his film *The Silence of the Lambs* (1990). But the complete palette of iconographic references to Christian art and religious history cannot hide the fact that there is really very little room for a deeper theological interpretation of Demme's dark world.[16] His sinister heroes "Hannibal Lector" and "Buffalo Bill" never suffer from the evil that they do. Conscience and guilt are completely foreign to them. Lector seems to be much too maniacal to function as a prototype of a "satanic individual" characterized by a "self-confident, free creation of evil."[17] He is more the incarnation of the freed beast that lurks in all of us, the "predator in man" of whom Nietzsche spoke. Lector looks like the vanguard of the "amoral period" that Nietzsche predicted, in which the "will for power" raises itself above every moral destiny.[18] Despite all of the dark fascination that Lector exudes (which is as irritating to the audience as it is to agent Starling), he is, in the end, only an apotropaic monster, apparently erected against the recurring popular flirtation with the *Übermensch,* or "master morality."

It is David Lynch who has, with special perseverance and fantasy, explored "the darker regions of existence,"[19] the "shadows" in the soul (Carl Gustav Jung), the stuff that nightmares are made of. As Lynch himself has repeatedly said, it fascinates him "to explore the subconsciousness of people, to dive into the depths of this endless zone" because "what is on the surface is only a part of the truth. It is what is beneath that, that I find interesting about life: the darkness, the uncertainty, the terrifying, the sickness. Every one of my films is about what is happening on the surface of life and what is hidden beneath that surface. It could be that I am possessed by the things that are hidden."

Because of this, Lynch's films are an amalgam of almost all facets of evil discussed here – evil in the dualistic mode, evil as external power, and also evil in the depths of the soul. They show strong gnostic traits, but also work with Christian ideas. This puzzle becomes most obvious in the popular TV-series *Twin Peaks* and in the film prequel, *Twin Peaks: Fire Walk with Me* (1992), that followed it. The references to diverse religious traditions cannot be overlooked, including Christian biblical motifs. In Luke's Gospel, it is the devil who takes possession of Judas and uses him as his tool, and whenever in the Gospels demons get someone under their control, uncontrollable violence is threatened (cf. Mark 5:1ff). In *Twin Peaks*, it is "Killer Bob" who embodies evil and takes possession of Leland Palmer, who, while dying, is able to make his grand confession and find his final peace in death. Other inhabitants of the supposedly "clean" small town fall prey to the temptations of evil and drown in a maelstrom of excess and violence without being directly overpowered by "Bob," as Leland was. Even the FBI agent Dale Cooper (and with him the "good") falls victim to evil in the end. His shadow, personified as his look-alike, triumphs – although Cooper, by putting his trust in spiritualism and recognizing powers other than simply the rational ones, had held in his hands the actual key to conquering evil.

Lynch's exploration of the evil that "is seething beneath the idyllic surface"[20] reminds us a lot of a Jungian journey into the zone of the collective unconscious. The archetypal characters and plots known from fairy tales and mythology are there: the "Black Lodge," hidden deep in the forest, giants and dwarfs, souls haunted and sold. In *Blue Velvet* (1986) and *Wild at Heart* (1990), it is the pattern of the purifying journey that expands the mythical horizon. Similar to the basic action in *Twin Peaks*, the pure-of-heart hero of *Blue Velvet* penetrates into the secretive night districts of the city and, thus, at the same time into the previously closed rooms of his soul. In the end Jeffrey, inwardly changed after his journey into the dark, like waking up from a "bad dream," as he says himself, returns to the bright surface of the everyday world. But now he knows its small joys as deceptive and fragile. He has seen the dark abyss, looked evil straight in the eye, and has withstood it through the power of love. Seen in this way, *Blue Velvet* is, regardless of its violence, a fairy tale for grown-ups. The fairy tale is even more apparent in *Wild at Heart*. Whereas in *Blue Velvet* it is only, ironically, a plastic robin that signals a return of a happiness that one does not really trust in, in *Wild at Heart* it is none other than the good witch of the north from *The Wizard of Oz* (1939) who waves to the archetypical lovers, Sailor and Lula, as they reach the end of their adventure-trip through a purgatory of violence.

A danger for Lynch and his films becomes most apparent here; namely, that they give away their topic through an eclectic game of quotations, motifs and styles, and slip into noncommittal vagueness. Yet it is through this kind of exploration of evil that he lucidly shows the fears, the perversions, and the violence of today. So his stories become more than just fashionable accommodations to the *zeitgeist*. And it is astonishing how explicitly Lynch again and again puts hopeful images of mercy and redemption into these stories permeated by evil – images that, despite all of the postmodern decoration and bold kitsch, let something be known of a deep desire of the present time. Through these signs, mankind's hope for redemption is freed from the bounds of a nihilism that wants scornfully to push it aside as being anachronistic.

Perhaps it is simply by accident or maybe an expression of his gradual discontent with too much bizarre and arbitrary syncretism, but, in Lynch's latest film, the signs of redemption more clearly point to a Christian iconography and symbolism. Despite their fantastic dimension, they are a trace more "realistic" in that redemption does not necessarily have to occur on earth. At the end of *Twin Peaks: Fire Walk with Me*, the soul of Leland Palmer, who was possessed by evil during his atrocious deeds, rises and begins to hover in the air as if free from the burden of sins. When "Bob" tries to force the floating soul into his power again, he is thrown back – his control is broken. And in a double guardian angel vision, the "fallen" Laura Palmer is reintroduced after her death. Her smile and her liberating tears in the beyond of the "red room" announce her redemption. Then, accompanied by Cherubini's *Requiem in C-minor*, the final credits roll down the screen. With this ending, Lynch counters the supposed victory of evil in the episodes of the previous series and breaks with their rather pessimistic conclusion.[21]

What the films of David Lynch often so drastically illustrate was not first spoken of by Kant in his discourse about "radical evil,"[22] it was already addressed in the basic articles of the Christian Credo, the baptismal confession, and the Lord's Prayer: the profound inclination of man to evil as a part of the *conditio humana*. Man's faith tells him that he is not left at the mercy of this inclination, but instead maintains, in an often seemingly defiant "but," his freedom to choose good and to hope for liberation. This hope of overcoming evil survives in Lynch's work as a feeling for the need of redemption, as a desire for it – even if it hides behind the mask of a playful quotation or a kitschy image. Obviously, in our days, many dare not speak about it in any other way.

IV. Stories of Repentance and Change

None of the variations of evil found in popular films looked at so far has been free of at least crypto-religious moments and mythical substructures. Sometimes their sediments have developed a clear-cut profile also on the surface of the plot and the visual images whereby the ideologically harmless references to archetypical mythical elements far outweigh the references to Christian tradition. In contrast to the numerous "philosophical" films of, in particular, the 50s and 60s, which either explored the question of evil and man's involvement in guilt, or left the question open with a merciless insistence that the problem lies in our very attempts at answering the question (one thinks here of the films of Ingmar Bergman and Luis Buñuel), today's films aim instead at satisfying our curiosity and tickling our nerves – or at the (supposed) pleasure of cathartic horror. Despite all of the evil that washes out onto the viewer from the screen, he will, only in the rarest of cases, go home in a state of agitated thought about guilt and forgiveness, freedom and responsibility. Instead, the viewer is given the pleasant happy ending or the genre-typical continuous existence of evil (leaving the door open for a sequel).

A film of exemplary quality for the discussion of evil on a deeper level is Robert Bresson's *L'Argent* (1982). Through Bresson's laconic direction, it becomes an oppressive, claustrophobic *Kammerspiel* and links together the past and present generations of religious film. Bresson masterfully visualizes the complex connections between personal guilt and evil as a "structural occurrence"[23] and, in a very restrained manner, the hope of overcoming evil. The counterfeit money that is foisted on the simple truck driver Yvon Targe sets off the avalanche of evil. Hardened by his unjustified prosecution – although given only a suspended sentence – Yvon refuses to ask his employer for his job back. Instead, he takes part in a bank robbery that fails, and lands in prison. His normal lower-middle-class life destroyed, Yvon endures also the death of his daughter and finally his wife's departure. He is saved from a suicide attempt and then, back in prison, becomes influenced by his new cellmate, a nihilistic, cynical young intellectual. Functioning almost as a "dark" alter ego, he gives Yvon's dull desperation rational expression – in the spirit of Dostoevski's Ivan Karamasov (Ivan-Yvon?), who, in the face of all those who innocently suffer, renounces God and the moral order founded on him – in the spirit of Albert Camus' address on the absurdity of the world after the death of God.

Immediately after his release from prison, Yvon "senselessly" murders the owners of a hotel. He tells the old woman whom he follows and who takes him in about his evil deed (and probably his life story). To her question about why he did it, he replies simply: "It was fun." That he can, of course, remember "all of the details" of his deeds and note that the victims looked "horrible" hints at the fact that he has not yet lost all of his human feelings. The woman reacts in a surprising way and that deepens their almost tender relationship of trust: "You will be forgiven. If I was God and it was only up to me, then I would forgive everyone." This makes the end of the film even more horrifying: One night Yvon breaks into the woman's house and as she answers his question – "Where is the money?" – with silence only, he kills her with an axe, just as he had killed the rest of her family earlier. The gruesome prayer that Yvon's cellmate imploringly whispered into his ear becomes reality: "Oh money, you visible God! What wouldn't we do in your name!" The film, however, does not end with a shot of the murder weapon thrown into the water. Yvon could have continued on with his murdering – as Henry, the serial killer, does (as we will see later) – but he doesn't. Instead he goes into a restaurant and admits his crime to a policeman, who by chance is there.

The heroes of Bresson's previous films have always been "confronted with the powers of evil."[24] The ending of his last film is as gloomy as ever. One could in fact suspect here the final failure of Christian hope, which Bresson has tested again and again, the hope that love once experienced will enable one to break through the vicious circle of evil and that forgiveness once experienced will encourage one to forgive. The forgiveness of the old woman and her quiet affection for Yvon are, without doubt, merciful gifts, even if they bear fruit only after his last murderous deed. Yvon finds his way back to the religious order through his willingness to take on the consequences of his deeds. Through his free confession of his crimes to the policeman, Yvon recognizes his guilt and acknow-

L'Argent, Robert Bresson, 1982

ledges evil as evil. The first step toward change has been taken, a step that creates room for forgiveness, which in turn transcends death.

As in so many of his other films, Bresson shows us what is important in a fragmentary, elliptical, almost casual style – here it is the confession. In the end, *L'Argent* thematizes evil *sub specie Dei* in the tension of fate and conscious decision against good. It moves into a religiously qualified connection between guilt, forgiveness and mercy, dependent on the degree of freedom that can be felt. As Yvon's path has shown, the freedom to do evil always includes the possibility of change, so that man himself (with the help of mercy) can break the bonds of guilt that often appear inescapable.

No doubt there is a world of difference between Bresson's informal, indirect approach and the glaring treatise about guilt and redemption that Abel Ferrara has "set into scene" with *Bad Lieutenant* (1992). A comparison of these two films can make evident what changes have taken place, on the one hand, in the public's taste and its feelings about life and, on the other, in cinema itself with respect to religious meaning within only the last decade. Despite its often loud gestures and evident toughness, Ferrara's story of the decline and possible conversion of a nameless New York cop deserves attention as a forceful study that seeks to measure evil in a Christian, or rather "orthodox" Catholic, perspective of guilt, mercy, repentance and redemption. In his recourse to the story of salvation, Ferrara sometimes seems almost too explicit. It is as though he wants to protest vehemently against the postmodern rejection of, among other things, the Christian "meta-story," as if he wants to insist that this meta-story still represents a decided axis of orientation in contrast to the boundless sea of the relativistic mentality or the fashionable syncretistic-eclectic mixture of religions.

In a way *Bad Lieutenant* reminds one of Ingmar Bergman – thematically as well as in the explicit nature of its images. In the context of today's conditioning of perception, it probably has a similarly stirring effect as many of the sequences from such films as *Tystnaden* (*Silence*, 1965), *Vargtimmen* (*Hour of the Wolf*, 1968) or *Skammen* (*The Shame*, 1968). The question of suffering, the uniting of evil with good, the silence of God in the face of evil – these big themes of Bergman have not disappeared, only changed their appearance. Whereas with the Swede there are only faint sparks of hope left, such as one's continuing life "despite it all" (as in the end of *Nattvardsgasterna* [*Winter Light*, 1963]), and only small signs of reform or traces of the good that have emerged from evil, the Italian-American uses a comparatively coarse brush to express his ideas. To his credit Ferrara also avoids cheap consolation where it should not be given. Due to the undeniable power of circumstances and the weight of accumulated guilt, the process of "turning back" is stopped before it can really begin and redemption can only take place through death. In that respect the fate of Ferrara's *Bad Lieutenant* – as well as the fate of his *King of*

New York (1990) – resembles the story of the hired killer in Alan Baron's *Blast of Silence* (1960). The killer here drops out of the circle of crime, but ends up paying for it with his life. Even Bresson's Ivon Targe seems to be a precursor. The character here reminds us of the rebel against every type of morality in the meta-historical episode of Pier Paolo Pasolini's *Porcile* (*Pigsty*, 1969), who in the end voluntarily walks into an apparent trap set for him by the authorities, which seals his fate. Afterwards he defiantly admits (though choking with tears, which belie his ostentatious gesture), "I have killed my father, I have eaten the flesh of men, I'm shaking with joy," and is crucified on the earth of a desert Golgotha to be eaten alive by wild animals.

    Blast of Silence and *Porcile* have only recently been screened widely in theaters, which is not completely by accident when we consider the context of the new interest in the question of good and evil. By using references to the story of Christ's suffering and resurrection, both films express the hope that even the most offensive misdeeds that lead man away from his real destiny can be forgiven as soon as evil is freely renounced, even if there is very little room for action left.

    Three further examples come to mind. The Georgian director Lana Gogoberidse demonstrates this in her film *Walsi Petschorase* (1992) through the character of a Stalinist officer who is the commander of a "death squadron"; when meeting up with the child of deported "enemies of the people," the officer experiences an inner change and finally places human kindness before duty. In doing so he signs his own death warrant, but he finds a peace that will outlast death. The other two films are stories of repentance and change that are not completed by the characters themselves, but await completion by the viewer in his own mind. In Krzysztof Kieslowski's *Krotki Film o Zabijaniu* (*A Short Film About Killing*, 1988), a young murderer experiences remorse and deep emotional shock for his misdeed. Consequently, the viewer is hopeful – yes, even almost certain – that the murderer will find a more merciful judge in heaven than on earth, where he ends up on the gallows. The viewer hopes the same for the abortionist in Claude Chabrol's *Une Affaire de Femmes* (*Story of Women*, 1988). In the beginning, the abortionist is motivated only by neighborly love, but then her motivation turns more and more to greed. Her heart, which had increasingly hardened over time, suddenly breaks open during the night in her death cell and unloads itself in a blasphemous prayer. God has once again become a reality for her even if this is expressed only in a lament full of abuse and curses.

    Certainly, it is not the rule in film that a dark ending always covers up all traces of hope. There are many examples of films that end differently, as was the case in the parable of the "prodigal son," who has his entire life before him after returning home (his conversion). Probably the best loved film metaphor for this is the journey "out of the dark and into the blue." The journey into a new future is, at least to an extent, already

A Short Film About Killing, (Long Version, *Decalogue V*), Krzysztof
Kieslowski, 1988

true in the case of the freed young criminals in *Bad Lieutenant*. It manifests itself too in the endings both of Sean Penn's *The Indian Runner*
(1991), whose substructure refers to the biblical myth of the fall and to
other religious motifs,[25] and of Pavel Lungin's *Luna Park*. This latter film
is a typically constructed story of hope about the transformation of a violent, hate-filled, ideologically-blinded young man, who, in the search for
his father, reveals the sensitive person he had secretly always been.

V. Absence of Good: Absence of God?

It is probably a sign of the times that films like the ones just mentioned,
with their more or less restrained pictures of encouragement and the "happy
ending," do not become cult-films, whereas a film like John McNaughton's
Henry: Portrait of a Serial Killer (1990) does, in which the end of the
journey becomes a deeper journey into crime. It is a terrifyingly hopeless
film: Henry, the main character, was greatly traumatized during his childhood. After murdering his mother, he continues to kill women, a prisoner
of his own hate and fear. For a short time, some hope is growing that he
could have experienced a cleansing shock in brutally beating to death his
murderous partner, Otis, when Otis begins to rape his own sister. But even
this faintest hope is destroyed. Henry does leave the city with Otis's sister,
but the next morning he checks out of a motel alone and, somewhere along
the open road, disposes of a bloody suitcase. There is absolutely no sign of
police activity that could stop him from continuing his murderous binge.

The success of *Henry* and other serial killer stories found in film and
literature can be interpreted in different ways. In the context of the "ren-

aissance of evil" taking place in our *fin de siècle*, the character of the serial killer stands "in simple terms . . . for radical individualism and the
urge of freedom," and thus takes "the American Dream to a bizarre and
terrible end."[26] In an environment that has been formed by a paralyzed
value system, the serial killer becomes "the deadly executor of the old ideals." Self-realization becomes a depraved and grotesque gratification of desire – destruction for pleasure. A part of the dark fascination for the serial
killer may stem from just this: "He is the unquestioned king in the realm
of desire" in a "coordinate system that seems to be very much in fashion
today." As was once the case with De Sade, who was celebrated by the
perpetually transgression-hungry surrealists, the emotionalism of an absolute autonomy reaches a new peak in some of the serial murder characters.
Freedom – insofar as it is compatible with psychotic traits – is the license
to do radical evil (or to imagine it). The serial killer thus becomes the incarnate antithesis of the Christian ideal of freedom – the freedom to
choose good. However, whereas De Sade raged against God and the do-
mestication of desire in an open revolt that is explained in the philosophical interludes of his works, God is not present at all in the the world of
the contemporary serial killer, not even as the butt of blasphemous jokes.
Morality, based on a fundamental decision for good, has become completely lost in this modern configuration.

In this regard, a film like *Henry* is certainly the complete opposite of
what is normally considered a religious film, even if it is relevant for the
theological reflection on evil, which must plumb even the darkest depths
of the *conditio humana*. Similar to Goya in *Desastres de la Guerra*,
McNaughton holds up a terrifying mirror to mankind, except that his war
is moved to the city and becomes a campaign of the individual.
McNaughton is able to show the potential for atavistic cruelty that can be
found in man and that can be set free in extreme situations, such as war or
psychological trauma, when the normal "safeguards" give way and supporting factors like anonymity lend help. McNaughton shows this especially through the character of Otis, who, once the last threshold of
violence is crossed, kills just for the fun of it. Christian anti-dualistic faith
in the one, good and loving God must defend against such mirrors; it must
be able to find answers to images presented in films like *Henry*, which
give a fresh and urgent impetus for a re-thinking of the problems of
theodicy that are of immense existential relevance for people today – problems that theology too often tries to evade because of their complexity.

It is not at all McNaughton's intention, as it was not Goya's, to support the pleasures of dread in portraying an inferno of evil. He explicitly
rejects any thought of complete determinism and hopes that his film can
"re-sensitize even the most hard-core 'slasher' film fan because it really
shows the ugly face of death."[27] A film like *Henry* allows the moviegoer
to see a cinematographic "secularization of hell," provoking such a deep
"existential uneasiness" that it is surely not suitable for everyone's view-

ing. But because it does hit the often deadened nerves of moral feelings, it can be an impulse for the "hard core" to do some healthy self-questioning. Analogous perhaps to the (seemingly) blasphemous *provocatio ad salutem*, the desire for overcoming evil does not find any room on the screen here. The thought of goodness is brought to mind only by the viewer's realization of its complete absence. Perhaps by radically withholding any hope, the film provokes a much stronger and more painful desire for it.

VI. Conclusion

Working against tendencies to weaken and delete evil, film sends us an urgent reminder of its reality. Indeed, it is film as the youngest of the art forms that most vividly articulates the feeling of a deep threat and uncertainty. Evil in cinema may have depressing and even terrifying traits. Of course, from the Christian perspective there is always the hope "that it won't have the last word." The wish that Pope John Paul II expressed in his memorable address to artists and journalists during his first visit to Germany is pertinent to this context. Without wanting to question the legitimacy and possibility of portraying evil in the arts, he nonetheless hoped that this would take place in a horizon that includes the idea and possibility of resisting evil – a context that allows traces of "the reality of good, redemption, and the mercifulness of God" to become visible.[28] This type of transparency does not mean that the reality of evil is in any way denied or simply neutralized by a larger good. All of the artistically superior films that bear signs of the belief that evil will not win in the end – signs that often do not deny their Christian origin – are aware of that.

Most of the films discussed in detail here are paradigmatic of the view that the "new image of religious film" is an image that, in most cases, can only be seen as being "religious" or (at least) relevant to theological reflection on a second viewing, but then possibly with even greater intensity. Many, oftentimes the most irritating, films are continuations of the old eternal questions about good and evil that are closely related to real life. By not merely opening itself to those films, but instead intensively questioning their contribution to dealing with the problem of evil, theology can regain some of the worldliness that it has often lost in the past. Remembering the often severe comments of the prophets of the Old Testament about their social environment, we realize that a critical position can also be a sign of serious dialogue.

Criticism from a Christian standpoint is advisable when the representation of evil turns into a surge of irrationalism, when its representation is merely an end in itself and only serves to satisfy the curiosity aroused by the eternal fascination with evil, or when the speculative exploitation of this fascination threatens to provoke aggression, cynicism and the contempt of human beings. On the other hand, belief and theology should be thankful for those films that do not minimize the problem of evil in favor of a quick satisfaction of the need for clear answers and unambiguity, but instead point to its disruptive interaction, to the ambiguity of good and evil, and thus to man's need for redemption, up to the last dimension that lies outside his power to possess. That is why, in the end, all of the films that do not, through their representation and narrative treatment, bury the questions of the human, of freedom, guilt and redemption, and finally of God, but keep them ever present – be it only through the painfully felt absence of good – are of great importance and productive potential for both faith and theology.

Endnotes

1. See K. H. Bohrer, "Das Böse: eine ästhetische Kategorie?" *Merkur* 39 (1985), 459-73; "*Die permanente Theodizee: Über das verfehlte Böse im deutschen Bewußtsein,*" *Merkur* 41 (1987), 267-86; J. Baudrillard, *Transparenz des Bösen: Ein Essay über extreme Phänomene* (Berlin: Merve, 1992).

2. See A. Chuller and W. von Rahden, eds., *Die andere Kraft: Zur Renaissance des Bösen* (Berlin: Akademie Verlag, 1993); C. Colpe and W. Schmidt-Biggemann, eds., *Das Böse: Eine historische Phänomenologie des Unerklärlichen* (Frankfurt am Main: Suhrkamp, 1993).

3. See D. Kamper and C. Wulf, eds., *Das Heilige: Seine Spur in der Moderne* (Frankfurt am Main: Athenäum, 1987); see also the current interest in the thinking of R. Girard, esp. his *Das Heilige und die Gewalt* (Frankfurt am Main: Fischer, 1992).

4. See R. Cosandey, A. Gaudreault and T. Gunning, eds., *Une invention du diable? Cinéma des premiers temps et religion* (Sainte-Foy-Lausanne: Les Presses de l'Université Laval-Éditions Payot, 1992).

5. W. Kasper, "Das theologische Problem des Bösen," in *Teufel-Dämonen-Besessenheit: Zur Wirklichkeit des Bösen*, ed. W. Kasper and K. Lehmann (Mainz: Grünewald, 1978), 46.

6. P. Ricoeur, "*Schuld, Ethik und Religion,*" *Concilium* 6 (1970): 384-93.

7. For a readable reflection on the intimate connection of evil and freedom, see P. Vardy, *The Puzzle of Evil* (London: HarperCollins-Fount, 1992).

8. *Gaudium et Spes*, n. 37.

9. Quoted in Bohrer, "*Permanente Theodizee,*" 280.

10. Ibid., 281.

11. See T. Peters, "The Selling of Satan in Popular Literature," *The Christian Century* 108 (1991): 458-62.

12. The Christopher interpretation I owe to P. Sloterdijk, "Sendboten der Gewalt: Der Mensch als Werfer und Schütze – zur Metaphysik des Action-Kinos," *Die Zeit*, 30 April 1993, 58.

13. Quoted in T. Gaschler and E. Vollmar, eds., *Dark Stars: 10 Regisseure im Gespräch* (München: edition belleville, 1992), 61-62.

14. Quoted in H. D. Rusche, "Die Bürde der Tradition," in *Martin Scorsese*, ed. P. W. Jansen and W. Schütte (München: Hanser, 1986; Reihe Film 17), 26.

15. H. W. Dannowski, "Scorsese/Schrader," *epd Film* 4, no. 11 (1987): 2-5.

16. See H. Niewöhner, "Mythisches Perpetuum Mobile: Das Schweigen der Lämmer – der Film und seine Betrachter," *Lettre International* [German edition] 19 (1992): 48-54.

17. Rosenkranz, *Ästhetik des Häßlichen*, 297.

18. F. Nietzsche, *Jenseits von Gut und Böse* (Frankfurt am Main: Insel, 1984), 44.

19. R. Fischer, *David Lynch: Die dunkle Seite der Seele* (München: Heyne, 1992), 10 (following quotations, ibid., 271, 264).

20. Ibid., 235.

21. For a more detailled analysis of the series (without the prequel): M. Verbeek, "It's the Mystery That's the Fun of Life," in *Aus Leidenschaft zum Leben: Film und Spiritualität*, ed. Z. Cavigelliet et al. (Zürich: Benziger, 1993), 171-95.

22. See I. Kant, *Die Religion innerhalb der Grenzen der bloßen Vernunft* (1793).

23. See J. Gründel, "Das Böse," in *Praktisches Lexikon der Spiritualität*, ed. C. Schütz (Freiburg: Herder, 1992), 168.

24. A. Eichenberger, "*Religiöse Dimensionen im neuen Film*," *film-dienst*, 30, no. 20 (1977): 5.

25. See my analysis: "Nach dem Sündenfall. Religiöse Momente in Sean Penns Indian Runner," *film-dienst*, 45, no. 2 (1992): 8-10.

26. U. Genzler, "Kill and Thrill: Kriminalromane heute – der Serienmörder als Held," *Süddeutsche Zeitung*, 14-15 August 1993, p. 113 (the following quotes, *ibid.*).

27. See Gaschler and Vollmar, *Dark Stars*, 87.

28. Pope John Paul II, "Ansprache an die Künstler und Publizisten im Herkulessaal in München am 19. November 1980," in *Papst Johannes Paul II. in Deutschland: 15-19 November 1980* (Bonn: Sekretariat der Deutschen Bischofskonferenz/ Verlautbarungen des Apostolischen Stuhls 25A), 189.

Part 3

Changes in
Religious Consciousness

6

The Religious Dimension of Cinematic Consciousness in Postmodern Culture

Sylvain De Bleeckere

In this cultural-philosophical essay on the religious dimensions of film, I regard culture as the anthropological phenomenon within which religion and cinema can be interwoven. Culture represents the world of human work and life, which develops in the history not only of mankind but also of the planet earth and even of time itself. The fact is that film is now situated in the middle of changing cultural patterns. One can question how this new center of culture is related to religion, that former center of the cultural scene. There is a great intellectual temptation to address that question without taking cultural and historical considerations into account. Culture, religion and film are indeed related to one another in, and not beyond, history.

Within the scope of this essay, I confine myself to discussing only one aspect of the basic question – namely, the postmodern cultural project that developed during the second half of the twentieth century. Increasingly, it took place alongside and even against modernism. I shall consider at length some important elements of postmodern culture. But, first of all, we must understand why the modern phenomenon of film could be mastered by modernism in the first decades of its appearance.

I. The Modern Medium of Film

Film is in the first place connected with the modern world of scientific research, technological machine construction and industrial capital. At the end of the nineteenth century, film grew like a ripe fruit on the tree of modern industrial society. A clear sign of that was the first film studio, called the "Black Maria." Film made its arrival through the gateway of industry, which was opened definitively and irreversibly by the modernism of the Age of Enlightenment. Consequently, film was not experienced in its early days as a new exponent of the artistic genius of mankind. Rather, it was initially understood as one of the manifold and growing expressions of the modern genius that was continuously expanding its scientific, technological and economic power over space and time. Even more than with photography, film allowed "the man of the new age" to enlarge his "Faustian" powers over time. He had now invented a magical instrument to record time itself. So, not surprisingly, the motion-picture camera was promptly claimed as its own by modernism. It forced film to take over a leading part in its greatest experiment on the cultural scene of the twentieth century.

With the breakthrough of the communist October Revolution in 1917, the modern film medium was charged with playing an important part in the realization of modernist objectives in the Soviet Union. Under the supervision of the Communist Party, Sergei Eisenstein formulated its first theory. The key to the theory is the concept of *montage*, better known in the English-speaking world as "editing."[1] Eisenstein borrowed the word *montage* directly from the industrial machine culture, the extension of which was a priority in the revolutionary policy of the Soviet party. That means, to begin with, that film was not considered as an artistic medium, even when it made use of the different arts. Film appeared as a cultural technological machine, the aim of which was to clear the mind of the oppressed people of all kinds of alienation and to lead it to the pure high point of dialectical insights. Seen in this way, film must be the adequate medium for the expression of the liberated and emancipated collective mind of the proletariat and so even of mankind itself. In that communist cultural plan, modernism reached its historical climax. The utopian aim of the Enlightenment to free mankind once and for all from *die Unmündigkeit* was now within arm's reach. Finally, it had become possible to realize this aim in a technical and strategic, i.e., efficient, way.

The immediate consequence of such a vision and practice was that films had to be dictated by a pure and enlightened reason. We can see the concrete implications of that *diktat* very clearly in the work of Eisenstein, which shows how film was a propaganda machine for the great truth, "the Pravda." Eisenstein names the true film, the Soviet film, "the intellectual film-art." He considered "the living man" as the greatest enemy of that true film-art inasmuch as he had in mind the Russian man in particular, attached to old folk customs, which made him intellectually underdeveloped and completely disqualified to understand the scientific truth about himself and his historical situation. That was the reason why the Russian people needed a thorough reorientation.

This massive program was to be accomplished by Soviet filmmakers. Seen from a stylistic point of view, the filmmaker uses the technique of the industrial assembly (*montage*) to forge film into the politically chosen instrument of cultural and educational policy. Film becomes an assembled image-machine, which can only be called a work of art because of its ingenious construction, similar to the structural works of the civil engineer. Like an industrial machine, film is composed of removable parts that are assembled together according to a fully rational procedure. In accordance with the strict regulation of modernism, only enlightened reason can produce real art. Eisenstein considered the intellectual film to be the last link in the chain of means necessary to accomplish the cultural revolution. This sort of film would bring to completion the final dialectical synthesis in the form of a monistic and all-embracing system encompassing the fields of collective education and teaching as well as all the arts. The intellectual film puts all the arts at the service of the absolute idea, which found its first historical figure in the Soviet society of "the Pravda."

The historical example of Eisenstein's work is of great importance for the comprehension of the relationship between modernism, film and religion. Modernism manifests itself here in its clearest cultural form, namely that of self-assured atheism. It proclaims religion to be an historical phase of *Unmündigkeit*, definitely overruled by the Enlightenment. In this sense it is highly significant that the communist revolution of 1917 recognized the painting *The Black Square* (1914-15), by the Russian painter Kazimir Malevich, as the icon of the new age. This is the period of the atheist who, with a single brushstroke, effaces all religious icons. Following the famous example of Malevich, Eisenstein promoted film as the art of the new atheistic man. As the master of the Soviet film, he stood at the cradle of the machine image of the communist revolution. The Soviet film in general institutionalized the heroic image of the industrial machine through many sequences exhibiting factory machines and large farming equipment in operation. From the point of view of modernism, the camera, seen as the machine of the moving image, naturally belonged to the industrial world of mechanized progress.

Soviet film is certainly significant as an historical paradigm for the study of the cultural relationship between film and religion. It shows that any form of modernism aims at using the new film medium in order to bring about the liberation of mankind. Thus, film always serves as an ideological instrument for the enlightened "idea of progress." Such an idea always labels religion as a cultural stage that must be surpassed in order to make planned progress possible. Through his films, the enlightened filmmaker can unmask religion for a broad public and propagate the enlightened lifestyle. With the collapse of the Soviet Union at the end of the twentieth century, modernism has lost, to be sure, its most extreme historic form. But elsewhere, too, it had begun to lose its ideological grip on culture in general and on film in particular.

Since the 1980s, a postmodern cultural consciousness has been growing. It creates a new place for a completely different cinematic consciousness because it has the will to contemplate the cultural relationship between film and religion in a constructive way. Thus, a new light shines on film and religion in postmodern culture. Both can now be seen, in many ways, as cultural correlates instead of as antipodes. I want to describe in detail the meaning of that postmodern correlation between film and religion in two different stages – first, by explaining the sense in which I use the notion of postmodern culture and second by discussing some fundamental aspects of the suggested correlation.

II. Postmodern Cultural Traces

I prefer to speak of "postmodern culture" rather than about "postmodernism." That makes it possible to modify the import of the notion of postmodern culture during the thought process itself, which follows three cultural traces of meaning, namely, the epistemological, the decentric, and the aesthetic. In my view, these traces give expression to a minimal agreement on the content of postmodern consciousness in contemporary Western culture.

The epistemological trace involves the thoroughgoing relativizing of the Pravda-concept or a general rejection of any ideological figure of truth that is written with a capital letter. The popular postmodern formula says that there are no longer any "great stories." The most recent one was that of a secular and atheistic modernism. A postmodern period shows great sensitivity to diversity in vision and behavior, i.e., cultural expression. It is interesting to note that, via the very different philosophies of Martin Heidegger and Ludwig Wittgenstein, the epistemological trace brings postmodern culture to an important revaluation of language. Postmodern philosophy concentrates on the emancipation of language from any kind of ideological restriction – an emancipation that occurs in the postwar period precisely when everybody concludes that language has forfeited its cultural dominance and is facing a deep crisis.

Up to the present, however, the epistemologic trace of postmodern philosophy has drawn attention to the medium of language without displaying any sensitivity for the new medium of the image and its own cultural value. Particularly by way of the cinematic image, the modern technological world creates a completely new medium for a mankind that lives and thinks in a world full of all kinds of machines. Such a positive understanding of the image culture is mainly developed outside the traditional academic world, which has occupied itself either with elaborating the technological language of the scientific disciplines or with defending almost desperately the classical literary function of the spoken and written mother tongue. By contrast, sound and image engineers under the direction of filmmakers in American and especially in European studios have explored the new intellectual field of the cinematographic image. Looking back on the first century of film history, it is clear that the will to explore the new image has always been stronger than the will to confine it within the epistemological limits of modernism.

I call the second trace of postmodern culture decentric, whereas modernism appears to be the last exponent of a centric culture. In modernism, the autonomous and pure reason of mankind is always, in one way or another, the center of attention. Postmodern consciousness looks upon such an anthropocentric middle as culturally extinct. Earlier, modernism had denounced any kind of supernatural center (mostly identified with God), placing, instead, enlightened man at the focal point of history. Now postmodern thinking has unmasked that modernistic center as a final illusion of a too self-assured mankind. Thus, the decentric trace of postmodern culture points to both religion *and* film. Religion is no longer considered as an expression of a not-yet emancipated, still infantile mankind because, in a postmodern society, the traditional churches and their theologies cease to constitute the big centers from which the religious life of mankind is managed and dominated. The postmodern development of film in the twentieth century is a sign of the two mentioned phenomena. Film can be seen as a privileged and decentered field for postmodern mankind, in which it can freely express its religious feelings and thoughts. Film creates an important extra-ecclesiastical and non-clerical, as well as non-modernist, space of religious evocation for the person who learns to live without all-too-human illusions. This also implies that in postmodern culture the fixed and traditional boundaries between cultural expressions cease being limits that exclude and metamorphose into points of encounter.

Also the stylistic boundaries between arts and genres, mostly laid down by the aesthetics of modernism, are fading away and even disappearing. Film thus becomes the preeminently postmodern medium. In the decentric trace of postmodern culture, it also becomes clear that the possible religious dimension of film decenters the traditional thinking of theology. The religious implications of film in postmodern culture go further than evaluating film as just a new hierophantic medium for theological truth. In the treatment of film and religion, ecclesiastical theology can no longer act as the third term, i.e., as the center that harmonizes the two other terms. Along the decentric trace in which the cinematic and religious expression displays its strength, no hierarchical approach to the relation between film and religion can any longer be applied.

The third postmodern trace in contemporary culture is aesthetic in character. The understanding of its own nature stems from the assessment that postmodern consciousness has manifested itself for the first time in an explicit way within the world of art itself. Indeed, postmodern culture is in a broad sense backed up by the will to liberate art from all kinds of ideological patronization. Thus, architecture has found its postmodern style by ridding itself of the fixed frame of modernistic architecture. Mark C. Taylor was the first theologian to present an explicitly postmodern theological interpretation of the situation in which architecture and other arts are expanding.[2] In his so-called postmodern a/theological interpretation of culture, the key word is "disfiguring," which signifies the postmodern refusal to represent or mimic aesthetically any sort of metaphysical essence. The postmodern artist does not want to copy any preexisting model. Plastic figuration refuses to be a copy of one or another existing model. The image receives its form from the refusal to re-present anything. For Taylor, this disfiguring rejects the traditional "theo-aesthetics," which is modeled by the will to imitate and realize the eternal, the divine, the absolute, in the transitory order of space and time. That utopian dream is even recognizable in atheistic modernism. Taylor's a/theology finds in postmodern architecture and art the paradigm of the postmodern endorsement of disfiguration. But a basic question is why film remains a blind spot in the vision of the a/theological, postmodern discourse. Does film still possess an inferior place in the rank of arts, in the eyes of intellectuals? The a/theological blindness for film is rather due to the unarticulated opinion that by nature film has too modernistic an essence. Is the visuality of the film image too strong to disfigure the illusion of representation? This question returns us, by way of the aesthetic trace, to a discussion of the aforementioned postmodern correlation between film and religion. Against the a/theological point of view, I see film as an essential medium in the postmodern situation of art. Therefore, in the following portion of this essay, I propose more closely to elaborate on the relevant exponents of the postmodern character of film.

III. The Postmodern Correlation between Film and Religion

In my wanderings through the cultural domain shaped by countless great films, I have pinpointed three roots or foci of the postmodern correlation between film and religion,[3] which promote not only a positive but also a desirable and productive dialogue between the two fields. In fact, the notion of postmodern culture receives its proper content through an elucidation of three foci: the biographical, the apocalyptical and the iconophile.

By the biographical focus, I refer to the postmodern significance of a number of successful, award-winning films like *The Mission* (1986) by Roland Joffé, *Romero* (1989) by John Duigan and *Daens* (1992) by Stijn Coninx. Although they are of different aesthetic quality, the three are valuable films acclaimed by large audiences. These films are highly relevant to the context of religion in postmodern culture. In cinematic language, their function can be described as a "flashback." Each one, in its own authentic way, retrieves and brings to the fore an important religious moment of a forgotten past. They are precisely relevant to postmodern culture because on the big screen of feature films they are significantly antimodern in two different respects. First, they give a vision of the history of the church that rejects the modernist attempt to portray religion as an outdated issue. Second, they remind modern man that religion cannot be plausibly conceptualized as an unequivocal and ideological appearance in history.

The contemporary audience is reminded, especially by films like *The Mission* and *Daens*, that in some important cases religion played a positive role in the social and cultural struggle of the eighteenth and nineteenth centuries. It was the period in which the Enlightenment with its modernistic ideologies of free-thinking liberalism and socialism scored triumphs, afraid neither of using violence in order to acquire political and economical power nor of manipulating the church and killing its priests. That occurred during the twentieth century in communist states, but also, as the film *Romero* shows, in nationalistic states where the church was tolerated only when it agreed to be a political servant. *The Mission* opens a dark page in the history book written by modernism of the period of Latin-American Jesuit missions, the so-called Reductions. Dictated by the modernistic idea of enlightened progress, this period had always been expunged from European memory. In turn, the film *Daens* brought about a public rediscovery in Flanders of a forgotten page of Belgian history, written during the liberal and anticlerical period of the modern Belgian state.

One distinguishing feature of these films is that they do not derive their content from any sort of premodern clericalism. Moreover, in them the postmodern cultural expression is in no way an alibi for "a return to traditional religion."[4] In each, religion finds authentic expression in the biographical postmodern focus, which reveals a very interesting postmodern way of presenting religion from the standpoint of a concrete man with existential roots in a particular time and world. In the contemporary postmodern situation, it is precisely the film image that has the power to signal, in a manner accessible and reliable for everyone, that religion is not a dried-up existential and historical source. In contrast with the vision of the industrial machine in Soviet films, church architecture in each of these three films appears as an enduring metaphor of religious culture. By making the architectural signs of certain historical churches an integral part of a biographical portrait, postmodern religious film can dissociate itself from the typical modernistic vision of churches as empty, dead archives.[5]

Each of the three films has in a sense an apocalyptic ending, which introduces a second important focus of the postmodern correlation between film and religion. Through the apocalyptic focus of postmodern culture, the possibilities of both film and religion are more closely related to one another. Particularly in the Jewish-Christian religious heritage, the apocalyptic experience is crucial, as was made clear by the historic decision to round off the Christian canon of the Bible with the Book of Revelation. The fact that the Book of Apocalypse, as it was formerly called, is written in a flamboyant and visionary style full of visual metaphors makes possible a correlation with postmodern film expression. Through their sensitivity to the realm of "the horizon of time," as I call it, the biblical Apocalypse and the film medium are structurally related to one another in their openness to time, encouraged by the will to see the life of man on the existential dividing line (horizon) between the known and the unknown – the past and present on the one hand, the future on the other.

Indeed, through its religious visionary openness, the Apocalypse is able both to take account of the suffering of man living on earth and to see in it an "advent" possibility and, by so doing, to liberate it from the despair of pessimism. The theologian Schillebeeckx rightly describes the biblical apocalyptic texts as a religious philosophy of life. Film can also develop into such a philosophy of life in a technological society. The requisite postmodern condition is that film frees itself from any kind of modernism, since modernism always cultivates an optimistic vision of human history that weakens the visionary power of the film image. But in the postmodern culture, film can both discover and explore its affinity with the religious apocalyptic vision inasmuch as film, with its visual composition and sense of movement, stands firmly anchored in time.

This has been very well understood by none other than the Russian director Andrei Tarkovsky, as is attested by his brilliant movies and his inspiring book on film theory, *Sculpting in Time*. Tarkovsky's film *oeuvre* opens with the feature film *My Name Is Ivan* (1962), in which he remembers the apocalypse of World War II, and closes with *The Sacrifice* (1986). In the latter, the apocalyptical sequences of the burning house empower the visual pregnancy of the whole film. His complete cinematographic work stems from a sharp eye for the continuous suffering of man in history, both in the industrial machine culture (World War II/*My Name Is Ivan*) and in the super-industrial consumption civilization (*The Sacrifice*). At the same time, the apocalyptic vision in Tarkovsky's films makes clear that there is an openness to the realm of time, i.e., to a coming renaissance that cannot be rendered in images. This openness can be found in the Berlin epilogue of *My Name Is Ivan* as well as in the sublime epilogue to *The Sacrifice*, with the child as waterbearer for the barren tree.

Tarkovsky's film theory also underlines the unbreakable link between the film image and living time: "The image is cinematographical if it lives in time and if time lives in it from the first shot."[6] The authentic relation between the film image and the facts of life is, he writes, "the *conditio sine qua non* and the real criterion for the plastic construction of a film."[7] In this vision, all the implications of the religious relevance of film are completely understood. It is totally opposed to the modernistic will to restrict the life of time in the image because of its intention to discourage, neutralize or root out religious belief from modern society. The films of Tarkovsky constitute a paradigm for the correlation between film and religion in postmodern culture. In his filmmaking, he rigorously draws the cinematic conclusions from the postmodern awareness of the all-embracing mystery of living time and gives the realm that transcends the human ego time to express itself. In the hands of a filmmaker like Tarkovsky, the camera – the paintbrush of film – takes the time needed to allow physical reality to speak its own language. It lets the director act as the first spectator of the visual story told by real things themselves. In its postmodern significance, the film becomes the visual medium that arises from a decentering of the organizing subject. The authorship of film permits itself to be decentered by the plastic power of the filmed elements.

In a decentric direction like Tarkovsky's, the camera preserves the life-value of time. It frees physical reality from the all-too-human objectifying gaze and extends its seal to moving time, to the reality of duration. The cinematic seal produces evidence of authenticity and delivers a charter that ratifies the life-value of what appears on the screen. At the same time, the Tarkovskian film image protects the reality of time against every wrongful breaking of its seals; just as in the biblical vision of the Apocalypse, it does not belong to man, and certainly not to the all-too-human ego-centered man of modernism, to open the divine seals of time. Only the Lamb of God has the right to break the seals of the Book of Life. Tarkovsky refers explicitly in his film *My Name Is Ivan* to this religious, apocalyptic openness of time with the image of Dürer's etching *The Four Horsemen of the Apocalypse*, and also in his film *Stalker* (1979) with the image of John the Baptist, from the famous Ghentian altarpiece painted by the brothers Van Eyck, and also with the literal quotation of a passage from the Apocalypse (6:12b-17). What is considered impossible in the vision of Taylor's postmodern a/theology finds outstanding expression in the postmodern film world: an intense and powerful "presence" that is not achieved by a merely human effort. Through the postmodern film image, presence can be sensed in culture and can offer significant authenticity to religious experience.

An excellent example of cinematic power in a postmodern sense can be found in Ingmar Bergman's masterpiece *The Seventh Seal* (1956) – a title taken from Apocalypse 8:1. This Swedish work stands out as the postwar representation of the quest of the medieval crusader Antonius

The Sacrifice, Andrei Tarkovsky, 1986

Block, for whom the target of real religious struggle is the absurdity of "Death," one of the four apocalyptic horsemen. Block discovers that the religious road runs along the paths of life, which are in turn revealed by the film image. Because of its revelatory nature, the film acquires an apocalyptic religious relevance in postmodern society, endangered as it is from within by the capacity for fatal destruction.

Another basic aspect of the apocalyptic focus directs our attention to the neverending struggle between good and evil in human history, in the heart of every person, and even in the elements of the earth. In the religious traditions of mankind, especially in Christianity, the experience of that struggle has always been a matter of great interest. From a secular perspective, this apocalyptic dimension can even be found in the core of modernistic and atheistic ideologies. But in a postmodern cultural situation, marked by the disappearance of a central, firm and unchanging moral code, film employs its special visual power to evoke the theme of good and evil. Postmodern film emphasizes the fact that morality's long history has not yet reached a happy ending. It portrays postmodern man as one for whom the reality of good and evil is not only an enormous problem, but also an indecipherable mystery.

Tarkovsky's films dredge up this existential mystery. Although imbued with a completely different style, the same argument also applies to more commercially successful American action movies such as *Grand Canyon* (1991) by Lawrence Kasdan, *Bodyguard* (1992) by Mick Jackson and *Falling Down* (1993) by Joel Shumacher. The postmodern cinematic eye for the apocalyptic struggle between good and evil emphasizes the point that film and religion are working with the same anthropological raw material and thus encounter one another as correlatives. This varies, of course, from director to director and from film to film.

Close resemblances and important differences are visible between the postmodern European films of Tarkovsky and the American films of Francis Ford Coppola and David Lynch. Within the described apocalyptic cultural context, the resemblance can be found in the absence of a fixed center, particularly of the character of the father. The difference centers on the fact that in Tarkovsky's *The Sacrifice* the father sacrifices himself because he has witnessed the increasingly apocalyptic power of evil, whereas in Coppola's *Apocalypse Now* (1979) and *The Godfather* saga (1971, 1974, 1990), as well as in Lynch's *Twin Peaks: Fire Walk with Me* (1992), the figure of the father represents good, yet brings about apocalyptic destruction. In the latter films, the complex interweaving of good and evil gives exemplary expression to the postmodern consciousness. It also implies the presence of religious raw material. The interconnectedness finds its most significant visual expression in the restrained sorrow of the cinematic gaze that observes the apocalyptic events and behavior.

As a result, these films place a narrative emphasis on the loss of innocence as the apocalypse unfolds. In *The Godfather* films, the young and innocent Michael Corleone becomes the dreaded and corrupt Godfather who finally causes the ruin of his family. And in *Twin Peaks: Fire Walk with Me*, an anonymous fortuneteller says to Laura Palmer, "When this kind of fire starts, it's very hard to put it out. The tender wings of innocence burn first and the wind rises and then all goodness is in jeopardy." In the next sequence, Laura cries while listening to someone sing a melancholy song: "Why did you go, why did you die away from me while the whole world seems to sing? Was it me? Was it you? Questions in a world full of blue. How can a heart that is filled with love start to cry? When the whole world seems so right, how can it die? Was it me? Was it you? Questions in a world full of blue." In Lynch's films, the postmodern sensibility quickly turns to images of a demonic and nihilistic nature. This is true of some sequences in *Twin Peaks: Fire Walk with Me* and of his entire film *Wild at Heart* (1990). In these cases, the postmodern apocalyptic view degenerates all too quickly into the nihilistic pose of someone trying to play a morbid game.

Tarkovsky and Kieslowski follow a completely different cinematic road. In the *Decalogue* cycle (1988-89), Kieslowski offers a very clear example of the mysterious, apocalyptic struggle between good and evil in the everyday life of contemporary man. In *Decalogue I*, he portrays a father who, self-assured in his modernistic belief in the scientific power of computers, unintentionally causes the death of his son. In its own special filmic way, the *Decalogue* cycle renders visible the incapacity of any kind of moralism to settle the catastrophic struggle between good and evil. It also makes clear that this struggle reveals the great mystery of life and death. Together with postmodern filmmakers, the spectator can see the contemporary religious image as an indispensable mirror through which he is intensely linked – *religere* – with the wonderful world of time and space. In the cinematic hall of mirrors, postmodern man learns to experience that world religiously through the sign of light, which opens the way to an understanding of the third focus of the postmodern correlation between film and religion – the iconophile.

In the detailed theory of the French philosopher Giles Deleuze, the *image-mouvement* and the *image-temps* emerge as the two defined structural elements in the substance of film.[8] Indeed, film draws its support from the fundamental reality of enduring movement and is, for that reason, also called a "motion picture." In the mirror of films like Tarkovsky's, the full power of the *image-mouvement* appears as *image-temps*. In the framework of my inquiry into the postmodern correlation between film and religion, I want to emphasize earthly light as the living source of both the *image-mouvement* and the *image-temps*. In my view, earthly light constitutes a focal point for the further understanding of the religious dimension of postmodern culture and its cinematic consciousness.[9] The postmodern development of the film image places religiosity in the sign of light. After all, the film image not only demonstrates the power of light, but also

Apocalypse Now, Francis Ford Coppola, 1979

brings light to power. Since their origin, film images appear fully as "light pictures," as sculptures of earthly light.

The religious experience of this life-giving power of light has received everlasting expression in the first chapter of the oldest document of the Jewish-Christian religion, the Book of Genesis. In the biblical myth of creation, light is the only element explicitly named twice, i.e., on the first and the fourth days of creation. And both times "God saw it was good." In the tradition of Genesis, the light of creation is a source of religious experience. But created light itself becomes an essential source of creation, bringing the earthly realm of time and space into light. The creative power of light shows the lifework of God himself. "Bringing to light" means "having a good eye" for the metaphysical wonder of being, which is not to be searched for in an abstract, invisible and supernatural world, but in the concrete world of earthly life. In religious faith, as expressed in Genesis, the earthly realm of light is a preeminent metaphysical place. Religion assigns man the task of not walking around blindly. On the contrary, he is called to keep his eyes open and to discover the wonder of the created "light images" sculpted by creative light.

Since the twentieth century, man possesses a completely new religious medium, the most light-sensitive machine that ever existed and of which former generations could only dream. The idea that the authentic film has a basically religious essence is confirmed by the leading cameraman, Henri Alekan. In his interesting study *Des Lumières et des Ombres*, he notes that "of all means of expression used by filmmakers, light is the most basic one."[10] In his opinion, the task of the contemporary filmmaker consists in organizing and rhythmically arranging light and shadow, although he is not the possessor of light's power. The director comes to the "living images" by integrating the creative nature of light into his personal point of view. When he lets the creative power of light take part in his images, then his film receives an authentic characteristic of religiosity.

Precisely in a postmodern culture, the understanding of light puts us on the right track for discerning the religious dimension of the film image. However, it is not obvious that each film automatically has a religious dimension. It can only clearly be seen in the iconophile focus of the postmodern correlation between film and religion, namely, the "worthy light image." By this I mean that an authentic image is the fulfilled work of creative light. In fact, the essential antithesis between modernism and the postmodern culture appears to be an important issue in the contemporary cultural confrontation that has the "worthy image" as its node. For that confrontation, the difference between Eisenstein and Tarkovsky, especially the difference between Eisenstein's *Alexander Nevsky* (1938) and Tarkovsky's *Andrei Rublev* (1966), is paradigmatic. Eisenstein ended an article presenting his film in 1939 with the words: "Patriotism – that's our theme." With his film project, Eisenstein went along with the ideological need of the Soviet Union at the time, mobilizing the people emotionally for the military defense of the régime against Hitler's attacking armies. To that end, the historical character Alexander Nevsky and the national feelings of the Russian people were fitted into the ideological figure of Stalin's communist dictatorship.

Tarkovsky's *Andrei Rublev* stands at quite a distance from Eisenstein's film. Tarkovsky's masterpiece also deals with the medieval period of Russian history, but not to promote any possible militaristic and nationalistic abuse of the film and its subject. The religious image – the Trinity icon of Andrei Rublev – is the main purpose of his lyrical epic. Tarkovsky wanted to help the spectator (re)discover the sublime icon. He succeeded in his enterprise by making his own the observing gaze of the painter-monk. Tarkovsky's main character is in no way a military hero who commands, fights, and triumphs. The painter-monk is a religious man who contemplates the divine creation with open eyes, following the paths of the revealing light. Tarkovsky's iconophile engagement with the authentic image also expresses itself in basic stylistic differences from Eisenstein's method. In contrast with Eisenstein, it is not the *montage* but the interrupted living image itself that is the cornerstone of Tarkovsky's cinematic construction. The style of the film is determined by the film image that sets itself free for the creative light of life. The modernistic usage of the film image relates to the iconographic expression of the same as does the darkness of night to daylight. The postmodern iconophile attitude lets the film image be itself. It is free to become an authentic image and sets itself free to experience creative light and its plastic, religious power.

The iconophile attitude provides an adequate outlook on twentieth-century culture with its abundant images. This does not mean that we already sense the advent of the worthy image culture; the first is at most a condition for the second. In our cultural situation, the postmodern way of both championing the worthy film image and developing an authentic religious culture can be seen as the same. The key role played by directors related to the Christian heritage in the history of filmmaking up to the present day shows us that the worthy film image in postmodern culture can be a religious act of faith. One basic aspect of it concerns the continuous fight with the audiovisual clichés attempting to dominate and even terrorize vision in our culture. In his essay on Cézanne (1929), D.H. Lawrence clearly argues that "the cliché is the deadly enemy" of a real image that emerges from the difficult "fight with the cliché."[11] Thus, we can understand why the contemporary filmmaker in the postmodern culture, with its predominantly audiovisual images, feels an affinity for the painter. He feels they are kindred spirits. He explores the inspiring history of painting with its many examples of painters fighting with themselves and their surroundings. Their life testifies to the spiritual care for the visionary power of the image, related to the inexhaustible creative power of the divine light of life.

That brings us to another stylistic feature of the religious dimension in the postmodern cinematic consciousness, which I define as the iconophile phenomenon of "the image graft." It consists of the creative integration of worthy pictures from the distant or near past into a film. In this case also, the *oeuvre* of Tarkovsky is an excellent postmodern example. He inserts a great number of visual quotations into his films, but I call attention here exclusively to the icon sequences at the end of *Andrei Rublev* and to the visual prominence of da Vinci's unfinished *The Adoration of the Magi* in *The Sacrifice*. Tarkovsky grafts the religious experience of the film image onto the creative power of valuable pictures from the past. By doing so, he weakens the argument of the dogmatic progress in arts as laid down in modernism that envisages the art of the past only as a museum piece. Tarkovsky demonstrates that worthy images from the past own not only aesthetic, but also spiritual qualities that can be rediscovered in a postmodern time.

Another iconophile aspect of "the image graft" can be seen in some recent films which focus on the work of a painter. I am not referring to films like Louis Malle's *Van Gogh* (1991), but rather to the likes of *La Belle Noiseuse* (1991) by Jacques Rivette and *The Quince Tree Sun* (1992) by Victor Erice. Rivette places the work of the French painter Bernard Dufour in the forefront; Erice follows the Spanish painter Antonio López with his camera. Both films respond entirely to what Pasolini called "*cinéma de poësie.*"[12] In the hands of both directors, the film image is grafted onto the contemplative work of the painter so that the spectator too experiences a liturgy of the gaze. In Rivette's film, the spectator is exposed to the possibility of looking at the naked human body in a religious way that stands in stark contrast to the countless films in which the human body is visually reduced to the level of a sex object. As for the film of Erice, the spectator's gaze directs itself meditatively towards the sublime play of sunlight on the leaves of a quince tree, and the painter celebrates an iconophile liturgy where the traces of the ancient religious experience of creative light, as captured in the verses of Genesis, once again make themselves felt. The spiritual eye of the two directors declares its solidarity with the painter who patiently and diffidently searches for a representation that does justice to the concrete mystery of being. In the postmodern view, such a picture is never completed, as we see literally in the final sequences of Tarkovsky's *Andrei Rublev* where the Trinity icon shows signs of destruction. In *La Belle Noiseuse*, the most important painting is never exposed, not even to the camera. And in *The Quince Tree Sun*, the painter is unable to follow and represent the cycle of the fruit. In each of these films, the film image emerges from the movement and emotion of the open gaze.

From the perspective of these three "movies," we can say that the postmodern religious picture is a process of seeing. In this context, I should recall Tarkovsky's observation in *Sculpting in Time*: "Mankind never created something disinterestedly, unless it was the artistic image. Is it perhaps in this way, that we have been created in the image and likeness of God; namely, capable of creativity?"[13] In response to that question, it might be meaningful to argue that in the postmodern time, as in no other, unselfish sacrifice acquires a religious significance in godly seeing. Looking with an open gaze on this creation was the work carried through by the Creator on the seventh day. Is it perhaps possible to experience the cinematic image that shines beyond the audiovisual cliché as the seventh day of human culture? During such a cinematographical day, the postmodern spectator can, even if only in the twinkling of an eye, surpass his all-too-human littleness and become a kindred spirit with the divine Spectator.

Endnotes

1. S. Eisenstein, *Montage: Het konstruktie-principe in de kunst* (Nijmegen: SUN, 1981), 30: "Film art is first of all *montage*." (My translation from the Dutch edition of Eisenstein's essay *Outside the Film Picture* [Moscow, 1929]).

2. Mark C. Taylor, *Erring: A Postmodern A/theology* (Chicago: University of Chicago Press, 1984). Mark C. Taylor, *Disfiguring: Art, Architecture, Religion* (Chicago: University of Chicago Press, 1992).

3. The argument that I develop here emerges from the studies I have published in Dutch (see bibliography).

4. Taylor, *Disfiguring*, 317: "Postmodernism that is not a disguised modernism does not involve a return to traditional religion."

5. Some significant films of the last two decades to be mentioned here are in chronological order: *Le Diable Probablement* (Robert Bresson, 1977), *Nostalghia* (Andrei Tarkovsky, 1983), *A Prayer for the Dying* (Mike Hodges, 1987), *Babettes Gaestebud* (*Babette's Feast*, Gabriel Axel, 1987), *Sous le soleil de Satan* (*Under Satan's Sun*, Maurice Pialat, 1987), *La leggenda del santo bevitore* (*The Legend of the Holy Drinker*, Ermanno Olmi, 1988), *The Navigator: A Medieval Odyssey* (Vincent Ward, 1988), *Jésus de Montréal* (Denys Arcand, 1989), *We're No Angels* (Neil Jordan, 1989), *Marcellino, Pane e Vino* (*Bread and Wine*, Luigi Comencini, 1991), *The Miracle* (Neil Jordan, 1991), *L'Annonce faite à Marie* (*The Annunciation of Mary*, Alain Cuny, 1991), *La Belle Histoire* (*The Beautiful Story*, Claude Lelouch, 1992), *Bad Lieutenant* (Abel Ferrara), *Sommersby* (Jon Amiel, 1993).

6. Andrei Tarkovsky, *Le Temps Scellé* (Paris: l'Etoile/Cahiers du Cinéma, 1989), 64. (My translation from the French.) English translation: *Sculpting in Time* (Bodley Head, 1986; U.S. ed. 1987).

7. Ibid., 67.

8. G. Deleuze, *Cinéma I: L'image-mouvement* (Paris: Minuit, 1983); *Cinéma II: L'image-temps* (Paris: Minuit, 1985), 7. Referring to Charles Sanders Peirce (1839-1914) and annotating *Matière et mémoire* (1896) of Henri Bergson (1859-1941), Deleuze elaborates a taxonomy of cinematic images and signs.

9. My point of view is different from that of Deleuze, who considers the *montage* as "*l'acte principal du cinéma*" that constitutes "*l'image du temps*" (*Cinéma II*, 51). For me the basis of "*l'image-temps*" is ontological rather than purely aesthetical.

10. H. Alekan, *Des Lumières et des Ombres* (Paris: Sycomore, 1984), 79. (My translation.)

11. D.H. Lawrence, "Introduction to His Paintings," in *Selected Essays* (Middlesex: Penguin Books, 1950), 337-38.

12. Pier Paolo Pasolini, "*Le cinéma de poésie*," in *L'expérience hérétique: Langue et cinéma* (Paris: Payot, 1976), 135-55.

13. Tarkovsky, *Le Temps Scellé*, 223. (My translation.)

7

From Eve to the Virgin and Back Again: The Image of Woman in Contemporary (Religious) Film

Diane Apostolos-Cappadona

It is quite appropriate, I believe, that the recent "Year of the Woman" provided an ideal opportunity to investigate more precisely what the phrase *the image of woman* means in terms of contemporary religious film. To avoid any initial misunderstanding, let me clarify that I employ the term *religious* not to connote a scriptural or ecclesiastical theological tradition, dogma, ritual or creed, but the larger more generic sense of religion as found in the writings of the historian of religions, Mircea Eliade. Hence a secularized society without a publicly avowed ecclesiastical or biblical faith may still be deemed and/or interpreted as religious. For Eliade, *the sacred* (his term for identifying the presence of the religious) camouflages itself in the secular culture of the modern world and manifests itself through the symbols and signs of the arts, including film. To heighten this awareness of the concept of religion and the religious, I will consistently employ the use of parentheses throughout this essay, as I have in the title, i.e., religious, to suggest the camouflage of the sacred in the modern world.

The celebration of the "Year of the Woman" at the 1993 Academy Awards ceremonies was ambiguous, with much acclaim given to the "great" female film stars of past generations and to the "behind-the-scenes" roles that women have played in the production of films. Yet a simple glance at the films nominated for "Best Picture" or the directors nominated for "Best Director" suggested that, despite the hype, Hollywood and thereby the film industry remain a bastion of traditional male values, hierarchy, and authority. In that light, then, the image of woman in contemporary (religious) film may be limited to – albeit in a politically correct re-vision – the traditional dichotomy of Eve and the Virgin, and at best only the occasional role for a unique actress like the female lead in *Who's Afraid of Virginia Woolf?* (1966) or *Agnes of God* (1985) remains the exception and not a norm, while the rare woman's picture like *Beaches* (1988) is simply that – a rare woman's picture.

We need to ask ourselves what elements are necessary to constitute or identify a film as both (religious) and feminist without impinging upon the integrity of either feminism or religion. For example, is it sufficient to suggest that a film like *The Prince of Tides* (1991) is a feminist film simply because the producer/director was a woman, or that Walt Disney Studio's *Beauty and the Beast* (1991) is a feminist film because Beauty (aka Belle) appears to rescue the Beast? Is there a clear distinction between a feminist film and what has traditionally been identified as "a woman's picture"? Is it possible to reflect upon and/or discuss the image of woman as separate and distinct from the image of man as in the current rash of "gender-bender" films such as *Orlando* or *The Ballad of Little Joe* (both 1993)? How do we safely categorize a film because as Jean-Luc Godard's *Hail Mary* (1985)? Is it a feminist film because its central character and storyline are about a typical contemporary woman who finds herself in an atypical situation and struggles to survive, or is it a (religious) film because of its consistent scriptural and theological allusions? Do we disregard its overemphasis on female nudity and/or its objectification of woman as passivity and obedience personified because it may be either a feminist or a (religious) film, or even possibly a feminist (religious) film? Whether viewed in a traditional movie theater or in the comfort of one's own living room, film has become one of the most powerful projectors of cultural values and attitudes.

In recognition of this fact, we must consider with care exactly how and why film has a formative, not simply entertaining, function in our contemporary society. Because film is a visual, not a literary medium, I will employ the terminology of "sight" and "seeing" as opposed to the literary critical terminology of text and reading in my discussion of the power of images, the images of woman in contemporary (religious) film, and in the development of a feminist (religious) methodology for the analysis of film.[1]

It is my contention that the fundamental transmitters of Western cultural values – the family, theological traditions, and educational institutions – have been supplanted in our contemporary society by the media, specifically film and television. One of the major cultural attitudes formed and communicated by the media is the identification of gender as opposed to sexuality. Since gender identity is directly related to the definition of being human, it raises immediate theological questions that are not necessarily ethical or moral issues. Thus, the media's manner and style of imaging woman suggest a fairweather barometer of the general culture's interpretation of the appropriate role of women in society and in ecclesiastical traditions or institutions. My examination of the power of images emphasizes the centrality of images as primary communicators of gender identification and theological values, the relationship between art and film or "moving pictures," and the specific parameters of the image of woman in contemporary (religious) film.[2]

Crucial to this analysis is my attempt to define a feminist (religious) aesthetic and to offer a feminist (religious) film methodology for the reading of contemporary (religious) film. To that end, I will survey the histories of feminist scholarship in art, aesthetics, and film studies; the relationship between images of woman and woman's images in both the visual arts and film; and the recent developments and interrelationships of a feminist aesthetics, feminist film studies, and feminist theology.

A film is composed of "moving picture" – frames that project both a series of recognizable images and a story. The narrative of the film tells us something about a person or persons, a place, an event. The images project both explicit and implicit messages to each viewer. The combination of the narrative and the images within a film is constructed by the film-maker, but the actual "seeing" of them is dependent upon the viewer. Each of us "sees" in a manner that is both singular to our individual selves and coordinated by the worlds – social, cultural, economic, political, and theological – into which we have been socialized. A major, if not central, element in that socialization process is the role of images. Our English word *image* is derived from the Latin *imago* meaning "a copy" and denoting imitation as opposed, for example, to an icon that derives from the Greek *eikon* meaning "likeness or portrait" and denoting originality. Images have power: power to please, power to shock, power to educate, power to convert, power to transform. In the classical world, the power of images was accepted as a dynamic force to be both respected and reckoned with. Consider, for example, this rather typical description of the power of images from Saint Augustine's polemic on divine creation:

> The tyrant Dionysus, . . . because he was deformed, did not wish to have children like himself. In sleeping with his wife he used to place a beautiful picture before her, so that by desiring its beauty and in some manner taking it in, she might effectively transmit it to the offspring she conceived.[3]

Such an attitude toward the power of images has not lessened in the modern world when "primitives" fear having their photograph taken lest they lose their spirits or souls, or when sophisticated moderns effectively alter their appearance in a portrait photograph, thus becoming more like what and who they want to be as opposed to what and who they are in reality.

As David Freedberg (the first art historian to have actually studied the "power of images" in terms of the response of the viewer/audience) explained,

> people are sexually aroused by pictures and sculptures; they break pictures and sculptures; they mutilate them, kiss them, cry before them, and go on journeys to "see" them; they are claimed by them, and incited to revolt. They give thanks by means of them, expect to be elevated by them, and are moved to the highest levels of empathy and fear. They have always responded in these ways; they still do. They do so in socie-

ties we call primitive and in modern societies in East and West, in Africa, America, Asia, and Europe.[4]

Images have a fundamental power that causes each of us to re-form or form our attitudes toward ourselves as individuals and as a community, and toward God. The root of an image's power is both its visual nature and the nature of the visual. Images evoke an aesthetic experience, which at its highest level can bring the individual to a moment of spiritual ecstasy or union or, more simply, a heightened sense of being. Images are capable of evoking such responses because images operate in the aesthetic realm. Etymologically, our English word *aesthetic* is derived from the Greek word *aisthetikos*, which is a variant of *aisthanesthai* meaning "to perceive," as in "to know," not simply "to see" through the senses. At its highest levels, the aesthetic brings forth all the senses of the human person, heightens a recognition of the self and of the body, and merges these heightened sensitivities with the engaged bodiliness and consciousness to bring the individual to a recognition of "knowing." In the aesthetic experience, then, heart, mind, body, and soul are excited and coalesced into a holistic identity and a renewed recognition of the self. The individual images themselves may have a great deal to do with the evocation of the aesthetic experience, and/or with the authority granted to the film as being real and true.

Images communicate authority and reality through what I have elsewhere identified as the process of visual analogy.[5] Simply enough, each new image presents a fresh and independent representation that is dependent upon an earlier classical image or traditional masterpiece on the theme of an individual or individuals of fame or power, or of an event that transformed history or ways of thinking. This background nurtures and supports, implicitly and unconsciously, the viewer's reception of the new image. Each of us has a history of visual images with which we were bombarded as children, including sacred images from church, the Bible, and such mundane items as Christmas or Easter cards. These images were invested with an aura of reverence and adoration due to their "sacred authority" – their ability to conjure up the holy, to heal, to transform, to bring about spiritual conversion, to be the site of the sacred, etc. For example, we need only to consider Zeffirelli's *Jesus of Nazareth* (1977). Throughout this film the costumes, backdrops, scenery, groupings of persons, and even the facial and bodily gestures of each character are presented with a caring and careful acknowledgment of the power of images inasmuch as each of these "episodes" or "persons" is modeled upon a traditional masterpiece of Christian art. These visual analogies to the works of Rembrandt, Michelangelo, Botticelli, Raphael, and Sebastiano del Piombo, to name only a few examples, simultaneously invest the film with an aura of authenticity and an acceptance as real, through the unconscious and subliminal manipulation of images. As the critic John Berger has noted, an image is a sight which has been recreated or reproduced. It is an appearance, or a set of appearances, which has been detached from the place and time in which it first made its appearance and preserved – for a month or a few centuries. Every image embodies a way of seeing.[6]

Similarly, we have an internal warehouse of secular images – many of which are premised upon traditional sacred images – and which also have a profound effect upon our manner of being in the world. In particular, images of men and women project our "proper notions" of maleness and femaleness, not simply in terms of styles of dress or hair styles, but also in attitudes of bodily deportment, gestures, and actions that delineate maleness from femaleness. For example, a child comes to realize by watching *Cinderella* or *Snow White* that being female involves a surrender to male action and wisdom, that love conquers evil, and that single older women – whether they be widows or old maids – can be identified as evil creatures by the deep tones in their voices, their tall and scrawny bodies, their lengthy fingernails, and their exaggerated gesticulations when speaking. Loving "feminine" women, on the other hand, have soft and sweet voices, short and plump little bodies, and an overall gentle demeanor that governs all they say and do. Handsome young princes will go to extremes in dangerous actions to save the "girl of their dreams." The contemporary cinematic interest in androgynous heroes and villains (I almost shudder to say "also heroines and villainesses") suggests a series of messages and signals about the meaning of gender identity. Clearly the 1990s have become a time of transition, including long-sought transformations in our cultural definitions of the appropriate roles for men and women, which began with the feminist movement in the 1960s. Redefinitions of the meaning and roles of parenting as opposed to the separate identities and duties of mother and father, the emerging acceptance of alternate lifestyles, including a variety of family compositions and sexual preferences, and the public recognition of the changing roles of women – both single and married – in the professional worlds of business, academics, and athletics have initiated a larger cultural examination of the meaning of "maleness" and "femaleness."

Images are central to the socialization process(es) by which each of us enters into that social and cultural order that we come to identify as "our world." This socialization process involves the simultaneous development of an individual, communal, national, theological, and gender identity. In this way, we enter both the public sphere and what the social historian Lois Banner identifies as the "history of the personal."[7] In our contemporary world, this socialization process is compounded by both the loss of an identifiable theological center and a "surrender" to the media.

The contemporary theological situation – that is, pluralism – can be defined as one without a center. There is no singularly identifiable or unifying ecclesiastical tradition or ethic that the United States or the Western world can identity with. Instead, we are faced with a world in which multiple faith identities survive and perhaps flourish side-by-side. Although there may be some commonalities among these traditions, they are further confronted by neighboring systems of disbelief (or perhaps better said, unbelief), including modern science, apathy, and a secular spirituality that advocates an optimistic faith in humanity and in the power of an unspecified sacrality. There is also present in this contemporary theological situation what might be labelled a postmodern spiritual nostalgia, which like postmodern art, architecture, and literature seeks a recognizable foundation or image from the classical tradition while packaging itself in a postmodern abstract collage. Given this variety of (religious) and non(religious) attitudes, is it any wonder that contemporary film images which seek to define gender identification or spiritual values flounder as if lost at sea? As Lois Banner suggests,

> culture is a mélange, a potpourri of messages which we both screen and by which we are shaped. Artists of substance both reflect and reshape those messages in epic ways, telling us what the world of images we inhabit is all about. Or, they give us the pleasure of receiving mixed meanings, so that we can exercise our own minds and imaginations.[8]

Two central interpretive tools that we need to aid us in our "seeing" of images are a recognition of theological values and of gender identification. Filmmakers, as artists following Banner's dictum, reenvision our sense of self and of others, and in so doing bring us to a recognition of our limitations as well as our aspirations.

When the camera was "perfected" in the mid-nineteenth century, the way human beings saw their individual selves as well as others was irrevocably changed, just as art was irrevocably transformed. Painting and sculpture were challenged to do something other than what the camera could do – to capture a moment, a person, an event and freeze it unaltered and truthfully for all eternity. Artists like the Impressionists turned their attention away from creating works of art that were objects to be "seen" toward works of art that were about the process of "seeing." As photography evolved into the black-and-white but silent moving "picture," the power of this medium and its ability to communicate through the visual image transfixed its audiences. It became the rage to walk like, dress like, look like one's favorite film star. As the silent film moved into the "talkie," and the black-and-white talkie into the full color film, cinema's popularity increased and it became more and more accessible to the modern viewer. In today's world, nothing is more accessible than the visual images of film that can be "seen" in theaters, classrooms, shopping malls, living rooms, bedrooms, even airplanes. That esoteric presentation of images known as high art, which was once reserved for the elite, has now become accessible daily fare for all economic classes through the "magic" of the camera.

As historical and contemporary narratives are "played out" in film, the images of men and women either support or rebel against those socially acceptable roles the viewer already knows. The art historian and iconologist Erwin Panofsky suggested that "images of women . . . are cultural symptoms" whose study can help identify the essential tendencies of specific cultural eras. Following Panofsky, then, I would suggest that a careful analysis of the image of woman in contemporary (religious) film can offer a meaningful entry into a discussion of the role of women in the contemporary social and ecclesial world. We need to study carefully the image of woman, not simply from an iconographical or symbolic perspective, or from that of visual analogies, but from an integrated examination of the image or images of woman projected by both the film's narrative and its visual depictions. We need to consider alternate "seeings," what many feminists and/or deconstructionist scholars would refer to as the re-"seeing" of the vision: the narrative and the visual components of the film.[9] We need to look carefully from several angles simultaneously to recognize that no visual image is so simplistic and that no audience or individual viewer "sees" identically as does another group or person. Rather, the multivalent and heuristic qualities of film provide for both its extraordinarily powerful influence as a shaper and transformer of values and identities, as well as its attraction as entertainment. One can "see" the same film, or any work of art for that matter, three or four times and, each time, "see" more than "just something new," but a whole new way of being in the world. For example, in her recent study *In Full Flower: Aging Women, Power, and Sexuality*, Lois Banner introduces her premise that the theme and variations of the relationship between older women and younger men have been present throughout human history, by analyzing *Sunset Boulevard* (1950) from a variety of perspectives. She offers not simply several "seeings" and re-"seeings" of her own, but also contrasts her initial "seeing" of the film as a young woman growing up in the 1940s to that of her current students at USC. Banner saw Gloria Swanson as a sad, crazy, perhaps post-menopausal and thereby old woman who was being manipulated by William Holden, whereas her students, children of the 1970s and 1980s, saw Swanson as an attractive, intelligent, and powerful woman who used Holden. Combining all of her "seeings," Banner suggests that the central theme of this film is the story of the changing balance of power in male-female relationships in a world premised on deceit and distrust.

Feminist scholarship in art history, film studies, and religious studies grew out of the feminist movement of the 1960s. Like the political and social movements of which they were a part, feminist studies initially were concerned with issues of economic parity, equality of representation, and issues of aesthetic and female consciousness. In art and literary studies, this latter issue was defined by the debates over the criteria by which the artist/writer and/or her work were to be evaluated – "greatness," "art vs. craft," "artistic achievement," and "nature vs. culture," perhaps better identified as "nature vs. nurture." The fundamental complaint was the question of patriarchal values and the standards of a male-dominated and male-oriented culture. Should women be judged by the same criteria? Should the culture and its patriarchal values/standards be allowed to continue without transformation? Or were women so distinctively and fundamentally different that they had to be evaluated by "a separate but equal" set of criteria?

For women artists in this earliest period of the modern feminist movement, there was a clear and definable category of "women's art." It arose out of a female consciousness and experience of the world that was distinct from what was male, and was straightforwardly and unabashedly exclusivist. This attitude led to the initial development of forms of feminist aesthetic criteria which included the analysis of women's historical and ideological position in relation to art, art production, and artistic intentionality. The first decade of feminist art can be distinguished by its public outcry of anger over centuries, if not millennia, of male oppression; a new sense of an identifiable women's art community; and an optimistic faith in art as both promoter and engenderer of a feminist or, in my opinion, female consciousness. This led to the developments of the second decade of feminist art, in which two thematic categories can be distinguished – visual political rhetoric and the quest for a feminist spirituality, especially in terms of the retrieval or recovery of the goddess. Feminist art -historians sought to uncover the history of women artists and prepared scholarly monographs on individual women artists, argued for the inclusion of women artists in basic art history survey courses and texts, and developed special courses in the history of women artists and women's art. The danger here – as in all specialized fields of the study of the marginalized – is the recognition that, for good or for ill, this is only "missing history" and must be combined with the larger survey of patriarchal history that is our heritage. If art created by women is treated as a separate history, the student and the teacher may come to conclude that the Baroque began and ended with Artemisia Gentileschi, and Impressionism with Mary Cassatt.

This latter intellectual inquiry led to the more contemporary (late 1980s to early 1990s) trend toward a total questioning of the discipline of art history as a normative definition of how artists operate, how works of art are made and evaluated, how iconographic and stylistic innovations occur. This intellectual rebellion against traditional patriarchal values led to a call for a radical re-visioning of the discipline from its foundation. In their iconographical and historical studies of the image of woman in Western art, feminist art historians began to ask questions that are of interest for this particular essay. Is there a distinction between female sexuality and the construction of the feminine gender? Are images of women in the arts, including the media, nothing more than a result of the male fascination or obsession with the female body? Can language, including the visual language of gesture and pose, be revised once it is recognized as a controller and producer of cultural meaning and values? Finally, is there an operable distinction between women's images and images of women, especially a significant and observable difference between those images of woman created by women as opposed to those created by men?

Feminist film studies and feminist film followed a similar historical path emerging from the women's movement in the late 1960s. During the 1970s, feminist film studies concentrated upon the development of the history of women's contributions to filmmaking, an exploration of the changing images of women in film, the development of theories related to female representation and reception, and the encouragement of positive attitudes toward womanhood and optimistic views toward social change. During the 1980s, one focus was on *the* feminist filmmaker who vacillated between documentary films, made from a woman's perspective on women's issues (e.g., rape, abortion, divorce, discrimination, abuse), and countercinema to "grand-scale" fictional films. Like their sister scholars in art and literary studies, feminist film scholars sought to deemphasize gender distinctions between men and women while recognizing the oppression of centuries of patriarchy and the need for inclusivity in film studies and filmmaking. In the 1990s, the focus has shifted toward an emphasis not only on the gender distinctions between male and female, but also on the multiple differences among women – including race, class, and sexual preference. Feminist documentaries continue to be produced with either an issues orientation (e.g., health care, rape, abortion) or a focus on individual women of achievement, outstanding historical role models, and women's roles in historical events.

Laura Mulvey's groundbreaking essay, "Visual Pleasure and Narrative Cinema," first published in 1975, has become the most influential and most recognized text in feminist film studies.[10] In her analysis, Mulvey proceeds to describe how men consciously and/or unconsciously create images of women that satisfy fundamental and oppressive male needs and unconscious desires. Women, thereby, are purely objects created by males, for male pleasure, and subjugated *by* as well as subjected *to* the male gaze. The female is as totally passive as the male is active. What might be termed feminism's standard definition of the normative hierarchy of male domination and of female debasement is supported by Mulvey's analysis. However, she also raises but does not answer the interesting question of the female spectator. Do women (irrespective of individual sexual preferences) take pleasure in looking at images of naked women – weak but alluring, oppressed but seductive, objects waiting to be controlled and taken by a man – or are they repelled by such images? Are women spectators interested in looking at comparable images of men? Is it possible for the female spectator to become active in the male sense of the term and allow a male object of desire to become passive in the female sense of the term? For Mulvey, a crucial but unpursued issue is that of female subjectivity in relation to female pleasure. If she is correct, and I would suggest that she is, that meaning is not found solely within a film but also within the relational exchange between the viewer and the film, then by what criteria or methodology do we evaluate that exchange? I would offer the methodological possibility of integrating iconological analyses of images of women and men with textual analysis and the multiple re-"seeings" of a single film as the beginning of this new process of feminist (religious) film studies, which might then allow us to place the (religious) film within its contemporary context as a transmitter of meaning and values.

The evolution of feminist theology has taken a similar path to that of feminist art history, literary criticism, and film studies, with two major – and perhaps telling – exceptions. First, feminist theology, both in practice and in theory, is predominately an American phenomenon. Second, in the 1990s, the dominant tone of feminist theology remains one of outcries against patriarchal oppression and seeks an exclusivist, in some cases separatist, female theological worldview, if not world. At its best moments, feminist theology has awakened historians and practicing theologians alike to a recognition of the need for a reclamation of Christianity as a spiritual resource for women through a recovery of the feminine references, imagery, symbolism, and personalities that have either been suppressed or denied by ecclesiastical authorities or texts over the last 1,500 years. Feminist theologians operate appropriately with a constant "hermeneutics of suspicion" as their *modus vivendi*. They have sought for the goddess, have denied the traditional imagery and models of the Virgin Mary, and have come to rediscover the "lost mothers" of Christianity, including scriptural figures, legendary saints, and historical women, especially those from the early Christian and medieval worlds. They seek not so much to reform the ecclesial institutions or hierarchy as to advocate a radical reinterpretation of Christian history and belief to form a new and, in their eyes, more historically accurate and spiritually appropriate Christianity and thereby ecclesiastical institutions. In recent years, there has been a "submovement" within feminist theology arguing that most feminist theologians are among "the privileged" – white, heterosexual, and Protestant – and that the reality of feminism should be re-termed "womanist" to incorporate the fullness of woman's experience, including *all* gender identities, sexual preferences, races, and social classes.

Beyond the outcries of anger brought about by years, if not generations or centuries, of injustice and frustration, feminist theology has much to offer for both the singular endeavor of this essay and the larger reality of our contemporary world. Feminist theologians have reminded us of the lost heritage of early Christian and medieval women who actively participated in the development of and/or establishment of Christianity, of the multiple scriptural references to female imagery and otherwise forgotten female personalities, of the powerful role that language has in spiritual (and personal) formation, of the historical reality of Jesus's attitude toward women as revealed in a rereading of Scripture through a feminist lens, and of a reasonable questioning whether the failures of Christianity are due to the patriarchal biases and domination of "the establishment," which may have erred too far in its "maleness." As the noted psychologist Carol Gilligan has indicated, "Given the differences in women's conceptions of self and morality, women bring to the life cycle a different point of view and order human experience in terms of different priorities."[11]

To interject a personal note here, I consider myself a feminist who would probably be defined as centrist by more politically affirmative feminist scholars. For me, feminism involves a moral commitment to gender equality and individual autonomy, as well as a scholarly commitment to the "hermeneutics of suspicion," especially in terms of the power of images. No image has been "seen" enough, studied enough, or analyzed enough; there is always room for one more interpretation, another way of "seeing" that may assist us in coming to "see" the reality of what that image intends. A variety of seeings (or, more fashionably put, re-"seeings") is in order, as is an acute sensitivity to the power of language and to its projection of meaning. It seems to me that an integrated analysis of both image and text will reveal more to us than separate analyses of image and of text. I also advocate a commitment to the reality that our humanness is divided into the two sexual identities of men and women, and that if what we are interested in is the fullness of meaning, then we need to look jointly at the images of man and of woman not as separated entities but as parts of one unified entity identified as humanity. Gender identities leading to sexual preferences do in fact come in more than two simple varieties of male and female.

I wish to look briefly at *The Age of Innocence* and *The Piano* (both 1993) as cinematic depictions of the image of woman with an eye to the development of feminist (religious) film criticism, against the definition of a scholarly commitment to the hermeneutics of suspicion, the power of images, the interrelationship between image and text, the missing history that is women's history, the interdependence of men and women in both reality and images, and an evolving interest in the female spectator. The central question, for me, is not whether *The Age of Innocence* and *The Piano* are about distinct and different forms of social behavior – Victorian New York or barbarian New Zealand – but rather how they are about two unique but interconnected ways of knowing and being in the world – male and female. These two films offer such a comparison; while each is based on a story written by a woman about women's issues, *The Age of Innocence* had a male director and *The Piano* a female director.

Ironically, both films are set in the nineteenth century, raising the immediate, if not obvious, objection to identifying either the characters, themes, images, or topics as within the purview of "the new religious film." Irrespective of the art medium in question, my response would be the same the nineteenth century is open to our critique and analysis because it is distant enough from our current situations to be termed "history," yet in reality close enough to the present to permit the type(s) of questioning of social, cultural, and political values that prove impossible in our own identifiable contemporary situations, which may in fact be "too" close for comfortable scrutiny. Further, nineteenth-century culture is the creator of our dominant models of gender roles, especially of that tradition identified as the Victorian oppression of female sexuality and the social entrapment of women, both of which were deemed to be dependent upon Jewish-Christian values. Additionally, I find several classic nineteenth-century and Victorian metaphors pertaining to women – the "female maladies" as a sign both of female frailty and its ensuing madness, the female identification with "inner space," and the "fallen woman" (or prostitute) with the heart of gold – that prove critical to the images projected by the central female characters in both *The Age of Innocence* and *The Piano*. Finally, in what may be termed a traditional nineteenth-century literary convention, if not obsession, both of these films fascinate us with, and have a fascination for, detail.

Nonetheless, the first and most immediate point of comparison is the more classical theme of the eternal love triangle upon which both films' narratives are based. Martin Scorsese's *The Age of Innocence* offers the more conventional triangle of a young man torn between the obedient virginal maiden and the more worldly siren, while Jane Campion's *The Piano* focuses on the triangulation of a plain and matronly woman caught between two men, both unknown to her, who represent the rigidity of the world she wishes to deny and the freedom of the new world she wants to enter.[12] The manner in which both films project gender identities through images distinguishes, for us as viewers, their power and quality as (religious) films. Costumes, postures, gestures, and settings are elements intrinsic to the development of images in all forms of visual media from painting to photography and film. The costumes in these two films both heighten our immediate awareness of the relationships between each member of the love triangle and also help us to place the "personality" within an identifiable gender category (not simply into men who wear pants and women who wear skirts).

In *The Age of Innocence*, the virginal maiden, May Whelan, dresses appropriately in white or pale colored garments with simple lines, high necks and long sleeves as well as large bonnets and gloves – all of which deemphasize her bodiliness while signifying her innocence, like the spring month for which she is named. The more worldly (read "morally questionable") Countess Olenska is garbed in deeper, richer colors with ornate details, close-fitting bodices, shorter sleeves, and low-cut necklines, and more often than not is "seen" removing or carrying her gloves and bonnet, thereby calling attention to both her bodiliness and her own recognition of her sexual nature. The object of their mutual affection, the proper young lawyer Newland Archer, is dressed with appropriate and social perfection, simultaneously indicating his social status and his personal esteem – he is the "perfect" man, the "image" of masculinity. In the world of manners upon which *The Age of Innocence* is founded, such attributes as appropriate costume are most serious matters. To tamper with or question the social or cultural rituals of an established society is as serious as if those rituals were ecclesiastical sacraments.

In particular, the carefully structured world of *The Age of Innocence* – evidenced by Scorsese's obsessive interest in the dinner settings, wall decors, and food – was dependent upon the continuation and careful execution of these rituals for its survival. Once a ritual, however mundane to the outside viewer, is disrupted or questioned, the whole fabric of the society is stained and thereby subject to ruin. The moral structure of this social hierarchy, a world in which all individuals knew their individual identities, social roles, and gender categories by the stability of the whole, was defined as patriarchal because of its clear lines of social divisions, moral categories of action, and seemingly public display of male (read "patriarchal") power. Anyone (read "any woman") who questioned or, by questioning, critiqued this established hierarchy of values was ostracized and identified as a person of dubious (or no) moral virtue. Without any dialogue at all, these notions are conveyed to viewers through more than the costumes worn by the lead characters. Consider the settings in which the virtuous and socially appropriate May is placed (with the exception of those scenes in which she is alone with Newland, thus signifying their unseen sexual intimacy): she is always within the context of a lush decor that is populated with well-dressed people, whereas the precocious and socially unacceptable Ellen is found regularly within a confining and otherwise vacant space, signifying her solitude and her separation from society. Here I recognize the nineteenth-century, if not Victorian, perception of "inner space," i.e., domestic interiors, as female, and "outer space," i.e., the world as male. In this analogy, the more confining the interior space, the greater the emphasis on that most internal of female spaces, thus signifying female sexuality.

As the "fallen woman" in this small, inbred, and privileged world of manners, Countess Olenska threatened both the structure of the whole as well as the individual destiny of the morally heroic Newland Archer. One of the most successful scenes in terms of visual communication in *The Age of Innocence* is the one in which Newland and Ellen are clasped in a variety of embraces in her sitting room, highlighted by the warm, i.e., emotionally and physically passionate, colors of the interior decor and the languid exoticism of the painting over the mantle. As the camera shifts perspectives, giving the viewer a simultaneous sense of intimacy, identification, and psychological distance, the coupling postures of this man and woman refer to well-known visual analogies in the history of Western art, from the classical sculptures of Greece through the erotic drawings of Picasso. Their physical and emotional intimacy occurs without dialogue, only with music. The silence is golden as the power of images dominates this scene. Recognizing that she must conform to this illusionary world of manners in order to survive, the Countess Olenska sacrifices both her passion and her alleged love for Archer. By this action, the countess conforms to the nineteenth-century convention of the "fallen woman" with the heart of gold who sacrifices her personal happiness by sending the young hero away.[13] As *The Age of Innocence* comes to its climactic dinner sequence,

The Age of Innocence, Martin Scorsese, 1993

it becomes apparent that this hierarchical, patriarchal world of manners is in fact an illusion that is created, controlled, and supported by women.[14] The innocence that is challenged and lost in this "moment of recognition" is not that of the virginal maiden or the cosmopolitan "fallen woman," but rather that of the moralistic and male hero. This transformation is signified not by words, but through the postures, gestures, and facial expressions of the characters: the dialogue has no relation to the reality of the action and the scene could have been just as, if not more, effective had it occurred in total silence.

The Piano is a film about the power of silence and, simultaneously, the power of images. As it unfolds, the apparent conflict between the brooding Ada and the rigid Stewart becomes a visual metaphor for the entrapment of female sensibilities and sexuality in a displaced Victorian world of manners. The dark simplicity of Ada's garments combines with the shadowy gradations of light, the drama of the ocean, and the meteorological dankness of New Zealand to signify the ambiguity of the disempowerment of her own personhood as well as her sexuality, while "playing" on the traditional symbols of female fecundity. In a symbolic conformity to Victorian models, Ada's self-enforced silence and her physical diminutiveness are characterized as female maladies giving voice to Stewart's fears both of woman and of this woman's "madness." Modern feminist scholarship has called our attention to the metaphor of female silence for sexual repression, but I suspect that Ada's silence signifies more than just sexual repression, but rather her own inability to act, to decide, and to want to act or decide.[15] She avoids all acting and all deciding in life by her silence and thereby places extra emphasis on the importance of facial and hand gestures as her mode of communication with others.

The piano – her "best" friend and symbolic voice – is a traditional symbol in western art for female sexuality.[16] This traditional symbolism is expanded to include Ada's total repression of self and sexuality from the initial visions of her struggling to touch the piano keys on the boxed about-to-be-shipped-to-New-Zealand piano, to the images of the piano abandoned on the beach, being washed by the waves. Ada's self-imposed silence and her employment of the piano become more than the problematic of this film; they become the controlling factors in the film's vision. The physicality of Ada's breaking through the boxed piano to play it on the beach culminates in the sacrificial transformation of one of the piano's keys into Ada's severed finger.

Thus, with a recognition of the piano as a symbol for female sexuality and of the natural world as signifier for the primal (read "liberated and classical") nature of being female, the ocean represents the female womb as the source of life and female sexuality. At the beginning of the film, the tempestuous ocean is a metaphor for Ada's internal conflicts, while the calm ocean at the end of the film reflects her decision to establish a new life with Baines. Furthermore, the drowning sequence, perhaps the most visually powerful scene in *The Piano*, signifies the "womb experience" of Ada's rebirth to a life without the dependence upon her external instrument as her mode of communication, but to one with an empowered sense of self and sexuality. This new life is symbolized by the world of light and voice found in the last sequence of the film. Ada's entry into new life is orchestrated by the mysterious Baines, who signifies the dimension "between" the traditional rigid world of patriarchal hierarchy from which Ada seeks to escape and the primitive (read "primal") world of the Maori, characterized by its sexual freedom and its respect for nature. This new worldview represented by Baines not only combines the "best" of the traditional with the primal, but also emphasizes the centrality of intuition – a category or mode of being normally considered female.

In these two films, then, I find a variety of images that build upon traditional nineteenth-century characteristics of gender identity, which, when recognized, permit the viewer to accept these cinematic worlds as authentic. In *The Age of Innocence*, Scorsese highlights traditional categories of female gender identity, i.e., costume, interior space, food, and arbitration of society, in a comfortably familiar manner. In *The Piano*, however, Campion subverts traditional categories of female gender identity, i.e., interior vs. exterior space, silence, female malady as precursor of madness, nature and darkness as female fecundity, water, and intuition.

Both filmmakers, Scorsese and Campion, by raising visual questions, bring us to different understandings of the meanings of being female and being free. For Scorsese, the traditional dichotomy of Eve and the Virgin symbolized by May and the Countess continues to be operative in separate individuals. For Campion, on the other hand, that classical pattern of interpreting woman through the image of virgin or whore is no longer appropriate inasmuch as Ada reflects the fundamental ambiguity and fullness of the female experience within one identifiable person. Thus, Campion brings to life in her film the multiple feminist theories of the nature of being female. She has created a feminist (religious) film, but not because she is a woman director who had a woman screenwriter. Rather, this Australian director brings to visual reality through Ada a single and complete figure who encompasses the totality of female character – she is both Eve and the Virgin and, more than that, she is fully human.

Endnotes

1. I am pleased to acknowledge my former student, Lucinda Ebersole, both for her helpful critique of my manuscript and for the impassioned reminder in her remarks at Cavalletti VII that we are dealing with the visual image, not "written" texts, when we study and analyze film.

2. In my own study of gender images in Western art and of the power of images, I have been influenced by John Berger's *Ways of Seeing* (New York:

Penguin Books, 1977) and by David Freedberg's *The Power of Images* (Chicago: University of Chicago Press, 1989).

3. As quoted in Freedberg, *Power of Images*, 2.

4. Ibid., 1.

5. See my "The Art of 'Seeing': Classical Paintings and *Ben-Hur*," in *Image and Likeness: Religious Visions in American Film Classics*, ed. John R. May (New York/Mahwah: Paulist, 1992), 104-116.

6. Berger, *Ways of Seeing*, 9-10.

7. Lois W. Banner, *In Full Flower: Aging Women, Power, and Sexuality* (New York: Vintage, 1993), 14.

8. Ibid., 28.

9. I am here affirming my commitment to the concept of the visual as a primary modality of being human and of evidence for cultural analysis, by replacing the terms *reading, re-reading*, and *text* with *seeing, re-seeing*, and *vision*.

10. Laura Mulvey, "Visual Pleasure and Narrative Cinema," in *Visual and Other Pleasures*, Laura Mulvey, ed. (Bloomington: Indiana University Press, 1989), 14-26.

11. Carol Gilligan, *In a Different Voice: Psychological Theory and Women's Development* (Cambridge: Cambridge University Press, 1982), 22.

12. *The Age of Innocence* is based upon Edith Wharton's well-known novel. The success or failure of the screen adaptation of the original story, although an important issue in the context of contemporary film study, is not at issue here.

13. Other typical "fallen women" (prostitutes) with hearts of gold in 19th-century literature and music include Thais, Camille, and Violetta as well as interpretations of Mary Magdalene. For a survey of this iconography, see Linda Nochlin, "Lost and Found: Once More the Fallen Woman," in her *Women, Art, and Power and Other Essays* (New York: Harper and Row, 1988), 57-85.

14. The emphasis, perhaps better said overemphasis, on food in *The Age of Innocence* could be interpreted as female activity. Feminist scholars such as Caroline Walker Bynum have studied the direct correlation between the gender identity of being female with food; for example, see her *Holy Feast and Holy Fast: The Religious Significance of Food to Medieval Women* (Berkeley: University of California Press, 1987).

15. For example, see Margaret Miles's interpretation of Susannah's silenced voice in her *Carnal Knowing* (Boston: Beacon, 1989), 121-24.

16. For example, see the late medieval northern paintings depicting women "of a certain type" seated at the virginal, the ancestor of the piano. For the iconography of the virginal in Western art, see Emmanuel Winternitz, *Musical Instruments and Their Symbolism in Western Art: Studies in Musical Iconology* (New Haven: Yale University Press, 1976).

Part 4

Theological Reflection
on Religious Film

8

Toward a Theological Interpretation and Reading of Film: Incarnation of the Word of God – Relation, Image, Word

Joseph Marty

(Translated by Robert G. Robinson III)

To speak theologically of the religious film today, it seems to me indispensable first of all to question both the world of film and the world of the religious by means of anthropology. My reflections, therefore, will focus at the crossroads of these two complex theological areas. Their encounter and their crossing call forth a problematic that is in certain aspects recent; it is that problematic which motivates this volume and is also one of the axes of my application of theory with its limits and weaknesses.

The well-weighed choice of "image" (*l'image*) and the "imaginary" (*l'imaginaire*) in their articulation with "the word" (*la parole*), despite the difficulties in delimiting such concepts,[1] seems to me to respond more than any other to the present questions, especially to those raised by the proliferation of the audio-visual in society and the church, as well as to the proposal of a religiosity not regulated by the Christian churches. At the outset I want to recall that only "Jesus is the visible image of the invisible God" (Col. 1:15) and that it is by the mystery of his incarnation – the union of divinity with humanity in the space and time of his personal body and his historical and ecclesiastical body – that I can envision the reality of cinema and the religious world. Always in search of the "seeds of the Word," to use the beautiful expression of St. Justin and St. Irenaeus, I shall deal with those points necessary to isolate some propositions for a theological reading of religious film. The cinema is one of the privileged places that reveal the functioning of human psychology *à propos* of the "imaginary," which itself merits greater precision because of its intimate connection with the religious.[2]

I. The cinema provides images and representations which are indispensable, but which are not reality.

There is no human life or faith without images because they are a fundamental reality of all language and culture. The image is not reserved to infancy, amusement, or pedagogy. We talk and write with images that are
words and letters, and we have images of the body, the world and God that
go back to our infancy. There is no thought, no poetry, no religion without
images. Jesus tells us who he is with unexpected images: the vine, the door,
the shepherd, the bread, and so forth. And when the believer is deprived of
them, that absolutely naked faith is still carried by the image of the night,
the dark night of the mystics.

The image is a "representation" that otherwise "presents." It makes
present that which is absent or invisible, but is not the reality "represented." More exactly, it is a little of what it represents while not really
being it. If the risk is great of assimilating them, it is also a bit of luck to
have "representatives" like the image, the media and the cinema. They
form bridges, create relationships, "bind" and, thus in a certain etymologi-
cal sense, assure a "religious" function. The image, the indispensable reflection of something else, always leads back to that referent, even if it is
hidden – because the human being, child or adult, wants everything immediately. Im-mediately, that is to say, without mediation, without delay or
relay. From birth on, a separation puts everything at a distance and the
more the infant grows, the more the separation deepens. Then immediacy
becomes tenuous, making indispensable the mediations of which the most
extraordinary – from the point of view of constituting the human being –
is language. It is by means of language that there is a humanity, and language comes also from nonimmediacy, from the absence that creates desire. The word brings things alive, permitting the separated beings to bind
together and face the lack. But the word binds at a distance; it creates
closeness without fusion.

Thence comes the temptation to live in the immediacy of needs as it
was lived before birth, to suppress the word by mediations – images – to
which one accords the status of reality by taking them for what they are
not. The thumb of the infant, the photo, religious images and films, so
many mediations threaten to replace illusorily the presence of the other!
To take the shadow or the reflection for the reality is a risk inherent in the
human condition because we can only live with mediations, while we forever dream of getting along without them. With the myths of the cave
(Plato, *The Republic,* Book VII) and of Narcissus and Echo, the Greeks
had already put themselves on guard against the dangers of confusing the
image and the original, the double and the reality. The play that takes
place in the cave could correspond to the screening of a film or a television show! An echo is only the babbling of the person talking and not
someone else who answers, just as the image is only a double and not the

presence. The Greeks understood that the image is not the reality of presence, and that love is the meeting of another, really alive and different. These myths can nourish reflection about our relationship to the cinema.

With movement and sound, cinema produces an illusion of reality that curiously resembles the original. It is a treasure because the opportunities for knowledge are developed, but the risk of confusion is heightened. Portraits or statues, even ones that are good resemblances, are different enough from their referents to be perceived as a representation. A photograph is much more identical and can actually reveal our identity, as in the photo of the same name, the ID. With the movement and the sound tracks of film, the illusion is immense. The person filmed moves and talks, but is nevertheless only a shadow and some noise! In 1895 with cinematography, humanity could, for the first time since its origins, see itself doubled, reproduced with exactitude. The objective lens gives a pseudo-objectivity that one easily takes for reality. It is a discovery that humanity ought to accept because it engenders a new relationship to the body, to the perception of the self, of others, of God. To see ourselves filmed, or to hear ourselves on a tape recorder, surprises us: it's us and it's not us! It will take some time to master this mediation that has numerous consequences – some not as yet realized.

The first people to see Lumière's film *Arrival of Train at Station* (1895) recoiled with fright that the train was hurtling over them. Still today, even if we know that it is just cinema, we cry or we rejoice. In the "projection" of a film, there is a projection and an identification that is immediate. That's the risk of a mediation that does its job so well that it can make us forget the representation. With massive development of the means of communication, our society lives more and more with representations. The image becomes more important than reality to the point that the artificial and the apparent are preferred to the thing itself, in order to give a good image of oneself and of one's group. This debate, which the church cannot escape, is rooted in the indispensable function of the "imaginary," which renders present what is not there. But this fictitious presence ought to open us to others, to the totally Other, and ought not to develop into a world in itself. The surrealistic painter Magritte saw this clearly. When painting an apple, he wrote beneath his canvas, "This is not an apple." Another painting of a pipe with the inscription "This is not a pipe" bore the judicious title "The Treason of Images." It is and it is not an apple, a pipe.

In this relationship something fundamental is at play that concerns faith and the relationship to God. The translation of images often betrays them to the point of making us contradict ourselves. Through the cinema we do not have access to symbols (like water, fire, earth, or air), but to representations of symbols. On the other hand, if the structure and the language (*l'écriture*) of film are symbolic, the spectator can open himself to the symbolic. Our time, more than any other, pushes us toward fusion, toward confusion – to the suppression of mediation in the name of the religious. It slips toward a fundamentalism in which the mediation of the letter is taken for the spirit of the text. Something of extreme theological importance is at stake here.

II. Through its technique the cinema
awakens the symbolic dimension of *homo religiosus*.

Cinema is at the crossroads of photography, theater, opera, and painting; it inscribes itself in the vast universe of art, even if it is also concerned with industry and commerce. The seventh art, it attracts to itself phenomena having to do with anthropology, the history of religions, of civilizations and of art, notably in the aspect of representation, doubles, *mise en scène,* liturgy, celebration, magic, mystery and the sacred. An anthropology of cinema and of the image must be developed to work out more carefully their bonds with the religious. Certain French works let us foresee a wider and more interdisciplinary approach, like those of Jean Mitry, Edgard Morin, Élie Faure, André Bazin, Barthélemy Amengual, Jean Epstein, Henri Agel, and Régis Debray. The arts have their origin in relation to the sacred, and if they have won an autonomy over against religious institutions, they are still bearers of a transcendence. The same thing is true of cinema, even if it was born at the same time as electricity.

In its language, cinema plays on and favors dreams, the imaginary, the poetic. In its beginnings it is a spectacle at a fun fair, and, although it can be tragic or moving, it is also tied up with laughter and dreams. Georges Méliès (1861-1938) is a magician who makes of cinema an instrument of illusion and enchantment. Auguste (1862-1954) and Louis (1864-1948) Lumière orient themselves more toward reporting, but a reporting inhabited by poetry because even if cinema reproduces exactly what it records, it immediately transforms it. To capture movement and to play with it creates something *un*-usual. To speed up or slow down, to back up, to suppress an image and let it fade into another, to dare double exposures and freezes, to make images appear and disappear – these are so many possibilities that have no place in reality, except when the weakened consciousness gives way to the dream, asleep or awake (often thought to be a messenger of the gods and, since Freud, of the unconscious).

To capture movement, rather than to record a gesture or a displacement, is to let us see the everlasting dance of our eyes and thoughts, a dance that in our normal states we do not perceive. It is to reconstruct a dream after finding its structure (*l'écriture*) apparently disordered, to bypass the conditioned, to take oneself for a god. The cinema can do it by making present the inner movement of the mind, of the thought of the heart. It uses this power even for rigorous documentaries like those of Resnais or de Rouche. Through editing, the images or sequences put into relationship acquire a new meaning. A piece of music transforms a place or a scene. The camera can even enter into the interior of heroes and render visible their secrets or wishes that will never see daylight. It is one of the difficulties of *The Last Temptation of Christ* (1988) by Martin Scorsese that it shows what Jesus did not succumb to. In *Perceval* (1978) by Eric Rohmer, Percival relives inwardly the passion of Jesus and we see him die on the cross on screen.

Even with a realistic subject, the cinema is not always totally realistic. Its language, its syntax, its grammar are from the beginning dreamlike and poetic. It carries with it, by its nature, a mysterious and surreal dimension. Film is to be not only understood, but also felt; before reaching our reason, it touches our senses. St. Thomas Aquinas, taking up a point of Aristotle's, reaffirms: "There is nothing in the mind that has not first been in the senses." This dream dimension, the shattering of a narrow realism and an emergence of the unconscious, belongs to the "imaginary." The imaginary brings together the not clearly defined territories of the religious and the sacred. It nourishes itself from the immemorial depths of symbols, from mythical tales, from ritualized celebrations, from the grand poetics that every culture elaborates to give meaning to the everyday and to overcome the absurd, evil and death. Many films that seem to be anecdotal find once more the power of the great tragedies, the ancient myths, the lyrical epics, the founding deeds in which the religious and the sacred dwell.

The conditions of "projection" amplify this even more. The spectator, comfortably seated in the dark, has his outer perceptions minimized while the screen comes to life and the sound wraps around him. His liberty and his consciousness are lulled because he is fascinated by the shadows, the lights, the rhythm, the actions or the passions presented. Other reactions set in. Emotion and sensibility are sharpened and he is as though hypnotized, in a sort of second state between waking and dreaming. He attributes his own feelings to the characters, identifies himself with their actions and empathizes with them all the more so because he is passive. Cinematographic "projection," as its name rightly indicates, always involves a submission to the images and an unconscious participation. It is, of course, always possible to escape it, but most of the time the viewing has impregnated and changed us.

Thus, in arousing sensibility, the symbolic and the sacred, cinema awakens *homo religiosus*. It enlivens human dimensions that are somewhat underdeveloped in our scientific, technological and, to the bitter end, rationalized cultures: the symbolic and the poetic, sensibility and emotion. It strengthens weakened possibilities that have to do in part with the religious. It brings back to life the sense of mystery by making us love what is not immediately perceivable, what is beyond appearance and evidence. It suggests the invisible. It broadens our outlook, our affectivity, our approach to the sacred. It provokes an awakening that puts us in a state of admiration and contemplation before scenes we marvel at. It makes the absent present, brings back to life what is dead and gone, reawakens the past and the memory, urges anamnesis (flashback) and rereading. All film is memory. It unfolds like memory, by leaps, fragments, lacks, holes; ellipses, associations, confusions, backtracking. But it also invites us to make an accounting and to celebrate the great figures and times that have disappeared in order to draw on their resources and quicken the present. It is therefore very close to the great liturgical and ritual initiatives that give direction to history by dynamizing and celebrating the human adventure and its stages, for it often proposes the evolution of character and transformation by trial, which are true passages of initiation or conversions. *La Strada* (1954) by Federico Fellini, *Madame De* (1953) and *Lola Montès* (1955) by Max Ophuls, *Wild Strawberries* (1957) and *The Seventh Seal* (1956) by Ingmar Bergman, *The Man Who Had His Hair Cut Short* (1965) by André Delvaux, *The Marquise of O* (1976), *Perceval* (1978) and *Le Rayon vert* (1986) by Eric Rohmer, *Jesus of Montreal* (1989) by Denys Arcand, *Night Sun* (1990) by Paolo and Vittorio Taviani, like so many others, give the spectator once more a sense of an opening to the meaning of life and to spiritual quest.

Thus, cinema binds us again with the poetic and religious expression of humanity, even through subjects that are profane, scientific or areligious; all the more so if it approaches the great experiences such as birth, love, work, hope, fidelity, joy, death, or their inseparable opposites treachery, lies, jealousy, hate. Everything that is human, every relationship to the world and to nature, treated artistically by the cinema becomes a poem, a tale, a re-reading, a proposal of meaning, a celebration – in short, something that resembles a first religious step. And this step may be blasphemous, contentious, provocative, pantheist, deist, mythic or revolutionary. Thus it is with *Intolerance* (1916, Griffith), *Seventh Heaven* (1927, Borgaze), *Peter Ibbetson* (1935, Hathaway), *How Green Was My Valley* (1941, Ford), *Day of Wrath* (1943) or *Ordet* (1954, Dreyer), *The River* (1950, Renoir), *Ikiru* (1952, Kurosawa), *Ugetsu* (1952, Mizoguchi), *Viaggio in Italia* (1953, Rossellini), *Pather Panchali* (1955, Ray), *Viridiana* (1961, Buñuel), *The Miracle Worker* (1962, Penn), *Oedipus Rex* (1967), *Teorema* (1968) and *Medea* (1970, Pasolini), *2001: A Space Odyssey* (1968, Kubrick), *The Virgin Spring* (1959), *Winter Light* (1962) or *Cries and Whispers* (1972, Bergman), *Johnny Got His Gun* (1971, Trumbo), *Andrei Rublev* (1966-1967), *Stalker* (1979) and *The Sacrifice* (1986, Tarkovsky), *Kaos* (1984, Tavianis), and *Babette's Feast* (1987, Axel).

As do all the arts, cinema can make a type of transcendence sensible. It is a call toward something more. But above all, more than the other arts, it summons and supports elements that belong to the religious dimension inherent in every human being. The *homo religiosus* defined and validated by Mircea Eliade is summoned by the cinema, almost independently of the content and themes dealt with. In very different aesthetic registers and ideologies, it is the blast of air that elevates the films of Bergman, Buñuel, Dovjenko, Eisenstein, Ford, Griffith, Lang, Mizoguchi, Murnau, Olmi, Pasolini, Rossellini, Sjöstrom, Tarkovsky, and the like. Cinema develops and enriches the human, awakening the living but forgotten forces of *homo religiosus*, and thus approaches a spiritual dimension.

III. The cinema, a reflection of society, is presently a mirror of the religious dimension that surrounds us.

All cultures are articulated according to a religious proposal that authenticates their validity and practice. It is quite recent that science, technology, and philosophy have dissociated themselves from religious thought. Without analyzing the complexity of this situation, I want to underline the secular practice that associates the artistic and poetic treatment of anthropological experience with the religious dimension.

From its birth the cinema has been interested in the religious, even though in France the law of separation of church and state was voted in in 1905. *The Life and Passion of Our Lord* appears repeatedly among the first films: one by Lear in 1897 in France, another by a collaborator of Lumière's; in 1898, the American Hollaman produced his, followed by Lubin's in Philadelphia, and in 1900 Topi's; in 1902 Zecca filmed Pathé's *The Life and Passion of Jesus Christ*. Biblical episodes were common – Samson and Delilah (Zecca, 1902), Joseph sold by his brothers (Nonguet, 1904), Moses and the flight from Egypt (1907), as well as stories of early Christian times – *The Sign of the Cross* (1897, Hagar) and *Quo vadis?* (1901, Zecca) – or lives of saints like Joan of Arc (1898, Hatot; 1900, Méliès; 1908, Capellani; 1909, Caserini; 1913, Oxilia; 1917, De Mille). These often repetitive films do not always correctly express the Christian mystery and tease us with tricks to emphasize the extraordinary. In 1899, Méliès films a *Christ Walking on Water*. Such confusion of the miraculous and the marvelous is still with us, and it is a point of theological discernment that cannot be neglected.

Today the cinema is again finding the religious sense that it had somewhat forgotten. Since the 1950s, critics with a Christian orientation (Amédée Ayfre, Henri Agel, Andre Basin, Eric Rohmer, Michel Esteve, Jean Collet, Claude Beylie) point to the particular bonds that cinema can have with the sacred and faith. But, on the whole, film criticism has utilized tools of analysis accenting other aspects of cinema, and the surrounding culture was carried along by currents of thought other than those concerning *homo religiosus*. It is principally with the cultural and economic crises that shook the west during the 1960s and in 1973 that other aspirations appeared. The cinema is a reflection of these, although it is only by drawing back that one perceives it better. The attraction of the east and of the far east (not new to the cinema) and the fascination with drugs (*More*, 1969, Schroeder, or *Les chemins de Katmandou*, 1969, Cayatte) broadened the horizon as well as the presentation of the figure of *Gandhi* (1982, Attenborough), the sacred atmosphere and misery of *Calcutta* (1968, Malle) and the benefits of Indian massage to children (*Shantala*, Leboyer). *Close Encounters of the Third Kind* (1977) and *E.T.* (1982, Spielberg) make the spiritual sense slip toward the bizarre, the unusual and the extraterrestrial.

It was in 1973 that *The Exorcist* by William Friedkin (from the novel by William Peter Blatty) brought diabolical possession back into style before *The Omen* (1976, Donner), *Exorcist II: The Heretic* (1977, Boorman), and their other sequels. These films signal the recurrence of the troubles of the religious sense in a world affluent and civilized, but in crisis. The following films had already appeared in troubled times: *Day of Wrath* (1943, Dreyer) in occupied Denmark, *The Seventh Seal* (1957, Bergman) in the postwar world shaken by Hiroshima, *The Devil and the Nun* (1960, Kawalerowicz) in the Poland of the 1960s, and *The Devils* (1970, Russell), which denounces trumped-up trials.

In *The Exorcist*, which came out in the middle of the oil crisis, a Jesuit archaeologist in the oil countries of the near east returns to the United States, where he is confronted with the problems of possession. The energy crisis is thus bound up with the arrival of diabolical troubles. The Jesuit, in search of the past and the meaning of society, resembles Father Teilhard de Chardin (so appreciated by certain members of the New Age). A theological approach cannot hide these traces inscribed in the filigree of ancient history and mentalities. To probe the depths of a land rich in buried history and resources is not accidental to reflecting on the economic crisis of a society that provokes spiritual and psychosomatic crises.

The same thing is true for the "return of the religious," which the west has known through the appearance and development of sects, of the "new religious movements," and of the New Age. For a dozen years films have had a more explicit religious content, which is to be attributed to the global phenomenon of society and its quest for the religious. The nearing of the year 2000 and of the Age of Aquarius has aroused millenarian reactions.[3] The collapse of the great ideologies, of marxism and the Berlin Wall; the liberation of the countries of the east; the rise of Islam; the flowering of fundamentalist and intergrationist movements; the climate of international economic crisis are many elements among others that must be studied. The election in 1978 of Pope John Paul II from Poland, whose international contacts with other religions were broadcast by the media, must also have played an important role. His meeting at Assisi in 1986 with the representatives of many religions remains one of the great events of his pontificate and of the history of the church: one will have to know how to read its cultural and cinematographic fallout.

IV. The religious belongs to humanity and not only to Christianity.

One must remember that secularization is not the source of the loss or rejection of the religious. Quite the contrary. After secularization, the Christian churches were no longer the dominant force in society, no longer the norm in questions of faith and morals. But the religious dimension, too long assimilated to Christianity, remains fundamental for every individual and every culture. Thrown out with the water of Christian baptism, the infant *homo religiosus* comes back in full force and looks for his points of orientation outside of and far from mother church, in practices and beliefs ranging from the most serious to the most illegitimate, fantastical or dangerous. Our society once again rediscovers, painfully, that the religious and the sacred are fundamental for human beings for human and culture, and this results in difficulties, improprieties and failures reflected in the cinema. How can a society legitimate the religious function outside of the churches, which up until now have been its regulators and depositories? The answer is by no means clear, yet humanity needs the religious and the sacred to inscribe life and all its deeds, great or commonplace, within a breadth that bears meaning and praise. Cinema, like music or theater, can be one of its vectors. Immediately, our attention is drawn to several factors.

Under the regime of secularization, laicization and democracy, we note that the sacred texts, biblical or others, such as the lives of the saints, form part of a common cultural patrimony. Every cinematographer can dip into them and inspire himself there without even consulting the church. Directors touched by works or lives put them directly on the screen without asking for the *Nihil obstat* or the equivalent of the *Imprimatur*, as is the case with Jean-Luc Godard's *Hail Mary* (1985), Alain Cavalier's *Thérèse*, which won the jury prize at the 1986 Cannes Festival, Roland Joffe's *The Mission*, winner of the Palm d'Or the same year, Maurice Pialat's *Under Satan's Sun* from the novel by Georges Bernanos, Palm d'Or winner at Cannes in 1987, and Denys Arcand's *Jesus of Montreal* (1989). The same was true, though with scandal added, with Martin Scorsese's *The Last Temptation of Christ* (1988) from the novel of Nikos Kazantzakis. Obviously, the church should never forget the need for dialogue, especially religious dialogue, and utilize these widely-released works for catechetical ends. Thanks to such popular works, people have access to riches that they do not immediately recognize and that the church can situate for them. There are also films, almost ignored by the church, of beauty, richness and spiritual depth that touch those who see them, like Gabriel Axel's *Babette's Feast* (1987) from the short novel by K. Blixen.

In a secularized world, one can also find types of Christian iconographics, diffused by the history of art, which serve from then on to express sacred experiences, though not necessarily Christian. Certain films take them up again to celebrate the sacred because their directors never had, or no longer have, other models, or because Christianity has imbued these icons with an evangelical connotation. It is often not self-evident that the image must necessarily be given a Christian interpretation. A woman with a child in her arms is not necessarily a nativity scene; nonetheless, the reception of the gift of life is not alien to the mystery of Christmas. Equally, a mother who holds the body of her son is not inevitably a Pietà, even if the reference to Mary can give the piece an added dramatic sense. Bergman's *Cries and Whispers* (1972) explicitly employs this image; in *How Green Was My Valley* (1941), Ford composes the movement of the crowd like processions, and the lifting of the bodies out of the mine shaft becomes a liturgical act. He impresses the seal of the sacred on them. The lyricism of the directors from eastern countries, even the Soviets, takes up again the structures of tableaux and of evangelical frescos, but do they celebrate the Christian faith? Discernment is necessary in order not to "baptize" hurriedly every allusion or every symbol, all the more so because it is today that they flourish, and publicity makes references to them for purposes other than evangelizing!

It is important humbly to rediscover the fact that the Catholic Church is not the only repository of the religious and the sacred. In order to evangelize, the church has sometimes grafted itself onto previous image systems, either suppressing them or turning them to its own uses. Without criticizing what the church has thought well to do at times other than ours,

Gandhi, Richard Attenborough, 1982

let us recognize that today the taproot is gaining strength again and reject-
ing the graft, and that the life force of religiosity belongs to humanity.

V. Christianity evangelizes the religious
and the sacred, summoning to holiness.

The sacred is a composite of human experience and of every group, culture
and religion, carrying their nuances and rules. To simplify somewhat, one
can say that it takes its orientation from a sort of shudder or thrill in the
face of a powerful situation or happening, the unleashing or calming of the
elements, the instinctive power of animality. Birth, love, deeds, death, the
body and sex. The face, tears, smiles, wrinkles. Violence, war and blood.
Revolt, justice, victory. Horror, the bizarre, the unusual, the disquieting.
The beautiful, the marvelous, the miraculous. The birth of the word, the
vow. The opening to the beyond and to mystery. One could apply titles of
films to each of these aspects.

The experience of the religious provokes simultaneously attraction
and repulsion, fascination and fear. But Christianity comes to convert it, to
"evangelize" it, to make of it one of the places of encounter with Jesus
Christ and his Father. Liberation, the opening to brotherhood, peace and
joy are signs of the Christian sacred. Trouble, fear, complacency, and aestheticism distance it. There is a sacred that elevates, humanizes, opens toward the more distant, toward what is greater and truer than we – and
another which lowers, bestializes, closes, reduces, alienates. A Nazi demonstration, a bullfight, a nighttime bombing, the opening of the Olympic
games, a festive parade, a pilgrims' Mass play within the sacred. They do
not all have the same effect. The cinema amplifies them. A form of the
sacred makes us vibrate in communion with cosmic, astral, and aquatic
forces; the success of *The Big Blue* (1987) by Luc Besson is both significant and disquieting. Animism, pantheism, deism, or a certain return to nature reappear here. But the Bible desacralizes nature, and the first
Christians, refusing to worship it, were accused of atheism. In fact, Christianity calls the religious and the sacred to a conversion.

The sacred is opposed to the profane and sets apart space and time.
This separation is sometimes useful, but with Jesus Christ, the incarnation
shocks and transfigures these frontiers. God is with us at every moment
and in every place. "Whatever you may say or do, let it always be in the
name of the Lord Jesus, giving through him thanks to God the Father"
(Col. 3:17). History and the body are the place of encounter with God. To
distrust them or flee them is no more Christian than to drown or lose oneself in them. And the relationship with one's brother is an obligatory path.
What is religious concerns all religions, but every rite is not a sacrament,
every communion is not a eucharist, every prayer and every celebration is
not Christian. A religious initiative can open toward God, but not neces-

sarily the one that Jesus Christ reveals as his Father. The sects, esoteric groups of initiates and certain masonic lodges are interested in the religious and propose a religious practice. Hinduism, animism, and voodoo are religions. Judaism and Islam are monotheistic, revealed religions.

But the revelation of the God of the Trinity – Father, Son and Holy Spirit – opens new perspectives that have nothing to do with deism. Christianity is not a gnosis, a saving knowledge reserved for an elite of initiates. God's love is offered to everyone, especially the poor in spirit, and the Gospel invites everyone, no matter who, to an initiation toward and in love. The call of God is the first gift of love. It is up to each of us to respond. Christianity is a religion of converts, the "evangelized," and thus not at all like the others. One can even wonder seriously whether the words "religious," "religion," and "sacred" suit it and can be used without risk of confusion. The theologian Joseph Moingt writes:

> The Gospel is not a code, nor a system of precepts, rites and beliefs, and in this precise sense, let us say even narrow sense, it's not a religion, it's more than that, it's something else. Even keeping in mind the sacraments – and there is certainly no question of forgetting them – it does not let itself be compared with any other organized religion or religious organization that we know nor does it let itself be enclosed in statutes.[4]

The perspectives of the Gospel propose something other than a submission to sacral and religious forces. Cinema does not always specify what religion it is concerned with; thus, inasmuch as it often evokes the religious by symbols, one must discern and await the annunciation of the Good News, though it be through metaphor.

1. God is not "constrictive" or "captivating," but liberating.

This is the heart not only of religious cinema, but also of the theological and spiritual initiative, because to confuse God and his images, or to take the images for God, is the great sin denounced by the Bible, the idolatry qualified as prostitution. The decalogue prohibits making images of God (Ex. 20:4-5; Deut. 5:8-9), and the whole Bible makes it clear that its images are also interior images that are more pernicious than the ones exteriorized by painting or sculpture. These images, taken for the reality of God, are the idols that must be destroyed, just as the golden calf. They are the projections of an imagination drowning in falsehood, the radical mendacity that makes us believe that the image-idol can talk. But it is lifeless because it can't talk. The prophets and the psalms recall: "[They are] the handiwork of man. They have mouths but speak not; they have eyes but see not; ears but hear not; noses but smell not; hands but feel not; feet but walk not! They cannot utter any sound from their throat. Their makers shall be like them, everyone who trusts in them!" (Ps. 115:4-8). To bind oneself to death, of which the image-idol is the sign, is to be a slave. The living God, whose love is liberating, frees us from this morbid and mortal slavery.

There are so many loves, gods, idols, stars, gurus or masters who are "seductive" or "captivating" that one might imagine that the Father of Jesus is too. The cinema can make Jesus, or the saints, so "attractive" that the viewers become their fascinated slaves. A religious film can be "captivating" to the point of making us "captives." The God of the Trinity is not "constricting": he undoes bonds, including the cunning and seemingly innocent ones that attract us to images. He comes to burst the chains that hold prisoners back, to shatter the mirrors that lose us in labyrinths of the image, to destroy imaginary things that do not refer us to the real, to break the mediations that do not open onto an elsewhere, to tear down the representations that make present only themselves and nothing else.

2. God liberates while speaking, and his Word initiates a Covenant.

God's Word loosens our bonds, opens us up, creates as on the first morning of the world (cf. Gen. 1). By speaking, God separates in order to give birth. He snatches us away from the confusion of chaos, from the slavery to death. By giving mankind speech, God allows it to grow in humanity, thanks to relationships that need mediation. The word is the most human of mediations. By creating a distance, it puts in perspective and reestablishes a mediation by exchange. It clears what is jammed, puts the paralyzed into motion, and resuscitates the asphyxiated. It snatches us away from the dead idol to make us live like a human beings capable of the word and of desire. To discover that the God of Jesus offers this liberation that gives us birth is the surprise of faith. It opens the heart to praise: "Before me you open a passage" (Ps. 31:9).

The biblical theologian Alain Marchadour writes:

> If one had to chose a word which differentiates the religion of Israel from other religions, I would take the word *separation*. . . . Separation does not mean infinite distance and absence. Between the fusion, that one finds so often in natural religions, and the infinite distancing, there is a middle term which is neither too far nor too near: it is the covenant, the word that separates, and creates a relation.[5]

If the Word of God separates and puts at a distance, it is in order to establish better communication and relationship (*relation*). God gives birth only in order to offer his word of love: it is the Covenant. "I will be your God and you will be my people" (Lev. 26: 12). The "deca-logue" (ten words) is a law that at the heart of differences establishes communion. No longer fusion, but exchange. There is no exchange without "inter-diction" (*inter-dit*), that cutting edge of the word dividing what is confounded, so that what is said (*le dit*) can be said between (*entre*) partners. The word can flow easily thanks only to the "diction-between" (*entre-dit*) that establishes the relation. It is "symbolic" in the strict sense (*sym-ballein*, "to put together, reunite") in that it connects and links what is at first separated or set apart.

This fundamental and indispensable dimension of Christianity can be discovered in numerous films by the presence or the absence of law, of prohibition, of exchange, of otherness. How do the themes of limit, frontier, threshold, of the door, the barrier, differences and, moreover, of listening, obedience, faith appear in films? Eric Rohmer's *Le rayon vert* (1986) is a good example of a film without religious content. How are proximity and bathing (in the sea, sun, crowd or music) dealt with? I attach importance to this, for in the enunciation [*l'écriture*] of these apparently innocuous realities, the deep structure of the film's message is delivered. When everyone bathes in sameness (*le même*), the all-devouring confusion of the diabolical (*dia-ballein*, "separate, disunite, deceive") is there, even if the intention is religious.

There is no true religion without the cutting edge of the word, of the law, of the interdiction. That is the very weakness of Arcand's *Jesus of Montreal* (1989), otherwise remarkable in so many ways, one of which was its restraint in relation to images. The character Jesus never makes reference to his Father and, when the character who is the immediate referent of that word (the priest who is the only one to be called "father") formulates the "interdiction" against performing the spectacle, Jesus and his troupe continue on. Refusing to obey this regulation (signifying the law), he provokes the catastrophe that radically modifies the theological sense of the passion. The Jesus of the film dies accidentally for his disobedience to the priest-father, while Jesus himself dies, condemned, obeying the will of his Father.

3. The word becomes flesh and sanctifies.

The incarnation is the great novelty of Christianity. "The Word became flesh and lived among us" (John 1:14). The eternal Word of God was made flesh in the body of history, and nothing is as it was before on the horizon of religions. By his resurrection, Jesus Christ assumes and transfigures the body and the world (cf. Rom. 8), and thereby fulfills the call to holiness present in the Old Testament. "To speak properly" – writes the theologian Claude Geffré in *"Le christianisme et les métamorphoses du sacré"*[6] – "one must say that the God of the Old Testament is not the sacred, but the holy one (the saint) who transcends the opposition between the sacred and the profane. The sacred proceeds always from God, but one must talk of a sanctification of man and of all creation, and not of a sacralization." And speaking of the incarnation, he says precisely:

> From then on, all the sacred mediation between man and God concentrates itself in the person of Jesus Christ, "the unique Mediator between God and mankind." Since God has been made man in Jesus Christ, all human existence is sacred and can become a site of sanctification. One can no longer, as in some other religions, distinguish in the life of mankind the zone of the religious and of the sacred, which does not always coincide with the moral, and also the zone of profane life. The privi-

leged category for the New Testament is that of holiness which transcends the opposition of the sacred and the profane, of the religious and
the non-religious, of the pure and the impure. And the will of God is
that man sanctify his whole life (*Ibid.*).

The Holy Spirit, divine breath of the Father and the Son, is the Spirit
of sanctification. With the Spirit, the differences and the communion of divine persons sing the absolute love in the Trinity of gift and of relation.
Certain aesthetics make us contemplate this mystery through their triune
rhythm. But dualistic oppositions, seductive because of their simplicity,
slip toward exclusions, Manichaeism, Jansenism or Catharism. Jesus Christ
is true God "and" true man. It is in the coordinating conjunction "and"
that the saving novelty of Christianity resides. That "and," a true gift of
the Holy Spirit, places us in the Covenant and offers the peace of the Res-
urrected. It sanctifies.

The films that make us participate in the mystery of grace also place
us in this articulation of contraries – the gift of Covenant, present in the
Spirit that resides in Mary and in the eucharistic offerings so that God, in
his son, comes to inhabit humanity and to save it. Bresson's *Angels of the
Street* (1943) and *The Diary of a Country Priest* (1951), Rossellini's *Open
City* (1945) and *Francesco – Giullare di Dio* (*Flowers of St. Francis*,
1950), Dreyer's *Ordet* (1954), Tarkovsky's *Andrei Rublev* (1967),
Rohmer's *Perceval* (1978), Cavalier's *Thérèse* (1986) and Axel's *Babette's
Feast* (1987) are marvelous examples of this. In the most humble way the
creations of Michel Farin for French TV's Catholic program *"Le Jour du
Seigneur"* – *Les deux témoins* (1984), *Le combat du roi* (1985) et *La
colombe et le serpent* (1993) – urge us to reread the Gospels with the understanding of faith and praise.

VI. The Church demands dialogue and mission.

Everything that emerges in reference to the specificity of Christianity
should be articulated in the light of the missionary needs clearly presented
in the dynamics of Vatican II. In order to experience encounter better, it is
indispensable to sharpen differences. The decrees *Unitatis Redintegratio* on
ecumenicism (1964) and *Ad Gentes* (1965) on the missionary activity of the
Church, as well as the declarations *Dignitatis Humanae* (1965) on religious
liberty and above all *Nostra Aetate* on the relations of the Church with
non-Christian religions demand attention and acceptance to prepare for the
"sowing of the word." The apostolic exhortation *Evangelii Nuntiandi* (Paul
VI, 1975), the meeting at Assisi organized by John Paul II on October 27,
1986 and his encyclical *Redemptoris Missio* (1990), as well as the document *Dialogue et Annonce* (1991), are a great opening into and engagement
with the questions raised by the cinema. I shall cite several extracts from
this last document:

Today . . . there exists a new awareness of religious pluralism. Religions do not simply content themselves with existing or even with surviving. In certain cases, they manifest a real revival. They continue to inspire and to influence the life of millions of their members. In the present context of religious pluralism, one cannot forget the important role played by religious traditions (no. 4), . . . the religions which, with Christianity, like to refer to the faith of Abraham, as well as the great religious traditions of Asia, Africa, and the rest of the world (no. 12) . . . . But this document does not deal with the dialogue with the members of the "New Religious Movements" because of the diversity of situations which they present and the need for discerning the human and religious values which they contain (no. 13).

For cinema too this specification merits attention. The text puts the accent on the "mystery of unity," binding together the whole human family, and is valuable for its cinematic approach. In fact, it is this "mystery of unity" that the cinema presents through images, symbols, gestures or rites of *homo religiosus*. The document continues:

It derives from this mystery . . . of unity that all those who are saved participate in, although differently, the same mystery of salvation in Jesus Christ through his Spirit. Christians are very aware of this, thanks to their faith, while others remain unaware of the fact that Jesus Christ is the source of their salvation. The mystery of salvation touches them, nevertheless, by ways known to God alone, thanks to the invisible action of the Spirit of Christ. Concretely, it is in the sincere practice of what is good in their religious traditions and in following the directives of their conscience, that the members of other religions respond positively to the call of God and receive salvation in Jesus Christ, even if they do not recognize him and do not confess him as their Savior (cf. *Ad Gentes*, nos. 3, 9, 11). [no. 29]

The cinema, reflection of similar initiatives, is a privileged place of interreligious encounter and dialogue by favoring discovery, listening, and theological research. These perspectives of the church in respect to religions obviously orient our manner of reading the cinematic treatment of the religious.

VII. Toward a theologial reading of film.

The theological reading of film attends to and critiques every expression of the religious and the sacred. It locates the specificity of Christianity because it announces a good news for the happiness of mankind and its liberation from everything that enslaves it, including the religious and the image.

1. Reading.

I propose the term "reading" (*lecture*) to signify something different from the simple spectacle of the film. The theological initiative implies an act of reason that goes beyond the feeling experienced during the projection. It is a distancing and a rereading of what has been seen, heard and felt. In order to avoid projecting into the film what we have in ourselves, it is indispensable to verify our impression by reseeing the film several times. To do that with others is an excellent school of asceticism and rigor – to pursue a detailed description of the shots, the sequences, the editing; to study the dialogue and the sound-image relationship; then, after having examined the significance of the surface, to locate what is at play in the depths of the construction of the whole. From the clash of images or of sequences, something implicit is suggested, and it is often there that the power of a film resides. This work of reading, very close to the task undertaken with a biblical text, rejects the first fascination and calls forth the word in the flux of seductive images. To read reintroduces the otherness, the confrontation with a difference which resists the emergence from the dream and from imaginary projections.

2. Are we to understand the reading as an opening or closing?

Do the script [*l'écriture*], the composition of the shots, the lighting, and the rhythm close in on themselves, or do they refer to something beyond themselves? There are aesthetics that conceal and others that open up. The various tools of film analysis help us to determine what the script communicates before we take on the content. Are the images "talking," above all in a talking film? The image "talks" if it assures its function of mediation by making us hear the mystery with which it is pregnant and that it can only suggest. Then it is open to the invisible that it makes present, and that must be understood, even if the director doesn't intend it to be. The image talks when it escapes the conscious motivations of the director in order to let slip through unexpectedly the word and the mystery. A reductive script, with images closed upon themselves above all by their beauty or their obviousness, possesses us. Seeing them, we "have been possessed," and it is a form of "possession." Closed images, those not open to the "symbolic," are "diabolical" and cannot be vectors of the word.

3. Is openness a gift?

The openness is of the order of structure and is not an entity that is a personal source of salvation. It is the effect of the Word alone, which opens and saves. Therefore, does the religious film cause the effect produced, or does it put us in relation to the otherness that provokes it? Does the openness come only from the aesthetic, the hero, the spectator, or the gift of the word? If the hero lives through a liberation, is it through his own efforts or by accepting a gift? A gift cannot be stolen, bought, manufactured! It is freely offered. By whom? By a witness of the word, a divine messenger, God? This perspective, concerning more the content, is important. All in-itiatory beginnings – gnostic, ascetic or heroic – are not necessarily a re-ception of divine grace. Does the hero hold on to his personal image? Does he strive to fashion for himself the image that fulfills his narcissism, or does he offer himself to what comes upon him without having wanted it? The true saints, receptive to grace and not puffed up by their image, sing with Mary, "The Lord has done marvels for me, and holy is his name!" (Lk. 1:49) A too heroic or marvelous manner of filming them can hide their openness of heart.

Bergman, in many of his films, treats death in images without always opening to the spiritual, but emptily and perhaps as an outcry. By this he shows that cinema has the possibility of piercing through the screen in or-der to open the image to the mystery of desire and of the word. It is also not by chance that Denys Arcand cites Bergman in *Jesus of Montreal* (1989), which denounces the traps of the image. The appeal of Mireille is astonishing. The word of the one who invites her to come into his follow-ing (Jesus) turns her away from the mirror of seduction where her friend has shut her up in the image of the woman-object. This turning away or conversion lets her continue by listening to the word that becomes flesh. The scenes where Mireille leaves the mirror, abandons her makeup and learns to talk are among the most beautiful and strongest in the film. It is also in that perspective that Farin in *Le combat de roi* (1985) shows the devil tempting Jesus by means of media, mirror, costumes, publicity, and success. The Spirit helps him by breaking the mirrors set up on Calvary. Death and resurrection are the shattering of the images that imprison the word made flesh.

4. Rereading in the present and in history.

This work on the film text does not exclude the historical and cultural con-text of its production and reception. During a rereading, this relationship to history gives meaning to the spectator-reader because a religious film that rests on an historical reconstruction is not only a word to the present but also a seduction of the past. The Christian message should allow us to live today from the strength of the resurrection. That's where the great difficulty lies in making films about Jesus, his miracles or his resurrection. How does one get from the narrative to the scene? The narrative is spoken, under-stood, integrated into prayer. The scene represented must keep the dimen-sion of being heard and of the narrativity proper to personal interiorization and rereading. A pruning of attention is necessary; if not, the door will be open to the spectacular, the melodramatic, false reporting and propaganda. There more than elsewhere, the word should come through the image. The symbolic, the parabolic, the metaphoric, the evocation or suggestion are to be favored. Sobriety and austerity strip away religious tourism and allow us to be touched by the Word of God, always present.

5. To savor the peace, the joy and the praise transmitted by the work of art.

This is not the narcissistic sentiment of pleasure, but the openness that resides in the word and makes us remain there. Only the word recreates us in joy. Films that engender fear, disquiet or violence cannot be Christian. "Don't be afraid" is the evangelical refrain when a strange event comes to upset our life. It is the sign of the presence of God who offers his peace. Zachary (Lk.1:30), Joseph (Mt. 1:20), the shepherds (Lk. 2:10), the women at the tomb (Mt. 28:5,9; Mk. 16:6; Lk. 24:36-40) and the apostles at the Last Supper receive this invitation to accept peace and to offer it (John 20:19, 21, 26). This criterion seems to me determinant and can come only from a work of art. If I have not brought out the qualities necessary for a film to be a work of art, it is because the same qualities seem to me indispensable to the religious film. The intention is not enough, nor the beauty of the content. The message comes across in the aesthetic, the rhythm, the writing (*l'écriture*), the *mise en scène*, the performance of the actors. To forget it or to disregard it is not worthy of the subject treated. "In order that a work of art have a sacred character, it is first of all necessary that the work have character," Father Regamey wrote in 1952 in *Art sacré au XXe siècle*.[7]

6. The Second Council of Nicea and image-mediation.

In conclusion, it is fitting to listen once more to the Second Council of Nicea (787), reminding us, during the iconoclast crisis, of the mediating function of images that are icons, not films:

> The more one regards frequently these imaged representations, the more those who regard them will be led to remember the original models, to be carried toward them, to witness them, kissing them, with a respectful veneration, without that being a true adoration according to our faith, which is fitting to God alone, . . . because 'the honor shown to an image goes up to the original' (St. Basil, *De Spiritu Sancto*, 18, 45). Whoever venerates an image venerates in it the reality which is represented there.[8]

On the anniversary of the Council, Cerf published the acts of the *Colloque international Nicée II, 787-1987, Douse siecles d'images religieuses*. In their Foreword, François Boespflug and Nicolas Lossky did not overlook "moving images" and, taking up the text of Nicea, posed these questions: "Which conditions should the image satisfy in order that the believer's intention be drawn toward him (the prototype, the original) and rejoin him? Are there not numerous cases, and entire areas of religious art, which, far from favoring this *transitus*, take the eye captive?" These are some of the conditions that I have wanted to make precise by putting the accent on what seems to me to be the first – namely, to remove the "confinement" or the "captivity" of the spectacle – for faith in Jesus is also to believe in him whom I do not see, but who has been mediated to me; to believe that the signs, the promises, the word of the Gospel and the church lead beyond to someone invisible but living. It is to hope that the transfiguration makes good all our disfigurations. And it is also to rejoice: "Happy are those who, without having seen, believe" (John 20: 29). "Happy are those who hear the word of the Lord and who keep it!" (Lk. 11:28).

Endnotes

1. I am inspired by the works of Denis Vasse, who along the lines of Jacques Lacan and Françoise Dolto pursues a personal anthropological reflection with fecund theological perspectives.

2. I permit myself to make reference to texts written for the *Centre National de l'Enseignement Religieux* (C.N.E.R., Paris) in the reviews *Catéchèse* 125 (October 1991), "*Les moins de 7 ans, enfants de médias,*" and *Initiales "Spécial cinéma"* 109 (May/June 1992).

3. See Jean Vernette, *Le nouvel âge: à l'aube de l'ère du Verseau* (Paris: Téqui, 1990).

4. "*Rencontre des religions,*" *Études* (January 1987), 102. Cited by A. Marchadour in "*La révèlation chrétiennne, un mode original de traitement du religieux,*" *Les représentations religieuses dans la tourmente des productions culturelles* (*Recherches et Documents, Institut Catholique de Toulouse,* February 1988). See also J. Moingt, "*L'écho du silence,*" *Recherches de science religieuse* 67 (1979).

5. *Ibid.*, 69-70.

6. Claude Griffe, "Le christianisme et les metamorphoses du sacre," in *Le sacré: Études et recherches* (Paris: Aubier-Montaigne, 1974), 147.

7. Regamey, *Art sacre au XXe siecle* (Paris: Cerf, 1952).

8. Cervais Dumeige, trans., *La foi catholique: textes doctrinaux du Magistère de l'Église,* (Paris: L'Orante, 1961), 311-12.

9

Theology, Discernment and Cinema

Michael Paul Gallagher, sj

One of the key tasks of any theological reflection on film is to identify what can be called the "spiritual tone" that is present. Paul Tillich used to say that each culture has a style, and that the style reveals a latent theology or stance before the ultimate. In today's culture, it might be better to say that each changing generation of artists both embodies and reflects the "tone" of the times. This does not mean that artists are merely mirrors, passive reporters of what is around them. They are creators and prophets in two senses – future-seeing and value-challenging. They serve as advance warning systems that sense troubles and potentialities. They offer an experience that can provoke people into a depth of response not often realized by the average churchgoer.

In the last twenty years there there has been a significant shift in how the religious element in film demonstrates itself. Previously, films by directors ranging from Bresson to Bergman contained an explicitly religious character. Now, while some excellent "religious films" in this sense continue to appear, attention has moved to a certain "anonymous religiousness" in seemingly secular movies. The basis of this shift lies in the intuition that a film which evokes fundamental questions cannot but be religious.

But this shift, obvious enough in itself, has been accompanied by at least two larger movements in contemporary culture as a whole. One is the increased primacy of the visual in people's lives. The other has to do with the transition from the comparative clarities of the "modern" to the fragmentation of the "postmodern."

The explosion of visual media is now seen as one of the key factors shaping contemporary sensibility, values, worldviews. It is something that is no longer confined to the "North" or richer world, but extends into the "South" or developing world. It is a planetary power that constitutes a revolution in perception and hence is of intense theological and pastoral relevance. This is not to deny that huge differences in cultures remain and indeed flourish healthily. At the Cavalletti Conference, an African commentator on an Ivory Coast film remarked that Africa retains a collective or communal culture, one that is still deeply and naturally religious in ways that have been lost in the "North." He added, insightfully and memorably, "From our point of view, the lonely individual involved in some spiritual search seems mad, and yet it is a typical image in the religious-inclined cinema of the rich world." Similarly, many Latin American or Indian films stay much closer to the rhythms of popular culture than their more sophisticated western equivalents.

I. Postmodern Gnosticism

That there are exciting differences between cultures hardly needs saying. It goes hand in hand with the fact that the visual is a new power influencing all cultures. Even though it applies much more to the "West," or Euro-American world, the other shift called postmodernism seems particularly significant for theological approaches to cinema. In fact, there are close parallels between the tendency toward anonymous religiousness rather than an explicit treatment of religion *and* the dominant "tone" of postmodern culture. As one commentator has put it, the disillusion with rationality that marks postmodernity links up with a new "primacy of experience in the search for God" and in this way a new postatheist mood can be interpreted as an "excellent preparation for Mystery."[1] In spite of all its possible ambiguities, this less explicit, shy spirituality seems more in tune with the fragmented lifestyle that dominates the urbanized and developed world.

No doubt there are questions to be asked about this tendency to prefer the indirect to the explicit. Positively, it can be a sign of a new if hesitant openness to religious horizons: after all the scorn poured on religion in the excitements of the post-Enlightenment or "modern" phase of culture, basic human hungers reemerge from suppression and seek some nourishment. Negatively, it could be symptomatic of a certain preference for vagueness, an avoidance of definite commitment, and even a distortion of the religious impulse into narcissistic self-satisfaction. There is more than a whiff of gnosticism in the contemporary sensibility, but it is not a question of pure doctrine. Instead, the gnostic problem is now a cultural presupposition that shows itself not only in the producers but perhaps more so in the receivers of movies and other art forms. A religious danger arises when the receivers are so impressed "by a world of vague symbols that they can give no credence to any other form of truth."[2] For example, is the finale of Spielberg's *E.T.* (1982) a genuine moment of vision and self-transcendence, liberating of the spiritual imagination, and even Christian in its echoes, or is it merely a soft manipulation of seemingly spiritual emotions, short-lived and lacking in depth?

In this light, one of the critical skills of the Christian tradition that is eminently translatable for the world of cinema is that of spiritual discernment. It can offer scaffolding towards a set of Christian criteria for evaluating films that might be less externalist than those in vogue in the 1950s or even later. The focus would be less on the displayed content than on the rhetoric toward the implied viewer. The tradition of rhetoric is even more ancient than that of discernment, and its analysis of arts of persuasion could be a useful tool for exploring the interaction between movie and audience. What is the relationship of influence between the visual "text," as shaped by its many makers, and the receiving audience? It is a question of making explicit what is often powerfully present in this complex zone of realized and collaborative experience.

II. The Discernment Tradition

Discernment offers another and more specifically Christian mode of hermeneutics: it involves interpreting the signs of the Spirit in human experience. The phrase "discernment of spirits" is used in two rather different contexts in the New Testament. St. Paul's letter to the Corinthians about diversity of gifts, the word *diakrisis* refers to a special charism not given to everyone (1 Cor. 12:10), but at the service of the community. In St. John's first letter, the term is *dokimasia,* and it seems rather a gift for everyone (1 John 4:1) in order to recognize those spirits that can be trusted as coming from God.

Apart from these two basic texts, several other expressions of St. Paul use the Johannine word *dokimazein,* as for instance in Romans where he speaks of their countering the culture around them with the ability to "test" what is God's will, what is the "perfect thing to do" (Rom. 12:2). Obviously, one should also mention the various promises of the Paraclete in the last discourse of John's gospel where Jesus describes one of the functions as showing what is wrong and what is right (John 16:8). What is striking in these and other texts of the New Testament is an underlying assumption of a context of potential deception, and hence the discernment in question is a double operation – a matter of seeing through illusion and making a wise choice, often in the teeth of temptations to be taken in by falsity. Positively, it is a matter of recognizing the genuine call of the Spirit within one's human freedom.

The figure of Ignatius of Loyola and, in particular, his *Spiritual Exercises* are historically central in the developing understanding of Christian discernment. For present purposes there is no need to rehearse all his subtle insights in this field. Two of them seem of particular relevance to the discernment of the film experience. The first is that consolation can "seem" to be genuine, but may not be so in reality. In our language a film may induce a certain satisfaction, even a felt enlargement of heart, but this yardstick of feeling is not in itself a valid criterion of authenticity. The second Ignatian contribution is his insistence on paying attention to the whole "process" of one's spiritual movements: not only to the moods of consolation but also to their overall orientation. This means a test of time and of asking where all this is leading the person. In the words of Ignatius, it calls for reflection on "the beginning and middle and end of the course of thoughts" and experiences.[3] If all the fruits are good and lasting, this offers the best available confirmation that the roots are in God.

In more modern language, discernment specializes in unmasking illusion and in offering skills for a deeper wisdom of judging reality. Thus, it has two aspects: first, one needs to recognize and remove obstacles to making a genuine choice, in order then to move towards a positive option for the good, ultimately of God's will. This involves the practical skill of sifting the genuine from the deceptive in spiritual experiences. In tune with many of the sensitivities of today, it values interiority, but it also insists on examining the direction of inner experiences, on seeking to recognize roots in terms of fruits, origins of desires and choices in terms of existential orientations and conversions. To use a metaphor, discernment involves a scissor's movement, a convergence of lights, from above and from below: in the Christian understanding, it seeks to unite the revelation of God in Christ with the here-and-now options of one's life and history.

Thus, the sorts of questions that the discernment tradition would pose to film are the following: Does this movie open or close the hearts of its audience to compassion? Does it seduce people into a vague "self-trip" of nice feelings (the solipsistic spiritual trap), or does it point them to an encounter with mystery? Does it serve the spirit of poverty that knows its own vulnerability and honestly tries not to hide it, or does it foster infantile fantasies of various kinds – power, pleasure, unhistoric play? Is it faithful to the spirit of incarnation, which means a reverence for the holy in the human? What quality of looking and receiving is evoked – voyeuristic or stunned, humble silence?

In all this the wavelength of communication called for and the disposition fostered are much more accurate indicators of genuineness than mere content. By their fruits you will know them, as the gospels say, and the saying is a foundation stone of spiritual discernment. The question is less what is being portrayed than where does this film lead its audience: toward spiritual freedom or toward stereotyped immersion in familiar images and reactions? When a wavelength of humility and wonder is evoked, we as audience are where Virgil leads or leaves Dante – on the threshold of a listening that might make faith glimpsable. But it is important to insist that cinema serve the disposition of openness (pre-evangelization of a kind), not necessarily the definiteness of evangelization. Indirectly, it can prepare the path for faith. Baptist-like, it can arouse a potential receptivity for an encounter with greater mystery.

Decades ago the Italian marxist literary critic Galvano della Volpe used to warn his fellow militants against *contentutismo*, meaning a tendency to judge a work's relevance exclusively by its overt content. The same warning may still be needed for some theologians, but not for all. Joseph Marty, in the previous essay, speaks of how cinema reaches a kind of religious transcendence precisely by its awakening of the sensibility.

III. Theologians and Art

In a striking way, recent theology has discovered the paradigm of art as a model for what used to be called the preambles of faith. For all their divergences, it is one of the points that links Hans Urs von Balthasar and Karl Rahner. Thus, Balthasar comments on what makes the perception of God possible: "We can understand this best from the astonished realization we experience in privileged moments and encounters . . . [that] elicit . . . wonder."[4] In Rahner's view there is a preparation that a person "must undergo to be or become a Christian, which turns out to be a receptive capacity for the poetic word." He sees this whole wavelength as being able to "reach the *heart*, the centre," where mystery becomes incarnate.[5]

Rahner has dealt with the theological or spiritual relevance of art in several major essays that span his whole career. Even though he does not make the link with cinema, what he has to say is easily adapted to that medium. His emphasis falls on the wavelength of communication opened up by art, rather than on any explicitly religious content. Poetry, he argues, "is one way of training oneself to hear the word of life." Equally, if a person who truly listens to revelation in depth "begins to be a man who can no longer be totally unreceptive to every poetic word."[6]

Thus, in Rahner's view there is significant common ground between the human capacity required for religious receptivity and for artistic experience. But in this respect he insists on the rich complexity of what is embodied in art as a criterion of value: "there is an intrinsic connection between a really great Christianity and really great writing. . . . Great writing is achieved only in those cases in which man achieves a radical self-confrontation, in which he realises what he himself is."[7]

In two essays written in the 1980s, Rahner develops this stance further. Some theologies will have little time for the artistic: those that seek to "devise a metaphysical anthropology" and a "religious knowledge which would not depend at all on sensory or historical experience."[8] But, on the contrary, "all peak experiences of every *sense* domain" open the door to a religious dimension.[9] The following is his strongest statement of the theological significance of art that at first seems non-religious:

> even an image that does not have a specifically religious theme can be a religious image, when viewing it helps to bring about, through a sensory experience of transcendence (if we may call it so), that properly religious experience of transcendence. . . . A naive theology will spontaneously think or silently presuppose that only explicitly religious acts . . . will bring about a salutary relation to God. But, theologically speaking, that is false.[10]

His other essay of the same period proposes that a "poetic theology" is needed and that it should be a "mystagogical theology" in the sense of encouraging people to discern the presence of the Spirit in their secular and artistic experiences. "If theology is the conscious self-expression of persons about themselves from the point of view of divine revelation," he wrote, "we might submit the thesis that the most perfect kind of theology would be the one that appropriates these arts as an integral part of itself."[11]

In Rahner's emphasis, theology needs to rediscover the challenge of the contemporary Areopagus – to overcome, like St. Paul, any merely dismissive attitude to the culturally embodied forms of religiousness and to discern what is spiritually valuable in the artistic expressions of the time. Indeed, theology needs to be pushed out of its sacred enclosures, to plug itself into other languages and other forms of knowing, engaging other questions than those that belong to its own territory. Film could be its forgotten or neglected partner for approaching contemporary culture.

Theology means many things to many people. What kind of theology would be interested in film? Probably not the kind that emphasizes a timeless zone of eternal truth. Nor the kind that lives in a world of documents, whether from scripture or church tradition. Both of these tendencies may pay lip-service to dialogue with history or culture, but in practice their interests lie elsewhere. The theology that takes human history and human experience seriously is one that needs to embrace film as a privileged witness in today's culture.

Thus, Bernard Lonergan in *Method in Theology* offers the following aphoristic observation: "As conversion is basic to Christian living, so an objectification of conversion provides theology with its foundations."[12] Film, like other narrative arts, thrives on conversion stories, not necessarily of an explicitly religious kind. If conversion is so fundamental for theology, film offers a huge store of images for theological reflection. It thus provides, to adapt another expression of Lonergan, "the horizon within which" mystery and its meaning can be apprehended.[13]

At another point Lonergan insists that "studies of human interiority" in general are needed to equip the theologian to approach his or her key field of "religious experience." He immediately adds that this entails a "spiritual development" in the person of the theologian in order to "enter into the experience of others."[14] In this light, one can argue that film today offers a unique field of spiritual development and a challenge to enter with sympathy into the consciousness and vision of another.

IV. Discerning Some Movies

Some examples of movies can exemplify the issues. Without entering into all aspects of these complex films, we can pose two questions about them. In what way are they spiritually or theologically significant? What is the audience rhetoric involved? The films we shall examine were the joint winners of the 1993 Venice award: Altman's *Short Cuts* and Kieslowski's *Three*

Colors: Blue, together with one of the popular successes of recent times, Bertolucci's *Little Buddha* (1993).

It is Bertolucci who is most openly concerned with religious issues. Ironically his film seems to me to be the cheapest of the three – which is not to say that it is a film without merits, as we shall see. What of their relative spiritual visions? Altman and Kieslowski approach such horizons indirectly, narrating respectively a story of apocalypse and a story of conversion. The world of *Short Cuts* is stark, fragmented, pitiless in its exposure of a void, a noncommunication, a brittleness of all relationships. Its focus takes in much more than the interpersonal realm, and the opening shots (the menacing helicopters spraying insecticide to protect crops against the scourge of the medfly) seem like a judgment on a whole world. This is a film of doom that, without ever being explicit about religious possibilities, seems to point towards more than an ethical crisis.

By contrast, Kieslowski is concerned more with one person than with a whole world. The central figure in *Three Colors: Blue* is the widow who survives a car crash that kills both her husband and daughter. The film is reminiscent of James Dickey's magnificent poem, "The Scarred Girl," which also begins with a crash and evokes a gradual emergence from horror and darkness into transfiguration of vision. In Kieslowski, what seems religiously significant is the slow rediscovery of compassion, initiated perhaps in the encounter with the prostitute who brings flowers to Julie to thank her for saving her from being thrown out of the apartment block. (Julie had refused to sign the protest more out of her chosen spirit of noncommunication and noninvolvement, but her refusal meant that the proposal failed.)

There is no need to enter into the details of the film: enough to say that it moves from closedness to forgiveness and generosity, and that the final scenes offer a sung Greek version of St. Paul's hymn to love (1 Cor. 13), set against a montage of previous moments of pain and disaster. It seems to suggest both transcendence and immanence, how love can (eventually) embrace the tragic, or how healing, like music, can (in time) reach all brokenness. A similar emergence from frosty isolation is at the core of *Red* (1994), the third in Kieslowski's French-flag *Three Colors* trilogy (1993-94). It too presents in secular settings what seem to be profoundly religious concerns: judgment, sin, betrayal, forgiveness, healing, and the crucial role of human relationships in mediating conversions of heart. Both these films reach a level of spiritual authenticity, perhaps mainly due to their indirection. Deep issues are delicately touched upon in an incarnate way.

By contrast, *Little Buddha* lacks this genuineness and falls, in my opinion, into a falsity of tone that is symptomatic of a certain tendency in contemporary culture. In order to make my point forcibly, while allowing for some overstatement in doing so, I would say that *Little Buddha* is New Age for children, and as such it appears spiritually and rhetorically false, even dangerous. It is appealing, simple, and smooth enough appeal to appear to an audience of both children and adults. But its version of religion is childish, not child-like. Its view of spirituality is of the do-it-yourself variety. Concentrate hard enough and you will overcome whatever demons there are. Enter deeply enough into your own self and you will find illumination. Besides, from a Christian point of view, this is gnosticism and pelagianism mixed: all is esoteric and all is ultimately up-to-me. The kind of religion imaged here lacks conversion of anything except consciousness. There is never a moment when anyone expresses social concern. The image of the poor man dying is presented as merely a spur for Siddhartha to undertake his narcissistic adventure to find his own meaning for life in the face of death. By comparison the other films have grit, pain, healthy pessimism, and, in Kieslowski at least, the uphill struggle of conversion toward compassion in action, not just compassion as a nice word or feeling.

I can imagine admirers of Bertolucci being offended with this judgment. They can say that it misses the subtle interplay of worlds that is the core of the film, the contrast between the empty world of Seattle glass and the poorer but wiser world of the east. There is, they will insist, much spiritual critique of the west in this film. Agreed, but I am more concerned with the vacuity of the positives and, more crucially still, with the rhetoric or impact of this film on less "subtle" viewers. I fear they will be left with a vague admiration of a spiritual culture that is presented as mere spectacle, not as struggle. Thus, they are being sold a cheap and trivial version of a great religion. From a Christian point of view, one can wonder about the absence of revelation, of salvation, of Savior, of social love (as opposed to a cosmic kindness).

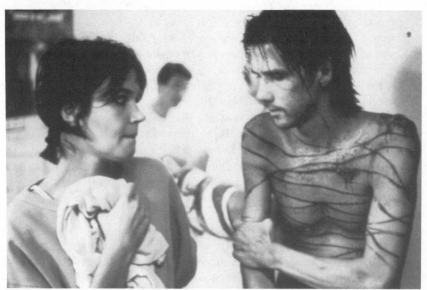

Jesus of Montreal, Denys Arcand, 1989

Bertolucci seems, with a certain honesty, to accept a necessary trivializing of spirituality, not only with his presentation of Buddhism in cartoon language, but through some revealing remarks in an interview about *Little Buddha*: "*Kitsch* is an essential part of talking today about Siddhartha: it is the resonance of the present in the past." In the same conversation, he describes his own current philosophy, after the shock of the collapse of the communist utopia, as rooted in an "emotional discovery of Buddhism." This reads like a classic case of postmodernity. The communist stance was "modern" in its cold clarity. The flirting with the spiritual as "emotional *kitsch*" is one of the dangers to be discerned in the "postmodern."[15]

V. Conclusion

In one of the finest reflective books of the last decade, Charles Taylor comments on an insidious "subject-centeredness" that inflicts contemporary culture, and adds that "overcoming it is a major task, both moral and aesthetic, of our time."[16] This essay has been a footnote to that judgment, arguing that in regard to cinema, it is in the reception culture surrounding movies that this vulnerability is mostly found. Movies may simply play into that narcissism of context, resist it, or even liberate people from it. Discernment, it has been argued, is about a spiritual rhetoric: it asks where the flow of experience is leading a person long-term. If it is Christian discernment, ultimately it wonders whether this work of imagination is somehow in tune with the "losing of one's life," which is for Christ a saving of life (Lk. 9:24). One is not calling for an art that is didactic, but for an art that provokes mystery and compassion, however indirectly, instead of providing fodder for fantasy. A celebrated poem of Rilke speaks of seeing a classic statue that challenges the viewer: "You must change your life." In this spirit there is room for reflection on how films may not only explore conversion (which was so in the Kieslowski examples), but may act as paradigms of how conversion is experienced as a source of more than short-term humanizing fruit. In this way the world of movies offers a crucial locus for theological reflection on culture.

The opposite of subject-centeredness is what the theologian Sebastian Moore has called "egophanic." Interestingly, he uses this term in an article where, among other things, he praises Denys Arcand's film *Jesus of Montreal* (1989) and speaks of "conversion" as taking place "in the dramatic pattern of experience." What he means by egophanic is that instead of collapsing the Jesus story into the blinders of the director or the audience, this movie, in spite of some theological ineptitude, attempts an alternative journey: it is an "expansion of our story into the Jesus story."[17] This essay has also tried to ponder that expansion-conversion experience in films, even where a specifically religious reference is not present. In our culture now it seems theologically significant that some secular movies are broaching a new and non-simplistic language of spirituality. Sebastian Moore would go even further. "Not for the first time," he claims, "the grammar for the next phase in theology is being hammered-out in non-theological, even in non-believing circles."[18]

Endnotes

1. José M. Mardones, *El desafío de la postmodernidad al cristianismo* (Santander: Sal Terrae, 1988), 25.

2. Michael Paul Gallagher, *Struggles of Faith* (Dublin: Columba, 1990), 115.

3. *The Spiritual Exercises of St. Ignatius*, ed. and trans. Louis Puhl (Chicago: Loyola University Press, 1952), No. 333.

4. Hans Urs von Balthasar, *Theo-Drama*, vol. II, *Dramatis Personae: Man in God* (San Francisco: Ignatius, 1990), 21.

5. Karl Rahner, "Poetry and the Christian," in *Theological Investigations*, vol. IV (London: Darton, Longman & Todd, 1966), 357-361.

6. *Ibid.*, 364.

7. Karl Rahner, "The Writer in Relation to Christian Living," in *Theological Investigations*, Vol. VIII (London: Darton, Longman & Todd, 1972), 119.

8. Rahner, "The Theology of the Religious Meaning of Images," in *Theological Investigations*, Vol. XXIII (London: Darton, Longman & Todd, 1992), 149.

9. *Ibid.*, 157.

10. *Ibid.*, 159.

11. Rahner, "Art Against the Horizon of Theology and Piety," *ibid.*, 163.

12. Bernard Lonergan, *Method in Theology* (London: Darton, Longman & Todd, 1972), 130.

13. *Ibid.*, 131.

14. *Ibid.*, 290.

15. Chris Wagstaff, "Bernardo Bertolucci: Intravenous Cinema," *Sight and Sound* (April 1994), 20-21.

16. Charles Taylor, *Sources of the Self: The Making of Modern Identity* (Cambridge: Harvard University Press, 1989), 429.

17. Sebastian Moore, "Four Steps towards Making Sense of Theology," *Downside Review* 383 (April 1993), 93,100.

18. *Ibid.*, 81.

10

Too Beautiful to Be Untrue: Toward a Theology of Film Aesthetics

Marjeet Verbeek

Theological reflection on aesthetics has varied widely throughout the history of Christianity. Sometimes the arts were considered to be sources for the experience of faith; at other times, aesthetic expressions and experiences were viewed theologically as mere illusions and therefore opponents of divine truth (*verum*), good (*bonum*) and beauty (*pulchrum*). Theologians and artists obviously have not enjoyed harmonious relationships during the ages, and they remain distrustful of each other. So, in the twentieth century, the relatively new image of film has not received a fond welcome in theological circles either.

In this essay I shall make an effort to overcome the theological distrust of the arts in general and of film art in particular. One of the basic questions that must be answered is whether the new image of film can be a source of faith experience. Or, in other words, can the theological notions of *verum, bonum* and *pulchrum* have a healthy relationship to the art of filmmaking and film-viewing?

This essay, however, will not be purely theoretical. My background includes ten years of involvement in and reflection on media education, of which film education is an integral part. This mainly pedagogical work has had its influence on my positive evaluation of film aesthetics because of its ability to enchance the imaginative powers and the faith experience in film-viewers. Therefore, I shall start my theological reflection on film aesthetics with an inductive approach, describing my experiences with film education. In the second part of the essay, these experiences will be put within the broader context of contemporary culture. The contemporary "spirit of the age" tends toward an increasing appreciation of the aesthetic experience in general and the film-aesthetic experience in particular. This phenomenon invites theologians to take film art seriously, since theology should always start from and be imbedded in its culture, however critical it might turn out to be toward this culture. In the third and last part of this essay, the tradition of a vacillating relationship between theology and the arts will be explored and directed towards answering this question: In what ways can this tradition offer critical insights for a contemporary theological reflection on film aesthetics?

In this essay I shall approach recent film as an art form – a form of aesthetic communication that is able to evoke experiences of faith in the beauty of creation. I do not approach film aesthetics through a specific film style, e.g., a formalist or realist style, with a view to defining which concrete images of film are more or less appropriate for communicating faith. This essay makes a plea for an openness toward all kinds of film styles. There are numerous ways of presenting film narratives in concrete images and sounds that might reveal faith in the beauty of creation. It is precisely the creative developments in film aesthetics that make film-viewing such a fascinating praxis, and that invite viewers to search for the faith-revealing potential of all kinds of new images in contemporary films. Thus, I shall appeal throughout this essay to a number of films that are variable in styles, though all of them in my opinion have potential to reveal faith. Whether a particular film will in fact evoke this for others is of course decided by the viewers themselves, experiencing the moving sights and sounds of the film narrative. The theologian interpreting and reflecting on films is in the end just one of the recipients of the film images.

I. Experiences with Film Education

Apart from my own experiences as a film-viewer, my students in film education taught me first of all that film should in fact be part of theological reflection because film can be faith-revealing, and that theological reflection should be done in dialogue with art studies because film is considered an artistic medium. Like all forms of art films are judged on their potential to communicate beauty.

The experience of beauty that film aesthetics is able to evoke does not, by the way, refer only to style – though as in all the arts the form of film is a fundamental component – but also to the "substance" or "content" of the chosen images and narratives. The experience of beauty in a film usually implies more than just the experience of the beauty of a shape, an exciting harmony, an appearance void of any substance. The aesthetic experience also includes an ethical moment when the viewer appreciates the substance or message the film shape is transmitting. Ethics and aesthetics are inseparable in filmmaking and in film-viewing. Moreover, the distinction, often the division, made in theological thinking between truth and morality on the one hand and the beauty of the arts on the other hand harms all three qualities. Thus, *verum, bonum* and *pulchrum* seem to me to be inseparable in the art of filmmaking and in film-viewing.

Many films aim at revealing something beautiful that goes beyond mere substance or style. The artist making a film wants his film to be beautiful in style as well as in substance, and the audience expects his film to be of that kind. Hence, the *splendor formae* of films usually reveals more than just enjoyable style without substance: both style and substance keep the curiosity and attention of the viewer going.

A central issue of substance in innumerable films is the self-transcending search for identity of the main character(s). Some of these films are able to articulate in an appropriate style the often painful and, at the same time, beautiful inner growth of the main character's slowly discovering responsible freedom of spirit. This happens to Travis in Wim Wenders's *Paris, Texas* (1984) while he is traveling through places and among people that contribute to and parallel his interior journey. In films like these, substance and style are integrated into the film's beauty.

Another film theme that has great impact on viewers is the revolt against violent culture and the search for a liberating praxis. When this substance in all its concrete variations is imbedded in harmonious film styles, it has the potential to reveal faith. Numerous, too, are the films with this communicative ability. One that I have worked fruitfully with over the years is Hector Babenco's *Kiss of the Spiderwoman* (1985), which reveals the repressive violence of dictatorial regimes pitted against human dignity, as well as the potential dialogue has for liberating the spirit in a dead-end situation. Aesthetically using the confinement of a Latin American jail as a metaphor for the "dark night" of the soul, the film reveals the potential of empathetic communication for the self-revelation and mutual understanding of two human beings who have no apparent reason for hope. The initial, but inevitable failed communication between the two prisoners yields to a dialogue that spiritually liberates both from their hopelessness. Films like this can in fact evoke experiences of faith in the beauty of creation.

The new images of film are obviously very much able to discover and articulate the religious sensibilities of our time: the self-transcending search for spirituality in, but also against, our culture that may reveal faith against all odds. This phenomenon is even more important because the institutional church is no longer a major interpreter of culture. In addition to the films I have mentioned above, a few others that I have worked with successfully are Sargent's melodrama *Choices of the Heart* (1984), a docudramatic film about the life and choices of one of the four nuns killed in El Salvador; Kieslowski's metaphorical film series *Decalogue* (1988); Arcand's multileveled Christ-movie *Jesus of Montreal* (1989); Madonna's audiovisual morality play in the music video *Like a Prayer* (1987); and even Lynch's surrealistic and stylistically complex television series *Twin Peaks* (1990).

Obviously there are all kinds of formats, styles, and harmonies – in other words, all kinds of *splendor formae* – to be found in the cinema that can lead to an experience of beauty that evokes imagination and the revelation of faith. One might even think of comedy as a dramaturgical style that, for obvious reasons, "uses" human conflict to reveal optimistic faith in its resolution. Though comedy is a popular film genre, it is seldom reflected on theologically, perhaps because at first sight it seems to contradict the seriousness of Christian faith. This, I believe, is a mistake. Comedy teaches us to laugh at life, to accept its vicissitudes, and to hope against all odds. It is a challenge to interpret films that also make you laugh, like Danniël's *Ei* (Egg, 1987) or Adlon's *Bagdad Cafe* (1988). Clearly, I believe there is, and should be, no universal prescription of styles to be required of films capable of revealing faith. Film aesthetics as concrete artistic audiovisualization is in development throughout time and culture. The new images of film, as well as the experiences they evoke are subjective creations in constant development because they are part of culture, even when they criticize culture. This potential for development is what makes film-viewing such a fascinating activity. It enhances the anticipated pleasure of being confronted with constantly renewed aesthetic approaches to hopeful artistic communication.

Now, because my role here begins as a viewer of films and a film educator, my interest goes out first of all to viewers of contemporary films. For this reason, before I come to speak about theology, I offer a description of what I believe to be an important aspect of the "spirit of the age" concerning the appreciation of the arts in general and film art in particular. I believe that in contemporary western society, at least European, the aesthetic experience is highly valued. A shift – one that has to be taken seriously in theological reflection – has taken place from the primacy of ethical evaluations of films to the primacy of aesthetic evaluation. That this may sometimes pose a difficult problem for the theologian became particularly clear to me when some Christian groups in the USA and later also in the Netherlands protested against Scorsese's film *The Last Temptation of Christ* (1988). While many viewers were "merely" complaining about the length and slow movement of the film, its real adversaries were more than troubled by the image of a Christ who was tempted by earthly love and sexuality.

II. The World in Fragments

At the end of the twentieth century, western European societies are often characterized as *post*modern. For better or for worse, the term postmodernism is, confusingly enough, used too for all sorts of contemporary developments that point toward a crisis in modern society. I use the term not so much in order to raise a discussion about its definition or even its validity, but to point out that, in the way it is often used, it refers to an *Unbehagen* with (which also suggests a replacement, or "post" of) the rationalism of the Enlightenment and the of industrial revolution. Contemporary Europeans have trouble in keeping up faith in rationalistic ideologies, like liberalism, socialism, and communism, that are optimistic about the human potential to create truth, virtue and salvation, because nowadays these ideologies are considered to have resulted in oppressive systems and institutions. This loss of faith pertains not only to political or scientific systems and institutions, but also to Christian churches, which are believed to have sold out to modernization, to a great extent. To put it in other words, the classical political, scientific and religious meta-stories or myths with their distinct utopian objectives concerning truth, virtue and salvation no longer play that central integrating role in the spiritual search of contemporary people.

To some degree this is due to the effort of science itself, which made an epistemological break with the past.[1] Metaphysical theology, as well as the physical and political sciences, presupposed a clear distinction between subject and object. Truth, virtue and salvation were not only objectives clearly distinct from human knowledge and experience, but also possible subjective areas of error that one tried to avoid. Such a distinction between subject and object is no longer realistic. The object as such does not occur in nature. Nature is even defiled as a myth. Now the object is seen as the result of human activity and vision insofar as the subject always interferes with the object. Human beings are not subjects opposed to objects, but are always connected with the object and, by means of experience and language, become subjects.

Therefore, the conclusions of religion, politics and science – especially their claim to be objective – have been heavily criticized, mostly by and since Nietzsche. This presumed objectivity gives their representatives the warrant to determine and dictate what truth, virtue and salvation for humanity are and should be. Thus, they have turned out to be opponents of the belief (including Christian faith itself) that the human spirit can transcend determination.

This epistemological break is one of the reasons that a majority of people in contemporary society consider notions like universal truth, virtue, and salvation as subjective or even illusory. Thus religion, politics, and science no longer exercise any objective, central integrative function in their spiritual search. Rather, people find fragments of them, as well as of by now subjectivized ideologies that are "up for grabs" in the pluralistic market of modern culture. Religion is part of that open market. Christian churches are also included in this process of fragmentation and subjectivization, which offers them a unique challenge. We might even say, quoting the French theologian Jacques Pohier, that God insofar as he is claimed to be Almighty is in fragments.[2]

If it is true that the classical meta-stories that created the communicative and symbolical environment of the modern world no longer play a central integrating role in the identity and spirituality of contemporary people. If it is true that people are now searching in the fragmented market of popular culture, then the popular media, as a major contributor to popular culture, are becoming increasingly important sources of identity and spirituality in the lives of people. We tend to be surrounded more and

more by a communicative or symbolic environment full of fragmented media messages.[3] Slowly, we have developed from an industrial to an information society that may also be "communicative." And here lies the
challenge for film, as well as for theological reflection on film. The totality of popular media, including contemporary films, reflects as a mirror
the subjective and fragmented (religious) images of truth, virtue and salvation that live on, and are lived according to, in our society.

Because the media images are multiple and often without any apparent mutual relationship, the popular media culture itself is fragmented,
though in many ways still related to the classical scientific, political and
religious meta-stories. In what direction these images are in fact heading
now is not clear. Our fragmented media environment reflects uncertainties
about or even loss of faith in the past, present, and future.[4] To that extent,
contemporary films demonstrate more often the search for rather than the
achievement of the goals of today's spirituality. In other words, asking the
right spiritual questions within is more important than finding the right objective answers outside.

In contemporary films, people are often considered to be projects
breaking through existence. Contemporary images of truth, virtue and salvation are put in a dramaturgical and narrative context of the subjective
search for (religious) identity and spirituality. One has only to remember,
for example, Wenders's *Der Himmel über Berlin* (*Wings of Desire*, 1987)
or Tarkovsky's *Andrei Rublev* (1966), *Stalker* (1979) and, in fact, all of his
other films, to get an idea of what is meant by this notion. Films like
these (and many others) invite the viewer's spirit to transcend political,
scientific and religious determination; they shed an aesthetic light on liberating human praxis.

1. In Search of Aesthetics.

Partly because of the loss of faith in the above-mentioned meta-stories, the
role of the audiovisual media has become more important in daily life. Obviously, the technological developments that brought television sets into
every home and gave popular artists the potential to create highly stylized
audiovisual messages are also reasons for their importance and success.
These technologies have only increased the ability of the audiovisual media
to use their appropriate aesthetic tools of mixing and editing specific physical, moving images, spoken language and music in order to narrate and
dramatize to the fullest. If audiovisual aesthetics is capable of something
more than appealing to emotions and evoking identification and imagination, the audiovisual media and their viewers favor artistic messages. And
since there is hardly any accepted (political, scientific, or religious) authority that tells people that they should be searching for this or that objective
truth instead of enjoying popular art, people nowadays tend to give in to
media's enjoyable aesthetic experience. In return, the audiovisual media focus more and more on aestheticism, tending to emphasize it as a value in

itself: the messages become more stylized, and they often implicitly or explicitly promote an aesthetic lifestyle.

One of the key aspects of the aesthetic lifestyle as a value in itself is design. Industrial products, like television sets, are no longer just created, promoted and enjoyed because of the constantly improving quality of the audiovisual images they transmit, but also because of their design. Philips, for example, advertises this way: when the television set is turned off, people should put an apple on top of it, so that the set becomes a work of art – a design that fits their lifestyle. The Dutch airline company KLM likewise sells aesthetics in its TV ads, by comparing its jets to beautiful, gracious swans landing on the water, rather than by touting cheap incentives for flying with them. This appeal goes beyond mere consumption; it also incites the audience to contribute creatively to its aesthetic environment.

Emphasis in the popular media on aesthetics as pure style is aimed at "lifestyling" audiences. The growth of the fashion, advertisement, architecture, pop music, film and television industries makes clear not only that the media are interesting for economic reasons, but also that enjoying the aesthetics of media is itself becoming a major cultural activity. The aesthetic media experience seems to be the key to every experience, including the experience of religious or political values. The arts no longer serve religion or politics; religion and politics tend to become servants of the media aesthetics people want to enjoy. For this reason theologians are often warning against the so-called hedonistic trend in contemporary society. The more pluri-sensorial media aesthetics becomes, the more it seems to have the potential for creating a fundamental experience of pleasure in a beauty that reaches beyond "style without substance."[5] Even audiovisual advertisements like to appeal to more than just the desire for a lifestyle. Although advertisements aim at selling lifestyles by focusing on aesthetics, the substance they appeal to is often derived from scientific, political and religious imagery.

Think, for example, of the controversies the Bennetton advertisements evoked. Did these advertisements for conventional fashion, by means of highly aesthetic images of the world's injustice, include an experience of idealism? Or were they "just" a tricky way of selling clothing by means of something that cannot be bought; namely, the wish to do right? This example sheds a certain light on the apparent victory of materialistic hedonism over spiritualistic idealism, which is not to say that idealism has disappeared from the minds of people, but rather that it seems to result from experiences of pleasure, evoked by fragmented popular media.

Within this context one can speak of the search in contemporary society for a so-called "aesthetic utopia," which means that the enjoyment of aesthetics is generally believed to lead to faith in truth, virtue and salvation.[6] One searches for the "aesthetic utopia" in popular audiovisual media that take up images of political as well as religious faith. The pleasure one draws from these media is believed to stimulate to creativity and intimate social contacts. Within this line of thinking, the religious film is also imbedded in a cultural context in which the aesthetic experience prevails.

For example, in 1992 the Thomas More Academy in the Netherlands drew a surprisingly large audience – by both their and Dutch standards – when it organized a film series about the search for, growth in, and loss of (religious) identity as imagined in contemporary film. As I lectured on Cavalier's film *Thérèse* (1986), I was struck by the kind of discussion this film, which portrays St. Therese of Lisieux as a bride of Christ, afterwards evoked. Most viewers were fascinated by the formalist style of the film, which in their opinion suited its substance, namely the purity of the faithful Therese. Clearly they thought the film was beautiful. For some, especially the younger ones, this aesthetic experience of both style and substance was enough. That was what they had come for and what they wanted to share with others. They were not bothered by what disturbed some others the most – the feeling of being tricked by an aesthetic film that exposed the destructive behavior of other nuns in the convent. This group did not want to see such things happening in a Carmelite convent, especially not the one a saint lived in. The majority, though, were simply fascinated by the film aesthetics that revealed for them the beauty of faith. Interesting discussions followed about the film's artistic ability to reveal faith in the facial expressions of the main character, and from there about the meaning of faith and mysticism.

What helped me to understand the phenomenon that enjoying media aesthetics can be a source for experiencing (religious) values is Wagner's notion of the so-called *Gesamtkunstwerk,* or multiple style media. Their goal is to try, by means of distinctive arts and styles, to give perspectives

Thérèse, Alain Cavalier, 1986

on political and/or religious issues, as well as to deliver a profound aesthetic experience by using different arts like choreography, music, singing, and drama.

The pop artist Madonna, for example, is a contemporary *Gesamt-kunstwerk*. Through her changing personal images, her music videos, her book, her multiple-style concerts, her print-mediated publicity, she has become a work of pop-art herself with great impact on large audiences. Through her multimedia approach, she tries to address audiences on social issues like racism, AIDS, female (sexual) initiative, religion and mysticism.[7] As a successful piece of pop art, she is probably Andy Warhol's dream come to life. Her beauty is a *splendor formae* of aesthetic as well as moral importance. Her music video "Like a Prayer," indebted to Wagner, clarifies my point. In this morality play, she has a religious experience in a black church after she has witnessed the rape of a young woman, committed by white men, for which an innocent black man who wanted to help the girl is arrested. The religious experience she has in the church converts her from being afraid to testify against these criminals to a trusting that results in liberating the victim. Her love for God and others overcomes her loneliness and helps her to make the moral decision to testify against the crimes of rape and racism. Aesthetically, this audiovisual morality play is well thought out. A harmony emerges from the interdependence and integration of color and symbols, dramaturgy and narrative, camera movement and editing, music and lyrics. "Like a Prayer" is, I believe, a fine example of what aesthetic and ethical potential music videos can have.

Another example is the multiple-style media spectacle David Lynch made out of his roughly thirty-hour television series *Twin Peaks*. Integrating comedy, detective story, mystery, horror and several audiovisual allusions to about sixty years of film history – together with the advertisements, publicity, maps and books about the town of Twin Peaks and its fictional inhabitants – the series tries to evoke imagination by giving enjoyment to as many senses as possible. By audiovisualizing religious myth, mystery and magic in an eclectic, surrealistic way, *Twin Peaks* surpasses mere entertainment, showing its viewers how dangerous it is to be fascinated by the destructive seduction of forbidden sexual pleasure. The only answer to this danger is to lead a spiritual life filled with human solidarity.[8]

Both Madonna and Lynch communicate aesthetically from a religious and spiritual point of view. Their popular media audiovisualize a search for spirituality and solidarity inspired by fragments of Christian (Madonna) and other religious, spiritual, mystical and sometimes even magical traditions (Lynch). But whereas Madonna is optimistic about human desire to do right, Lynch wonders whether the frighteningly seductive power of evil is not so immense that it will always impede our search for virtue. The contemporary multimedia like Madonna and *Twin Peaks* try through their

focus on aesthetics to evoke enjoyment *and* imagination concerning religious images of truth, virtue and salvation. The results are *Gesamt-
kunstwerke* that, in my opinion, go far beyond appearance void of
substance. Popular artists like Madonna and Lynch are actually creators of
a pluri-sensorial audiovisual aesthetics that tries to evoke pleasure as well
as religious imagination and even faith.

2. How Popular Can Beauty Be?

Media created by popular artists like Madonna and Lynch, who obviously
are not embarrassed to work in television, raise another question about the
evaluation of the contemporary appreciation of aesthetic experiences. Is the
popularity of a film (or television program) proportionate to its aesthetic
level? In other words, how popular and entertaining must films be in order
to be considered artistic? Very often true beauty is still believed to be
found only in the timeless and universal higher arts. Popular television and
films are considered to be of a lesser artistic quality, more bound to time
and locality. In this line of thinking, high art is considered to be transcultural, whereas pop art is culturally bound.

Accidentally or not, popular media aesthetics are well appreciated by
large audiences. Many people, coming from what are often euphemistically
called different "aesthetic communities," enjoy and are moved by the same
kinds of television programs and films. They watch, for example, *LA Law*,
The Cosby Show, *Twin Peaks* and *Decalogue* on television. They might
like Madonna's music videos and *Nederland Muziekland* (Netherlands Mu-
sicland) at the same time. They could go out to see Verhoeven's *Basic Instinct* (1992) or Demme's *Silence of the Lambs* (1992), but also to the
Rotterdam Film Festival to see Cavalier's *Thérèse* (1987), Axel's *Babette's
Feast* (1987) or Boughedir's *Halfaouine* (1990). They go to art galleries
and folk festivals; they buy Vivaldi's *Four Seasons* together with Prince's
Kiss. It seems that the borders of traditional aesthetic communities are being crossed and that the high arts are becoming more and more part of
popular culture.

Thus, one of the classical approaches toward judging aesthetics – the
so-called "aesthetic relationalism" – now seems unrealistic. And maybe
this is for the better, because this approach has often led to elitism, to a
schism between high and low culture, between works of art and works of
culture (which would include most television programs and films). Such
schisms are based on presumptions that are hardly valid any more: (1) a
romantic myth of the (unpopular) artist and his public (hard to believe in
and live by now because of the cooperative way most popular artists work
together for a large audience) and (2) an elitism by people who judge
themselves superior because they are able to appreciate the more abstract
aesthetics of the arts.[9]

Milôs Forman's film *Amadeus* (1984) illustrates this point. When it
came out, it packed theaters in Amsterdam for a whole year. All kinds of

people, young and old, more or less educated, more or less informed or in favor of classical music and opera, went to see the film. My students in media education, who by no means came from one particular kind of "aesthetic community," enjoyed and were moved by the film. They liked its exuberant aesthetics, seeing the baroque dramaturgy, the decadent decor and costumes, and the theatrical way of acting as a perfect accent for the jealousy of the decadent court composer Salieri, envying the free-spirited Mozart. They experienced how perfectly Mozart's music was integrated with the images of Salieri's view of Mozart's life. They enjoyed these film aesthetics because they seemed to be very much in harmony with the film's substance, namely the destructive nature of jealousy.

Because they were unfamiliar with the story of Mozart, some of my students were shocked by the film's portrayal of his infantile behavior. Yet most of them were happy to see a film that portrayed Mozart as someone with a spirit free enough to compose his beautiful music. His unconventionality, especially towards his authoritarian employers, helped him win the sympathy of the audience. My students also found some comfort in the fact that the story, told through the eyes and ears of Salieri, who was a representative of the Vienna Court, reveals the upper class snobbishness concerning Mozart's music and the appreciation common people had for Mozart's vaudeville *Die Zauberflöte*. The film shows that Mozart's artistic talent as well as his religious and spiritual sensibilities (that attributed large music to the action of divine grace) were as much liked by great audiences then as they still are today. This film clearly criticizes the presumed distinction between high and low culture.

Amadeus might also be interesting from a theological point of view. Viewers can identify with the universal human problem of being jealous of divine beauty in creation (the source and result of divine inspiration and talent) and with the danger of a destructive response to that jealousy: Salieri's murder of the presumed incarnation of God's beauty, namely Mozart, when in fact the beauty is to be found in Mozart's music which did not die. But also the aesthetic experience people have watching the film might reveal that such a jealousy can be overcome by a grateful and loving attitude toward the moving token of grace that Mozart's music, because of its beauty, still is.

Whether the film itself will be of that quality remains to be seen. Only time and sociocultural circumstances will tell. The recognition will be achieved though by bringing the film before the eyes of the public and keeping it there, like Mozart's music, which, because of this film and other popular media, is becoming better known to larger audiences these days and not just among the privileged, for whom it was meant by the artist for economic reasons only, as the film tries to tell us.

In the final analysis, media aesthetics are for the sake of those recipients who want to experience pleasure while being entertained. They are in fact also searching for a beauty that goes beyond pure shape, void of any substance. This beauty, I believe, is not just to be found in cinema meant for small audiences. Popular media too can be "pearls of revelation." As we approach now our third and last endeavor – an effort to bring theology and the arts closer together – it should be clear that some of our insights to date into the function of aesthetics in culture will be particularly helpful. If contemporary people do in fact see fragmented audiovisual, popular media as major sources of aesthetic experience, and if the aesthetic experience is never without a moment of ethical appreciation, then the theological reflection on film should never separate aesthetics and ethics. Moreover, films that are able to integrate style and substance in order to help us imagine the beauty of the human desire to transcend determination and to liberate the spirit are certainly worth reflecting on theologically.

III. Theology in Search of Beauty in the Arts

The contemporary "spirit of the age" here described may at first look like a complete reversal of a religious and theological tradition that let the search for objective, divine truth and goodness prevail over the search for the aesthetic experience of beauty in the arts. Often the arts and the experiences of beauty did not even come within the scope of theological reflection. Theological reflection on the mysteries of faith preferred to use the analogy of truth being beautiful instead of the beautiful (aesthetics) being truthful. The arts were all too often considered to be inferior to philosophy and the Scriptures concerning their respective potential to reveal truth and goodness. Usually the arts, especially the pictorial and plastic arts, were given only a limited pedagogical function for the masses who could not read; they became "Bibles for the poor."

Taking the contemporary "spirit of the age" into account, should not theology reflect self-critically on its tradition concerning aesthetics? Are the arts, especially those that are pictorial and plastic (and film aesthetics has a clear connection to these traditional art forms), in fact inferior sources of faith relevation? Some critical work has already been done. Sylvain De Bleeckere, for example, provides interesting cultural and philosophical reflections on the reasons why the pictorial arts were usually considered to be of inferior value for revealing truth.[10] Throughout European history, theological and philosophical thought presumed that God's revelation is related almost exclusively to the spiritual hearing of his Word, which may result in a mystical seeing of God, unmediated by pictorial images. The "apparent" transcultural Word of God as revealed in the Scriptures and explained in theology was considered of greater potential for the experience of faith than the more culturally bound images of God found in the pictorial arts. Because of this longstanding metaphysical distrust of images, it is somewhat understandable that up until now many theologians have had problems in taking film aesthetics very seriously.

However correct this reflection on the traditional relationship between metaphysics and aesthetics may be, it must also be said that philosophers and theologians were not always of one mind concerning the arts. Throughout the history of European theology, there has been confrontation as well as harmony in the relationship between aesthetics and theology. For example, whereas Plato saw a conflict between divine truth and the apparent and misleading "truth" of the arts, Aristotle and later, in the Middle Ages, Thomas Aquinas found a harmony between aesthetic truth and divine truth. In the Renaissance there was a conflict between the medieval theological view of religious art as an objective image of divine creation and the "modern" view of the artist as an "alter deus," as the human subject whose task it is to reveal truth in spite of reality. It is obvious that philosophers and theologians have always considered it to be important to describe their relationship to aesthetics. A. Grözinger has formulated some theological issues emerging from the history of theology and aesthetics that might enlighten the way toward a contemporary theology of film aesthetics.[11]

1. The question of truth (*verum*) in the arts throughout history has often been put in the perspective of doing right (*bonum*), of human praxis. Aristotle and later Thomas Aquinas first formulated this "purpose" of aesthetics. For these thinkers the arts are important since it is the human desire for the divine beauty in creation that one can experience in aesthetics, that motivates us to a liberating human praxis. Because beauty (*pulchrum*) is the norm of aesthetics, profound representations (*mimesis*) of divine creation (reality) can be found that mediate a liberating (cathartic) praxis. Obviously, this harmonious relationship between aesthetic and theological thinking comes forward out of the conviction that the human desire for beauty motivates people to a liberating praxis. Since the arts are able to communicate divine beauty, they are considered to be important mediators of the motivation to do good. Beauty is more than style: it is also substance that mediates liberating action. Therefore, a theology of film aesthetics should aim at relating *pulchrum* to *bonum*, aesthetics to ethics: the beautiful being good, the experience of beauty liberates us to do good. Clearly, this approach meets my concern that a theological reflection on film aesthetics is directed towards the search for beauty in substance as well as style.

2. Throughout the history of the interrelationship between theology and aesthetics, there has been the recurring question concerning aesthetic truth. For Plato the "truth" of the arts was an illusion. Aquinas, on the other hand, saw the arts as objective and truthful mediations of divinely created reality. Since the Renaissance, artists themselves were considered to be creators of objective truth. Twentieth century philosophers like Adorno and Heidegger, however, no longer see the artist as a producer of

objective truth. They consider the arts to be mediators or revealers of truth, though no longer the objective truth of the Middle Ages or the Renaissance, rather the subjective truth of contemporary artists who are able to (re)create creation as it should be and thus mediate a liberating praxis. From the point of view of subjectivism, today's philosophy formulates a view on the arts that has this core – the truth-revealing potential of the arts, in common with the metaphysical view on aesthetics in the Middle Ages. When theological reflection takes subjectivity seriously, it may accept the contemporary insight that the arts have the potential to reveal truth in a fragmented and subjective way.

3. History has shown that the arts can stimulate theological self-criticism, as once the Renaissance artists did by criticizing the metaphysical view on art as an imitation of nature (*analogia entis*). Their revolt consisted in trying to reveal the sinful dimension of nature, by defiling it as a cultural myth instead of calling it divine creation. And in fact contemporary films often revolt against the religious thinking that confirms violent cultural myths (also about nature). Maria Luisa Bemberg's film *Yo, la peor de todas* (*I, the Worst of All*, 1990), where the oppressive religious myth at the time of the Spanish Inquisition concerning the "nature" of women is exposed and criticized, is a case in point here – also Oliver Stone's popular Vietnam movie *Born on the Fourth of July* (1989), which rejects the total integration of Catholicism with the nationalistic myth of needing, even if necessary, to defend violently American cultural superiority.

These issues from the history of philosophical and theological thought about aesthetics are, I believe, helpful for contemporary theology reflecting on film art. The pleasure in aesthetics comes out of the human desire to realize beauty in creation. Aesthetic beauty is understood, therefore, as a possible source for liberating action. Within this line of thought, beauty is neither an outward shape without any substance nor necessarily a fact of life. From a theological point of view, the desire for beauty comes from a desire to realize good. The relationship between aesthetics and truth is, therefore, not the ability of the arts to reveal the facts of life which are already truthful and good, but to show how truthful and good life can be. A film is a work of art when it is able aesthetically to motivate a liberating praxis.

In film aesthetics and the experiences they evoke, beauty is the central term. Beauty is what human beings are searching for when they are creating, experiencing and (theologically) interpreting films. J. Wissink, whose title I "borrowed" for this essay, helps to further clarify the theological notion of beauty.[12] In theology, beauty is not a term that applies only to the arts. All creations, not just artistic ones, are potentially beautiful and may evoke aesthetic experiences. But the arts are privileged aesthetic creations that are able to render transparent the beauty of creation. They are mediators of beauty in creation. But when is a creation beautiful? In other words, can beauty be defined? According to Wissink, the beauty theologians search for and find in all sorts of creations, including film aesthetics, cannot be defined because beauty as well as truth and good are, theologically speaking, transcendentals, which means they are characteristics of God and of everything in creation that is ordered toward God. Beauty, though part of concrete and particular creations, at the same time transcends them and thus escapes definition. The theological notion of divine beauty in creation can, however, be circumscribed, and this is what Wissink does.

His circumscription of beauty, which he basically connects with the thinking of Thomas Aquinas and Francis of Assisi, starts with a theology of creation. Beauty in creation is what God makes things to be. This means that it is not simply a fact of life, but a gratuitous gift from God to creatures so that they will recognize beauty and create beautiful things, which means ordering them toward God. Beauty, therefore, depends on the human attitude toward his own creation and the creation surrounding him. To realize God's gift is to make the things in creation become beautiful by analogy with his beauty.

For Wissink, the mystical writers have best circumscribed in their poems what this attitude toward creation should be in order to realize the beauty of it: a loving openness toward the things God brings into being. The realization of the beauty of creation depends on the loving openness of human beings towards creation of which they themselves are part. Wissink uses this analogy: a human being who loves God and others realizes himself more than one who closes up within himself. A loving openness toward creation implies that one no longer greedily grasps at creation in order to put it under personal control. Obviously it is love toward creation that seems to be the key term for creating beauty. As an example, Wissink refers to Rembrandt's painting *The Old Woman Praying*, which shows the loving openness and free spirit of the old woman praying. Rembrandt's creation mediates the beauty in creation.

Once human beings are able to have a loving openness towards creation, they are able to "experience" its beauty. Theologically this means that the experience of beauty in creation is, first of all, the result of a loving praxis that comes to rest in an aesthetic experience. The realization of beauty in creation and the experience of its beauty come together in one experience that has an ethical as well as an aesthetic moment: *pulchrum* and *bonum* in creation are inseparable.

A few films, already mentioned in other contexts, that, in my opinion, exemplify these thoughts are *Ei*, *Thérèse* and *Babette's Feast*.[13] All three offer pure and intimate portraits of their main characters, who are visualized as beautiful people capable of a loving attitude and openness towards the creation surrounding them – their fellow human beings, the flora and fauna, their daily work and the tools they use. It seems that their lives are an aesthetic experience of the beauty in creation. Because of their loving openness, they are also able to open up the people around them, tempting them to let go of themselves, and never again to close in on themselves and grasp greedily at the creation surrounding them. All creation, therefore, is seen as God made it to be and thus becomes beautiful. These three films are aesthetic creations that make the beauty of creation transparent. Such films are an artistic ode to beauty in creation and to the people who are able, unselfishly, to receive as well as produce the beauty that goes far beyond mere shape. Their pure styles and substances, moreover, make it possible to experience faith in the beauty of creation. Their film aesthetics mediate a liberating praxis that may evoke an aesthetic experience of the beauty in creation, depending on the ability of the viewer to see and appreciate this beauty in a positive way.

In Wissink's theological approach to beauty, there is finally no division between subject and object. All creatures are intersubjectively interconnected. Their freedom and beauty depend on the loving openness they have toward one another. For this reason, Wissink can state that the highly subjective realization of beauty in creation and the experience of that beauty in creation are at the same time a highly objective realization and experience.

For me, Wissink sheds an interesting light on the relationship between beauty in film and the experience of beauty in film. Both the artist creating the film and the viewer need to have a common ground in order to understand each other, otherwise the film will not communicate beauty. Theologically speaking, the artist creating the film as well as the person experiencing it depend on the same loving openness toward creation in order to be able to mediate and experience the beauty of creation through film aesthetics. In other words, neither the director, nor the viewer, nor the theologian reflecting on the film will meet when any one of them closes in on himself. The artist needs to have a loving openness toward creation in order to make a beautiful film and his audience, including the theologian, needs the same attitude in order to experience the beauty of creation in the film.

That such a common ground between artists and audience, including theologians, can and should exist so that the beauty of creation in film can result in an aesthetic experience of this beauty I know from my own personal experiences in media education, as well as from a recent interview that I saw on Dutch television with Peter Sellars, an opera producer and filmmaker in New York. In this two-and-a-half-hour session, Peter Sellars was questioned about what he believes to be the ideal audiovisual aesthetics. He answered by trying to put into words what can scarcely be expressed for the obvious reason that he was talking about sounds and images; then he demonstrated convincingly what were, in his opinion, good and bad audiovisual fragments chosen from all sorts of television programs and films, in order to make the point that ideal audiovisual aesthetics demand a total integration of image, sound and message. Although I believe Sellars is right in defining audiovisual language this way, his definition was general, as he was very well aware. He ended the interview by showing the last fifteen minutes from a film that he thinks represents the sum of audiovisual beauty – Andrei Tarkovsky's final film, *The Sacrifice* (1986). In the last thirty minutes of the interview, I witnessed what I believe to be an encounter between the beauty of creation in Tarkovsky's film and Sellars's experiencing this beauty. I saw him watching and obviously experiencing the aesthetic beauty of *The Sacrifice*. For Sellars, the ending of the film demonstrates what film aesthetics should be, sacrificing the beauty of Bach's *Erbarme Dich* to the beautiful image, and the beauty of the image to the beautiful music in order to bring some wisdom into the contemporary world. Film aesthetics should, as in *The Sacrifice*, communicate a perspective on the possibility of faith in the beauty that creation can be. In that way, all the viewers in search of aesthetics in our media world may actually find the beauty of creation they are looking for.

This is a thought too beautiful, I believe, to be untrue.

Endnotes

1. Frits Tillmans, "The Theologian's Role in the Communication of Faith," *Media Development* 4 (1981), 46-47.

2. Jacques Pohier, *Dieu fractures* (Paris: Seuil, 1985).

3. Bert de Reuver, "Labyrinth: Typography of a Method," *Verbum* (1993).

4. See the essay in this volume by Reinhold Zwick.

5. Michel Onfray, *L'Art de jouir* (Paris: Bernard Grasset, 1991).

6. Bart Tromp and Willem van Rijen, "Oude en nieuwe utopieën," in *Onderstromen en tegenliggers, wijsgerige reflecties bij het nieuws*, ed. Peter van Hoof (Kampen: Gooi en Sticht, 1992), 127-42.

7. Joost Zwagerman, *Collega's van God* (Amsterdam: De Arbeiderspers, 1993), 38-73.

8. W. de Bruijn, *Peaks Experience: Vademecum* (Amsterdam: Amber, 1992); Marjeet Verbeek, "It's the Mystery That's the Fun of Life," in *Aus Leidenschaft zum Leben* (Zürich: Benziger, 1993).

9. Joli Jensen, *Redeeming Modernity: Contradictions in Media Criticism* (Newbury Park: Sage Publications, 1990); also A. De Zwaan, *Kwaliteit is klasse* (Amsterdam: Bert Bakker, 1985).

10. Sylvain de Bleeckere, "Filmkunst en spiritualiteit," in *Geloof en communicatie*, ed. H. van der Wouw (Utrecht: KTU, 1991).

11. A. Grözinger, *Praktische Theologie von Ästhetik* (Mainz, 1987), 29-71.

12. J. Wissink, *Te mooi om onwaar te zijn: theologisch vragen naar het schone* (Vught: Radboudstichting, 1993).

13. Marjeet Verbeek, "Portret van een bruid," in *Zin in beeld* (Nijmegen: Thomas More Academie, 1992).

Part 5

Developments in
Mass Media Studies

Film Education in a Christian Perspective: Some Contemporary Approaches

Henk Hoekstra

The underlying thesis of this collection of essays is that perceptible developments in the relationship between film and religion have occurred during the last fifteen to twenty years. There have also been considerable developments regarding education in film and religion. These developments concern attitudes toward film itself as well as toward education, its objectives and methodologies.

Film education can focus mainly on imparting more systematic information about the fundamentals of the film medium: its history, genres, techniques, language, worldviews, aesthetics and ethics. This type of film education situates itself more on the cognitive level of knowledge about film. Film education can also focus on the analysis of and reflection on film experiences, on film evaluation and appreciation in the context of film group work. This type of film education situates itself more on the emotional-affective level of the reflective and systematized film experience. Both types have their own possibilities and limitations. Parts of one type are often combined with and integrated into the other. This essay focuses is more on the second type of film education.

There are many different "schools" of film education.[1] They are all inspired by a certain, more or less explicit point of view or world vision (*Weltanschauung*). World vision is understood as a fundamental vision, orienting and influencing in decisive ways the experiences, interpretations and evaluations of films. I approach film education here from a *Christian* point of view, offering this working definition: This viewpoint is (1) inspired and guided by the Christian world vision, (2) goal-oriented and systematic, (3) educational and "dialogical" (in a group process), (4) through which the involved participants (5) develop and grow (6) in understanding and appreciation of (7) the film medium, which takes into consideration (a) its stories, (b) its audiovisual language, (c) its history and genres, (d) its views on life, humanity and world, (e) its mirroring of culture and the spirit of the time, and (f) its disclosure of the essentials of life and society.

First of all, I shall explore the main characteristics and dimensions of film education as defined above (I), then describe new thematic approaches to "film and religion" in this type of film education (II). My main intention is to delineate some promising new developments in film education from a Christian perspective, and thus to broaden and deepen the already-existing rich visions and methodologies.

I. A Concept and Model of Film Education from a Christian Perspective

There are, in my opinion, four key terms in a practicable model of film education – *film, education, Christian point of view* and *dialogue.*

1. Film: A Medium of and on behalf of Communication and Culture

Film is a complex sociocultural communication phenomenon. It is a "medium" of (mass) communication similar to radio, television or print media (newspapers or books). It can also be understood as an "audiovisual language," as the forms in which film stories and film messages are expressed and received. Finally, it can be used as a term for distinct film "products"[2]: *Paris, Texas* (1984) by Wim Wenders, *Cape Fear* (1991) by Martin Scorsese or *Thérèse* (1986) by Alain Cavalier.

Film education must deal with these three different meanings. Film as an audiovisual "medium" – not identical with television, but similar to it – is a medium of communication and a medium on behalf of communication, a product of culture as well as an expression or mirror of culture. Film speaks an "audiovisual language." Words (audio) and images (visual) enter into a new marriage through the instrumentality of electronics (camera, microphone, editing, and so forth). The audiovisual language of film combines and integrates the moving, colored images on the image track with the words, music and sound effects on the soundtrack to communicate stories to audiences.[3] The principal potentiality of the film medium and its language is to dramatize stories, to offer visions and interpretations of life, of humans and society in audiovisual narrative form. Film speaks an emotional and affective language in a broad range (love and hate, intimacy and aggression, anxiety and guilt, desire and fear, fascination and rejection). It actualizes these visions and emotions differently in its various genres (romantic comedies, musicals, detective stories, westerns, action films, science fiction, and so forth). In this sense film functions as a mirror of culture and as an expression of the spirit of the time.[4] Viewers are fascinated by film stories that speak to their experiences, emotions and imagination. They interact with them in their own distinctive ways, from the viewpoint of their life stories and situations. Films not only show all kinds of communication between people in and through their narratives, but also invite and generate communication among the viewers.[5]

Film as medium, language and product is influenced in its character and form by technological developments. We understand film first of all as ciné-film or "public" cinema – the film screen in movie theaters. However, public cinema changed profoundly with the rise of television and the availability of videotapes, both of which promoted the emergence of "home" cinema. Films on television and videotapes recorded from television, bought or rented, change the presentation, the reception and the experience of the film profoundly.[6] We will understand film in the broad sense here, of public *and* home cinema, as it affects education.

2. *Film Education: A Goal-Oriented and Systematic Process*

Film education situates itself on the side of the viewer, of the public. It takes its starting point from the ways in which the viewer watches film – the attitude he develops regarding it and the manner in which he deals with it. Thus the starting point of film education is film *reception.*[7]

Film education enters into dialogue with viewers about their reception of films. In this dialogue the viewers are searching for more clarity about the language and the story, the influences and the effects that films can have on people. They also reflect on the interactions they have with the film and on the meanings they give to the film from the viewpoint of their own life situations and their biography. These elementary issues – the relationship between films and their viewers, and particularly the two-way communication between them – belong to the heart of the film educational project.

Film education, therefore, has eyes and ears for the film itself as well as for the viewers and their mutual relationships and interactions. Furthermore, the educational approach implies that there is a consciousness of an ideal, optimal or more desirable film reception – a process from film *reception* to film *perception.* What does this mean? Quite often there is much to improve in our film reception. Unseen possibilities are missed. Opportunities for greater joy and more intense pleasure are enlarged by deeper experiences, more sensitive appreciations, a greater capacity for discernment, more relevant knowledge, and clearer insight in film reception. A guided, goal-oriented and systematic dialogue and exchange concerning specific films in small groups can support this process from reception to perception, as we will see later on. The meaning that the film may have for the viewer is broadened and deepened. Thus, film education does not limit itself to research and discussion of *factual* film reception and attitudes; it wants to be and to do something more. It intends to provoke qualitative changes by its activities – to change viewers by forming and educating them.[8]

Because film education deals with change and formation, it is constantly in search of ways to realize this formation in a more goal-oriented and systematic manner through the use of adequate methods. Film education takes place nearly always in a kind of stimulating group setting. The group, its members, its facilitator, its dynamics contribute substantially to film formation. Particularly, the group dialogue about the many different aspects of a film and the different forms of film experiences of the group members belongs to the heart of film educational methodology.[9] Furthermore, didactic methods such as observations, guiding questions, and role play have a fundamental place in penetrating the content and form of the film. The information shared by the leader and the group members about films, trends, aesthetics, genres and forms must contribute essentially to film understanding, insight and knowledge; this is an essential part of the film educational approach. We shall concretize goal orientation and the systematic approach later in the section on film dialogue.

Finally, film and film education do not function in an historical and sociocultural vacuum. They are formed by and embedded in sociocultural life and in concrete social situations, undergoing the influence of technological, historical, sociocultural, economic and religious events and developments. Moreover, they show enormous developments and differences in emphasis in the course of time. There was, of course, a tremendous difference in the study of film education during the time of the rise of the film as opposed to the film education taking shape in periods when people and society are gradually becoming more familiar with the phenomenon. In the latter cases one has more factual insight into the character, role, and impact of the film, as well as more research-based film theory. Thus, all these developments make film education a "contextualized" sociocultural phenomenon.[10]

3. A Christian Viewpoint or Perspective

Film education confronts us with at least three different levels of world vision or philosophy of life. First of all, world visions – which affect the educational process itself – can be more or less implicit and hidden, or explicit and open. They imply or express a system of values about life, human beings, society and church, about film, education and ethics, and thus inspire, sustain, orient and influence film education in all its dimensions. Indeed, they are fundamental to the conduct of film educational activities. Philosophies of life can be quite different in origin, character and perspective. They can have, for example, humanistic, liberal, Marxist, religious, Christian, or so-called neutral roots.[11] Hence, film education seeks to make explicit and also to reflect on its "chosen" worldview – its origins, guiding forces, and concrete forms. The vision that informs this essay is, as I have said, a Christian one.

Second, film education itself is inspired and guided not only by its own chosen worldview, but also by the philosophical preferences and values *in* film stories themselves. These are expressed in the way the stories are told – through film aesthetics, the development of characters, the solution of problems posed. They take concrete form in the behavior of characters and in the context of the stories.[12] World visions on this level can also be of quite different origin and nature. For example, the film stories of *The Sacrifice* (1986) by Andrei Tarkovsky and *Wild at Heart* (1990) or *Twin Peaks* (1992) by David Lynch show considerable difference in this regard. Film education also has to be aware of these differences, making them explicit and clarifying them as part of the educational process.

Finally, there are also the world visions of the film viewers themselves, who are by no means *tabulae rasae*. They have their life histories, experiences, motivations, visions, values and norms related to life, human nature and society, in short their own worldviews. These phenomena play an intervening role during the viewing and evaluation of a film. They cannot and should not be neglected. Film education implies also a process of confrontation and exchange between "the world" of the film and the "worlds" of the film viewers.[13]

How do we understand film education from a Christian point of view? Such a film education constructs its identity, projects its goals, and develops its methodology in the light of the Gospels. What does this mean? Seen historically, we can trace some clear developing lines in the views of Christians regarding film. These shifts have their roots in media-technological developments, in the changing spirit of the time, and also in the changed attitudes of Christians with regard to the medium of film. From an originally ambivalent through a negatively-inclined attitude, we can observe nowadays, at least in principle, a positive attitude.[14] The contemporary attitude does not question cinema as such. It is accepted as a sociocultural phenomenon. The usual film criticism from a Christian perspective today is concerned with critical analyses and evaluations of the stories – the presentations, messages, implications, aesthetics and ethics of the films viewed.

The world vision component of film education from a Christian point of view must take into consideration the following elements: (1) Christianity aims at constructing a worldview and a culture in which life and death are meaningful for all people. The theology of creation as well as the Christology of Bethlehem (incarnation), Golgotha (suffering and death) and Emmaus (resurrection) are crucial points of reference for the Christian worldview, for the understanding, interpretation and appreciation of human life. Film education from a Christian viewpoint, taking creation and redemption as its frame of reference, thus interprets and values films and their stories in the light of the Christian faith.[15] (2) This film education is aware of the contemporary image culture, called into existence and developed by the audiovisual media – film, television, and video. Image culture, quite differently from literary culture, requires an audiovisual language to express and to experience life, human nature and society. As Christian film education values the image culture in a more positive way, it furthers an "iconophile" attitude, developing a sharp eye for the unique cultural value of the image and for its spiritual force. It stimulates the appreciation of films with aesthetic and spiritual dimensions, and helps us to discern films of varying degrees of value.[16] (3) Thus, film education in a Christian perspective makes an option, in principle, for a constructive attitude toward the world of the film, for a genuine dialogue with this world, for the development of an affirmative sense of human life, and for the value of being human via film education.

4. The Religious Film Dialogue

Viewers develop relationships *sui generis* with films and their stories. As we have already noted, film stories touch the emotions, the heart and the imagination of the viewers. Quite often, films inspire viewers to one or another form of dialogue about life experiences – those portrayed in the film story as well as those that viewers themselves have experienced and that the film provides the occasion to recall. Dialogue as a typical form of interpersonal communication is different from a debate or discussion. The debate has the character of an argumentative struggle between the parties (*se debattre,* a verbal war). Discussion is a form of interpersonal communication in which partners analyze their subject on a more objective level. Dialogue partners have open ears and eyes, attitudes that are receptive to the deeper (religious) inner experiences, feelings, and thoughts of their partners, while revealing themselves too on a more personal, existential and religious level.[17] We understand film dialogue in this latter sense. It means, first of all, that the film and its director can be partners in this dialogue.

The film as partner. The viewing of film stories offers moments of self-recognition to viewers. Forms of identification with or rejection of characters, their situations or behavior initiate and reinforce the processes of self-recognition. In this way the viewer dialogues with the story, the lifestyles portrayed, the visions, options and preferences of the main characters, as well as with the director of the film. This dialogue with the filmmaker and the film story as partners can take place on an intrapersonal, interpersonal or group level.[18]

The intrapersonal dialogue. The intrapersonal dialogue implies a communication of the viewer with him- or herself about the film story. The viewer becomes the sender and receiver of messages at the same time. He or she reflects on the film in silence, and this meditation leads to introspection, self-confrontation and self-recognition. Such intrapersonal dialogue is an excellent way to get inspired as viewer and to cultivate one's own life of the spirit. It offers a possibility to link film and life experiences, to integrate them both into one's own life in a new and mature way. Filmmakers like Fellini, Godard, and the Tavianis make a plea in their films for these forms of silence, introspection, meditation, even spirituality and ascesis.

The interpersonal dialogue. Film stories can equally stimulate an interpersonal communication between viewers (within a group) – about what they perceived regarding lifestyles, visions, options and preferences, in both the form and the content of the film story. The film story also functions as an occasion for the viewers to dialogue about their own experiences, life styles, options, and so forth. Such interpersonal reflection on the film as well as their own experiences thus nourishes and supports the spiritual and moral life of the viewers.

The religious film dialogue in the context of small groups. Dialogue can also take place in organized groups, discussing a film from the perspective of the Christian world vision, under the guidance of a facilitator or group leader. Through the exchange of experiences and the responses to questions raised, a group member becomes aware of fragments, shots, images, scenes, texts, that she did not see or observe. She also hears the interpretations of the other group members, which perhaps she did not think of. A group leader facilitates, steers and regulates this process of religious dialogue. The Christian view of life makes an active contribution to this process of viewing, reflection and dialogue. Since the group members have a common religious history, they share a vision of human life from the viewpoint of the Gospel. They live in the context of Christian faith and spirituality, and use the Bible and tradition as frames of reference and models of explanation.[19]

Combination and integration of the four forms of dialogue. These four forms of dialogue can be coordinated easily. Film stories have the function of showing, involving, engaging, motivating, informing us about what is going on in life and society, always of course through the language of the film. Moments of personal reflection after the viewing of a film serve as a first individual reflection on the experience as well as a preparation for the dialogue with another or within the group. The contributions of the individual group members are stimulated and recorded. The group dialogue has mainly the function of deepening, broadening, and clarifying differences in visions and experiences, of developing a collective meaning, of evaluating and integrating. Each of these four forms has also its own place and role in the total process of communication, continuing through several successive stages. They support and reinforce one another. It is in this sense that we can speak about a goal-oriented, systematic and guided group dialogue about film stories from a Christian point of view.

We are now in a position to formulate the following main goals of the religious film dialogue in small groups:

Comprehension and understanding. Group members, sharing their experiences and perceptions in a more systematic and goal-oriented way, reflect on the content and form of the film in such a way that they get a deepened and broadened comprehension and understanding of the film, its story, its language and its message – as a result of the guided group dialogue.

Reflection and confrontation. The group members are not religious or moral blank slates; they have their experiences, visions, values, religious/Christian frames of reference. As such, they enter into dialogue with the stories and the characters of the film, the implied options, visions, values and ways of life, and also with themselves and with others. So there develops an intended process of analysis, reflection and confrontation in and through this guided group dialogue.

Order, interiorization and integration. Each one contributes what he or she experiences concerning the film. The other group members, by listening attentively, broaden and deepen their own experiences and visions of the film story, learning to appreciate and to evaluate the film and its message more for its own value (or lack of it). The group members thus begin to interiorize and to assimilate their experiences and visions, putting them in order, digesting and integrating them into their own concepts of life.

Development and growth in sharing Christian meaning. The film dialogue that is animated by a Christian view of life implies a clarification and explanation of the ways in which a religious person looks at and deals with the stories reflected on. Religious film dialogue should result in a caring involvement with the religious visions of others, a growth in sharing Christian meaning. "Religion lives by communication. Unless it can be shared, it dies."[20]

To implement the formulated goals, we can use the following five steps.[21] This methodology indicates at the same time the main tasks of the facilitator during the successive steps.

1. *Viewing the film.* Brief information about the film and its director and some questions for viewing will be helpful. At the core, though, is the screening of the film and the encounter between the film and its viewers.

2. *Viewer-oriented film discourse.* The focus here is on the expression and sharing of film impressions by the viewers. It is the process of intra- and interpersonal communication, in which the personal role of the viewer is reflected on and the impact of his own biography is experienced and discussed.

3. *Analysis and reflection-oriented film discourse.* Attention here turns to the film itself, through an analysis of the film story, its content and form. Group communication is systematic and goal-oriented. Methods and instruments for analysis are used.

4. *Confrontation of film story and Christian worldview.* Here the focus is on reflective analysis of the film from a Christian point of view, with principal emphasis on creation and redemption, as discussed above – leading to a formulation of Christian viewpoints and positions.

5. *Reflection on the dialogue processes.* Up until now, the focus has been on the dialogue within the group. A kind of *meta*-communication about the film as "good news," as well as a reflection on the results of the dialogue and their consequences for the future, comprise this last step.

The film education I have described involves a growing comprehensive understanding of cinema as a cultural phenomenon, group dialogue as a collective process of sharing meaning, the interpretation and evaluation of the film "in the light of the Gospel," and the formation of critically autonomous viewers. Film education, in this vein, reveals "liberating potentialities."[22] It also implies the need for a Christian identity, a professional approach and qualitative work. Comprehension and understanding, dialogue and interpretation, autonomy and liberating power are situated in and oriented by the Christian world vision.

II. New Approaches to Film Education from a Christian Perspective

1. Film Media as Supermarket, Public Forum, Areopagus

Once the Western world was more or less homogeneously Christian. The dominant world vision was a "given," so to speak, and not therefore a matter of public debate. This situation has changed radically in recent times, in part because of the growing presence and influence of the audiovisual media, television and film. Now the Christian faith and church often find themselves in a marginalized situation, at least in western Europe. Many different world visions announce themselves and are dominantly present in public life, even if often expressed by the media in more or less incoherent and fragmented ways. The modern world looks like "a supermarket of world visions or *Weltanschauungen*" or like a "public forum in which all the relevant public issues are thematized and discussed."[23]

Pope John Paul II made some remarkable contributions to the discussion in his encyclical *Redemptoris Missio*.[24] Film and television for him are not only technical instruments, but also and above all "a culture of their own," meaning that they are creative expressions of a specific way of life (feeling, perceiving, thinking, speaking, judging, acting, relating, communicating, etc.). The pope calls these media "the first areopagus of modern times" (referring of course to St. Paul's experience in the Areopagus of Athens concerning the unknown God[25]). The areopagus is the marketplace or forum, the "religious" forum, in which questions about the meaning of life and the existence of God are debated. Christians, says John Paul, feeling themselves to be in the forum of these media as St. Paul was in Athens, find that it offers them the possibility of knowing what other contemporaries think, say and do, what motivates and inspires them, what they fear, desire and hope. The areopagus becomes for Christians a relevant source of information about the spirit of the time. Faith and church must inform themselves and must reflect carefully on what the media offer concerning meaning, religion, ethics, spirituality through their productions – not only "what" they are offering, but also "how" they are doing it in terms of their own audiovisual language.

2. Film and Worldview, Religion, Spirituality, Morality

Christians thus find themselves in a pluralistic dialogue with actual religious, spiritual and moral issues and questions. The forum can stimulate a truly fascinating process of exchange, confrontation, negotiation, clarification, growth, and renewal regarding the relationships between cinema and worldview, religion, spirituality and morality, but it can also create situations of tension, conflict, confusion, incoherence, and fragmentation. Koole comments on the considerable discomforts or troubles today because of the "analphabetism of worldviews."[26] Thus, the media and film areopagus is both a chance and a challenge as well as a cause of tension and conflict between the Christian worldview and the multitude of visions and ideologies regarding human life.[27] It creates also the need, even the necessity for people in general and for Christians in particular to pay explicit attention to and to reflect on issues of world visions.

Although it would be instructive at this point to present film educational approaches to "Film and Worldview," "Film and Religion," "Film and Moral Formation," and "Film and Spirituality," space necessitates a choice; hence, I shall restrict myself to a presentation of "Film and Spirituality." The endnotes provide references to the descriptions of the others.[28]

3. Film Education: Film and Spirituality

There are two main reasons for dealing with the question of spirituality and film. First of all, the phenomena of spirituality, spiritual life and spiritual values play a more central role in the lives of people today, who experience this new call for spirituality very strongly, living as they do in a fragmented, incoherent and secular culture.[29] Spirituality becomes a kind of necessity in order to survive in the cultural milieu of today. The growing attention given to this phenomenon must also be understood from the perspective of this new cultural background.

Second, until recently the phenomena of spirituality have been expressed and experienced mainly in forms of verbal communication, the spoken, written and published words in the print media – books, magazines and periodicals. However, the audiovisual language of the film medium, television and video has become culturally predominant, taking over the prior role of the print media, becoming the preferred language of the majority of people today. Can those spiritual phenomena also be expressed and experienced in the language of the audiovisual media, especially in film? The film education approach to "Film and Spirituality," situated from this background, explores the medium of film, its language and its products as possible sources and reservoirs of spiritual phenomena and processes. Its educational perspective tries to stimulate and to guide people searching for spiritual issues and meanings in the language and in the stories of specific films. Needless to say, this approach to "Film and Spirituality" implies a positive vision of film and its language, as well as the need for a revision of the traditional and existing concept of spirituality. Film and its language will give expression to spiritual phenomena according to their possibilities and limitations.

Three questions concerning film education's approach to "Film and Spirituality" are of vital importance, and will be treated in sequence: How do we understand the word "spirituality"? What are the possibilities of the audiovisual film language for expressing and experiencing spirituality? How can we sensitize people to the spiritual phenomena in film?

A few key terms are constitutive of a concept of spirituality. Together they build a kind of search model for spirituality,[30] which can also be used in the search for spirituality in the audiovisual medium of film and its concrete products, as well in the group dialogue about film, as we will see. The key terms are:

1. *Spiritus*: spirit, breath, inspiration, aspiration, motivation; by which spirit we are driven, pushed or motivated

2. *Experience*: ordering, putting on line, integrating the many different life experiences, and creating unity are the more or less conscious activities of the human spirit, very necessary in our time of fragmentation, incoherence, pluralism; experiences of the deeper dimensions of life include transcendence, boundaries, liminality, *mysterium tremendum* and *fascinans*, the holy, the sacred, the *mysterium*, saints, Jesus Christ, God

3. *Sociocultural context*: humans do not live in sociocultural vacua, but in certain periods of history, in the context of particular societies – cultural, social, and political organizations – and in all kinds of groups, influenced by and interacting with them

4. *Conscious process*: life is a process of change and growth; the human person is more or less consciously and actively living his or her life, directing self-developments, cultivating the life of the spirit (e.g., meditating, reflecting, praying, communicating, criticizing, exercising)

5. *Viewpoint/perspective*: the guiding, orienting vision on the phenomena of human life, the world, society, from which one sees, interprets, orders, integrates life experiences – worldview, religion, Christian faith

6. *Transformation*: spirituality changes and transforms life in the direction of integration, unity, fulfillment, solidarity, humanity

7. *Mysticism*: a burst of consciousness, an awareness that there is another reality of which one was not conscious before; although different in forms but in essence the same in all religions and cultures, mysticism knows from experience that all phenomena of life belong together, that they all are one in their origin[31]

8. *Working definition*: spirituality is a conscious, dynamic process of cultivating of one's own life of the spirit from a Christian perspective. These key elements are the necessary and interdependent components of a concept of spirituality.

Now the audiovisual language of the film medium is the language of word and image, of camera and microphone, of compositing and editing images and sounds – in short, of audiovisual electronics. It is also the language of story and drama insofar as it tells stories and presents dramas about living persons and groups, about their dynamics, conflicts, crises, points of no return, fundamental decisions and final solutions. It expresses imagination, associations, emotions and affections. The characters and the milieux of the stories are shown as incarnations of worldviews, spiritual and moral values, representations of love and hate, tenderness and violence, fulfillment and failure, struggle and harmony, life and death, good and evil, and so forth. These stories and dramas touch also the feelings and the hearts of the viewer. The viewer enters into interaction and negotiation with these persons, stories and milieux, doing this from the viewpoint of his own biography and concrete life situation. The film personalities can function as figures of identification, as examples for imitation, and as models of life.

What then are the characteristic possibilities of the film medium and its language for "expressing" spirituality (as sender) and "experiencing" it (as viewer)? The following are important to note:

1. Spirituality takes the form of a story or drama, of dramatized life stories. So spirituality in film is mainly on the narrative rather than the argumentative level.

2. Spirituality is always expressed in the form of a concentration/condensation of crucial life events: ruptures, conflicts, crises, points of no return, fundamental decisions, and processes of transformation.

3. Spirituality is always situated in concrete sociocultural contexts, showing confrontation/conflict with the existing culture/spirit of the time, and criticism of and/or protest against the existing dominant culture.

4. Spirituality has its roots in religious or secular events or developments like the socioreligious context of the end of the 19th century in Cavalier's *Thérèse* or the sociopolitical context of the 1980s in San Salvador in Duigan's *Romero*.

5. Spirituality is always individualized and incarnated in living persons. It is a living or lived experience.

6. Spirituality quite often takes the form of an audiovisualized life journey. Spiritual life and development are shown in the form of a quest, a journey.

7. Spirituality implies visions/appreciations of life, human nature, world, and being – often very different and conflicting – and interpretations/evaluations of them.

8. The audiovisual language of film has at its disposal its own facilities to "express" spirituality and spiritual values, and to "experience" the same.

9. Spirituality in the context of film dialogue is a "dialogical" spirituality: it concerns spirituality and spiritual values implied *in* the film story, and explored/discovered *through* the dialogue in the group about the film's spirituality.

The spiritual group dialogue is the communication within the group about spirituality embodied in the film story *and* about the specific spirituality of the group members in their dialogue about the film. Spirituality develops also during this dialogue. It is a "dialogical" spirituality, born in and through the dialogue with the film, with oneself and with the others in the group. This spiritual group dialogue can be practiced in all kinds of settings: religious education, spiritual formation, retreats, reflection meetings, community meetings, spiritual film sessions, seminary education, etc.

Films that lend themselves admirably to this spiritual dialogue are characterized by the following: an interesting life story, drama, or spiritual journey; strong inspiration, aspirations and motivations; a clear conversion, transformation, or reorganization of life; a demythologizing

The Mission, Roland Joffé, 1986

and revelatory character; an openness to the mystery of life, *mysterium tremendum et fascinans*; liminal experiences, crises, ruptures, and points of no return; and critical attitudes vis-à-vis the dominant culture and religion.

In our seminars on "Film and Spirituality," we screen and reflect on films like *Yeelen* (*The Light*, 1987, Souleymane Cissé), *The Decalogue* (1988-89, Krzysztof Kieslowski), *Paris, Texas* (1984, Wim Wenders), *Jesus of Montréal* (1989, Denys Arcand), *Romero* (1989, John Duigan), *Andrei Rublev* (1966, Andrei Tarkovsky), *Ei* (*Egg*, 1987, Danniël Danniël), *The Legend of the Holy Drinker* (1988, Ermanno Olmi), *Babette's Feast* (1987, Gabriël Axel), *The Gospel According to St. Matthew* (1964, Pier Paolo Pasolini), *Under Satan's Sun* (1987, Maurice Pialat), *Thérèse* (1986, Alain Cavalier), *The Mission* (1986, Roland Joffé), *The Kiss of the Spider Woman* (1985, Hector Babenco), *Wend Kuuni* (1982, Gaston Kaboré). Periodicals like OCIC's *Ciné&Média* offer a lot of information about these kinds of films. Concerning the goals, methodology and guidance of the spiritual film dialogue, we refer here to our earlier descriptions of the process, which offer the needed information concerning spiritual film dialogue.

4. Summary and Conclusion

The film medium makes available a very differentiated, attractive language for expressing and experiencing the central phenomena of human life and of the spiritual life. It is able to touch the hearts of all people. Goal-oriented and systematic group sharing about all kinds of film stories leads to the development of a "dialogical" spirituality. Moreover, film education contributes to this dialogical spirituality by sensitizing people to a more comprehensive understanding of the medium and its language as well as by clarifying the phenomena of the journey of the spirit. This is a new perspective. One must learn to experience it.

Endnotes

1. *Communication Research Trends: New Approaches to Media Education* 3 (1982), 2; *Communication Research Trends: Media Education – Growth and Controversy* 6 (1985), 4.

2. Jean Marie Peters, "Media en mediakunde," *Onderwijs en Media* (1981), 1346ff.

3. Pierre Babin, *Language et culture de médias* (Paris: Collection Communication Éditions Universitaires, 1991), 57-68.

4. Robert R. Snow, *Creating a Media Culture* (London: Sage Publications, 1983), 169-209.

5. See John Fiske, *Television Culture* (New York: Methuen & Co, 1987), 62-83.

6. Sylvain de Bleeckere, "Filmkunst en Opvoeding op School: Een Filosofische Mare," *Media Film* 142 (1983), 13-31.

7. See Robert A. White, "The Role of Film in Personal Religious Growth," in this volume.

8. Len Masterman, *Teaching the Media* (London: Comedia Publishing Group, 1985), 18-37. See also note 1.

9. Henk Hoekstra and Karin Zöchbauer, *Massamedia en Kommunikatie Agogiek: Theoretische en Praktische Grondslagen* (Bloemendaal: Nelissen, 1980), 37-78.

10. Len Masterman, "An Overview of Media Education in Europe: Media Education, Future Strategies," *Media Development: Journal of the World Association for Christian Communication* 1 (1991), 3ff.

11. See Helmuth Benesch, *Warum Weltanschauung? Eine Psychologische Bestandaufnahme* (Frankfurt: Fischer Verlag, 1989), 297-347.

12. Johan G. Hahn and Frits Tillmans, eds., *Kijken naar Levensbeschou-wing* (Hilvesum: Gooi & Sticht, 1989), 81-110.

13. Henk Hoekstra, "Het Media Gesprek: Het Groepsgesprek over Media Boodschappen," in Johan G. Hahn and Henk Hoekstra, ed., *In Gesprek over Film en Televisie: Over de Theorie en de Praktijk van het Mediagesprek* (Kampen: Uitgeversmaatschappij Kok, 1991), 55-66.

14. Patricia Mittchell, "Approaches to Television in Religious Education," in T. Inbody, ed., *Changing Channels: The Church and the Television Revolution* (Dayton: Whaleprints, 1991), 98-112.

15. See Wesley Carr, *Ministry and the Media: Society, Role of the Mass Media, Christian View Points* (London: SPCK, 1990), 3ff.

16. See Sylvain de Bleeckere, *Het Licht van de Schepping: De Religiositeit van de Beeldcultuur* (Averbode/Helmond: Altiora, 1992), 11-31.

17. M.C. Doeser, "De mogelijkheid van de dialoog bij pluraliteit van levensvormen," in *De Dialoog Kritische Bezien: Studies over de Waarheidsvraag in de Dialoog met Geloven van andere Culturen* (Baarn: Ten Have, 1983), 77ff.

18. Robert Cathcart and Gary Gumpert, "Mediated Interpersonal Communication: Towards a Typology," in Gary Gumpert and Robert Cathcart, eds., *Inter Media: Interpersonal Communication in a Media World*, 3rd ed. (New York: Oxford Univesity Press, 1986), 26-40; Brent D. Ruben, "Intrapersonal, Interpersonal and Mass Communication in Individual and Multi-Person Systems," *ibid.*, 140-160.

19. Frits Tillmans, "Die Augen des Glaubens: Theologische Überle-gungen zum Mediengespräch," in Michael Kuhn, Johan G. Hahn and Henk Hoekstra, eds., *Hinter den Augen ein eigenes Bild: Film und Spiritualität* (Zürich: Benziger Verlag, 1991), 139-140.

20. S. Hopkinson, "Religion Goes on the Air," *Picture Post* 26:7 (1945), 24.

21. Maria Engelhard and Udo Schaufelberger, "Filmgespräche: Methodik für die Auseinandersetzung mit Spielfilme," in Zeno Cavigelli et alii, ed., *Aus Leidenschaft zum Film: Film und Spiritualität* (Zürich: Beziger Verlag, 1993), 229-44.

22. See the editorial on "Media Education," *Media Development* 1 (1991).

23. Horace Newcomb and Paul M. Hirsch, "Television as Cultural Forum," in Horace Newcomb, ed., *Television: The Critical View* (New York: Oxford University Press, 1987), 455-70.

24. Encyclical of John Paul II, *Redemptoris Missio* (1991), nos. 37-38.

25. See Acts 17.

26. Wim Koole, *Kan televisie troosten? Levenshulp als Pastorale Bijdrage* (Amsterdam: Doctoraal Scriptie Vrije Universiteit, 1984), 44; also Helmuth Benesch, *Warum Weltanschauung?*, 303-4

27. Chris Arthur, ed., *Religion and the Media: An Introductory Reader* (Cardiff: University of Wales Press, 1993). Many contributions in this collection thematize the tensions between the Christian view of life and media worldviews.

28. See Jan C. G. Braun, Henk Hoekstra and Frits Tillmans, *Mass media en levensbeschouwing: Thematische Verkenningen vanuit een postacademiale cursus* (Amsterdam: IWC, 1982), 31-50; also Henk Hoekstra and Marjeet Verbeek, "Possibilities of the Audiovisual Narrative for Moral Formation," in Philip J. Rossi and Paul A Soukup, eds., *Mass Media and the Moral Imagination* (Kansas City: Sheed & Ward, 1994), 212-233.

29. Leo Laeyendecker, "Spiritualiteit en Moderne Cultuur," in Jurjen Beuemer, ed., *Als de hemel de aarde raakt: Spiritualiteit en Mystiek, Ervaringen* (Kampen: Uitgeverij Kok, 1989), 79-108.

30. Otger Stegging and Kees Waayman, *Spiritualiteit en Mystiek: Een Inleiding* (Nijmegen: Uitgeverij B. Gottmer, 1985), 79-108.

31. Bruno Borchert, *Het verschijnsel: De Geschiedenis, De Nieuwe Uitdaging* (Haarlem: J. H. Gottmer, 1989), 10-39; English translation published as *The Mystic: The Phenomenon, the History, the New Challenge* (New York: Samuel Weiser, 1993).

12

The Role of Film in Personal
Religious Growth

Robert A. White

It is widely assumed that films, especially if they have manifest religious themes, can influence or at least play some part in the religious ideas and ideals of audiences. But there is no clear conception of how this might occur and very little evidence that film viewing does or does not play a role in religious or moral development. This essay attempts to bring together some of the current research on how individuals and groups use the mass media to construct the meaning of their lives. From this it is possible to construct a kind of model of how the audiovisual mass media can play a role in the unfolding of the religious dimension of people's lives.

The study of film has for the most part focused on the text and the author, following a tradition of artistic and literary interpretation. The typical analysis moves from the text – the central evidence – "back" into the artistic and cultural intentions of the producer/director and "forward" into the likely interpretations of the audience. The audience is assumed to be seeking to understand and re-experience as closely as possible what the author has experienced and "written into" the text, and the text is the point at which the audience and author meet. Rarely has the study of film been concerned with the "autonomous" readings of the audience that may perhaps take the film as the starting point but then move to constructions of meaning that respond much more to the personal and cultural interests of the members of the audience. In recent centuries we have seen the aesthetic autonomy of the artist – a form of cultural demiurge – as far more important than the autonomy of the audience, more important in fact than the mass popular audience that most films are produced for. It is assumed that the audience has little to say; instead, it needs to be educated and uplifted by the great artists.

One of the most interesting developments in media studies in recent years has been the steady move away from the "powerful media effects" assumptions toward the new conception of the autonomy of the audience constructions of meaning. Already in the 1960s it was substantially proven that almost never is the text simply reproduced in the members of the audience by exposure to media and the direct processes of psychological learning. But not until the 1980s did the application of the descriptive approaches of the cultural anthropologist and the ethnographer to audience studies begin to produce models of the conditions and ways in which audiences "pick and choose" elements from the media to construct their own life stories.

I. From "Powerful Effects" to the "Active Audience"

One of the first major studies of media effects in the USA – and probably the first in the world – was carried out in the 1920s and dealt with the supposed harmful effects of film on youth.[1] Many public leaders – especially parents, teachers and clergyman – assumed that one of the major factors influencing the "breakdown of morals" of the time was the first truly "mass" popular medium, film. Throughout the 1920s there was a growing demand for a study of film influence as a basis for public controls on film producers, and in 1928 the National Committee for the Study of Social Values in Motion Pictures (later called the Motion Picture Research Council) obtained relatively lavish funding from the Payne Family Foundation to carry out an exhaustive study of film's effects on children. Like so many similar studies, the Payne study never proved anything definitively, but it did have lasting influence in setting up the method of later studies of harmful effects of film, radio and television: one must first do a content analysis of the text to find out what the message is and then test to see whether that text is reproduced in the attitudes and behavior of the audience.

In 1960 a landmark book reviewing hundreds of media effects studies discredited this line of research with the conclusion that "mass communication does not ordinarily serve as a necessary or sufficient cause of audience effects, but rather functions through a nexus of mediating factors."[2] This turned audience research toward the cultural sciences and literary theory to understand better audience interpretation of media and the sociocultural contexts in which audiences produce different kinds of interpretations.

II. The Cultural Studies Tradition[3]

Most accounts of the development of conceptions of the audience's subjective interpretations of media begin with Raymond Williams, professor of drama and literary criticism at Cambridge University, who suggested that the media be studied as a literary "text" not simply to reveal the meaning of the text in itself, but as an indicator of the cultural issues and debates in which this text is embedded. Williams was leading a generation of young British critics away from the adulatory Victorian admiration of the purity of the classics and their power to "uplift" the masses. He suggested that "readers" from the popular classes need not be "civilized" by the mass media (as Lord Reith of the BBC maintained). Already Williams was shifting the emphasis not just to the reader of the text, but to the people who were actively creating a culture in that moment and who have left us an authentic specimen of their thought that we might rework to develop our own "text."

E. P. Thompson and Richard Hoggart, also coming from a background of literary criticism, carried the perspective of Williams a step further in their studies of how the English working class interpreted popular literature from their own sociocultural – and political! – perspectives as part of the creation of a self-confident and independent popular culture in the nineteenth and early twentieth centuries. Thompson and Hoggart established a tradition of looking at the working class interpretations of media "from the inside," the way it appeared to the mass audience – not from the perspective of the social scientist asking functionalist questions about effects, or the persons worried about the degrading influence of the media, or the views of those trying to improve the "tastes" of the masses. They also introduced an ethnographic approach that started with the cultural system of the audience as an integral way of life and then asked what was the role of the media within that culture or subculture. They showed the mass audience as agreeing with some aspects of the media, disagreeing with and ignoring other aspects, and how this audience could be co-opted by the media.

In 1964 Richard Hoggart became the founding director of the Centre for Contemporary Cultural Studies at the University of Birmingham that encouraged studies of how youth and other subcultures actively reinterpreted the media to fashion symbols of their own cultural identities, and thus started a new trend in audience research. For Stuart Hall, director of the CCCS from 1969 to 1979, the central question was an acceptable intellectual explanation of how audiences can resist the preferred readings of the media and develop their own antagonistic decodings often quite different from the manifest meaning. In the 1970s, however, the CCCS was still focusing on the text, especially applying French and Italian linguistic, semiotic and structuralist conceptions in order to explain how the signifying practices of language and the formation of worldviews could become an arena for the audience's struggle over meaning.

In 1979 a member of the CCCS group, David Morley, carried out a study of audience interpretations of a BBC news commentary program that attempted to test Stuart Hall's thesis that audience decoding will largely depend on their social identifications (especially social class).[4] Instead, he found that individuals draw upon a composite of often unrelated and even contradictory social and personal histories in their readings. Morley suggested that a much more open-ended audience ethnography, quite independent of social science categories, is needed to understand how viewers negotiate with the preferred reading.

III. The Interaction of the Author's Story and the Audience Members' Life Stories

It is widely accepted that media are a leisure-time, storytelling activity and that television and film have an essentially narrative meaning structure. It is also widely accepted that narratives "work" because of the complicity of the audience. In the classical narrative structure (most popular drama follows this structure), the storyteller invites the audience to enter into the entertainment by first posing a problem or question that the public can see as its own problem, and then linking the problem with some moral culpability of the community. This opens the door to villainous evil and destruction, presents problem solvers that the audience can identify with, and then stimulates the audience to "try out" imaginatively various solutions. Some of the most interesting studies of autonomous audience construction of meaning demonstrate how members of the audience individually "pick and choose" elements of the narrative to work out the plot of their own life stories.

Narrative is an attempt to organize meaning around certain "moral" outcomes – the way the world "should" be. The audience's work with narrative texts, in my opinion, brings us closer to the religious dimensions of audience construction of meaning because it involves people's "life commitments." The "religious" usually refers to what transcends our cultural construction of reality and to our life commitment to reality that transcends the realm of culture.

The analysis of film as a mythic structure of meaning seems to open up to audience construction of meaning much more easily than a purely semiotic analysis of film narrative like Christian Metz's which emphasizes the director's activity. The analysis of dramatic narrative as an example of cultural myth construction in the fashion of Lévi-Strauss implies that the storyteller is performing a function of reconciling the contradictions of meaning in the culture for the whole community. The story-teller is continually implicitly "asking" the audience, "Does this make sense? Do you agree? Would you have the story end this way?" Often the great film directors are working through particular issues of cultural meaning in film and after film. The critics and, in a secondary sense, the cultural analysts function like the chorus in Greek drama that comes on at intervals to comment and wonder at the action. Like the chorus, the critics are stand-ins for the audience, echoing as best they can what the public is debating.

Roger Silverstone argues that television, especially television drama, today carries out many of the processes of mythic stories in reconciling contradictions in our culture and producing acceptable explanations to the great questions of meaning of our time.[5] The narrative structure enables the major characters to enact visibly the conflicts and contradictions everybody senses in the culture, especially what is new, esoteric and seemingly irrational. Most popular art satisfies the quest of the "layman" for an acceptable answer in "common sense language" (the language shared by everybody in the culture) so that ordinary people can go on living their everyday lives. All of us are now professionals in some areas, and more elite drama is aimed at philosophers and particular sectors of the professional question-askers (the scientific researchers in this area). But mass popular media presuppose that because the drama is dealing with a general sociocultural issue, all of the members of the audience can enter into the drama with some sense of the contradictions being reconciled.

Silverstone suggests that the meeting point of storyteller and audience to build an integrated meaning in the lives of all involved is in the selection of cultural codes that have powerful connotations in the memories and imagination of the audience. For example, Oliver Stone's film *Born on the Fourth of July* (1989) uses a religious code, a geographical code, and many other narrative codes with great connotative and symbolic power for the members of the audience. Stone, like all good storytellers, has a powerful rhetorical message primarily for his American audience, but also for all people who have lived through the wars of this century; namely, that the mixture of patriotism and militarism is a cultural contradiction that can only be resolved with a personal transformation. He attempts to show this contradiction in the religious code of *Born on the Fourth of July*, especially the 1950s crusade of Catholicism against communism. In the climactic scene of the film, Stone again uses religious imagery to portray the symbolic transformation of the hero. He has the young warrior, tormented by the guilt of his militarism, "confess" to a family that he killed their son and innocent people in Vietnam. Stone, of course, is inviting the American people to "confess" that they have killed their own sons and innocent people in Vietnam with their misplaced patriotism. The elderly mother of the boy killed forgives the hero with words of "absolution," and the confession has a sacramental power of healing, reconciliation and interior peace that gives the young man new purpose in life. Stone is inviting his audience to be "healed" by identifying with the hero and to "recover" the deepest values of the American culture, finding national meaning not in militarism but in peacemaking.

The selection of cultural codes that are symbolic more than literal invites the audience to enter into the reworking of these codes around the particular questions and concerns of different members of the audience. No two people who see the film *Born on the Fourth of July* will experience the same sort of highlighting and integration of meaning. The film takes up all of the emotionally unresolved contradictions of a generation: religious conflicts, political conflicts, family conflicts, and so on. Horace Newcomb suggests that the storytelling of the media provides a "liminal" space, apart from the pragmatic world, that we can enter into to "entertain" or "try out" possible alternative scenarios of life, and then return to the pragmatic world with some selection of these scenarios.[6]

None of these authors is suggesting that drama presents heroes and life scenarios that the audience simply imitates. Members of the audience and the audience as a whole are constructing their own life stories and patterns of meaning out of the pieces of meaning in their lives. Whatever combinations emerge will be the unique combinations of whatever has been happening throughout each individual lifetime. What these stories do is to pose problems of meaning that at best will touch quite different problematics of life, and stimulate a search for meaning. Second, the stories recall and highlight connotational symbolic codes in the imaginations of the audience that combine with other life contexts in quite unpredictable ways. Third, these stories suggest formulas for the reconciliation of contradictions of meaning in our lives. For example, I doubt that many people rushed out to become pacifists after seeing the transformation of Tom Cruise in *Born on the Fourth of July*, but I suspect that the formula of humble admission that "I was wrong in my whole worldview and that I will find peace and personal integration by publicly confessing this to the people I have offended" did nestle into the imaginations of people and may have found some application in whatever major meaning contradictions they were facing at the time.

But does the audience construct meaning in that way? If so, how? In the numerous studies of the audience experience of television drama, what people remember most and "work with" most are the major characters. Members of the audience enter into the intentions and the decisions of these characters and identify with them in developing the story of the plot. A recent highly-regarded study of audience construction of meaning in television drama confirms that the most salient aspect of characters is their morality, that is, whether they are "good" or "bad" people.[7] This is not understood in the sense of living up to some set of external moral norms, but rather whether the main characters contribute to making other characters in the plot happy and whether they contribute to resolving the problem of the plot in a way that creates social harmony. The other aspects of the characters' personalities (cleverness, beauty, attractiveness, etc.) tend to be evaluated in terms of what they do with these capacities – again, an evaluation in terms of their morality. For the author of this study and for others doing similar research, this confirms the thesis that audiences tend to construct the meaning of drama in terms of the dominant mythic formulas. People want order and integrated meaning in their worlds.

Such studies are equally applicable to film audiences inasmuch as they indicate how audiences construe the meaning of a given text. Nonetheless, they only hint at how people integrate this meaning into their own lives. To understand the interaction of the narrative structure of drama and how people are constructing the "plot" of their own lives, we need a model that takes as its central point not the text but the *context* of their lives. The remainder of this essay will be devoted to this quest.

IV. The Pleasure of Resisting Media and Defining One's Own Personal and Cultural Identity

In the early 1980s media studies began to question the assumption held with equal fervor by both the Marxist left and the moralist right that the mass media are inevitably a manipulative, corrupting, and alienating influence. It was evident that all classes of people could both engage in quite militant social press and, at the same time, deeply enjoy tele-novellas, soap operas and action adventures. Are we to conclude that all these people are "cultural dopes," or is enjoyment of media a form of defining one's own cultural identity or even a form of "popular aesthetic" quite as "legitimate" as the canons of high art? Audience research argued that we must ask with some objectivity why people enjoy the media so much and what this enjoyment of popular art might mean in the construction of personal value systems and cultures.[8]

A strong recent trend in audience studies is the ethnographic description of the friend groups and discourse networks that build up around a particular genre such as daytime soap operas, sports events, police adventures, or any of the other multiplying genres of mass media.[9] This research calls into question the widely-accepted model of the lonely, passive viewer easily manipulated by the media. Rather, most construction of the meaning of media is carried on in groups, with very considerable debate among members of these groups and with the group identities as the reference point of interpretation.

Particular genres of film and television become the meeting point between the producers who know that a particular genre is certain to draw a particular type of audience and an audience that knows particular genres will be the source of particular pleasures. Genres and formats are the point of the most active "negotiation" between the media and audiences. And audiences know their power in this process of negotiation.

V. Media as Mediation

As media studies delved more deeply into the audience's negotiation of the meaning of the text, however, they discovered that much audience meaning construction has relatively little to do with the narrative, the symbols or the mythic background.

One approach sees media as, at best, a "site where individuals and groups construct the meaning of their life situation."[10] Audiences tend to form communities of interpretation that are attempting actively to construct a cultural identity in a particular context. The group interaction and process of meaning construction become the "mediation" of the role of media. The media has a certain power to "convoke" an audience and draw people together, but the meaning construction is carried on almost in spite of the media. It is the group or interpretative community that will often determine the symbolic significance of the media or filter and reinterpret the meaning of a particular media message.

For example, discos are places that attract young people, yes, to hear the music, but primarily to talk to other young people. The music itself, and not the lyrics (which cannot be heard or understood), creates an atmosphere, a style of life, and above all a place where other young people come together to establish the identity of their generation, to differentiate themselves from older or younger people, to define their social class, to find a ritual moment of being in contact with their own interior and to "commune" with the mysterious common spirit of their friends in the "public sphere" where the moguls of musical culture are making things happen.

The same can be said of many genres and types of films. Why did millions of people go to see *Jurassic Park* (1993)? The young film producer Thomas Schüly, who feels himself to be in competition with Spielberg, commented to me that Spielberg has an uncanny ability to catch at the right moment the "mood" of young people and to create a style, a place where they want to be if they want "to be with it" and "to be where everybody else is!" In the 1950s, two films, *Blackboard Jungle* and *Rock around the Clock*, helped to make the history of a new teenage generation. In the summers of 1955 and 1956 respectively, every young teenager "had" to see those films and hear that music to "be with it."[11] Those films were an important site for creating the meaning of life for many young

Malcolm X, Spike Lee, 1992

people, a prelude to what many consider a major cultural shift in western civilization. Did the rock music or the films of that era contain information that "caused" this meaning? It is very unlikely. The young people created the new meaning, but the music and quite a few films were "sites" that brought young people together to interact and, in the interaction, to create something that was ready to come into existence.

VI. Religious Media as a Mediating Site for Constructing the Meaning of Life

Unfortunately, there are virtually no audience studies in which the media text is religious film. The best example from religious genres is, instead, a study of the U.S. televangelist Pat Robertson, a personality and a topic that, for better or worse, have attracted more media research than all of the rest of religious media research put together. Stewart Hoover's study, *Mass Media Religion,* is of special interest because it is one of the few audience ethnographies that uses life histories and places the interpretation of the meaning of media texts in the lifetime search for religious meaning.[12]

Hoover asked forty members of Pat Robertson's 700 Club (the organization of thousands of loyal supporters whose contributions insure that the broadcasts will continue) to recount in some detail their life histories, with emphasis on the religious life histories. The study was interested in the role that Robertson's broadcasts played in their lives, but the research focused on a much broader issue; namely, the patterns in the construction of meaning in their life histories by these admittedly loyal followers of Pat Robertson.

Many did not watch the program every day or even regularly, and few could cite a specific example to show that some program content of Robertson's broadcasts had changed their attitudes or behavior in a specific way. The theory of media effects explains relatively little of the importance of Pat Robertson for these people. Yet all have a very strong identification with Pat Robertson and the neoevangelical movement, and all will say that Pat Robertson has been one of the most important influences in their lives. The immediate matrix of their beliefs is in the small groups of evangelical friends who have been brought together around Pat Robertson as a "symbol of identification," and with whom they are involved in various forms of Christian outreach. Even for those who have never met Robertson personally or who do not have the time to watch his programs, his broadcasting center itself has become a kind of geographical focus for their movement. Some give large amounts of money because they feel that the program is absolutely essential. And they are right, because the program is the public, visible symbol of this movement of so many people who are in search of this kind of belief system and have found the movement precisely because of this public "symbol."

The broader matrix of beliefs is the Pat Robertson evangelistic movement that these people identify with and which they "take their life cues from." This movement and the still broader movement of the evangelical-fundamentalist tradition become the link with the culture and the national social system: political movements such as the new right movement that people of evangelical background such as Reagan led, the economic policies of these movements, the conceptions about education and the mass media, etc. The broadcasting program is the mediating link to all of this for them and the televangelists have been one important symbol of identification for these movements.

When we come back to the "patterns" in the life histories of these people and the way they have constructed the meaning of their lives, we note the following similarities:

1. Most started off life with an evangelical or "devout Christian" (some Catholic) orientation and learned the basic evangelical religious language so that they could understand or identify with the language of the evangelical movement without too much difficulty.

2. The life experiences of most carried them into ever broader circles of culture and social institutions, and with each cultural shift toward the "mainstream" of pluralist modern America through education, experiences in the armed services, business or family careers, etc., the "center of gravity" shifted further away from their traditional Christian roots.

3. Most went through a long period of "searching" in which they experienced a kind of lack of integration of meaning in their lives.

4. Virtually all went through a certain "crisis" of meaning in their lives, an especially painful and often tragic moment when something happened that made them wonder what life is about. This intensified their search for meaning and integration.

5. For all of these people, the evangelical movement as it is in America and in the world today provided an integration of meaning that finally "made sense" to all of them. They feel that they now have a much more integrated, happy life, especially in their activities of "outreach" to less fortunate people (prison inmates, the addicted, broken families, the emotionally depressed, and so forth).

6. The point of conversion for these people came in the use of their talents in life for the service of others rather than just for their own personal enrichment and fame.

7. What makes sense to them is the fact that a televangelist like Pat Robertson (graduate of Yale University, symbol of intellectual prestige in the US, and a wealthy senator's son) as well as the successful businessmen, sports figures, and television and film stars involved with him show symbolically how one can integrate "success" in the mainstream American system with being evangelical.

In the background is the fact that the evangelical movement world-wide realized some forty years ago that it was becoming marginal and that it would have to "inculturate" more to survive. The lives of the forty people in this study by Hoover are a microcosm of the growing evangelical movement worldwide. Clearly, the human structures of conversion here can be discovered without great difficulty in the narrative patterns of many, if not most, mainstream American feature films.

VII. A Model of Religio-Spiritual Development in the Symbols of Mass Media

Studies of the media audience have so far provided only small pieces of a model of the role of media in religio-spiritual growth. I would like now to take those pieces and fill out the gaps with various phenomenological analyses of religious conversion and profound religious experience where media is described as part of the experience. Some of the best evidence is in autobiographical accounts such as the one of Ignatius of Loyola, who describes the role of the imaginative symbols of St. Dominic and St. Francis that he found in reading popular religious books. The autobiography of Ignatius is particularly valuable because he gives us a detailed description of his life story before the experience, the crisis that forced him to rethink his life, how the symbols presented in some of the first mass media had a impact on his consciousness, how he debated within himself, his description of the mysterious influence of grace, how he finally came to a decision and then the unfolding throughout his lifetime of those symbols from the initial experience. In this account we are able to locate the "religious media experience" in a life story, taking advantage of the enormous biographical literature about Ignatius to fill out this description. It is evident that the combination of previous life searches, the popular religious culture of his time, but especially the imagery in the books he was reading influenced the imagery that Ignatius used in the *Spiritual Exercises* and in the conception of the religious order he founded. Here we can see that the symbolic imagery of the mass media was of great importance in the religious development of a person and in religious history.

Four clusters of factors are particularly important in such a model: (1) the social-psychological dynamics of the development of personalities; (2) the cultural context that provides the integrating symbols for developing a life story; (3) the role of crisis context and of symbolism in the central integrating experience of a life; and (4) the faith response of the person to the experience symbolized by paradox and parable in the moment of the central integrating experience and throughout a lifetime.

1. The Social-Psychological Dynamics

At the core of the personality is the "self-concept," my concept of who I am and how I am different from others, which develops from the first awareness of what I like and what I don't like, what is pleasurable and un-pleasurable – a concept of myself as an individual built up in no small part from the responses and reactions to me from persons around me.

A second dynamic element is the continual search for what I want to be, "my life meaning," in terms of the symbolic meanings that the culture puts before me and rewards or punishes me for selecting. This is a kind of mediating principle between my self-concept and the culture around me, a continual dialogue between what I feel deep down I like doing and what the culture makes available and possible for me. It is also a striving to-ward integrating the meaning of my life, an integration that the singleness of the self-concept demands in the face of the multiplicity of possibilities the culture offers.

A third dynamic element is the sense of the "given" of existence, limits that reality imposes, and the "musts" that seem built into existence. This produces a basic sense of reverence and awe for the reality that "we" have no real control over. This awareness of the structure of reality pro-vides the basic moral sense, the sense of "ought" in the dynamic of the personality. How I construct the meaning of my life, therefore, is not just a matter of total whim but has a set of "limits" and "musts" to it.

2. The Cultural Context

When I confront the culture to "select" symbols and meanings around which to organize the "story of my life," I do not just confront a random mass of interesting possibilities, but a highly integrated system of symbols – from history, literature, the science of the day, religion, everyday heroes, the economy, sports, and so forth – organized around the central "myth" of a particular culture. The organizing principle of the myth is the sense of origins and historical destiny that makes it worthwhile for this people to continue as a community. What lies outside the rationality constructed by this myth is considered foreign, strange, irrational, unnatural, inhuman and irreligious. Myths are backed by political power. As new expert knowledge comes into the realm of cultural myth, the myths must be reorganized. A completely consistent set of mythic meanings is always just beyond our grasp. According to many, the mass media are a central mechanism for con-tinually reorganizing our myths so that they "make sense" to all in the cul-ture.

Our great rituals of renewal are the means of dramatizing our myths and passing them on to another generation. Not surprisingly, myths present to all young people ideal role models and offer all sorts of rewards for these roles. Most of us tend to build our life stories around the cultural myth.

A second element in the cultural context is "popular culture," those aspects of the culture that form a "language and way of life common to all," the opposite of the esoteric specialized languages of the experts. This is the contrast between theology and popular religiosity. Where the myth presents the ideals we are striving for but may never quite attain, the popular culture presents the reality we live with – pragmatic, humorous, tender, earthy, disrespectful, quirky but lovable, disorganized, full of magic and fatalism, but also of celebration and human love.

A third essential element of our culture is the mass popular media that mediate between the myth and popular culture. They are "mass" because they are for everybody and because they recount stories that we all know and want to hear over and over again. They are "popular" because they are couched primarily in the language of popular culture. They are "media" because they are a text – that is, a story that has become formulaic and has become the property of the community, not just a particular author. The mass popular media tend to insinuate the myth into popular culture, but are always resisting, eluding and subverting the myth. They are an area of neverending negotiation between the myth and the popular culture.

3. The Context of Crisis and Central Integrating Symbols

Every person, in the effort to construct a life story in a relatively integrated fashion, comes to a time of choices. No one can do "everything." A person can simply choose what the myth offers and rewards, but our self-concept is never completely satisfied with that. Moreover, the myth is full of contradictions and, in spite of its continually rationalizing the irrationalities, the personalities organized around the dominant myths find themselves never quite together, or they find themselves torn between one world of myth that is in contradiction with another. Then there are the realities of the popular culture that are never quite in harmony with the myth. In the face of all of this confusion and contradiction, the ordinary person comes to the mass popular media with its stories that are trying to get it all together.

The mass popular media are some of the major sources of symbolic role models and symbolic meanings for integrating our life stories. In the stories and in the framed liminal space of popular fables, we can find heroes who are not the exalted gods of the myths, but the flawed human heroes of popular culture. Thus, the media present something of the myth, but also something humanly possible. Here we find solutions that are not "forever," but for the time being.[13] They also present a model of how we can negotiate meaning in our lives and get along the best way possible. Popular culture brings the analogical imagination that David Tracy speaks of into the reality of everyday life.

The important element is the symbol that integrates our lives because it represents the point of intersection between all the dynamic elements: the self-concept, the history of my life so far, the personal moral sense of "must," the current proposals of the myth, the popular culture and the mass popular media. With so many factors involved, most life choices are quite unique. But when is the formulation of this central integrating symbol likely to be religious?

4. The Relation to the Transcendent through Symbols of Paradox

Although many contemporary theologians stress that our relationship to God is sacramental, "in and through" the symbols revealing a transcendent reality, I prefer to look for the religious in the limit areas of human consciousness where the constructions of human rationality in myth end and the transcendent has an opportunity to express itself in the form of cultural symbols. The "kingdom" presented by Jesus in the Gospels is the classical affirmation of the aspirations for meaning embedded in the structures of reality. The kingdom is what all await, yet the kingdom is not of this world of myth.

This is the area where cultural myth is confronted with cultural paradox and parable, where we experience the inability of the myth to comprehend and express the transcendent. Paradox affirms that all of the human cultural aspirations to find ultimate meaning are quite moral and justifiable, but denies that meaning will be found within the limits of the cultural construction, especially in the rational construction of myth. This is a form of the classical theological *via negativa.*

Paradox and parable choose not an expert language, however, but the language of popular culture and mass popular media, in the ordinary stories and sayings of everyday life. The saying "unless the seed fall into the ground and die it shall not bring forth fruit" is the typical paradox that can only be responded to by faith. As Crossan argues in *The Dark Interval,*[14] parable affirms human aspirations for meaning in the beginning of a story like the parable of the Good Samaritan, but then reverses the outcome to suggest that the meaning of the Kingdom of God is not something that is produced by myth. The Good Samaritan appears on the scene – unpredictable, mysterious, like a miracle, so astounding in his overflowing goodness that we can only contemplate this in awe. Likewise the generosity of the father in the parable of the prodigal son is unpredictable in terms of the myth that says that this son should be punished – thus so mysterious and miraculous that we can only grow quiet with reverence.

These symbols of paradox and parable – the classical religious symbols not only in Christianity, but also in all great religions – open human desire to transcendence and call forth a leap of faith. In a sense one must cross the limit out of the bounds of rational myth to reach the source of this unbounded goodness and love that is symbolized in the Good Samaritan and in the father of the prodigal son. These symbols both affirm human aspirations and deny that they will be found in the culture.

A common element in the life stories of most people who have had rather strong integrating religious experiences is a crisis in life that has exposed contradictions or has introduced contradictions that open them up to "rethinking" the meaning of their lives. Often the crisis of meaning is the crisis of the cultural myth in one's life or a revelation of the contradictions of the myth. The crisis frees the person from belief in the power of the myth and, in a special way, opens the person to paradox and parable.

The questioning of the myth does not mean, however, that the person will have access to stories of parable and paradox. Some people in crisis simply go from one myth to the other. Oliver Stone in *Born on the Fourth of July* presents a character in crisis who leaves one myth, but takes up another. There is only a hint of a leap of "religious" faith.

Most of the great paradoxical symbols reveal such an unfathomable love and freedom that they transcend all myths and political utopias. They are so concrete and yet so connotative that they seem to respond to dissimilar people in different historical and cultural contexts. The religious classics such as the Gospels are normative, yet these symbols seem to come alive when they are translated into the contemporary popular culture. What would have happened if Ignatius had not, by chance, come across the books that were so influential in his life? He did not read the Bible, but rather popular lives of the saints and a popularized life of Christ. What provided food for his imagination was the imagery of Francis of Assisi and Dominic. For days, in his own reflections, he teetered back and forth between a choice of the myth of the Spanish culture, which had offered and still offered personal success, *and* the leap of faith.

Can we say that the symbols of Francis, Dominic and Jesus of Nazareth "caused" his conversion? Where does that leave God's spontaneous intervention and call to freedom for Ignatius? What about all of Ignatius's sociocultural context?

How does the person know that this leap of faith really leads to union with the transcendent? We can only know this in the unfolding of the paradoxical symbol in the life of the person. If, in every major decision that the person makes, the paradox and the parable become ever more apparent, we can be surer that the transcendent is present there. Ultimately, the person becomes a living paradox: a person that has nothing of the glory of the myth but is so resplendently beautiful, whole, loving and fulfilling of the meaning of human existence that we have to say, "This person is a miracle." This is usually what we say of the saints. They are living miracles that command our awe and reverence because we know that something holy is in our presence.

Endnotes

1. Willard Rowland, Jr., *The Politics of TV Violence: Policy Uses of Communication Research* (Newbury Park: Sage Publications, 1983), 92-99.

2. Joseph Klapper, *The Effects of Mass Communication* (New York: Free Press, 1960), 8.

3. Graeme Turner, *British Cultural Studies: An Introduction* (London: Routledge, 1992).

4. David Morley, *The "Nationwide" Audience* (London: British Film Institute, 1980).

5. Roger Silverstone, *The Message of Television: Myth and Narrative in Contemporary Culture* (London: Heineman, 1981).

6. Horace Newcomb and Robert S. Alley, *The Producer's Medium: Conversations with Creators of American TV* (New York: Oxford University Press, 1983).

7. Sonia M. Livingstone, *Making Sense of Television: The Psychology of Audience Interpretation* (Oxford: Pergamon, 1990).

8. David Morley, *Television, Audiences & Cultural Studies* (London: Routledge, 1992), 32-36.

9. Mary Ellen Brown, *Soap Opera and Women's Talk: The Pleasures of Resistance* (Thousand Oaks, CA: Sage Publications, 1994).

10. J. Martin-Barbero, *Communication, Culture and Hegemony: From the Media to the Mediations* (London: Sage Publications, 1993).

11. Steve Chapple and Reebee Garofalo, *Rock'n'Roll Is Here to Pay: The History and Politics of the Music Industry* (Chicago: Nelson Hall, 1977), 37.

12. Stewart M. Hoover, *Mass Media Religion: The Social Sources of the Electronic Church* (Newbury Park: Sage Publications, 1988).

13. Roger Silverstone in *The Message of Television* provides a clear differentiation between literature that touches on the more transcendental mythical level and the level of more popular "fairy tales." Film is a language closer to the mythical level while television is closer to the entertaining popular story.

14. John Dominic Crossan, *The Dark Interval: Towards a Theology of Story* (Sonoma: Polebridge, 1988).

13

A Methodology for Finding the Filmmaker's *Weltanschauung* in Religious Films

Johan G. Hahn

Several years ago I published a method for the analytical interpretation of audio-visual products.[1] It contains the methodological basis for theologians and philosophers to work with films and television programs on the very same academic level of exactness as they do with texts. Both theology and philosophy deal with the visible and the invisible world in which we live by reflecting upon our primary reality on the basis of mainly written cultural products, while reflection on films and television programs goes no further than a more or less general level of cultural reflection. More detailed theological and philosophical reflection on the reality and cultural space of our audio-visual heritage has scarcely begun. Only a few theologians and philosophers dare to discuss films, much less television programs, in the same detailed way they do the written text. Caftani©,[2] the Microsoft Windows© version of this method, is designed to solve this problem.

At the outset I addressed the fundamental question of the specific nature of an audio-visual product – film or television – and its difference from linguistic texts. This so-called "basic analysis" resulted in an overall "phenomenological view" as well as in five different fundamental views on the nature of the audio-visual product. Each of these five views leads me to a group of specific analytical tools.

The complexity of the audio-visual product[3] resulted in what can best be compared with a toolbox, containing all sorts of different instruments (called "modules"), each of which can be used to analyze different elements of the three basic aspects of the film (as of any work of art): form, content and function. By answering the analytical questions that are formulated in each module, the researcher can reveal the complexity of film. He can thus come to a deeper level of general and detailed understanding of a film's "dramatic form," its "iconic content," and its so-called "narrative cultural function." This leads to a coherent, synthesized researcher's view of film, grounded in analytical arguments and providing the basis for the researcher's interpretation of a film. Before getting into the principles of Caftani, however, I must explain some theoretical presuppositions of this project, as well as the basic principles of the subject we are dealing with – the specific nature of the audio-visual product.

I. Theory

1. Reception and Perception.

Sensual perception is the basis of all human knowledge. This means that all scientific insights, even from the domain of theological and philosophical reflection, are grounded in sensual perception. The use of more or less complicated technological and electronic devices only underlines the importance of sensual perception. In the process of developing a workable method for scientific research, the limitations of the possibilities of sensual perception have to be taken into account. By stressing the methodological importance of sensual perception for film and television analysis, I am implicitly stressing the centrality of the human being in the research process. The human viewer is the one who perceives the film and formulates the questions to put to it, and in the process chooses the most suitable and workable methods, by selecting composite elements out of a large methodological toolbox. The actual method in use – the concrete tool – has to be adapted to the specific questions of the research project and never vice versa. Whereas quantitative methodology uses standard procedures, qualitative methodology develops new or adapts existing instruments during the research process. Only then can a dynamic research process be developed in which the different elements – the question, the researching subject, the object under analysis, and the method of analysis – play an equal and mutually dependent role. Research then becomes a total, "holistic" process, instead of a "reductionist" endeavor. This is especially true when films are the objects of research because the film as a whole is more than the sum of its elements.

2. Perception, (Film) Theory and Film Analysis.

The possibility of perceiving a film depends on our ability to "see" and "hear," and to interpret correctly the impulses coming to us from the screen. Film analysis and interpretation is a methodologically grounded way of systematically perceiving audio-visual material and processing this perception according to given methodological rules. This very complicated relationship among the elements sketched above – question, interpreter, film, and method – must in any research report be made clear so that other parties are able to control the analytical and interpretive results. "Controllability" is, according to Alvin Gouldner, a central feature of scientifically sound research descriptions. This does not imply repeatability, inasmuch as changing situations make analytical repetition useless. It means, though, that a third party ought to be able to check the research process and the way in which given arguments and procedures are used. Only in this way can a scientifically sound dialogue between different interpretations of the same film take place. Even the assistance of complicated electronic instruments such as video recorders, computers, and so forth emphasizes the centrality of our eyes and ears in the scientific debate. It is my view, therefore, that film and television analysis can never be "dehumanized." Its results are always related to the person of the researcher.

Because film and television are at the very core of our culture, the "humanization" of this field of research seems evident. The development of Caftani is one step in that direction. The analytical interpretation of audio-visual material can bring us at last to the point where we can establish a theory of the audio-visual, more specifically a theory of the relation between *Weltanschauung* and the audio-visual. Any film, as a product of human activity, contains traces of the *Weltanschauung* of the maker. Caftani aims at finding these traces and making them part of a wider cultural theory about the value and place of audio-visual (secondary) reality in our dominant (primary) reality.

A theory is a set of interrelated options and visions that can be used to explain certain aspects of the reality in which we live. It is composed of synthesized details that come from the systematic observation and analysis of reality. Scientific theory is thus a result of methodic human perception. Methodology makes a theory scientific, which in turn means that a theory is neither "true" nor "false," just more or less "in line" with the given "facts" and their (subjective) perception. If a theory is correctly constructed – that is, if it is grounded on "correct" perceptions and according to the given "rules" of argumentation – then it is defensible. And if it adds culturally and socially relevant knowledge to the available knowledge of the moment, it is also valuable and usable.

So theory is never unquestionable; it can always be adapted or changed. It is flexible and depends on multiple factors such as the quality and the result of human perception, the actual sociocultural context, and so forth. As soon as a theory becomes dogmatic, hardened into law, it narrows our capability of perception (like rigid fundamentalist religious belief) and has fatal consequences for the development of human knowledge.

The scientific method presented here gives different opportunities to reflect in a self-critical way on the results of the research project. It is an open methodological system, which means that it is adaptable to concrete research situations, avoiding a frustrating theoretical *tour de force*. An "open methodological system" gives space to other methodological options and has a "democratic nature," whereas "closed methodological systems" are dictatorial in nature because they block other options out and often deny methodological debate. It should be clear that a humanistic methodology will never be found at the heart of a closed system.

Any new field of research has to define its specific "subject," develop its own "method" and build its own "theory" first. Insofar as these three basic elements are not analyzed and described in depth, the new field cannot be called independent. Since we regard "film and television studies" as an independent field of research, I shall focus my initial scientific efforts on the development of a reliable method of research in combination with the definition of the subject and the development of a film and television theory.

II. Caftani

Caftani builds upon a fundamental phenomenological analysis of the audio-visual product and stands in the tradition of Herbert Blumer's[4] "symbolic interactionism" and the "development of grounded theory," as described by Glaser and Strauss.[5] Both methodological strategies start with human perception and give way to an open methodological system for film and television studies. This means that neither the verification nor the rejection of any given hypothesis is the main goal of film and television studies, but the effort to develop a grounded theory of our audio-visual culture on the basis of a methodological "survey and control" of concrete audiovisual products

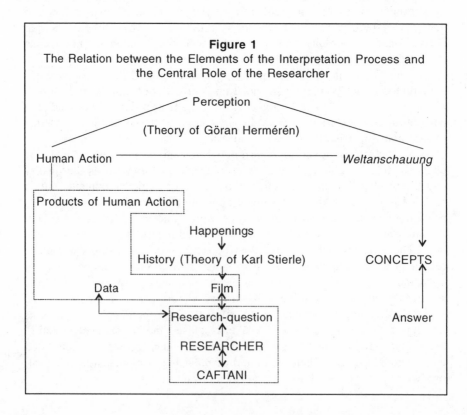

Figure 1
The Relation between the Elements of the Interpretation Process and
the Central Role of the Researcher

in the light of the research questions. The basic outline of the methodological principles of Caftani are given in Figure 1.

Grounded in methodological insights from different research areas, Caftani distinguishes six views on the nature of film. Most fundamental is, of course, the general "phenomenological view," in which film is regarded as a technologically produced cultural product of a highly complex and composed nature. It focuses the researcher's attention on all the composite details that are of any importance for a correct interpretation and gives a working definition of what film really "is." Out of this basic phenomenological view on film, we derive three more specific views (dramatological, iconological, and narratological) and two subviews (symbological and mythological).

The "dramatological view," which focuses mainly on the "form" of film, examines film as a complex, multileveled composition of formally dramatic human actions that can be analyzed with means adapted from the field of dramatology. I would stress here that the word "form" has no absolute meaning since it cannot be separated from its counterpart "content." The form of a film consists of those more or less technical elements that are independent of the content, but become meaningful only in relation to a certain content. The same form can shape different contents into different meanings, as the same bottle can contain several liquids; without the form (bottle), the content (liquid) has no shape. However clear it is that form and content cannot be separated, they have to be methodologically distinguished.

The "iconological view" regards film as an electronic icon, the provisional end-station of a neverending cultural development that started with the prehistoric cave paintings of Lascaux and Altamira and continues on up to High Definition Television today. From this viewpoint film is a moving two-dimensional picture, and we will focus here on its "content," without disregarding "form," with tools adapted partly from the field of iconology. A specific subview of the iconological is the "symbological view," which focuses on film as a complicated composition of interrelated symbols on different levels of symbolization.

The "narratological view" sees film as a composition in the narrative tradition of oral culture and analyzes it with tools derived from the field of narratology. Central to this view is the "cultural function" of film as narrated reality. A subview here is the "mythological view," in which film is seen as consisting of numerous ancient and modern myths that transport manifold cultural contents to the spectator.

1. The Phenomenological View – What Is Film?

The question fundamental to the construction of an analytical "toolbox" is this: What is the basic nature of film? The answer to this question is discovered by regarding film as it is presented to the spectator in as unbiased a manner as possible. Such a perception leads to certain insights.

Film is a two-dimensional picture, consisting of moving visible information in combination with audible information. On both its visible and audible levels, film shows recognizable, inseparable but analytically distinguishable elements of form, content and function in a triangular relationship. Four general aspects of "form" concern us: (1) "subjective movements," induced by factual and imaginary movements of the camera, (2) "pictorial frames," provided by the camera (focal length of the lens used) and/or the situation in the screening room (like dimensions of the screen and visibility), (3) "points of view," suggested by the position of the camera in relation to the objects shown, and (4) "duration," experienced in the length of the shot, through editing cuts (objective duration) or dramatic decisions by the director (subjective duration). Each of these formal elements will lead us to specific analytical questions. Similar distinctions can be made regarding sound, e.g., between synchronous and non-synchronous sound, natural and artificial sound, direct and indirect sound, music and spoken language.

The sum total of formal elements (see Figures 2a to 2c) gives the filmmaker an unlimited range of possibilities for shaping the content of his film. With them he will try to evoke in the spectator certain emotions. Using for instance a particular point of view or certain framing devices, he can focus the attention of the spectator. By his editing decisions, he can evoke relations between objects, build up suspense, suggest intimacy or distance, etc. It will be clear that the analysis of these basic principles is of utmost importance for the researcher who wants to come to a correct interpretation of the film.

a) The Recognizable Analogy. Regarding the "content" of the film, the first analytical question is whether the spectator is able to recognize a certain content element or not – because the perception of a film lies not only on a conscious level, but also and mostly on a subconscious level. Information will be consciously recognizable by the spectator only if there is a so-called "recognizable analogy" between the content of the film and something in the dominant reality of the spectator in its broadest sense. Since perceptions can be stored and remembered, perceptions from the past can be part of that reality and will influence the viewer's perception of a film. The "recognizable analogy" is a *conditio sine qua non* for the perception of all audio-visual information. Thus we have our first general clue to the discernment of "religious" film: only if there is a "recognizable analogy" between the film and a (previous) religious experience of the spectator, can a film be religious for him. On first view, therefore, a recognizable religious analogy can be found in profane films. Whether a spectator takes Superman, Batman or Terminator as "the savior of the world" depends to a certain extent on his religious (i.e., Christian) socialization.

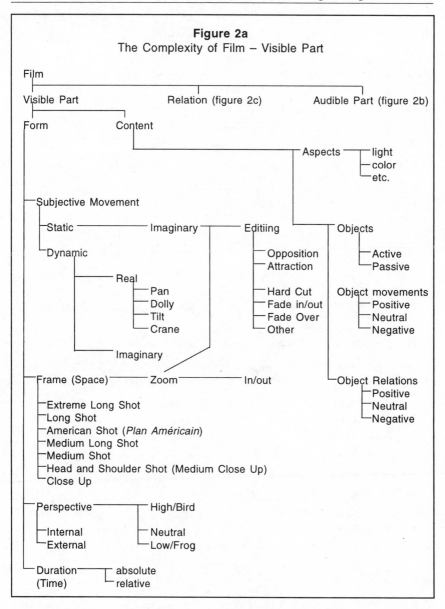

Figure 2a
The Complexity of Film – Visible Part

To establish a relation between the spectator and the film's characters, the filmmaker must try to construct "recognizable analogies" between
the content of his film and objects or experiences that the spectator already knows or has had, or that he can actively remember. Weird objects
or unfamiliar points of view, for instance, make recognition difficult. The
"recognizable analogy" allows us to "see" and experience any object or social situation as real, although we see only its audio-visual reproduction. If
we are familiar with something we see the filmic reproduction of (for in-

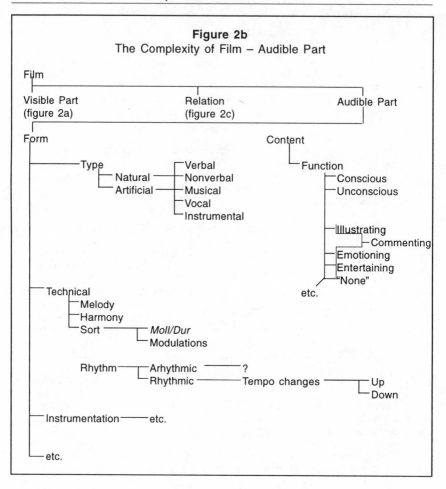

Figure 2b
The Complexity of Film – Audible Part

stance, a photograph of parents or a typical social situation), it can evoke emotions affiliated with our original experience. Here the analyst must be aware of the fact that most of our knowledge of the world depends on the information we have gathered during our lifelong process of socialization.

b) Only Objects in Film.

Film research, apart from considerations of "form," also has to deal with questions concerning the actual nature of the objects shown in the film, i.e., the film's content. Here we distinguish: (1) "shown objects," which can be either acting (active) or acted upon (passive); (2) "object movements," which can be either positive (directed toward another), neutral (parallel to one another) or negative (directed away from the other); and (3) "object relations," which can, on the basis of good arguments, be either positive (with mutual intentions), neutral (without clear intentions) or negative (without mutual intentions).

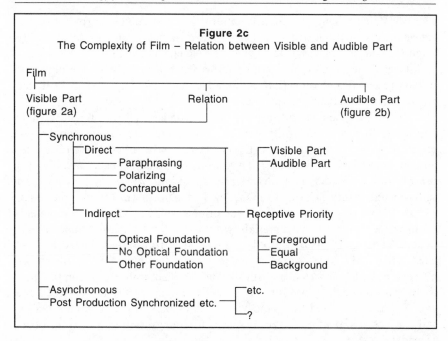

Figure 2c
The Complexity of Film – Relation between Visible and Audible Part

At this point it becomes evident that the borderline between pure analysis and interpretation is always vague. During the whole process of analytical interpretation, the researcher must be aware of the fact that he is looking for evidence, just as the detective looks for clues to solve a crime. In fact, the analytical interpretation of film can best be compared to the work of a detective collecting, analyzing, and interpreting evidence.

The phenomenological approach gives us the basic tools to analyze film from different points of view. Film is composed of individual, distinguishable elements and details. We can use the different views to focus our analysis on the details of (form) and within (content) the actual film. We do so in a step-by-step process that leads us through a series of analytical modules that have been developed within each of the five subdivisions of the phenomenological view. Inasmuch as Caftani is an "open system," the development of new modules remains a possibility for the user. The subdivisions of the phenomenological view in fact actively support further development of the system through the construction of new, tailor-made modules. The complex nature of film is illustrated in Figures 2a-2c.

b) Film: Representation of a Reality.

Film shows multiple levels of reality. As a two-dimensional reproduction of primary reality, it is to the viewer a part of his personal primary reality. In the meantime, in its audio-visual form, content and function, film is a representation of another absent reality, and thus it is a secondary reality. It also can contain symbolic representations that add another level of reality. An audio-visual product can in fact relate to at least four levels of reality (Figure 3), which the average viewer has never learned to distinguish. This multilevel dimension of film has, as far as I know, never been the object of serious research and reflection, although it plays an important role in the process of analysis and interpretation.

When we look at the primary and secondary levels of reality, it is important to stress that only primary (fundamental) reality can be approached by all our five senses. Every "lower" level of reality reduces the possible approach by our senses. Audio-visual reality appeals to only two senses: our eyes and ears. Practically speaking, we are not aware that audio-visual reality is of a different level of perception. On the one hand, we are strongly attuned to film's emotional impact. On the other hand, audio-visuals give us the materials with which we construct some of our images of primary reality. Both realities, therefore, are strongly interrelated. This looks like a paradox, but our everyday audio-visual life shows how we have learned to deal with it. Audio-visual reality is a combination of fiction and reality; we live emotionally on the borderline between the two. We have accepted the audio-visual sea as part of our dominant reality and adopted a sort of audio-visual survival strategy in the maelstrom of its secondary reality.

The professional audio-visual producer, managing a production-collective that cooperatively produces the audio-visual product under his artistic guidance, is very aware of this paradox and uses the emotional effects of the audio-visual material to influence the feelings of the viewer, as for instance big fund-raising programs like "Band-Aid," the American electronic churches, or the emotional effects of the film *Love Story* (1969) demonstrate. Only by a thorough analysis and interpretation can we at last understand the many possible ways these influences are working. It is the advantage of Caftani that it is not only usable for the analytical interpretation of films and television programs in relation to questions concerning *Weltanschauung*, but also that any question that can be answered by an analytically grounded interpretation can be dealt with.

d) The "Maker's Version" and the "Viewer's Version" of a Film.

With its double level of influence, film can under no circumstance be seen as a monolithic object. Although not directly influenced by postmodern theorists, I agree with their objections to monolithic interpretations of culture. Regarding the way we perceive our fundamental reality, we also perceive the audio-visual reality on the basis of all our former perceptions. Perceiving, being a constant process of learning, makes every viewer reconstruct the audio-visual material according to his or her own personal perceptive background: the viewer makes his or her own version of a film. Thus we have to differentiate between what I call the "maker's version" of

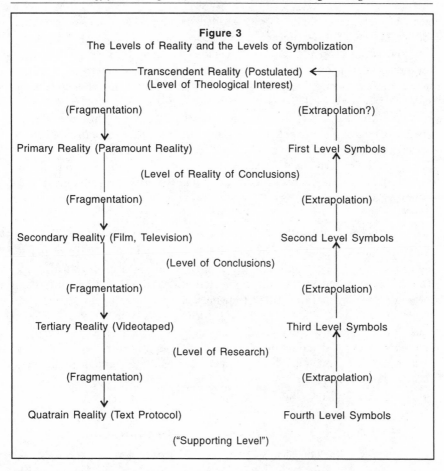

Figure 3
The Levels of Reality and the Levels of Symbolization

Transcendent Reality (Postulated)
(Level of Theological Interest)

(Fragmentation)   (Extrapolation?)

Primary Reality (Paramount Reality)   First Level Symbols

(Level of Reality of Conclusions)

(Fragmentation)   (Extrapolation)

Secondary Reality (Film, Television)   Second Level Symbols

(Level of Conclusions)

(Fragmentation)   (Extrapolation)

Tertiary Reality (Videotaped)   Third Level Symbols

(Level of Research)

(Fragmentation)   (Extrapolation)

Quatrain Reality (Text Protocol)   Fourth Level Symbols

("Supporting Level")

a film and the "viewer's version." Our interpretation of film is always the interpretation of our "viewer's version." Caftani gives us the tools to relate our viewer's version methodologically to the maker's version.

The analytical part of Caftani guarantees an optimal reference to the maker's version, whereas the viewer's version develops through the process of synthesis. On the other hand, the maker's version as such exists only as viewers' versions. Without the spectator a film does not really exist. So the maker's version as the product of the filmmaker stands in a paradoxical relationship with the viewer's version: it exists only by the grace of the viewer's version, but loses its existence from the very moment the viewer's film comes into being.

We can say, therefore, that if a film is seen by different people, they all reconstruct their own versions of the film they saw. The one maker's version of the film is mentally reconstructed into thousands, sometimes millions, of viewers' versions, which, though deriving from the same maker's version, differ one from another. The interpretation of a film consists of the reconstruction of what could more or less be called the "greatest common denominator" of the viewers' versions in a concrete sociocultural context. This reconstruction is based on film analytical arguments, derived from the film during the process of analysis. On the basis of analytical and interpretative arguments, a scientifically sound discussion even of different interpretations of the same film is possible. Different interpretations result from different interpreters, their different backgrounds and social-cultural contexts. Different interpretations can all be correct if they are based on sound and, therefore, discussable arguments. There is never "one and only one" interpretation as time goes by; everything is in the process of development, including the reception, the reconstruction of the viewing, and the analytical interpretation of a film.

2. Dramatological Principles – Film as Drama

Any analytical interpretation of a film takes its starting point from the insight that film is drama in one form or another, and it uses theatrical forms. The reality depicted in the film is by definition a dramatized reality. Even the most "documentary" kind of film must, by the very nature of the electronic production devices used, be regarded as drama in at least a general sense.[6] The camera "stages" reality and presents it as if it were acted out. The characters in front of the camera play roles, as they do in ordinary, camera-free life situations. Just as drama is constructed around its dramatic forms, the dramatological modules of film analysis focus primarily on the formal elements of the film:

D-1) Formal analysis: what formal type of film we are dealing with? This module is central to any comparative diachronic research.

D-2) Surface structural analysis: what is the inherent formal structure of the film? This structure is found in various formal criteria that have to be clearly defined.

D-3) Shot analysis: the determination of the smallest formal units (shots) of the film. What principles govern cutting and editing?

D-4) Program analysis: the determination of the boundaries of ultimate unity. What is the smallest combination of shots that yields an internal significance or sense? "Ultimate unity" cannot, like the "shot," be defined outside the film. It has only internal film boundaries.

D-5) Ultimate unit analysis: the analysis of the ultimate units determined in the previous module. What is their meaning? the significance of their relationship?

D-6) Point-of-view analysis: how did the filmmaker depict primary reality? What camera viewpoint did he or she take? What camera movements are used? What do these express?

D-7) Editing analysis: what relations between shots are established by the editing process? What relations between content-aspects are established? To what purpose? What does the relationship express?

D-8) Audible form analysis: what form did the filmmaker give its soundtrack? What is the sense of the sounds used?

3. Iconological Principles – Film as Icon

This principle, built on the iconological analysis of paintings developed by Erwin Panofsky and others,[7] takes the audio-visual product as an "icon," that is, as an object that represents another object on the basis of a general or precise resemblance between the two. The description of what actually can be seen and heard in the film is our main goal here. The iconological principles also focus on questions related to the different symbolic layers found in the film. Symbol here is understood as something perceptible that points to something nonperceptible. Film can be seen as a complex "total-symbol" containing numbers of other basic symbols, each of which has to be analyzed in itself and in its relation to the other levels of symbolization. The iconological and symbological modules are these:

I-1) Visible content analysis: what do we actually see? On the basis of "recognizable analogy," we can come to a description of the visual content of the film: (1) the "pre-iconographic description," or the basic level of identification of objects seen; (2) the "iconographic description," the level of the interrelationship and composition of the film's visual content; (3) the "iconographic interpretation," the level of the deeper (eventually symbolic) meaning of the film, as intended by the filmmaker; (4) the "iconological interpretation," or the ultimate cultural meaning of the complete picture, probably not consciously meant by the filmmaker.

This module is central to the whole method, even if other modules go deeper into elements discerned here. Frame-by-frame projection and multiple re-viewing will reveal details hidden from our first viewing.

I-2) Audible content analysis: what do we actually hear? All aspects of the soundtrack can be analyzed and described – dialogue, sound effects, music. A verbatim transcription of the film, a screenplay or the equivalent is often of great help, as is the assistance of a musicologist. The German computer program FILMPROT©, developed at the University of Marburg, can help construct such a film protocol.

I-3) In-depth structural analysis: the filmmaker's attempt to establish a strong internal cohesion among all elements of the film constitutes what I call the film's "credibility." How is this internal cohesion of the visual and aural material achieved?

I-4) Figure analysis: a description and analysis of all the characters (their external as well as internal aspects) that play a role in the film.

I-5) Interaction analysis: built on the results of the previous module, the interaction processes between all (central) figures are described and analyzed. How do these processes develop and to what purpose?

I-6) Setting analysis: in what settings, concrete as well as abstract, do the figures (I-4) develop?

I-7) Sound-picture relationship analysis: often films show a nonsynchronous gap between the visual and the aural information in the film. What is the relation between the two? and its significance?

I-8) Induction and recursion analysis: editing generates new meanings for materials otherwise meaningless in themselves. The "principle of induction" gives meaning to shots placed in a series. The "principle of recursion" makes us understand film as we "remember" meaningful details that come back later in the film. Induction and recursion make film what it is: a sensible pictorial-audible flow in time suggesting (primary) reality.

I-9) Rhetorical analysis: the power of a film results from its visual-aural rhetoric. How are rhetorical principles used in the film, and with what "effect"?

I-10.1) Formula analysis: the analysis of the filmic as well as cultural formulas used in a film.

I-10.2) Syndrome analysis: the analysis of the form-content constellations that characterize a specific film genre.

I-10.3) Editor's action analysis: if an editor has cut a film (e.g., to fit it into a television program slot), how and why was that done? What was added, what is missing?

I-11) Theme analysis: what is the theme of the film? Only films appealing to the same theme can be compared. For diachronic research projects, this module is as vital as module D-1.

S) The symbological module involves symbol analysis: a symbol is an object from our primary reality that refers to something in a reality that we cannot perceive with our senses. What symbols are used in a film and why? What do they refer to? How do they relate to one another?

4. Narratological Principles – Film as Story

In the "narratological view," film is a narrative. Culturally, the audio-visual media function as the great narrators of our time, and the actual situation in which they are presented can also be seen as a narrated situation. This central cultural function provides the scope for these narratological modules, derived from principles of narratology:

N-1) Storyline analysis: every film has a storyline along which the (manifest) story develops and which yields the (latent) "concept," transferred to the spectator. What is its storyline? its story?

N-2) Central/peripheral aspects analysis: how and why does the storyteller intermingle the story's central and peripheral aspects?

N-3) Narrator analysis: the "narrator/focalizer" can be in- or outside the story. The camera can be the storyteller or just the witness, a passer-by. Who is telling the story, and for what purpose of the filmmaker?

N-4) Narrated figures analysis: in the film (living as well as nonliving) figures are brought to life. What narrated figures do we meet in the film? How are they characterized? What are their roles? The analogy here is to module I-3, but the focus differs.

N-5) Context analysis: characters play their roles in a certain narrated context, which gives them shape and prominence (the figure/ground principle). How is the context narrated? The analogous relation here is to module I-5, but once again the focus of the research changes.

N-6) Conflict and tension analysis: any story develops around a conflict, with initial harmony/disruption/saving action/new harmony as standard stages. How is this done, and with what result?

Moreover, a narrative (i.e., a film) can be seen as a reproduction of the larger, general whole we call "history." Film is encoded "history," which means that "history" in film is restructured according to certain cultural "rules and regulations" that I call "concepts." "History" in turn is the encoded and restructured form that mankind gives to a larger whole, by nature diffuse and unstructured, called "events." Humanity reshapes these diffuse "happenings" into a concrete "history." By narrating this "history" in a structured way (i.e., through filmic means) and from a certain point of view, concrete "history" takes the shape of a narration, i.e., a film. Human structuring of actions gives meaning to the history.

This meaning can be placed within a wider context, derived from a set of general principles that the filmmaker consciously or unconsciously uses, the "concepts" (see Figure 1). These concepts lie at the basis of what I call the *"weltanschauliche* implications" that give the film its personal *weltanschauliche* color. In addition to "concept," I use the term "theme" to refer to the actual content of a film. The difference can be illustrated by an example: the "theme" of Akira Kurosawa's *Rashomon* (1950) is rape and murder, whereas the "concept" appeals to the fundamental question "what is truth?" The narratological modules try to trace evidence in a film that can lead to conclusions about its *weltanschauliche* implications. Central to this view is the assumption that myths are reproduced in films, that transport, construct, confirm, and induce cultural values.

M) The mythological module involves analysis of the film's myths. Myths are all those stories that tell about the real nature of things and how things became the way they are. Film and television constitute our modern cultural myths by explaining the extreme complexity of our reality, how things came into being. Although film and television tell myths, they are themselves mythological *means*. The mythological module analyzes the mythologizing function of the audio-visual media and traces the basic cultural myths these media tell us, deconstructing, so to speak, the way in which our reality is mythologized by the media.

Six characteristics of (audio-visual) myth play a central role in this module: (1) myth has narrative form, (2) it is bound to a cultural tradition, (3) its narrator is extremely motivated, (4) narrating a myth satisfies a passion, (5) myth is part of two separated and uncombinable realities it mediates between, and (6) it consists of a "sacred" story that is related to some (rudimentary, often no longer traceable, internal or external) "ritual."

Figure 4 shows an overview of the modules of Caftani© as they have thus far been explained.

III. Film and *Weltanschauung*

The six basic views allow the researcher to analyze any audio-visual product. But this analysis would be senseless without a concrete question. Although very different sorts of questions can be answered with the help of Caftani, generally speaking it is best suited for questions concerning the "concept" the filmmaker tried to suggest in his film. Although it may seem that only the narratological modules refer explicitly to the film's concept, it is important to stress here that all modules relate to it, inasmuch as a film is a composition of myriad details put together to express the filmmaker's concept as a kind of hidden message. The fundamental relation between a work of art and the details of it cannot, as the German theoretician Walter Benjamin has shown, be underestimated.[8]

The general word "concept" is related to the more specific word *Weltanschauung*, which refers to the way one looks at (*anschauen*) the world (*die Welt*), our primary reality. *Weltanschauung* refers to the complex and personal "knowledge system" that one uses to interpret reality, our frame of reference for understanding reality. Every individual sees the world in which he or she lives in a different way. The way in which we see reality is the basis for our "worldview" (*Weltanschauung*).

I define *Weltanschauung* as "the total of implicit and explicit presumptions, beliefs and general concepts concerning oneself, other human beings, nature, culture and the whole universe that give a more or less coherent explanation of the phenomena related to the primary reality of an

Figure 4
An Overview of Caftani©

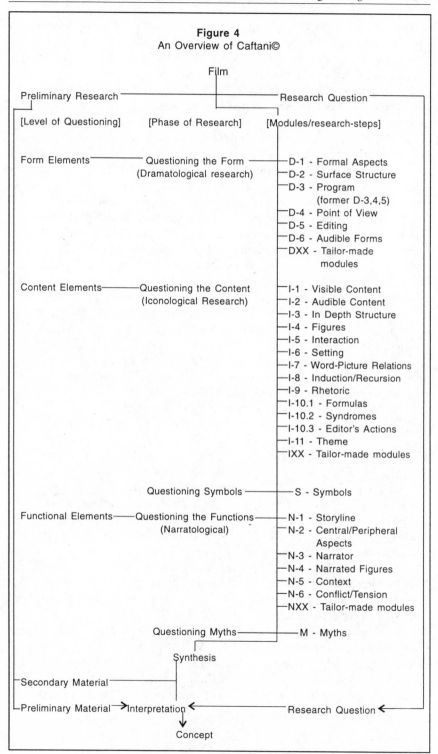

individual." It is a very complex partly-conscious, partly-unconscious knowledge system, the result of an ongoing adaptation process of socialization and resocialization. In my view the *Weltanschauung* of an individual structures the way in which he or she perceives reality and acts within it. If the actions result in cultural products, then the products contain the hidden sparks of the producer's *Weltanschauung*, especially if they are artistic products in which the maker implicitly and explicitly expresses much of his or her view of the world. Films are apart from other specific examples of creative products (see Figure 1).

Caftani makes it possible to bring these hidden sparks of *Weltanschauung* to daylight. For the study of *Weltanschauung* in film, the researchability of the audio-visual product is mandatory: The film has to be fixed on videotape to make repeated and often very detailed slow motion viewing possible; thus, the evanescent and constant audio-visual flow is translated into a nonevasive, interruptible, repeatable and therefore scientifically researchable flow of video frames. Moreover, any film analysis using a video version of a film must deal with the complicated problems concerning the extrapolation of the results of the analysis of a video-taped version to the level of the evanescent film or television product. In my opinion, this aspect of the theory is widely neglected in the analytical literature on film.

The way the *Weltanschauung* as a product of creative human action is found in a film is an open question whose answer is not simple because *Weltanschauung* normally does not take any visible shape. It comes into the film as wrapped in traces in minor details or implications (Latin *implicatio*, "wrap in") that have to be researched in depth to bring the traces to daylight. The Swedish art historian Göran Hermérén has shown that it is possible to analyze works of art and come to conclusions about the *Weltanschauung* of the painter. The same sorts of conclusions can be drawn by analyzing films with the tools of Caftani. The best way to do this, of course, is to go from the analysis of the film to the synthesis of the analytical results into an overall interpretation of the film. Whereas analysis attends to the details of the film, the synthesis puts the details together into a coherent overall view of the film.

Only methodological purity can guarantee argumentative correctness. The *Weltanschauung* of the researcher is not at stake, only the *Weltanschauung* of the artist filmmaker. In the process, of course, the *Weltanschauung* of the researcher can, but should not, interfere with the *Weltanschauung* hidden in the film. Only by giving a well-argued synthesis-interpretation on the basis of exact analytical data can a methodologically correct and controllable "*weltanschauliche* interpretation" of the audio-visual material be guaranteed. Caftani makes correct analysis, synthesis and interpretation of audio-visual material possible, as a number of high quality publications show.[9]

IV. Analysis and Synthesis

To use Caftani means to start always with the exact formulation of the question and a well-argued first selection of the tools (modules) necessary to answer it. As with any toolbox, not all tools are always in use. Caftani prescribes that the free selection of the tools to be used must always be clearly justified. The researcher will discover that the process of selection will develop as he proceeds with his research and that he has to add supplementary modules. Tools that are necessary, but not found in the toolbox, can be developed according to the general rules for the construction of Caftani. By going through Caftani's toolbox selectively and step by step, one can gather a complex, detailed knowledge of the film in relation to the question. The final synthesis and interpretation of all this material will at last lead to a methodologically-correct, question-related interpretation of the film.

The correct interpretation of a film is not an easy task. The often complicated and time-consuming work can be compared to that of text analytical research, inasmuch as a "close reading" also takes a lot of time and energy. Like a jigsaw puzzle, the bits and pieces representing all different views and subviews of aspects of the film have to be put together to reconstruct the film in its synthesized viewer's version. That is to say, after the process of deconstruction, of "analysis," comes the process of reconstruction, of "synthesis." When the synthesis is completed, the "research question" leads the interpretation to an answer.

Only then can the "preliminary" and "secondary" information be taken into account. "Preliminary information" was gathered in the preliminary Module VR, which was aimed at collecting all the analyst's first impressions and feelings about the film. With the help of a series of very concrete and personal questions, the analyst is invited to write a sort of personal viewing diary that he can use during the analysis-and-synthesis-process as a corrector for his biases. His first impressions function as the explication of his presumptions that can eventually negatively influence the interpretation of the film. Only after these presumptions have been explained does control over the results of the interpretation become possible. "Secondary information" is information from other sources about the film – the filmmaker, the genre, the country of origin, encyclopedia knowledge, and so forth.

This part of the research process sounds rather simple, yet it demands a great deal of discipline from the researcher. The results of his project depend entirely on the precision of his work. Only maximum conscientiousness can lead the researcher beyond the traps that line the way. Clean analysis is impossible; interpretation follows human perception, but the awareness of this can help the researcher constantly to purify his way.

The "greatest scientific sin on earth" is to neglect the weaknesses of a method and to use it dogmatically as an omnipotent tool. Such arrogance leads to dangerous "un-knowledge." It marginalizes science in our culture and ultimately destroys what men have created. Analysis and synthesis as aspects of Caftani are but means to dispel the fog that surrounds one of the most intriguing questions in cultural studies; namely, how do products of human activity reflect the *Weltanschauung* of their producers?

1. Analytical Interpretation: The Hermeneutic Spiral.

Caftani has much in common with biblical exegesis and general text analysis, especially its accent on the detail as the meaningful element. Without attention to even the minor details, no text analyst can come to a scientific result. Biblical exegesis has known this for centuries. The exegesis of film till now has lacked a usable method to deal with the same level of detail. Caftani fills that gap, starting with the assumption that any interpretation takes place within a hermeneutic process: details of a film can be understood only in relation to an understanding of the whole film, but the total film can be understood only through an understanding of all the details. This analytical interpretive movement, in which the details are reflected in relation to the totality, I call the "hermeneutic spiral." The term "spiral" is in my opinion preferable to "circle" because it emphasizes better the progressive and cumulative nature of the hermeneutic process. A spiral moves up to higher levels, whereas a circle is like a snake biting its own tail.

In the hermeneutic tradition, we acknowledge the fact that the analyzed text or film is part of a tradition, a sociocultural context, which the analytical interpretation takes into account. Caftani can be adapted to different contexts and still function as a useful toolbox; variety and adaptability are important characteristics of its openness. Open systems adapt themselves to changing research conditions – different researchers, other questions, or different types of objects. Change makes possible a better fit of the system to the researcher's question. Moreover, modularization makes it possible for the researcher to construct his own research process along the lines generally prescribed by basic scientific research and by Caftani in particular.

2. Some Fundamental Conditions.

Working with Caftani requires certain conditions for the researcher and his work if the project is to be successful and the results scientific. Because the question of the researcher is the central object-directed element in the research process, the importance of a correct, clear and short question is obvious.

The researcher must have the flexibility to incorporate different methodological modules in his research and to give these a proper, complete, and equal place in the totality of the project. He must also give proper attention to seemingly minor details in the material, which often provide the final clue to an interpretive solution, just as minor traces can lead the detective to the criminal. Often minor details that seem to have no meaning on their own gain central importance to the understanding of the "concept" of a film in proper combination with other minor details.

The researcher must work as a person of honor – be as unbiased as possible – to come to sound interpretations that can be defended "in the court of science," and thus to ensure the controllability of the process. The project must be reported in a way that makes review of it possible by other researchers (who may come to other conclusions!). Repetition does not mean imitation.

The researcher has to be open in his system of norms, values, and options (including his religious preferences) to the extent that these can negatively affect the "scientific" results of his work. He must explicate his personal vision of the film he is working on, again to maximize the controllability of the results. Any interpretation should be built upon a "positive relation" that the researcher has with the film; a film one detests can never be honestly interpreted.

Finally, working in an open methodological system claims openness toward all possible methods that can help toward greater knowledge – including other disciplines that can better explain aspects of a film. To choose this system is fundamentally a choice for a humanistic science in which man is the measure of knowledge rather than the physical reality he has created around himself.

3. Perspectives.

It becomes clear, moreover, that the choice of an analytical interpretation of film is a choice for a broad perspective of humanistic social and cultural studies. Only if we place man in the center of all sciences, including the so-called "exact sciences," will he disclose a new and human face. Humanistic science, even if it builds upon a religious or Christian philosophy, does not reduce human beings to the demeaning level of an operator of the buttons on electronic switchboards. It gives man centrality in the research process, allowing him his lawful place in the building of human knowledge. In my opinion, it is time to present human-centered alternatives to the reductionistic philosophies and methodologies in science. Mankind needs scientists who can function on the borderlines of different disciplines, accepting scientific knowledge as unified human knowledge and as leading to unified human wisdom. It is at once the weakness of all scientific work and its power. In its powerful weakness, science can build a humanized future.

Endnotes

1. Johan G. Hahn, *Het zout in de pap: Levensbeschouwing en televisie* (Hilversum: Gooi en Sticht, 1988). A German summary of the method was published as Johan G. Hahn, "Die Bedeutung des kleinsten Details: Bausteine zur analytischen interpretation sich bewegender Bilder," in Michael Kuhn, Johan G. Hahn and Henk Hoekstra, ed., *Hinter den Augen ein eigenes Bild: Film und Spiritualität* (Zürich: Benziger, 1991), 91-130.

2. CAFTANI© is the protected name of the Computer-Aided Film and Television Analysis and Interpretation Program that is currently under development.

3. I refer here to the audiovisual product as film, thus including television programs.

4. H. Blumer, *Symbolic Interactionism: Perspective and Method* (Englewood Cliffs: Prentice Hall, 1969).

5. A. Glaser and B. Strauss, *The Discovery of Grounded Theory: Strategies for Qualitative Research* (Chicago: Aldine, 1967).

6. E. Goffman, *Interaction Rituals: Essays on Face to Face Behavior* (New York: Anchor, 1967).

7. E. Panofsky, *Meaning in the Visual Arts* (New York: Doubleday, 1957); R. von Straten, *Inleiding in de Iconografie* (Muiderberg: Coutinho, 1985); E. Kaemmerling, ed., *Bildende Kunst als Zeichensysem I: Ikonographie und Ikonologie – Theorien, Entwicklung, Probleme* (Köln: Dumont, 1979).

8. Walter Benjamin, *Gesammelte Schriften* (Frankfurt/Main: Suhrkamp, 1972-89). See also S. Buck-Morss, *The Dialectics of Seeing: Walter Benjamin and the Arcades Project* (Cambridge: MIT Press, 1990), 2.

9. Els Speet, "Solaris: Het geheim van spiegels" (master's thesis, Catholic University, Amsterdam [KTUA], 1989); Michael Kuhn, "Hill Street Blues," (master's thesis, KTUA, 1989); Anne-Martha Becker, "Alle Wege führen zum Tod; Analyse des Films Der Bauch des Architecten (The Belly of the Architects) von Peter Greenaway," in *Aus Gleicher Leidenschaft*, ed. Z. Carigelli, J. Hahn, T. Henke, and M. Kuhn (Zurich: Benziger, 1993), 121-46; Dorothea Welle, "In Rendezvous mit der Geschichte verloren; Dialog zwischen *Der Bienerizüchter* ('*O Melissokomios*), von Theo Angelopoulos und Theologie," in *Aus Gleider Leiderschaft,* 147-96; Johan Hahn, "The Answer is Inside of the – Die virtuelle Realität von *Twin Peaks*," in *Aus Gleicher Leidenschaft.*

Part 6

Religious Film
in the Third World

14

India's Cinema:
Home and World, the Foci of Religion

Ray Kancharla

In India, the visual codes date back thousands of years. The cave paintings of Ajanta and Ellora, reflections of Buddhist monks – the creative sparks of never to be outmoded pieces of art in form and content – are from the sixth century B.C. There are further references to earlier visual codes in Central India (Madhya Pradesh), dating back to the tenth century B.C. They are indeed the archetypes of religious experience and individual meditation in pursuit of icons or images of communication and communion. The visual is an obsession with a point of view; the strength of the visual challenges a response and motivates life's activity.

From this earliest period in the history and experience of the image, we leap over several stages of human civilization to the time of the cinematic image. Ever since the cinematic image came to light, culminating in the experiments of the Lumière brothers, completing a process of evolution and invention, India has extensively integrated into its life this image culture. At the outset, one must say that the assessment of the creative effect this image culture of cinema has had on the social structures and cultures in India is questionable and negotiable. Cinema in India has, nonetheless, come to be an important medium in the lives of individuals and societies, of which the family is the basic model.

"The bulk of the Indian cinema is produced for the family," writes Gaston Robergé, who goes on to say:

> Film producers and exhibitors aim at obtaining a "U" (universal) certificate of exhibition for the largest possible audience. That audience often comprises family groups, or at least members of a family belonging to different age groups. The films they see portray stories that feature the family, usually the joint-family of grandparents, parents and children with their wives, and a number of uncles and aunts. Thus, the Indian Cinema is twice over a family cinema: it is a cinema of the family, for the family.[1]

Three important concerns dominate the understanding of the family in India:

237

1) *Samsaram sagaram* means "family is an ocean." The word *samsaram* stands for the "family" and the "world." It is also the subject of cinema in India. Family in India is the most visible nucleus of the society and the country. The family is a joint, interwoven network of relationships of kinship: kith and kin.

2) The word *legacy* qualifies the family. A family legacy is not merely an accumulation of material wealth and prosperity. It is a bodily whole of the genealogy of sons and daughters, grandchildren, grandparents and great-grandparents, uncles and aunts, symbolized as a "family tree." It is also an ensemble of relationships, spiritual values, family rituals and traditions upheld rigorously by everyone. These in their entirety form an unbreakable "sacred trust." From time immemorial, this view of family has been the common denominator of the eastern Semitic tradition (the Jewish-Hebrew family tradition) as well as of the Vedic philosophical and religious traditions of India.

3) A third concern is the question of *dharma*. The word *dharma* is defined as that which "sustains and ensures the progress of all." The expression "family *dharma*" is a derivative. A narrow meaning of *dharma* would be religion. At this juncture, the family is placed at the heart of the religious system.

Moreover, a four-tiered approach to family has evolved from the hierarchical structure of society. The four important stages in Indian family life are the following:

Stage 1: *Upanayana*, in which a male child is initiated into manhood.

Stage 2: *Brahmacharya*, in which a man lives the life of a bachelor, learning and practicing works that will bring him livelihood.

Stage 3: *Vivaha*, in which a man is married and embraces a family life.

Stage 4: *Vanaprastha*, in which a man and woman in their old age leave the property and entire household to their sons and retire into seclusion.

In all this, the focus is on the male. The woman is in the background as part of man – a system, obviously, that is essentially unequal and male-dominated. Supporting this hierarchical understanding of the family are the mythologies of *Ramayana* and *Mahabharata*, the great epics of the land. In recent times, these epics have dominated the life of the people. Many an Indian has taken an attitude of returning to a fundamentalist understanding of these epics, which have had their recognizable effects on the family in India, a majority Hindu society.

In this changing scenario, one can see the emergence of an intellectualism that has tried to reform and restructure the family and society. An intellectual such as Raja Rammohun Roy[2] in the preindependence era stands out as a pioneer in this regard. In addition, the humanism advocated by Rabindranath Tagore[3] through his numerous writings is a landmark in the evolving understanding of home and world from the Indian perspective. In more recent times, the dialogue over secularism has been pushed to the center stage of society.

From our perspective in the modern world, we can say that the family in the preindustrial era was composed of at least four generations: grandparents, parents, children and grandchildren. This exists in the rural sectors of India even today. The industrial era brought in a nuclear family where, for the most part, parents and unmarried children live together. In the new technological era, where communication and travel have made the world a global village with "microelectronics," "biotechnology" and "contraceptive technology,"[4] the configuration of the family has become even more diverse. Hence, today the family in India is a complex reality enhanced by the deep structure of specific cultural balances inherited through legacy and tradition.

I. Two Decades of Indian Cinema (1971-92): Family, Society, Values

Indian cinema is considered synonymous with Hindi cinema. It is unfortunate that regional cinema receives little or no attention. The three branches of Hindi cinema – mainstream cinema, which is the popular cinema; parallel cinema, also considered the New Wave cinema; and off-beat/middle-of-the-road efforts – have effectively been growing together recently, after suffering a hiatus of development in the eighties. My focus in this essay will be principally on popular cinema and New Wave cinema.

The journey that a creative director takes is by nature an undefined road. Mrinal Sen's *Bhuvan Shome* (1969) is the takeoff point for New Wave cinema. Of its newness, however, Satyajit Ray, the dean of Indian filmmakers, demurred. "The kind [of newness] looks a bit like its French counterpart," he commented, "but is essentially old-fashioned and Indian beneath its trendy habit."[5] Shyam Benegal has also excelled in issue-based narratives, typical of the New Wave, from his first film *Ankur* (*The Seedling*, 1974) on. The narrative structure employed by the New Wave filmmakers enabled them to portray a true-to-the-core picture of society. M. S. Sathyu and Govind Nihalani have also journeyed along these roads.

This first decade (1971-80) witnessed a remarkable change in filmmaking and introduced another film grammar and genre of narrative. While the narrative cinema of Shyam Benegal, Saeed Mirza and Govind Nihalani attempted to portray a realistic picture of society, the mainstream or popular cinema tended to glamorize such things as violence, smuggling and a rich lifestyle.

This period saw the healthy growth of New Wave cinema besides the emergence of new tides of popular cinema. The subject of "home and world" was explored in depth in the village, in the slum, in the town, and in the city. Additionally, the subject of woman in the family and the issues that confront life today, such as migration and modern culture, were portrayed creatively. The mainstream cinema, on the other hand, gave birth to new hero images glamorized under the banner of violent rebels in society and projected the images of a rich lifestyle as a value to be sought after.

In 1980, some remarkable family dramas appeared, covering a rich diversity of national life. A true landmark of the year was Govind Nihalani's *Aakrosh* (*Cry of the Wounded*), a hard-hitting film with innovative cinematic language that portrays the "culture of silence" through the story of a tribal family. One is left with a sense of wonder at the human person and with a feeling for the divine. Does God make all men and women his equal children, but some more equal than others, as the saying goes? Om Puri, the film's star, chilled audiences with his powerful though nearly wordless performance. *Aakrosh* was the first art film to become a commercial hit.

K. Balachander is another contemporary director who has made films reflecting the sociology of religion, adventurously proposing a revolutionary change of the traditional forms of life and outmoded values, patterns and beliefs of the people. His film *Akalirajyam* (*The Kingdom of Hunger*, 1980) is a good example of this approach.

In the following decade (1981-92), only a few of the 150 films made annually were successful. Rivers of blood flowed over the screens with a blend of vulgar songs to top the iceberg of stereotypical characters. However, Muzaffar Ali's *Umrao Jann* (1981), a quintessential courtesan film, was one of the surprise achievements of this decade in the New Wave cinema. Themes of love dominated the minds of filmmakers with a desire to provide a scenario where new ways of expressing love in the present-day modern culture invading the urban and semiurban population are pursued. Many popular films succeeded with young audiences and family viewers.

The mainstream cinema is presently undergoing a change. A new culture is emerging. It has deep effects on the way filmmakers address their viewers. In his dozen or so years of filmmaking with an equal number of films, the commercially successful director Mani Ratnam has made some noteworthy films, especially *Anjali* (a psychological treatment of the handicapped child) and *Roja* (a popular film successfully adapted into three languages). Mani believes in flexibility in handling form and structure, grounded in life-experience, rich in personal instinct, and designed for the eye of the average viewer – his triangular parameters. He proves that the commercial cinema need not be crude or harsh in color or texture to relate to the audience. A human interest story with strong emotional treatment and a sound cinematic craft will do the trick, bending the existing formula genre to the advantage of theme and cinematic technique. Soulful music becomes a central motif.

The pioneers of the New Wave are pushing the boundaries even further. Mrinal Sen in *Antareen* (*The Confined*, 1994) and Shyam Benegal in

Suraj Ka Satavan Ghoda (*Seventh Horse of the Sun*, 1993) have deliberately departed from the narrative style of storytelling. Both are deeply in search of an incarnation of the concept of "total cinema," i.e., form that fits the content. The Polish director Krzysztof Kieslowski's treatment of the language of cinema in his *Trois Couleurs* trilogy – *Blue*, *White*, and *Red* – is of vital importance in understanding this new image of cinema. In *Antareen*, it is the recluse poet, a woman and the telephone that lead one from fantasy to reality, moved by circumstances. The process of introspection is the underlying theme. R. Tagore's story *Khudita Pasha* (*Hungry Stones*) was Sen's inspiration, functioning as the film's backdrop. *Suraj Ka Satavan Ghoda* is structured like an onion. It is based on a powerful novel by Dharam Bharati, through which Benegal seeks a new genre of cinematic communication. The protagonist is the storyteller whose relationships in varying degrees with his wife and others form the main substance of the story. "The beauty of the film lies in what our narrator does not reveal. Every now and then he peels a layer of the onion that reflects himself. It is not that he lies. It is just that he does not want to reveal the entire truth, in the way he chooses to tell the story,"[6] Ajit Dwara observes.

II. The Films of Satyajit Ray

Inasmuch as, worldwide, the name Satyajit Ray is almost synonymous with Indian cinema, it would no doubt help to set in perspective our assessment of current trends in treating religious themes focused on the family if we review the centrality of "home and world" in his films. "Home and world" are indeed the foci of religion in India.

The subject of "home and world" permeates the thirty-five films of Satyajit Ray. His *Apu Trilogy* (1955-59) is an existential exposé of life in the village in its simplicity and subtlety. In the first film, *Pather Panchali* (*Song of the Road*, 1955), Ray proposes the paradigm of struggle in an impoverished rural family, and closes with migration to the city as the only alternative left for the brahmin Harihar, who is seeking a better living through his priestly duties. The promised land is the temple city of Benares. In *Aparajito* (*The Unvanquished*, 1956), the family situation actually deteriorates. Harihar dies, leaving his wife and their young son, Apu, destitute. After being initiated into the priesthood in the steps of his father, the unhappy Apu leaves his estranged mother for school in Calcutta. Although they are eventually reconciled, his mother dies while Apu is away at school, and he returns home to find no traces of her left. He stands alone in the world as the only survivor of the family, leaving home for the last time to pick up the threads of his new life.

Apur Sansar (*The World of Apu*, 1959), the conclusion of the trilogy, finds Apu back in Calcutta, struggling to meet his obligations while facing a multiplicity of choices. His world of hope collapses when Aparna, his young wife whom he loves dearly, dies giving birth to their first child. Apu stands defeated and shattered. In his twenty-five to thirty years of life, he is a witness to five deaths in the family and a victim of disappointments and disillusionment. How can one transcend death? All of Apu's five closest relatives who have died – the elderly aunt, his sister, his father and mother, and his young wife – simply cease to be. The only legacy of the family at this point is the memory of the dear dead ones whose visible marks are seen in the face of Apu. If death is the dominant experience of his family, hope is implicitly modulated by the ambivalent desire to go on. Grief-stricken, Apu is at first unable to care for the child whom he blames for Aparna's death. But when he finally breaks out of his prison of despair into the light of hope, he must – and does – win his son back.

Although Ray used two novels of Bibhuti Bhushan Bannerjee as his source for communicating his artistic vision in the trilogy, the story of *Apur Sansar* conveys in large part his own feelings about life. As critics Shampa Banerjee and Anil Srivastava note, "*Apur Sansar* has neither the documentary realism and epic dimension of Ray's first film, nor the camouflaged intensity and personalized impact of his second. In many ways it is a far simpler story [than the first two films], presented with greater technical ease, with an archetypal Bengali romantic as its protagonist."[7]

The theme of "home and world" continues to dominate his works from the Apu trilogy through to the period of his prolonged illness. During this time, Ray delved into the works of Bengali literature in order to express his artistic vision, as Pritiman Sarkar reports.[8] His film *Ghare Baire* (*The Home and the World*, 1984), based on a novel by Tagore, opens a new treatise on the family in modern and postmodern culture. As Ray himself has reported, the offer of doing *Ghare Baire* was made to him during his studies in England, which he had to end prematurely. A clear shift is perceivable in the period after his illness. Though he could not make films for five long years, he kept writing and gave himself more time for contemplation. During this time the only film he made was a documentary on his father, *Sukumar Ray* (1987). His illness imposed a limitation on his style of filmmaking. Most of his work had to be indoors. Sarkar explains the effect of illness on Ray's creativity:

> His illness also sharpened his sensitivity to his surroundings. So it is natural that he would not be satisfied with making films of stories written by others which might not satisfy his new requirement of comparative stasis. That is why, with his heightened sensitivity and his contemplative mood, the requirement of a different type of script and story, he declared that he would be making films from his material only.[9]

Due to the constraints of the situation he found himself in, Ray's last three films possess an uneven quality of production. *Ganashatru* (*An Enemy of the People*, 1989), an adaptation of Ibsen's socially-conscious melodrama (despite Ray's protestations to the contrary), seems somewhat tentative. *Sakha Prasakha* (*The Branches of the Tree*, 1990) exudes greater assurance, and *Agantuk* (*The Stranger*, 1991) takes on a strange mystic magical quality. It is said, "Ray transcends Ray" in his last films, given the fact that these films convey their concern for the human condition; their exposure of a corrupt, closed, polluted, strife-torn technological society and its quest for truth, beauty and magic touches us in the innermost core of our being and transforms us forever with their feeling for eternity. The latter two films, *Sakha Prasakha* and *Agantuk*, the last film before his death, have shown a new Ray, whose vision of contemporary family in modern and postmodern India reaches perfection.

In *Sakha Prasakha* (1990), Anand Majumdar, the principal character of the film, is the father of four sons. He started his career as a junior officer of a factory and advanced in life through hard work. "Work is worship" and "honesty is the best policy" formed the mottoes of his life. Anand enjoyed the affection of the people of the township of Mico. In fact, the township is renamed after him as Anand Nagar.

As the story unfolds, Anand lives with his second son, Prashanto, at one time a brilliant and promising young man, now an invalid, due to an unfortunate accident while he was studying in England. Prashanto's love for western music is noteworthy. On Anand's 70th birthday, the people of the town come to celebrate with him, during which time he suffers a heart attack. His three sons come to see him: the eldest son with his wife, the second son with his wife and son; and the youngest of the family who is not married yet. The home is now a home and a hospital, and a place for the world coming to be revealed.

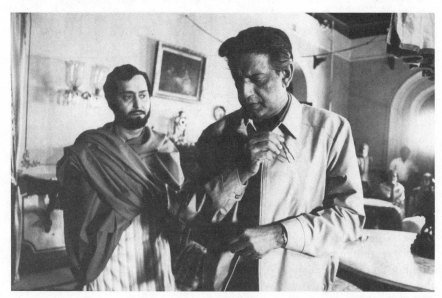

The Home and the World, Satyajit Ray, 1984

A major part of the film transpires in the inner rooms of the house and at the dining room table. Here, slowly, the corrupt practices of the married sons are revealed. They have good positions in society because of their ill-gotten wealth, and they begin to accuse one another about it. The youngest son has rebelled against corruption and has given up his job in search of a creative vocation in the theater. The good relationship between him and his older brother's wife has become a cause of suspicion to his brother. Serene in the belief that his sons have established themselves through their honesty, Anand gets a jolt when he learns about their corrupt practices through the rumblings of the child Dingo.

One goes through a claustrophobic experience during the major part of the film that take place in the house. The most relaxing scene is the picnic that the three visiting sons, their wives and Dingo go on. This had been the traditional family picnic spot. It is here that they are able to open up and reorient themselves amicably to one another. In the entire story, we know nothing about the mother and her role. During the time when the other brothers are at home, Prashanto does not enter his father's room, however intense his love for him may be. The opening of the film, in the long conversation between Anand and Prashanto, reveals the background of their relationship.

Ray has clearly portrayed the relationships of the sons and their wives to the father. The married sons are genuinely estranged from their father, while their wives have drawn close to him. The youngest son is journeying out of his inner darkness, while Prashanto's darkness within is suffused by the flow of intense love for the father and his love for western music. The finale leaves us with the experience of unanswered questions. Anand lies serene and waits, not knowing the terrible moment of revelation to come, only to be soothed by the presence of Prashanto, whose hand rests on his father's chest.

Satyajit Ray's last film – *Agantuk* – tests the time-honored assumption that blood is thicker than water. The story, set in Calcutta, is about the homecoming of a thirty-five-year-old wanderer. Has he come to get a legacy, or to give one? How metaphorically autobiographical is Ray being, one wonders, in his farewell film?

In *Agantuk*, Ray establishes the contradictions present in modern society, using sharp contrasts. Modern civilization is built on a misunderstanding of the past. Mitra, the principal character, remains friendly to the past by his deep attachment to the tribal wisdom and customs of that world. He is sensitive to its aesthetic and innocent originality. As such he remains a friend of his grand-nephew Satyaki. A critic of modern civilization is provided at a high point of the film by Mitra in the presence of Prithviraj, the antagonist, as well as of Bose and Anila. The main family meeting hall is its venue. Mitra alludes to the annihilation of the lives of the young by drugs and the destruction of cities through technology. Where does the future lie? Genuine love and pretence contemptuously coexist and are revealed through confrontations. Suspicion and certitude are constantly interactive in the entire ambience of the film.

Prithviraj is a sign of the human arrogance of knowledge, an essential by-product of the pride of technology and an assumed "I know it all" standpoint. The song of love by Tagore, sung by Anila, precedes the discussion of *dharma* and the future life of the world. *Dharma* is understood by different participants at various levels of meaning. It is strictly a religious practice bound by rituals for Prithviraj, but for Mitra it is that "which ensures the peace and unity of all."

In *Agantuk*, Ray proposes a sharp critique of postmodern family life and a theology (an understanding of God) reflected from the grassroots, present in the hearts of people who keep the spark of love alive despite the engulfing winds of human arrogance. The attitudes of Anila and Bose toward Mitra reflect this. Anila has gently articulated their growing distances from one another and her growing nearness to Mitra, her uncle. Satyajit Ray and Rabindranath Tagore, the filmmaker and the poet, are in creative unity. The words of Tagore have taken on visible flesh and blood here, in their journey towards transcendence:

> We can never go beyond man in all that we know and feel. Man must always be a music-maker and dreamer of dreams. He must never lose, in his material quests, his longing for the touch of the divine. Today, all barriers are down and the God of humanity has arrived at the gates of the ruined temple of the tribe.[10]

Mitra, the protagonist, articulates this in his dialogue before the tribal dance starts. "There is no more to say, there is only fresh air to breathe." Then the sound of a drum is heard and the scene of the tribal dance opens. Family is the transparency of the hearts of relatives. When semiurban families live by peaceful coexistence alone, the parameters of relationships measure only material attachment. Only the heart of the relative rightly sees the truth about love. This is rewarded dearly: the legacy of a family lies in this truth.

III. Two Other Special Films

Experience of film in India is still primarily, as we have said, a family event. Films seen by family members motivate them to expose their beliefs practiced through the generations, and to dialogue about the changing situation of their faith and their social values. There is a particular genre of film that could be called the family genre, and A. K. Vishwanaath is especially associated with it. In his quarter century of filmmaking, he has never forgotten what seems to be his cardinal principle: a film that cannot be watched by the whole family – where three generations are seated together – is not worth making.

His film *Swathi Muthyam* (*Precious Diamond*, 1984) is the story of a family, rooted in a rural family religious tradition, that asks the question whether marriages are made in heaven or are the result of one's environment. And even if the film cannot preserve a vision of the family that he makes his films for – in order to be true to reality – it is nonetheless a film to be seen by the traditional three-generation group.

Lalitha, a rich woman whose husband dies very shortly after their marriage, leaving her a son, is rejected by her father-in-law and harassed by her sister-in-law. Befriended by Sivaiah, a young semi-invalid whose devout mother attends to the cleanliness of the temple premises, Lalitha finds a protector for herself and her child. Sivaiah's day consists in helping his mother clean the temple steps, playing Ek Tara (a single-stringed musical instrument), and finding occasions to do good to others. His mother looks after his physical needs and instructs him in goodness from the lives of Lord Rama and Sita, his wife.

In Lalitha's presence, his voice awakens to new heights of music, a symbol of mutual flowering, as she feels drawn towards him too. In their earlier meetings, they sang a song that reflects the future chart of their life. Then, during the nine days of the Sri Ram Festival, he ties the Thali (from the principal marriage ceremony in rural India) around Lalitha's neck, as a mark of being her protector. After his mother's death, Sivaiah and Lalitha live a penurious but happy life in the temple precincts.

The nuclear family of grandparents, parents and children, living under the same roof, is already breaking up. Essentially, family is centered around the religio-cultural experience, situated in a group of diverse families. A believer is protected by his God through good works. The innocent and weak, especially women, suffer in life, yet receive their satisfaction. Genuine love surpasses all barriers, religious and sectarian, and seeks communion for people with their *sitz-im-leben*.

In *Swathi Muthyam*, Vishwanaath has vigorously blended reality and fantasy in the character of Sivaiah. The key questions raised are: Is this true? Is this real? Are love and life like this? The dialogue of the viewer begins here. Subtly and slowly, the film harps upon the truth that an average family is buried in the humdrum existence of everyday life, and it is thus emptied of the essence of family life, which is love. The poor carry a joyous smile on their faces in the worst of life's situations. They are a sign of the life to be revealed.

Vishwanaath, who falls into the category of regional filmmakers who unfortunately receive little or no attention in the all-encompassing world of Hindi cinema (equated with Indian cinema), has devoted a lifetime to making family films in the Telugu language, the third most widely-spoken Indian language. Like the films of Ray in Bengal, Vishwanaath's films have a remarkable popularity and draw incredibly large audiences of all ages. Music of every form – so central to his films – can help human beings to arrive at innermost unity and, at the same time, liberate them from the divisive structures upheld by the societies. His masterpiece is perhaps *Sankarabharanam* (*The Jewel of Shiva*, 1979), certainly a landmark in his own way of filmmaking, in terms of its concern for human culture and the crisis in civilization. In his later films, one sees a new concern for the neglected arts that play a role in shaping society and a greater need to recreate a society free from enslaving systems.

The other special film, from a religious point of view, is Rajkumar Santoshi's *Damini* (*Truth*, 1992). *Damini* (the name of the film's main character) presents another picture of contemporary Indian society. That the administration of justice by the courts of law provided to the weak and marginalized is inadequate is the film's crucial theme. Damini, who comes from an economically poor family, is put under house arrest by her wealthy husband, for fear that she will divulge the identity of his brother, as the man who raped their maidservant. Despite threats, she tells the truth, and her brother-in-law is convicted. People recognize Damini as the ideal Indian woman and joyously celebrate her courage.

Damini tackles one of the burning social issues that affects more than half of humanity. The attitude of law and justice to sexually-assaulted women and the data related to them are more than alarming. In 1992, the statistics showed that roughly thirty women are raped every day. The definition of rape and consent is unclear under the law, often treating the woman as the accused. The woman's agony is intensified by the insensitivity and sexist bias of the legal system. *Damini* highlights the problem but remains unrealistic about the way the solution is found.

Santoshi exposes the corruption prevalent in society, in simple yet clear terms. The absence of a hero in this film is striking; individually, a woman is seen as a weak and vulnerable person. Yet, the persistent effort of Damini, the main protagonist, and the potent image of a woman capable of "changing" things are clearly portrayed, while men remain idealists or contributors, but mostly continue the system as it is – with no actual change.[11] The crux of the story of Damini, addressing every active viewer, can be summed up in this aphorism: "The point is not to pocket the truth, but to chase it."

IV. Conclusion

Indian cinema continues to sing. The song in cinema is the instrument that achieves for the viewer the artistic conversion of fact into fiction, of the present tense of the camera eye into the past and the future of the audience's sensibility. Somehow it becomes the transcendental element in the language of the popular cinema. A song in the rural folk tradition lives as a cultural tool for expressing and explaining to people the gospel of their lives, the truths of the individual's life in relation to the society and the universe – besides, of course, providing cinema's aural enchantment.

The medium of song in Indian cinema is the way the filmmaker expresses the inexpressible. And the manner in which the song is treated reinforces the film's power to ignore the demands of realism. Song is like divine speech, a theological articulation, an expression of faith in life and humanity as well as in God.

Endnotes

1. Gaston Robergé, *The Ways of Film Studies* (New Delhi: Ajanta Publications, 1992), 185.

2. Raja Rammohun Roy was a Bengali who pioneered the revival of Hindu society. "The founder of Brahmoism and, for virtually all historians, the founder of modern India, [he] was particularly attracted to Unitarianism's social gospel" (Ben Nyce, *Satyajit Ray: A Study of His Films* [New York: Praeger, 1988], 60).

3. Rabindranath Tagore was a Bengali poet (1861-1941) whose illustrious work *Gitanjali* won him a Nobel Prize (1913).

4. Robergé, 185.

5. As quoted in Sumita S. Chakravarty, *National Identity in Indian Popular Cinema, 1947-1987* (Austin: University of Texas Press, 1993), 244.

6. Ajit Dwara, "The Story of the Shadows," *Illustrated Weekly of India*, June 12-18, 1993, 6.

7. Shampa Banerjee and Anil Srivastava, *One Hundred Indian Feature Films: An Annotated Filmography* (New York: Garland, 1988), 36.

8. Pritiman Sarkar, "Satyajit Ray's Third Trilogy," *Deep Focus* 5 (1993), 32 ff.

9. *Ibid.*

10. R. Tagore, *The Religion of Man* (London: Allen, Unwin, 1963), 64.

11. Rohit Brijnath, "The Second Rape," *India Today*, February 15, 1994, 120-25.

15

The Religious Film in Latin America

José Tavares de Barros

This essay about the religious film in Latin America has an evident similarity with its companion pieces coming from Asia and Africa. Each serves a "particular" purpose in the totality of studies, proposals and opinions expressed in these essays about the "general" theme of cinema and spirituality.

Questions about the concept, the anthropological dimensions, and the theological aspect of the so-called "religious film" will not be raised here, since these ideas have been sufficiently and deeply studied by other contributors to this volume. Rather, I shall focus on the theme of the religious presence in certain historical periods of the Latin America cinema, seeking to interpret its function starting from the broader relation between cinema and society in the so-called Third World countries.

I. Film Expression of a Particular Cosmic Vision

Jorge Sanguinez, the most famous Bolivian filmmaker, states that the creators of the "close-up" – from the transparent communication of David Wark Griffith to the dialectic experimentation of Sergei Eisenstein – are linked to the occidental Hellenic-Christian culture and are descended from Aristotle, Homer and Esquilo: "They opened their eyes to a world dominated by the idea of a human-god. They adopted individualism as the axis and aspiration of their lives."[1]

Sanguinez means that the individual and the particular take on an exceptional connotation in the Western world. Based on its own foundations, this dominant culture is opposed to the telluric and universal dimension that characterizes the wide vision of the Bolivian people, especially those living in the heights of the Andean mountains. Due to his choice of continuous filming (the *plan séquence* or sequence shot) as an alternative to the "close-up" for capturing more precisely the life of the Aymara culture, we can say that Sanguinez replaces the concept of the human-god with that of the nature-god. Consequently, he develops a type of cinema prepared more accurately to represent the customs, the rituals, the relation be-

tween life and death – that is, all the transcendent dimensions – that constitute the sum of everyday existence of his people. When we link the narrative options of his films to the expressive Bolivian culture, autonomous
and particular – in which transcendent values are privileged – Sanguinez
becomes at the same time a genuine *auteur* and the creator of a truly religious filmography.

II. Latin America: A Dominated Cinema

The Latin American cinema, in its origins, could not escape the connotation
of underdeveloped production imposed by the film industry of the developed countries. After some small-scale local, independent film production
emerging in the beginning of the twentieth century in some countries – especially Argentina, Brazil and Mexico – it coexisted with the dominant distribution of foreign films from Europe and the United States. In the absence
of European films due to the first World War, an increasing domination by
Hollywood emerged. Unable to keep pace with the technological developments in cinema production, particularly after the advent of sound, and
dimmed by the strong marketing of films "Made in the U.S.A.," Latin
American cinema production was suffocated.

Surprisingly, as the critic Paulo Emilio Sales Gomes observes about
Brazilian films, the domestic cinema always had to beg for its exhibition
space, as if the filmmakers were foreigners in their own land. The situation was the same in other Latin American countries. It is widely observed that the "gringos" won spectators from Mexico to Tierra del Fuego,
thus imposing the inclination toward identifying the American films as the
tout court movies. Facing the uncertainty of available technical and human
resources, heroic filmmakers were trying to escape the image of penury by
imitating the fashionable North American model.[2] This happened at the
high point of the silent movie era, but it became harder with the advent of
sound movies at the end of the 1920s. In order to overcome the language
barrier, Hollywood experimented with Spanish versions of important films
such as the famous *Dracula* (1930) by Tod Browning. Very soon the com-
promise of subtitled films prevailed, autocratically imposed on a public
with a significant rate of illiteracy. Alternatives to this prevailing situation
were provided by some isolated filmmakers through the production of
modest films, generally based on the popularity of comic actors coming
from radio and theater, and later from television. But conscious opposition
to foreign domination of the market would happen only through a collective movement emerging in the early 1960s, which made possible other
projects and innovations regarding language and content.

III. Religion in Latin America

Not only the people of the Andes but those of other sectors too looked to protagonists in many countries of the continent who presented new approaches to a traditional view of Christianity, based specifically on the discussions opened up by postmodernism. Maria Clara Berminger, a Brazilian Catholic theologian, says that the movements in favor of the black minorities, the women's rights movement, and the defense of popular cultures (in some countries, the Indian cultures) represent "the essence of historic Christianity, questioning its remarkable male configuration of thought and organized on the model of European society, white and developed."[3] Ecology also, says Berminger, questions the anthropocentric dimensions of modern Christianity and makes possible a broad reflection on the totality of creation, emphasizing other aspects of the Christian worldview, not just its anthropological aspect.

In spite of its coincidence in many ways with the origins of the so-called "theology of liberation," this new experience of religion in many countries of the continent, based at the same time on both the individual and the collective, presents itself in a natural and spontaneous way as a condition of the spirit. Through this religious sensibility in which both the social components and the emotional dimensions are extremely relevant, insists Berminger, it can be said that the quest for God becomes part of daily life. In other words, this new spiritual condition does not favor the forms of intellectual elaboration, conscious and organized, that generally show an inclination toward establishing a gap between the appeals of the transcendent and the material struggle for survival. It is from this complex framework that an objective and consistent approach to the religious cinema in Latin America must be constructed.

IV. Forms of "Pious" Cinema

"Pious" cinema refers to a literal view of religion that was introduced in Latin American cultures at the very time that the invention of Edison and the Lumière brothers became popular in urban centers at the end of the last century. In most cases, the religious themes suggest an acknowledged commercial and financial resource. When evangelization is considered, the good intentions of the producers are generally a mixture of evident naivete and a low level of professional quality. "Pious" cinema is divided into two groups. The first is constituted by reports of and short documentaries about religious events involving pilgrimages and other types of mass population concentrations. The other is made up of fictional stories about the lives of saints and similar subjects.

In the category of religious documentaries, we can mention by way of example, considering only the time of silent movies, ten consecutive versions, produced from 1897 through 1930, about the feasts of Our Lady of Penha, a sanctuary in the outskirts of Rio de Janeiro, Brazil. Among the Venezuelan films in this category, *La Fiesta de la Virgen de la Candelaria* (1966), a 30-minute, 16 mm documentary, was recently restored. The film's synopsis is instructive: "The devotion to the Virgin is an old tradition in the state of Mérida. It has originated from the discovery of a printed picture of the Virgin in the house of a poor woman. The festivities are celebrated with balls, processions and Masses."

Regarding this type of documentary film, it is also important to mention some interesting fictionalized accounts of the activities of witch doctors and miracle miracleworkers. Common characters in Latin American folklore, these people attract the simple believers, using a mixture of Catholic rites with practices of African and Indian religions. One such silent film is about an illiterate black woman who has attracted crowds of people to southeast Brazil, offering them the benefit of cures and other miracles. A more recent Venezuelan film, produced in 1962 by Blanca Guzmán, explores the personality of Miguelón, a well-known spiritual figure of the Andes region. Ever since he was a child, he had devoted himself enthusiastically to singing the "*Paradura del Niño,*" a religious song about the child Jesus. Invited to sing for an urban audience, Miguelón realizes the loss of the tradition and the public's ignorance of the song. As a result, he refuses to sing and thus fails to confirm his religious reputation.

Despite their limited number, these fictional films had a significant effect on current religion practice. Mexico, a country that has maintained its popular entertainment cinema against the Hollywood onslaught, provides a good example. At the beginning of the sound era, the film *La cruz y la espada* (1933), starring the singer José Mogica, became a big success. It tells the story of a Franciscan monk who sacrifices himself to make the wedding of a friendly couple possible. Mogica himself converted and entered the order of Saint Francis. Once a priest, he continued to act in films, to the delight of his fans.

Another important line of films that deals with the life of Christ began with the primitive productions of Charles Pathé and Ferdinand Zecca. Although limited aurally to a few sound effects and to background music, these films brought crowds to public movie theaters, especially during Easter. Miguel Martinez's *O martir do Calvario* was released in Mexico in 1951 and distributed throughout Latin America. In the same vein, a new version of the life of Jesus Christ was made in 1971 by the ex-seminarian José Regattieri, using a stage production annually held in a small town in the state of Espírito Santo. The film attained its commercial goal, despite being a naively-conceived animated illustration of the *via crucis*, without rhythm and somehow grotesque. The critic Miguel Pereira observes that the religious effect of these films is very close to an experience of the sacred common among Latin American people: "The ignorance, illiteracy and the sub-human conditions of the people favor and develop this diffuse and mythical form of religion."[4] Incapable of a more universal and critical view of the facts of life, the common people assume a conformist attitude and promote religion as an "ally" of their tendency to escape from the real problems of daily existence. The priests themselves also promote this conformist attitude. One frequently observes goodness associated with economic and political power, and evil with sex, disobedience and disrespect towards authorities, even when these authorities are arbitrary and violate basic individual human rights. This is obviously an older stance that has been partially overcome, mainly due to ideas associated with the political confrontations of the 1960s.

V. The Revolution of the 1960s

Ideological questioning marked Latin American society in the beginning of the 60s, stemming mainly from the dialectical opposition between capitalism and Marxism. This contributed to a reorientation of the focus of the relationship between religion and cinema, at least among intellectuals. Many films from this period were marked by the creative style and original ideas of the filmmakers themselves, especially in Argentina, Brazil, Cuba and Mexico. They offered a new approach to cinema in which religion criticizes the beliefs and fanatical mysticism of the common people. Contrary to what happened on other continents, very few movies focus in an orthodox way on the religious problematic of the individual believer.

In this context, it is pertinent to mention the Mexican phase of Luis Buñuel (1946-64), which showed the obsession with ritual and the deformation of religious phenomena. I refer specifically to *Simon of the Desert* (1965) and *Nazarin* (1959). This latter film was analyzed with precision by Octavio Paz:

> In *Nazarin*, with a style that avoids complacence and suspicious lyricism, Buñuel tells the story of a quixotic priest who in his conception of Christianity opposes the church, society and the police. The priest Nazarin belongs to that great tradition of Spanish fools inaugurated by Cervantes. In his madness, he takes seriously great ideas and sayings, and tries to live according to these rules. Like Don Quixote, who would see Dulcinea as a peasant, Nazarin realizes the echo of divine love behind the erotic frenzy of Beatriz.[5]

Although Buñuel's work, especially its irreverence toward traditional aspects of Catholicism, is taken as unique in the world history of the cinema, it nonetheless coincides with the new phase of Latin American religious cinema in which the relationship between cinema and religion changes radically.

In Brazil, this changing interrelationship is particularly significant. Two films illustrate perfectly, each one in its own special way, the criticism that the cinema of the 1960s directed toward some aspects of religious phenomena. The first is *The Given Word*, directed by Anselmo Duarte

and made for the general public; it was awarded the Palme d'Or at Cannes
in 1962. The film is based on Dias Gomes's original stage play *O pagador
de promessas* and bears no specific signs of the director's ideological intentions. It tells the story of a peasant who receives a special grace from
God and decides to carry a wooden cross from his small hometown to the
interior of the church of Senhor do Bonfim (Lord of Bonfim) in downtown
Salvador, Bahia. The disapproval of the parish priest and the local bishop
catches the attention of the press and the curiosity of people, transforming
this simple peasant into a hero and a symbol of the fight for freedom.
When he is shot by the police, his body is placed onto the cross he was
carrying and is brought in glory by the people into the church, to the altar
of Senhor Bom Jesus. Catholicism is shown here as a target of the fight
between classes that nourished the political options of a society that, in
1964, would be dominated by a military dictatorship for twenty years. The
grotesque presence of the church personalities represents a preconciliar
conservatism, blind to the convictions and spontaneous expectations of the
people of God.

The other film – *Deus e o diabo na terra do sol* (1964) by Glauber
Rocha – represents the type of cinema that is marked by the strong influence of the director as *auteur* in terms of ideology and narrative style. Insofar as the film portrays the tragic contradictions inherent in Brazilian
society, it can be considered a stimulus to a whole generation of filmmakers. It is the story of the cowboy Mañuel, wanted for the murder of his
boss, who gets protection from a fanatical group headed by a religious
leader called *Beato Conselheiro*. In actuality it was a social group that
lived isolated in the interior of the country, adopting the lifestyle of a utopian community; in Brazilian history the episode is known as *Guerra dos
Canudos*. Its prestige threatened, the central government ordered a military
raid. After some initial resistance during which the community reacted
with courage, the utopia was totally annihilated in 1897. In Glauber's film,
the leader tells his followers about the promised land where everything is
green, and there is water and food for everybody. "The hinterland will become sea and the sea will become hinterland," he says. Popular religiosity
is treated in the film as a deformed mysticism, and is shown to be as insane as the structures of social injustice. The land belongs to men; it does
not belong either to God or to the devil, the lyrics of one of the film's
songs insist.

Thirty years later, this critical vision of many filmmakers, about religion confused with popular piety, still continues in Latin America. I refer
specifically to a film made in Cuba by the Argentinean director Fernando
Birri, based on a story by Gabriel Garcia Marquez, *Un señor muy viejo
con unas alas enormes* (1991). In the mode of magical realism, the film
shows how a false angel is welcomed into a small, poor village and
quickly becomes a focus of popular pilgrimage. Thousands of people line
up in front of the angel, hoping for a miracle, while unscrupulous busi-

nessmen sell the naive populace figurines and pieces of St. Theresa's cloak!

VI. Religion in Contemporary Cinema

Apart from this critical tendency of certain films to offer caricatures of popular beliefs, it can safely be stated that the *explicit* religious theme is not common in current Latin American films. This phenomenon can be verified by the history of the winners of the Margarida de Prata Prize, annually awarded in Brazil by the Bishops' Conference to films of outstanding thematic and artistic quality. If a number of good films with religious themes had been produced, it would be reasonable to think that the selection committee would give preference to those with explicit religious approaches. This was not the case, however, between 1967 and 1993, and I can give my personal testimony to this as a member of the committee composed of critics with a Catholic religious upbringing, nominated by the Social Communication Department of the Brazilian Bishops' Conference. In my twenty-six years of uninterrupted participation, the films honored by the committee have dealt with social and psychological problems, focusing on the issues of land distribution, urban injustice, street children and the marginalization of the mentally disabled. The emphasis of the majority of these films is placed on human solidarity and points towards courage, optimism and hope – all basic Christian values.

Deus e o diabo na terra do sol, Glauber Rocha, 1964

The following are representative examples of this pattern. *Som e forma* (1971), by Joaquim Assis, shows the problem of self-affirmation and personal integrity in a institution for the blind. Eduardo Escorel's *Lição de amor* (1976), based on a classic of modern Brazilian literature, reveals the hypocrisy of a bourgeois family, closed on itself in an individualistic way, reinforcing its egotistic view of society through its descendants. *Em nome da Razão* (1980), a documentary by Helvécio Ratton, presents a realistic and creative journey through the universe of the mentally disabled from the poorest level of society, who are abandoned by their families and by government authorities. *Meninos de rua* (1988), a short film directed by Marlene França, is a high-level documentary that combines an articulation of urban life and the solitude of homeless children and adolescents with a vigorous denunciation of the same. The filmmaker lived with these deprived youth for several weeks, gaining their intimate and sincere testimony about the negative view they have of the society they live in.

Although such films could certainly be included in a broader definition of religious cinema, it is important to note that religion has been directly addressed in a few films that have received the Brazilian Bishops' Conference prize. There are many short films about evangelization that cannot be mentioned here,[6] as well as the video productions of a variety of organizations that have exploded lately upon the scene in Latin American countries, mainly in Argentina, Bolivia, Brazil, Chile and Colombia.[7] We must note, though, the 1980s documentaries that followed the trajectory of the so-called "progressive church" and its actions defending, together with other segments of Brazilian society, social and individual freedom against abuses of the military dictatorship.

Jorge Bodansky's *A igreja dos oprimidos* (1986) gives the people a potent voice. Filmed in one of tensest regions of Brazil, it focuses on the daily struggle for control of the land, with gunmen killing settlers and their families upon the request of powerful landowners. The film delves into the action of the church in defense of the people's cause. Bishop Don Alano Peña gives this testimony in one of the sequences of the film: "When I went to the Araguaia-Tocantins region, I took with me a lot of religious thoughts and ideas, but it was there that I realized their contrast with cruel reality." Through the statements of authorities and ordinary people, *A igreja da libertação* (1985), directed by Silvio Da-Rin, tries to explain the transformation that has occurred within the church, viewed not only as a religious institution, but also as a participant in the social and political life of the country. Da-Rin's film favors this church that was silenced many times and had some of its members killed, imprisoned, exiled and expatriated, mostly because they stood on the side of social justice. Paralleling these films, but with emphasis placed on the "base" communities and the popular modes of religion practiced by the people, Geraldo Sarno's *Deus and Fogo* (1987) tries to address the theoretical principles of the "theology of liberation" and its echoes in various countries on the continent. The testimony of Don Pedro Casaldáliga, Bishop of São Felix do Araguaia – an area of Brazil with the most troubled relationship between the big landowners and the extremely poor – is definitive: "The option for the poor must be a lived option, not just a formulated one." Finally, *Pé na caminhada* (1987), by Conrado Berning, is a documentary recording events, manifestations and actions of the church in Brazil, always seen through popular participation.

VII. Evangelization and Indian Culture

During the celebration of the 500th anniversary of America's discovery, aside from the direct discussion of the role the church played among the invading armies, some films showing this problem from a different point of view were produced. *Amerindia* (1991), the second full-length film from Verbo Films, produced and directed by Conrado Berning, became a domestic and international success. Filmed on location in Mexico, Ecuador, Peru, Bolivia and Brazil, it introduces material from the 1950s that was shot by the Belgian scientist Gesko von Puttkaner, documenting the daily life of Indian tribes totally isolated from civilization. *Amerindia* is a testimonial documentary at once tender and aggressive, a lyrical essay about the indigenous cultures of the vast Latin American continent. But it is also a haunting picture of the history and results of five hundred years of evangelization as seen by Indian leaders who speak for their communities and touch upon the effects of their long historical encounter with Europeans. Nursing her six-month-old baby, Ana Maria Guacho talks against the backdrop of the monolithic Andes in Ecuador. "They are speaking about commemorating 500 years of the discovery of Latin America," she says. "What did they discover? What did they see that was new? They did not discover; they covered up. They destroyed our lifestyle, they stole our richness, they exploited us and they killed us. Is this what they mean by discover?" The voice-over narration of the film is limited to some poetic texts that try to interpret and reinforce the beauty of the images, always seen from the pre-Columbian civilization's point-of-view: "My culture dates back millennia, as ancient as the sun. A culture as great as the mountains and rivers of Amerindian. I knew time as day and night, as the sun and moon, as rain and wind. My time was time itself, without hours."

On the theme of the discovery and evangelization of Latin America, three other films must be mentioned. Each one in its own way opens up the discussion of the historic problematic of culture and faith. The first one, *Jerico* (1988), directed by the Venezuelan Luis Alberto Lamata, tells a story of reverse evangelization. Santiago, a Dominican monk, conscious of his role as a missionary, arrives in the New World in 1537. Taken prisoner by an Indian tribe, he keeps his faith and his religious rites. However, the reality of the ambience he is living in is stronger. Little by little the tribe's customs and, above all, the drugs the Indians take from the plants make Santiago renounce his past and his Christian life. Later, found by a Spanish expedition, he presents himself as a naked white Indian, painted by his tribal companions. Incapable of taking the old religious habits back, he is considered mad and, under the laws of the Inquisition, kept isolated from civilized Catholic society. Corrosive and critical, *Jerico* is an important film because of the way that it deals with the theme of the cultural and religious conflict between the European and Amerindian civilizations.

Directed by the Mexican Nicolás Echeveria, *Cabeza de Vaca* (1990) describes the spiritual odyssey of a shipwrecked Spanish sailor in the sixteenth century, who becomes the prisoner of a terribly hostile tribe. He is called Cow's Head and becomes the slave of a medicine man, learning the secrets of the Indian religion and developing a strong curative power. When he cures the young chief of a lethal wound, he becomes respected and loved by the whole tribe. In another situation, Cow's Head follows the ritual of the burial of an teenager. Adorned as a princess with paint and necklaces to comply with the wishes of the gods of death, the girl is taken to a cave. The Spanish medicine man approaches her dead body and touches it with a stone considered to be miraculous and, under the scared glances of the Indians, cries out for her life. The response comes slowly and the girl, trembling and starting to breathe, stands up and joins the great feast of the tribe as Cow's Head is carried in triumph. The theory of Claude Lévi-Strauss, which notes the strict relationship between the science of the cure and the capacity for leadership of groups in primitive society, is confirmed here.

Later on, when Cow's Head divulges the diary he wrote about his experience, it becomes clearer that he is not telling everything he saw because he fears being taken for a liar or being condemned of heresy. On the other hand, his companions, considered less compromised by the ecclesiastical and military authorities, are free to create myths and to forge dreams in the heads of the soldiers around the campfire, easy targets for the most fantastic stories. They will be told and will believe in stories about single-footed creatures and about one with a single eye in the forehead, like Homer's Polyphemus. All literary inventions are permitted, provided they do not challenge the dogmatic truths of the dominant religion. This seems to be one of the messages of Echeverria's film, which also probes the community life of the missionaries facing the systematic massacre of the Indians. In the final sequence of *Cabeza de Vaca*, hundreds of Indians, running across the immense expanse of a beach, carry a huge wooden cross to place it on the top of the tower of a cathedral under construction. The camera takes a panoramic view that is quicker than the procession and finds on the horizon the black clouds that herald a coming storm. The question posed by the image extrapolates from the historical period, raising the doubt whether there is any hope at all for the primitive populations (nowadays underdeveloped and poor) of the countries in Latin America.

In this same quincentennial timeperiod, the Chilean film *La cruz del sur* (1992) by Patricio Guzman was also released. Evoking the arrival of the Spaniards and describing the spread of the Christian faith, the film integrates documentary realism and fiction, working at the same time with descriptions of religious manifestations and with testimonies from theologians and church authorities. Guzman creatively presents the theme of the discovery of the continent and the ambiguous relationship, in many cases, between the cross of the missionaries, the political ambitions of the representatives of Spain and Portugal, and the instinctively submissive stance of the Indian populations. In the film's first sequence, a tribe helps the army of Cortes to beat its local enemies in the name of the beliefs and the honesty of the white people. Disappointment soon yields to betrayals and cruel revenge. The director's intent is neither neutral nor indifferent to the rights of the people subdued by the military power. Interspersed throughout the main portion of the film is a series of statements about religion, politics, and cultural identity, together with powerful images about the religious mixture existing in Brazil, Cuba and other countries. Guzman's subtext is about the influence exerted by the people of God in determining the destiny of the religious life of the continent, which constitutes half the Catholic population of the world. In the final analysis, *La cruz del sur* is a hymn to the power of the Latin American church and the announcement of a new evangelical message based on the life, dreams, and hopes of the people. It is important to note that these three films, singled out for their artistic achievement relative to other productions, focus seriously on the problematic of the Christian faith's inculturation, leading spectators to reflection and debate.

Among the films that touch on the subject of Spanish evangelization, I am aware of only one that is based on a deliberate distortion of Catholic religious history, tradition, and teachings. It is the Mexican Gabriel Retes' *Nuevo mundo* (1987), an anticlerical lampoon of the history of the Virgin of Guadalupe. The film portrays a conspiracy between the church, represented by the head of an unidentified religious congregation, and civil authorities to delude the good faith of the people. Director Retes does not propose an open discussion, but simply practices his own prejudicial authoritarianism, the exact opposite of the "religious" cinema referred to above. It is an evident demonstration of an anticlerical posture that has dominated Mexican culture until recently, which is being slowly reversed.

VIII. Other Tendencies of the Contemporary Cinema

In the beginning of the 1990s, a general crisis arose in film production in a majority of the countries in Latin America. A typical case is Brazil. Ever since the initiation of the Cinema Novo, with its revolutionary ideas and aesthetics represented by such films as Glauber Rocha's *Deus e o diabo na terra do sol*, an industry with reasonable competitive power had been slowly developing, which produced about one hundred films in some of the best years. The mechanism of production and distribution was based on strong state support, with procedures in place that would not favor the commercial strategies of privately-owned companies. On the other hand, the majority of the film theaters were under the control of businessmen eager for North American films that guaranteed good financial returns. In March 1990, President Fernando Collor de Melo (who was impeached in 1992) abolished federal funding for all the cultural institutions that had supported his opponent. This presidential act struck at the heart of film production, which slipped to an all-time low in 1990 and 1991. With such a lack of material to appraise, it would be unlikely that the National Bishop's Conference could find films with strictly religious themes.

In 1993, the Margarida de Prata Prize was awarded to the film *A dívida da vida*. Its director, Octávio Bezerra, provides a spectrum of matters that touch the national conscience, not only exposing the foreign debt of the underdeveloped countries, but also questioning its causes and consequences. The film shows the tragic effects of the impoverishment of Brazilian society, both in rural areas and in the great urban centers: on one side, there is the quest of abandoned children and resulting violence; on the other, the destruction of the environment. Also honored in 1993 was the short film *A babel da lus* by Silvio Back, which provides the surprisingly beautiful revelation of a eighty-year-old woman, reciting her poems with a child's emotions, exposing without shame the intimacy of her soul. It offers a kind of existential experience of the balance between peace and beauty through a cinematic language in which poetry and its images melt into a unique composite, which I would call poetic cinema – indeed, religious cinema also.

Argentina, a traditionally strong producer of movies, maintains a constant presence at International Festivals. Some of its most important filmmakers, such as Eliseo Subiela, Fernando Solanas, Adolfo Aristain and Maria Luisa Bemberg, have had their films recognized by OCIC's ecumenical juries. Out of a total of more than ten films produced during this period, only one film, however, has an explicitly religious theme – Bemberg's *Yo, la peor de todas* (*I, the Worst of All*, 1990). It tells the story of a Mexican sister, Sor Juana Iñes de la Cruz, who had abandoned the world to dedicate herself to literature, her greatest passion. The director pushes the limits of simple biography to attain a profound level of discussion of such diverse issues as the limits of science, a woman's role in society, and religious freedom.

The pattern of finding films that are religious in the wide sense only is repeated in other countries – in Chile, for instance. Ricardo Larrarin

Pinedo's *La frontera* was awarded the OCIC prize at the 1992 Festival in Havana, Cuba. The commendation of the Chilean film reads as follows:

> The film is more than the simple story of a professor who is banned for having reported the disappearance of his friend. It shows the inhuman mechanism of such a system for the innocent victims that fall into its hands. The story brings forth themes about solidarity as well as devotion inspired by love, hope and faith in the future. Even though the film is his first, it demonstrates the effective use of cinematographic means, although we may think that it underlines too heavily the political discourse.[8]

The confirmation of the above-mentioned tendency can be found in the choices and motives for the prizes awarded in 1992 by OCIC to Latin American films presented in international festivals. The Ecumenical Jury of the Cannes Film Festival gave an honorable mention to the Argentinean film *El viaje* by Fernando Solanas, with the following justification: "Through a journey from south to north in the Latin American continent, Solanas paints a large political fresco made up of symbols and metaphors. This film is a denunciation and a call to justice anchored in a real search for identity." The OCIC prize at the San Sebastian Festival was given to *Un lugar en el mundo* by the Argentinean Adolfo Aristain, "for its honest and realistic treatment of contemporary social issues, featuring a sincere, sensitive approach to human values like friendship and family life." In Amiens, the award from OCIC went to *La cruz del sur*, already mentioned. The jury commented: "In the context of commemorating the discovery of Latin America, this film questions links existing among religions, cultures and powers." *La frontera* received the OCIC prize at the Havana International Festival

> because this film is a tender manifestation of love, a solitary love, a deep devotedness, a simple and sincere search for the meaning of life, transcending everything until death. This film exalts the presence of a Mother-Church that welcomes all human beings without exceptions. It brings forth an irresistible hope that fills those who love the truth.[9]

The examples referred to above enable us to point out with certainty two main tendencies in the thematic interaction of cinema and religion in Latin America in the last decade and a half. On the one side, there are films explicitly designed to propose and discuss issues related to church, religion and popular religiosity, generally motivated by concrete historical circumstances. In the case of the 500 years of America's discovery, the motivating issue for the films was the dichotomy between boastful celebrations and the shameful memory of the church's involvement in the plans of the European invaders. On the other side, there are those films of excellent artistic quality that deal with deeply-rooted humanistic themes founded on faith and Christian life – hope for a better future, solidarity with the people and communities who live in subhuman conditions, fraternity, and the light that shines on the environment. The journey of the human person in search for God appears more frequently in Latin American films as a hope that involves a whole segment of society, contrary to what happens in some European films that privilege the description of the solitary struggle of individuals.

The issue, however, is not as simple as this division may suggest. In an editorial of the magazine *CinémAction* about religious films, Philippe Boitel states that there are films essentially religious although they do not show religiosity, while others that pretend to be religious are offensive to the person of faith:

> We have used as criteria the films in which history, faith, and the religious search are the reason for choosing the script, whether the director is a person of faith or not. There are two ways in which a director can deal with an genuine religious film: from the outside, considering the theme externally as a spectacle or a melodrama, or from the inside, trying to face closely the truth of a being and to observe its soul in the most intimate way.[10]

Another factor that broadens this discussion of religious film is the theme that runs through a number of these essays; namely, that rather than trying to discern the essence of the religious film as such, it is much more appropriate and functional to leave to the spectator the task of discovering for himself the religious sensibility of a film. In this context, it is helpful to recall that the real concept of religiosity has less to do with the plot or theme than with the effect of the story itself on the audience insofar as there are many filmmakers who are not conscious of the aspects of their films that appeal to a sense of transcendence.

IX. Conclusion

It seems appropriate to conclude this essay with an insight from Roland Barthes, originally applied to literature, which he defines as "an unfulfilled technique of meaning." "The writer," he goes on to say, in words that seem equally applicable to the director of a film, "is concerned to multiply significations without completing or closing them, and that he uses language to constitute a world which is emphatically signifying but never finally signified." This "constitutive ambiguity" of language explains why an artistic work – literature or film – has such a power of posing questions to the world without, however, answering them. No masterpiece is dogmatic, he insists. Barthes's reflection points out the impossibility of creating an authentically religious film if the filmmaker has a materialistic view of the audiovisual milieu. The same reasoning applies as well to the critic: "The work is not an object external to the psyche or to the story of those who question."[11] I am convinced that the parameters proposed by the French philosopher can truly support those who, in the cultural diversity of the continents, occupy themselves with a religion incarnated in the sounds and images of the cinema.

Endnotes

1. Jorge Sanguinez, *"El plano secuencia integral,"* *Imagen: La Revista Boliviana de Cine y Video* 6 (1989), 22-27.

2. Paulo Emilio Sales Gomes, *Cinema: trajetória no subdesenvolvimento* (Rio de Janeiro: Embrafilme, Editora Paz e Terra, 1980), 76.

3. Maria Clara Berminger, *Alteridade e vulnerabilidade – experiencia de Deus e pluralismo religioso no moderno em crise* (São Paulo: Edições Loyola, 1993), 45.

4. Miguel Pereira, *"A religiosidade popular no cinema brasileiro,"* *Revista de Cultura VOZES* 7 (1974), 563-568.

5. Georges Sadoul, *Dictionnaire des Films* (Paris: Microcosme, Seuil, 1990), 225.

6. I refer especially to short films about religious and social themes produced in São Paulo, Brazil, by Verbo Films.

7. The work of small companies and isolated Latin American producers ("Creators of Christian Images") is related in the book *La imagen nuestra de cada día: La situacion del video pastoral en America Latina* (Bogotá: Ediciones Paulinas, FSP, 1992).

8. Ivan Rodrigo, "Critica," *Cine&Media* 1-2 (1993), 7.

9. Quoted in *Festivals: Prix OCIC oecumenique* (work in progress), passim.

10. Philippe Boitel, *"Rendre visible l'invisible?,"* *CinémAction* 49 (Paris: Corlet), 5-7.

11. Roland Barthes, *Essais Critiques* (Paris: Seuil, 1964), 256; also *Critical Essays* (Evanston, IL: Northwestern University Press, 1972), 266, 268.

16

Recent Developments in the Religious Film in Africa

François Vokouma

It is almost impossible to undertake a study of African cinema without dealing with the question of "colonization," which makes it advisable to extend our analysis beyond the narrow framework of African cinema, thus dealing more precisely with the beginnings of filmmaking in Africa. As a matter of fact, if we limited our study to an assessment of African cinema only, we might forget that the first movies produced on the African continent were made by Europeans and that, up until 1960, there was no recognizably indigenous cinematographic structure in Africa itself.

My approach to the topic of recent developments in the religious film in Africa, therefore, will be to treat in succession the following topics: the context of the beginnings of African cinema, the evolution of African film production and, finally, an analysis of films that can, in the context of this collection of essays, be called "religious" films.

I. Africa in the Context of Global Film Production

From the point of view of most Europeans, the mosaic of small republics that Africa is composed of remained a distant vision without much variety. Postcards reinforced this vision by showing only the touristic and exotic side of the continent. The film industry has done little to correct this misunderstanding. To the contrary, it has been more persuasive in supporting the status quo. As a result, films about Africa have been erroneous and over-simplified portraits that reinforced the image of a land full of wild animals and "noble savages." Africa became almost synonymous with *Tarzan* movies; in effect, those first films depicted Africans in situations that provoked laughter if not hostility from Europeans. Since such subjects and themes found a thriving market, producers did not shrink from perpetuating the prejudiced impressions that were building up against Africa. This distortion perpetrated by cinema, which rarely showed the reality of Africa, gave rise to further calls for "civilizing" the continent, a situation that lasted until 1960, the year of independence for fourteen new African states. Thus, sixty-five years after the invention of cinema, not a single feature film had been written, acted in, shot, produced, and distributed by black Africans speaking their native languages.

In effect, African cinema as such started in the late 1950s and the 1960s, when African intellectuals, needing to settle matters with Europe, started to question the global perception of Africa and to assert their own identity. The first African directors like African intellectuals were almost always marked by the trauma that the continent itself had experienced, the shock of "civilization" and the introduction of foreign religions. In this context, we witnessed the genesis of an African cinema born outside the continent – an art, a technology and an industry at the same time. African cinema did not find a propitious, indigenous environment for its growth.

II. Evolution of African Film Production

Afrique sur Seine (*Africa on the Seine*, 1957) is the evocative title of the first film conceived and produced by the African filmmaker Paulin S. Vieyra, a Senegalese student working in Paris. Thus, African film production was born in Europe, and all its pioneers have been trained there. Thirty years later, it can still be said that African production has regularly been funded with European money, processed by European technicians in European laboratories.

In their first films, African filmmakers seem to have had the conviction of being entrusted with a mission, to deliver a message to their people. They were mostly didactic films, moralistic and critical. Their themes generally related to the life of Africans in Europe, to the clash between two cultures, the city versus the countryside, modernism versus tradition. It is not surprising, therefore, that African filmmakers rarely dealt with popular comedy-type movies. Yet the African continent is an inexhaustible resource of human adventures, epics, legends, myths and magic – an endless supply of themes and possibilities that the African filmmakers could have been interested in. In the last decade, some African films have actually attracted an audience on the European continent. Such was the case with the film *Yeelen* (*The Light*, 1987) by Souleymane Cissé of Mali, and with *Tilaï* (*A Question of Honor*, 1990) by the Burkina Faso director Idrissa Ouedraogo. Both films are typical of a recent trend in African film that avoids overt anticolonial political themes, preferring a search for precolonial African traditions – a genuine return to native sources.[1] Yet in spite of some real success during this period, African cinema remains a marginal and marginalized cinema.

As we have seen, up until nearly 1960 there was virtually no African film produced entirely by Africans. Thirty years later, what is the situation in black Francophone Africa – Benin, Burkina Faso, Congo, Ivory Coast,

Mali, Niger, Tchad, Burundi, Central Africa, Gabon, Cameroon, and Togo? Though there has been some tentative national funding, most films have been produced entirely by the will and ingenuity of individual filmmakers and producers themselves. As a nation, Senegal has the most film producers and the highest rate of film production, thanks to its National Company of Cinema (SNC) created in 1974 (unfortunately, dissolved in 1977). Mali, Benin, and the Ivory Coast have also tried to set up production policies, but unfortunately with no success. Curiously, it is Upper Volta (Burkina Faso today) that seems to have been most successful in organizing its cinema. It sponsors the famous Panafrican Festival of Film and Television of Ouagadougou (FESPACO) and is also the place where the headquarters of the Federation of Panafrican Filmmakers (FEPACI) is based. It was again in Burkina Faso that, in 1977, UNESCO helped create the African Institute for Cinematographic Training and Education (INAFEC). FESPACO remains the internationally acknowledged framework that stands as a barometer of African film production. Nonetheless, in spite of the establishment of an efficient production complex in Ouagadougou, the majority of African films still continue to be funded by European countries.

Statistics made available by FESPACO from 1969 to 1991 suggest the significant growth of African film production in the last two and a half decades. In 1969, when the first festival was held, there were five African countries participating, with fourteen films produced, reaching an estimated audience of 10,000. A decade later, sixteen countries were participating in FESPACO, producing 62 films, reaching an audience of 100,000 people. By 1991, 60 African countries were participating, with 55 films (from 1981 to 1983, production had reached 69), with an estimated audience of over 400,000. At the present time, when all categories of films are taken into consideration (short films, documentaries, fiction feature films 16mm or 35mm), African film *production* is estimated to be in the vicinity of 400 films, directed and produced by about 200 filmmakers.

Nonetheless, the general assessment of the state of African cinema at the 1995 (14th) FESPACO was not encouraging vis-à-vis the possibilities for the *distribution* of African films to general audiences. Clement Tapsoba, noting that very few of the films screened at the festival had found distributors or buyers, filed the following report: "At a time when the whole world is celebrating the first century of cinema, [African cinema] continues to exist solely in the non-commercial circuit made up of festivals and other cultural events dotted around Europe."[2]

III. Cinema and Religion

As we began by noting, colonization remains a basic element to be taken into account in the analysis of any subject related to Africa. Political and economic domination naturally included cultural domination. We noted too, with regret, that the first films set in Africa aroused civilizing sentiments in Europe. Even if it was a fact that the conquest of new territories aimed to take their wealth away, religion was also one of the main reasons given to justify colonization, using quotations from the Bible like Matthew 28:18: "You, then, are to go and make disciples of all the nations and baptize them in the name of the Father and of the Son and of the Holy Spirit." Superstitious black people, it was felt, must be converted to Christianity in order to halt the spread of Islam.

As early as 1917, the Belgians presented at the Exposition of Ghent dioramas depicting the missionaries' presence in Africa and their accomplishments to date, especially in terms of church buildings. Present in the field at the same time as the explorers, therefore, were the missionaries, who would even produce some films in order to further their work; i.e., to raise money for their missions. It seems, however, that they failed to follow up on their early cinematic initiatives. From my analysis of African films, it would appear that the Christian religion is remarkable by its absence, whereas Islam is present almost everywhere. This may be a reflection of the fact that most filmmakers come from Muslim countries or countries that are predominantly Islamic (Senegal, Mali, and Niger, especially). It is worth noting, moreover, that if Islam seems omnipresent in African films, it is also almost universally criticized.

Nonetheless, when we attempt to classify African films according to the place they give to religion, they fall into three predictable categories: two about the imported religions – Islam and Christianity – and the third dealing with traditional or black African religions.

1. Islam

Islam has stood as a bulwark against colonization. Is this perhaps one of the reasons for its popularity? The fact remains that many of the best filmmakers have dealt with it in their works. The Nigerian director Oumarou Ganda's *Le wazou du polygame* (*The Polygamist's Moral*, 1971) – which won first prize at the 1972 FESPACO – is a powerful satire against the Hadji (Muslims who have made the pilgrimage to Mecca) who take advantage of their social and religious position to deceive the faithful. By satirizing the manners of a pilgrim to Mecca, Ganda is also making a statement against the values of Islam (polygamy). A pilgrimage to Mecca, his film clearly proposes, does not change a man.

Another filmmaker from Niger, Mustapha Alassane, has produced a film about a crook who acts as a filthy witch and a marabout (a dervish in Muslim Africa believed to have supernatural power). In Alassane's 1972 film *FVVA* (*Femme Villa Voiture Argent [Wife Villa Car Money]*), the main character, presented as an ardent believer, is in fact a dreadful person. The director is warning viewers against those false devotees of religion who use their faith as a screen for undertaking less commendable actions. In *Njangaan* (*The Koranic School Student*, 1975), the Senegalese director

Mahama Traore also depicts unscrupulous marabouts who, for their own profit, exploit the children they are charged to teach by sending them out to beg. The plight of Koranic school children is a theme that had been treated three years earlier in another film, *Cinq jours d'une vie* (*Five Days in a Life*, 1972) by Souleymane Cissé of Mali.

In many films, Islam is presented as an unacceptable social hypocrisy, a sentiment that Ousmane Sembene, another Senegalese director, scarcely disagrees with. His image of the Turkish slippers aligned at the entrance of the Mosque as a herd of sheep lining up behind the village chief to pray is aimed at exposing the rigid conformism of Islam in Niaye. In his film *Ceddo* (1976), Sembene questions the intrusion of Islam as well as of the Catholic religion and foreign business in Africa.

In *Pour ceux qui savent* (*For Those Who Know*, 1970), Tidiane Aw, also Senegalese, exposes maraboutism, its corruption and nepotism. The director introduces a mysterious figure, arriving in a pirogue and robed in black, who denounces all of the fraud and embezzlement that he witnesses. This godlike judge, who comes from the sea, suggests the sacred character of justice.

2. Christianity

The Christian religion is portrayed less frequently in African films. Because it was associated with European explorers colonizing Africa, it met with strong opposition from Africans. Through their missions and schools, the Christian clergy has trained mainly the elite of African leaders, who themselves very soon grabbed the power. Contrasted with Islam and the African religions, the Christian religion does not have an important place in African culture.

However, there are some films in which it has been the principal theme. *Bonjour Balthazar* (1972), the title of a film by Louis Mebaley, is in fact a representation of the theme of nativity. Pascal Abikanlou produced a medium-length film called *L'Afrique au rendez-vous de l'année sainte* (*Africa Gets Ready for the Holy Year*, 1975), which reports on the Holy Year ceremonies at Lourdes, Rome, Nazareth and Jerusalem that African representatives participated in. In *Identité* (*Identity*, 1972), Pierre-Marie Dong from Gabon presents a character named Pierre (Peter, intentionally as we soon discover) who reacts against the Catholic community he feels lost in. Revolted by the memory of the water that made him a Christian as well as by the first name that was bestowed on him, he goes back to his village and undergoes an initiation into the Bwili cult.

Jean-Michel Tchissoukou, a now deceased Congolese filmmaker, produced his first feature-length film, *La chapelle* (*The Chapel*), in 1979. Set around 1930 in a village in Congo, the sacristan-catechist runs afoul of the village witch. The priest arrives on a bike and demands that the Christians in the village build a chapel. The opposition between the two factions is such that the chapel is ravaged by a fire. In retaliation, the Christians burn the witch doctor's hut. *La chapelle* makes a strong case against institution-alized religion. In his film *Wendemi, l'enfant de bon dieu* (*Wendemi, Child of the Good God,* 1993), Pierre Yameogo from Burkina Faso tells the story of a "natural" child who happens to be the illegitimate son of a local priest – as yet another example of the abuses of organized religion.

Gnoan Roger M'Bala from the Ivory Coast tackles the problem of mushrooming Christian sects in *Au nom du Christ* (1992). The film tells the following story: the hero, Magloire the First (played by Pierre Gondo), a former hog breeder with strange practices, becomes a kind of prophet. He speaks in the name of Christ, his "cousin," preaches the Good News, is able to do everything and takes the liberty to do it. Having accomplished many "miracles" (curing a madman, fecundation of a sterile woman) and trusting in himself, he behaves as if he were Christ, if not better than he, even to the point of wanting to die on a cross. Magloire I reaches his apo-gee at the point that he thinks he is immortal. To prove his immortality, he instructs his hunters to shoot him: "Put your bullets in my body, and I'll collect them in my palms." Well, the prophet does not, as we anticipate, survive the gunshots. Magloire I dies from the bullet wounds.

This film comes as a warning in this period when all kinds of sects are rising up, with their "messengers from God," so-called latter-day mes-siahs. Gnoan M'Bala demonstrates the inabilities of the revealed religions to solve the problems of their believers. Sects are mushrooming and thriv-ing, and self-proclaimed prophets are being born to take advantage of peo-ple's naivete and despair. In awarding the film a "Special Mention" at the

La chapelle, Jean-Michel Tchissoukou, 1979

1993 FESPACO, the OCIC jury noted: "This film raises the danger of exploiting the credulity of people for secret ends. It invites the established Churches to be more attentive to the deep and real needs of peoples."[3] *Au Nom du Christ* is one of the rare films produced by a team composed almost entirely of Africans: the script was written by Marie Adiaffi, a talented writer from the Ivory Coast; the music is by Paul Wassaba, the cameraman was Kakou N'Gouan, and Gnoan Roger M'Bala was assisted as director by Bertin Akaffou.

One of the truly remarkable (and rare) African films that portrays Christianity positively is Ousmane Sembene's *Guelwaar* (1993). The film portrays a Senegalese Catholic activist who denounces corruption and the new ways of Western imperialism in his country. When Guelwaar dies, his family and friends prepare for an elaborate funeral only to discover that his body has been mistakenly buried in a Muslim cemetery. Sembene also shows in his film the sensitivity and harmony that can be achieved between Christians and Muslims.

3. African Religions

The attitude of African filmmakers toward their local religions is quite complex. Some of them advocate African religions, while others reject them for their inefficacy. In Mustapha Alassane's *FVVA*, that we have already mentioned, the ineffectiveness of the crooked marabout's amulets is clearly depicted. On the other hand, in *Identité*, Pierre-Marie Dong seems to suggest the efficacy of traditional African values. However, after his initiation into the Bwili cult, the hero Pierre, instead of staying among his people, takes his car and returns to town, as if the initiation was not a definitive solution. We have the same feeling of failure in Henri Duparc's *Abusuan* (*The Family*, 1972): a "bewitched" sheep beguiles a poor civil servant so that he will help two of his nephews succeed in town. The two young people end up in prison and eventually return to their village.

Pascal Abikanlou from Benin shares the ideology of advocacy of traditional values in *Sous le signe du vaudou* (*Under the Sign of Voodoo*, 1975). We are shown the structures of voodoo, its priests and its manifestations. The Senegalese filmmaker Ababacar Samb-Makharam, popularly known as Samb, presents in *Kodou* (1971) the great power of traditional religious cults. The young woman of the title, having decided to have her upper lip tattooed, is unable to bear the pain. She runs away from home and, rejected by everyone, goes insane. When the European psychiatrist she is taken to fails to help her, she is cured by a native medicine man. On the other hand, the Cameroonian director Daniel Kamwa portrays in *Akum* (1979) a happy coexistence between the Christian religion and the traditional worship of the earth and its fecundity. We see the faithful, after church, returning to their fetishistic practices.

To deal with traditional religion in their films, film producers often use natural symbols and resort to the repetition of character types. A type frequently presented is a character who plays the role of a prophet, a visionary or a priest. He makes claims and gives witness, yet is "fearful" when he deals with the "sacred." Water is typically a symbol of traditional values; thus, the lovers in *Sous le signe du vaudou* decide to go back to the village to avoid the gods' revenge. It is at the seaside that the young woman will be freed from the spirit that has possessed her.

IV. Conclusion

In the final analysis, African filmmakers themselves often surprise us when they talk directly about religion. Pascal Abikanlou of Benin says: "I am a practicing Catholic, but for us people from Benin, voodoo is sacred." Ousmane Sembene from Senegal is quoted as saying: "I respect all believers, but I think all religions are opiums. I am Marxist and without faith." Pierre Condo, the lead actor in *Au nom du Christ*, claims: "I am an animist, yet I believe in God." He is an animist who, in illusion, thinks that he is Christ. Gnoan M'Bala, the film's director, says simply: "In my family, I am considered *faithless*." Whatever they say, they invariably confirm our impressions of the diversity of religious attitudes in their films – and in Africa.

Endnotes

Editor's Note: The *Directory of African Film-Makers and Films*, compiled and edited by Keith Shiri (Westport, CT: Greenwood, 1992) and Nwachukwu Frank Ukadike's *Black African Cinema* (Berkeley: University of California Press, 1994) have been very helpful to me as authoritative sources for the spellings used here for African films and their directors.

1. Manthia Diawara, *African Cinema: Politics & Culture* (Bloomington: Indiana University Press, 1992), 160-64.

2. Clement Tapsoba, "FESPACO 95: After the Celebrations, What Future for African Cinema?" *Écrans d'Afrique* 4:11 (1995), 36.

3. See Robert Molhant, "Célébrer la diversité culturelle," *Cine&Media* 14:6 (1993), 13.

Selected Bibliography

Agel, Henri. *Un art de la célébration*. Paris: Cerf, 1987.

_____. *Le cinéma a-t-il une âme?* Paris: Cerf, 1952.

_____. *Cinéma et nouvelle naissance*. Paris: Albin Michel, 1981.

_____. *Métaphysique du cinéma*. Paris: Payot, 1976.

_____. *Le visage du Christ à l'écran*. Paris: Desclée, 1985.

Agel, Henri, and Amedee Ayfre. *Le cinéma et le sacré*. Paris: Cerf, 1953.

Ayfre, Amédée. *Le cinéma et la foi chretienne*. Paris: Arthème Fayard, 1960.

_____. *Cinéma et mystère*. Paris: Cerf, 1969.

_____. *Le cinéma et sa vérité*. Paris: Cerf, 1969.

_____. *Conversion aux images. Les images et Dieu. Les images et l'homme*. Paris: Cerf, 1964.

_____. *Dieu au cinéma, problèmes esthétiques du film religieux*. Toulouse: Privat, Presses Universitaires de France, 1953.

Altheide, D. L., and R. P. Snow. *Media Logic*. Newbury Park: Sage Publications, 1979.

Amengual, Barthélemy. *Clefs pour le cinéma*. Paris: Seghers, 1971.

Arnheim, Rudolf. *Art and Visual Perception: A Psychology of the Creative Eye*. Los Angeles: University of California Press, 1954.

_____. *Visual Thinking*. Los Angeles: University of California Press, 1969.

Arnold, James W. *Seen Any Good Dirty Movies Lately? A Christian Critic Looks at Contemporary Films*. Cincinnati: St. Anthony Messenger Press, 1972.

Babin, Pierre, and Mercedes Iannone. *The New Era in Religious Communication*. Minneapolis: Fortress, 1991.

Banner, Lois W. *In Full Flower: Aging Women, Power and Sexuality*. New York: Vintage, 1993.

Becker, Howard S., and Michal M. McCall, eds. *Symbolic Interaction and Cultural Studies*. Chicago: University of Chicago Press, 1990.

Bédouelle, Guy. *Du spirituel dans le cinéma*. Paris: Cerf, 1985.

Benesch, H. *Warum Weltanschauung? Eine psychologische bestandsaufnahme: Geist und Psyche*. Frankfurt: Fischer Verlag, 1990.

Berger, John. *Ways of Seeing*. New York: Penguin, 1977.

Blumer, Herbert. *Symbolic Interactionism: Perspective and Method*. Englewood Cliffs: Prentice Hall, 1969.

Boomershine, T.E. "Doing Theology in the Electronic Age: The Meeting of Orality and Electricity." *UTS Journal of Theology* Vol. 115 (1991), 5-16.

Boyd, David. *Film and the Interpretative Process*. New York: Peter Lang, 1989.

Brown, Mary Ellen, ed. *Television and Women's Culture: Politics of the Popular*. London: Sage Publications, 1990.

Butler, Ivan. *Religion in the Cinema*. New York: A. S. Barnes, 1969.

Carey, James. "Mass Communication and Cultural Studies: An American View." In *Mass Communication and Society*, ed. James Curran, Michael Gurevitch and Janet Woollacott. London: Edward Arnold in association with Open University Press, 1977, pp. 409-426.

Cavigelli, Zeno; Johan G. Hahn, Thomas Henke, and Michael Kuhn, eds. *Aus gleicher Leidenschaft*. Zurich: Benziger, 1993.

Cooper, John Charles, and Carl Skrade. *Celluloid and Symbols*. Philadelphia: Fortress, 1970.

Cosandey, R.; A. Gaudreault and T. Gunning, eds. *Une invention du diable? Cinéma des premiers temps et religion*. Sainte-Foy/Lausanne: Les Presses de l'Université Laval-Éditions Payot, 1992.

De Bleeckere, Sylvain. *De horizon van de tragische mens. Even cultuurfilosofisch gesprek met set filmoeuvre van Andrei Tarkovskij*. Antwerpen: De Nederlandsche Boekhandel, 1984.

_____. "Filmkunst en opvoeding op school. Een filmfilosofische mare." *Media Film* (1983), 13-31.

_____. *Het licht van de Schepping. De religiositeit van de beeldcultuur*. Averbode: Altiora, 1992.

_____, ed. *Zin in beeld. Identiteit en zingeving in hedendaagse films*. Baarn: Gooi en Sticht, 1992.

Debray, Régis. *Vie et mort de l'image. Une histoire du regard en Occident*. Paris: Gallimard, 1992.

Epstein, Jean. *Le cinéma du diable*. Paris: Jacques Meulat, 1947.

_____. *Esprit de cinéma*. Genève/Paris: Jeheber, 1955.

Erens, Patricia, ed. *Issues in Feminist Film Criticism*. Bloomington: Indiana University Press, 1990.

_____. *The Jew in American Cinema*. Bloomington: Indiana University Press, 1984.

Ferlita, Ernest, and John R. May. *Film Odyssey: The Art of Film as Search for Meaning*. New York: Paulist, 1976.

————. *The Parables of Lina Wertmuller*. New York: Paulist, 1977.

Fore, W.F. *Television and Religion: The Shaping of Faith, Values and Culture*. Minneapolis: Augsburg, 1987.

Forshey, Gerald E. *American Religious and Biblical Spectaculars*. Westport, CT: Praeger, 1992.

Freedberg, David. *The Power of Images: Studies in the History and Theory of Response*. Chicago: University of Chicago Press, 1989.

Friedman, Lester. *The Jewish Image in American Film*. Secaucus: Citadel, 1987.

Gaschler, T., and E. Vollmar, eds. *Dark Stars: 10 Regisseure im Gesprach*. Munchen: Edition Belleville, 1992.

Getlein, Frank, and Harold C. Gardiner. *Movies, Morals and Art*. New York: Sheed and Ward, 1961.

Gibson, Arthur. *The Silence of God: Creative Response to the Films of Ingmar Bergman*. New York: Harper and Row, 1969.

Giles, Paul. *American Catholic Arts and Fiction: Culture, Ideology, Aesthetics*. New York: Cambridge University Press, 1992.

Gonzalez, Jorge. "*Frentes culturales.*" *Estudios Sobre Culturas Contemporaneas*, Vol. 2, No. 4-5 (1987), 41-100.

————. "*Ferias, memorias urbanas y frentes culturales.*" *Estudios Sobre Culturas Contemporaneas*, Vol. 4, No. 12 (1991), 11-46.

Greeley, Andrew. *God in Popular Culture*. Chicago: Thomas More, 1988.

Grossberg, Lawrence. "Strategies of Marxist Cultural Interpretation." *Critical Studies in Mass Communication*, Vol. 1, No. 4 (1984), 392-421.

Hahn, Johan G. "*Afbeelden, verbeelden, uitbeelden. Over de ontologische status van het televisiebeeld.*" In *Kiiken naar Levensbeschouwing*, ed. Johan G. Hahn and Frits Tillmans. Hilversum: Gooi en Sticht, 1989, pp. 60-80.

————, "*Het belang van de kleinsb details. Bouwstenen ten behoove van de analytische interpretatie (exegese) van bewegende beelden.*" In *ibid.*, pp. 11-37.

————. *Het zout in de pap: Levensbeschouwing en televise*. Hilversum: Gooi en Sticht, 1988.

Hahn, Johan G., and H. Hoekstra, eds. *In gesprek over film en televisie: Over de theorie en de praktijk van het mediagesprek*. Kok. Kampen, 1991.

Hall, Stuart, et al., eds. *Culture, Media, Language*. London: Hutchison University Library, 1980.

_____. "The Rediscovery of 'Ideology': Return of the Repressed in Media Studies." In *Culture, Society and the Media*, ed. Michael Gurevitch, Tony Bennett, James Curran and Janet Woollacott. London: Routledge, 1982, pp. 56-90.

Hasenberg, Peter, et al., eds., *Religion im Film: Lexikon mit Kurzkritiken und Sachworten zu 1200 Kinofilmen (Untertitel)*. Koln: Kath. Institut für Medieninformation, 1992.

Hennebelle, Guy, ed. *Le film religieux de 1898 à nos jours*. Special edition of *CinemAction* and *Notre Histoire*. Paris: Corlet, 1988.

Hermeren, Goran. *Representation and Meaning: A Study in Methodology of Iconography and Iconology*. Lund: Scandinavian University Books, 1969.

Hill, Geoffrey. *Illuminating Shadows: The Mythic Power of Film*. Boston/London: Shambhala, 1992.

Hoekstra, Henk. "*Cinéma et spiritualité*." In *Communication et spiritualité*, ed. C. Martini, et al. Paris: Fayette, 1991, pp. 81ff.

Holloway, Ronald. *Beyond the Image: Approaches to the Religious Dimension in the Cinema*. Geneva: World Council of Churches, 1977.

Hoover, Stewart. *Mass-Media Religion: The Social Sources of the Electronic Church*. Newbury Park: Sage Publications, 1988.

Hurley, Neil P. *The Reel Revolution: A Film Primer on Liberation*. Maryknoll, NY: Orbis, 1987.

_____. *Theology through Film*. [Republished as *Toward a Film Humanism* (New York: Delta Paperbacks, 1975)]. New York: Harper and Row, 1970.

Inbody, Tyron, ed. *Changing Channels: The Church and the Television Revolution*. Dayton: WhalePrints, 1990.

Jensen, J. *Redeeming Modernity: Contradictions in Media Criticism*. London: Sage Publications, 1990.

Kahle, Robert, and Robert E. A. Lee. *Popcorn and Parables: A New Look at the Movies*. Minneapolis: Augsburg, 1971.

Ketcham, Charles B. *The Influence of Existentialism on Ingmar Bergman*. Lewiston, PA: E. Mellon Press, 1986.

Keyser, Lester J., and Barbara Keyser. *Hollywood and the Catholic Church: The Image of Roman Catholicism in American Movies*. Chicago: Loyola University Press, 1984.

Konzelman, Robert G. *Marquee Ministry: The Movie Theater as Church and Community Forum*. New York: Harper and Row, 1972.

Kuhn, Michael, Johan G. Hahn, and Henk H. Hoekstra, eds. *Hinter den Augen ein eigenes Bild: Film und Spiritualitat*. Zurich: Benzinger, 1991.

Kuryluk, Ewa. *Veronica and Her Veil: History, Symbolism, and Structure of a "True" Image*. Cambridge: Basil Blackwell, 1991.

Lauder, Robert E. *God, Death, Art and Love: The Philosophical Vision of Ingmar Bergman*. New York/Mahwah: Paulist, 1989.

Leach, Edmund. *Culture and Communication*. Cambridge: Cambridge University Press, 1982.

Le Fanu, Mark. *The Cinema of Andrei Tarkovsky*. London: British Film Institute, 1987.

Lexikon Religion im Film. Katholisches Institut für Medieninformation. Koln: KIM, 1992. (Also available as a computer program.)

Ludman, Rene. *Cinéma: Foi et morale*. Paris: Cerf, 1956.

Lull, James. *World Families Watching Television*. Newbury Park: Sage Publications, 1988.

Lynch, William. *The Image Industries*. New York: Sheed and Ward, 1959.

Mahony, Roger M. "Film Makers, Film Viewers: Their Challenges and Opportunities." *Cine&Media* 3 (1993), 13-22.

Malone, Peter. *The Film*. Melbourne/Sydney: Chevalier, 1971.

_____. *Films and Values*. Melbourne/Sydney: Chevalier, 1978.

_____. *Movie Christs and Antichrists*. New York: Crossroad, 1990.

Martin, Joel W., and Conrad E. Ostwalt, Jr. *Screening the Sacred: Religion, Myth, and Ideology in Popular Film*. Boulder/Oxford: Westview, 1995.

Martin, Thomas M. *Images and the Imageless: A Study in Religious Consciousness and Film*. East Brunswick: Bucknell University Press, 1981.

Martin-Barbero, J. *De los medios a las mediaciones: Communicacion, cultura y hegemonia*. Mexico: Editorial Gustavo Gili, 1987.

May, John R., ed. *Image and Likeness: Religious Visions in American Film Classics*. New York/Mahwah: Paulist, 1992.

May John R., and Michael Bird, eds. *Religion in Film*. Knoxville: University of Tennessee Press, 1982.

Medved, Michael. *Hollywood vs. America: Popular Culture and the War on Traditional Values*. New York: HarperCollins, 1992.

Menozzi, Daniel. *Les images: L'église et les arts visuals*. Paris: Cerf, 1991.

Miles, Margaret R. *Image as Insight: Visual Understanding in Western Christianity and Secular Culture*. Boston: Beacon, 1985.

Morley, David. *The Nationwide Audience: Structure and Decoding*. London: British Film Institute, 1980.

_____. *Family Television: Cultural Power and Domestic Leisure*. London: Comedia, 1986.

Newcomb, Horace, and Robert S. Alley. *The Producer's Medium: Conversations with Creators of American TV.* New York: Oxford University Press, 1983.

Nochlin, Linda. *Women, Art, and Power and Other Essays.* New York: Harper and Row, 1988.

Ong, Walter J. *Orality and Literacy: The Technologizing of the Word.* London: Methuen, 1982.

Paglia, Camille. *Sex, Art, and American Culture.* New York: Viking, 1992.

Pavelin, Alan. *Fifty Religious Films.* London: A. Pavelin, 1990.

Peters, J. M. *Het filmisch denken. Of de binnenkant van de beeldculuur.* Leuven: Amersfoort, 1989.

Postman, N. *Wij amuseren ons kapot. De geestdodende werking van de beeldbuis.* Baarn, 1985.

Roth, Wilhelm, and Bettina Thienhaus, eds. *Film und Theologie.* Diskussionen Kontroversen-Analysen. Stuttgart: Steinkopf, 1989.

Schillaci, Anthony. *Movies and Morals.* Notre Dame: Fides, 1968.

Schorb, B., ed. *Medienerziehung in Europa. Auf dem Weg zu einer Europaischen Medienkultur.* München: KoPad, 1992.

Schrader, Paul. *Transcendental Style in Film: Ozu, Bresson, and Dreyer.* Berkeley: University of California Press, 1972.

Silverstone, Roger. *The Message of Television: Myth and Narrative in Contemporary Culture.* London: Heinemann Educational Books, 1981.

Stierle, Karlheinz. *"Die Struktur narrativer Texte."* In *Funkkolleg Literatur I,* ed. H. Brackert and E. Lammert. Frankfurt: Fischer Taschenbuch, 1977, pp. 210-21.

Tavares de Barros, José. *La realidad imaginada: El video en America Latina.* Bogota: Paulinas, 1994.

Thorburn, David. *"Television as an Aesthetic Medium."* *Critical Studies in Mass Communication,* Vol. 4 (1987), 161-73.

Traudt, Paul J., and Cynthia M. Lont. *"Media-Logic-In-Use: The Family as Locus of Study."* In *Natural Audiences: Qualitative Research of Media Uses and Effects,* ed. Thomas R. Lindlof. Norwood: Ablex, 1987, pp. 139-160.

Wall, James M. *Church and Cinema: A Way of Viewing Film.* Grand Rapids, MI: Eerdmans, 1971.

Wissenschaft und Praxis in Kirche und Gesellschaft. Pastoraltheologie, Vol. 81, No. 12 (1992). [This issue of the scientific journal is dedicated to religion and film.]

White, Robert A. "Cultural Analysis in Communication for Development: The Role of Cultural Dramaturgy in the Creation of a Public Sphere." *Development,* Vol. 2 (1990), pp. 23-31.

_____. "Mass Media and Religious Imagination." *Communication Research Trend,* Vol. 8 (1987).

Zeitschrift für Padagogik und Theologie. Der Evangelische Erzieher, Vol. 44, No. 6 (1992). [Under the title *Religion im Film,* this issue of the scientific journal is dedicated to religion and film.]

Zwick, Reinhold. *"Blasphemie im Film. Motive und Probleme der Bewertung."* *Katechetische Blatter* 116 (1991), 540-49.

_____. *Montage im Markusevangelium.* Stuttgart: Katholisches Bibelwerk, 1989.

_____. *"Pfade zum Absoluten? Skizze einer kleinen Typologie des religiosen Films.* In *Theologie und asthetische Erfahrung. Beitrage zur Begegnung von Religion und Kunst,* ed. Walter Lesch. Darmstadt: Wissenschaftliche Buchgesellschaft, 1994.

About the Contributors

Diane Apostolos-Cappadona is professorial lecturer in religion and the arts at Georgetown University. She is the general editor for the twelve-volume series *The International Encyclopedia Dictionary of Women* and for the six-volume series *The International Encyclopedia of Religious Art*, both being developed for publication by Continuum Publishing Company. Dr. Apostolos-Cappadona has edited and coedited a number of books, including Jane Dillenberger's *Image and Spirit in Sacred and Secular Art* and Mircea Eliade's *Symbolism, the Sacred, and the Arts*, as well as *Art, Creativity, and the Sacred* and *Art as Religious Studies*. A contributor to *The Dictionary of Art, Encyclopedia of Comparative Iconography*, and *Harper's Dictionary of Religion*, she is the author of numerous articles for scholarly journals and of the forthcoming study *The Spirit and the Vision: The Influence of Christian Romanticism on 19th-Century American Art*. She is currently preparing *A Dictionary of Christian Art* and two new anthologies, *Theologians on Art: Documents and Sources in the History of Christian Art* and, with Lucinda Ebersole, *On Creating: Women in the Arts*.

Sylvain De Bleeckere completed his doctorate in philosophy at the Catholic University of Louvain in 1977. He is professor of philosophy of culture and art at the PHL-Department of Architecture (Campus Diepenbeek) and dean of Leuven's AGORA, Institute for Christianity and Philosophy, where he lectures on metaphysics and the history of contemporary philosophy. Since 1980 he has been an editor of *MediaFilm*, the Dutch journal for cinema studies. Interested in film in relation to the philosophy of art, Christian culture and spirituality, Dr. De Bleeckere has written and edited books on a wide variety of subjects – Andrei Tarkovsky and Krzysztof Kieslowski (including *Levenswaarden en levensverhalen,* a study of the *Decalogue* cycle), film and spirituality (*Zin in beeld*), and the religious dimension of our image culture. His most recent book is *Shadowlands: Van woord naar beeld in de menswording.* Every year in the city of Hasselt, he organizes a Day of Religious Film with the Kinepolis Group. He is also a member of the board of the Catholic Film League of Flanders, responsible for its film pedagogical policies.

Ambros Eichenberger, a Dominican priest, pursued his philosophical and theological studies in Vienna, Paris, and Fribourg. While extensively involved in the field of journalism and in youth pastoral ministry, he was director of the Swiss Catholic Film Center in Zurich from 1972 to 1994. As president of the International Catholic Organization for Cinema and Audio-visuals (OCIC) from 1980 to 1990, he promoted structures for church-related film-cultural activities in developing continents. The co-initiator of the project "Cinema and Spirituality" with various European universities, Father Eichenberger is currently a member of the Montecinemaverita Foundation, which is linked to the international film festival of Locarno. The author of two booklets on film (*Third World against Hollywood* and *Neither Western Nor Eastern: The Other Asian Cinema*), he contributes regularly to European film journals such as *ZOOM* and *film-dienst*, emphasizing East-European film cultures and the new cinema of Latin America, Africa and Asia.

Michael Paul Gallagher, a Jesuit priest, is a native of Sligo in Ireland. After studying literature and languages at universities in Dublin and Caen (France), he entered the Jesuits, pursuing further studies in Oxford and Belfast and at Johns Hopkins University, earning higher degrees in both literature and theology. For nearly twenty years he lectured on modern English and American literature at University College, Dublin. In 1990 Father Gallagher went to Rome to work in the Vatican, first with the Pontifical Council for Dialogue with Non-Believers and then with the Pontifical Council for Culture, while teaching theology part-time at the Gregorian University. During his Dublin years, he was film reviewer for the cultural quarterly *Studies*. Aside from many articles in the area of literary criticism, his main books are in spiritual theology, including *Help My Unbelief, Free to Believe, Struggles of Faith* and *Losing God*.

Johan G. Hahn, after a fourteen-year academic career, is managing director of a Netherlands-based group of public relations consultants, while continuing to lecture on public relations and audiovisual communication at both the University of Utrecht and the Catholic Theological University of Utrecht. He has also lectured as a visiting professor at various universities in Germany, Austria and Switzerland. His main areas of interest are public relations and questions related to the borderline of communication studies and religious studies: the communicative aspect of religion and the relation between audiovisual communication and religion. He has published on issues related to both fields and is developing a computer program for assisting with the analytical interpretation of films and television programs.

Peter Hasenberg studied English and German literature and film semiotics at the Ruhr University of Bochum, completing his doctoral degree in 1981. As an assistant lecturer at the university from 1978 to 1987, he taught courses for undergraduates on Shakespearean and modern drama, as well as popular fiction and theories of the novel. During his university years, he began his career as a film critic. Currently, he is responsible for the coordination of Catholic activities in the fields of film publications, film education and film politics for the Central Office for Media of the German Bishops' Conference. In addition to published articles on major film directors such as Wenders, Rivette, Kieslowski, and Gerrara, he has contributed to a project of the Catholic Film Commission, of which he is president, entitled *Religion im Film* (1992) – an encyclopedia of 1,400 films classified according to their religious content, with a database version for personal computers.

Henk Hoekstra, a Carmelite priest and a native of northern Holland, has studied philosophy and theology in Holland and communication sciences at the Catholic University of Louvain, and has taught mass media and group dynamics for the Catholic Theological Faculty of Amsterdam. He has been a member of the Department of Study and Research of Catholic Broadcast Holland (KRO) and is a senior staff member of the Catholic Media Center in Holland. Father Hoekstra is currently president of the International Catholic Organization for Cinema and Audiovisuals (OCIC), a member of the Pontifical Council for Social Communications, and also president of the Catholic Media Council in Aachen, Germany (CAMECO). The coauthor of *Media and Religious Communication* and *The Media Dialogue about Film and Television*, as well as author of many articles about media education, he now teaches media education, and film and spirituality at several universities and institutions.

Ray Kancharla holds degrees in art and theology. He is presently Communications Officer for Caritas India. For the last fifteen years, he has been teaching film criticism and leading workshops in media language and analysis. He is also a producer of video documentaries and a consultant for planning and achieving communications services in the context of church and society. He is currently the Vice President of OCIC Unda India – an affiliate of the international Catholic association for radio, TV, cinema and audiovisuals. His latest involvement is in communications research.

Peter Malone, an Australian Missionary of the Sacred Heart, is president of the Pacific Region of OCIC and a member of the International Directors' Board. While working in seminary formation and lecturing in Old Testament studies and theology, he has reviewed films since 1968 in the monthly *Annals Australia*. His books include *The Film, Films and Values, Movie Christs and Antichrists, The Australian Video Guide, Traces of God*, and *Myers Briggs Goes to the Movies*. Father Malone coordinated the publication of *Discovering an Australian Theology* and *Worth Watching: 30 Film Reviewers on Review*. He has edited the Australian theological journal *Compass* since 1972. He also works in adult education and spirituality at the Heart of Life Spirituality Centre, Canterbury, Victoria.

Joseph Marty, who has earned a *Maîtrise* in theology and a doctorate in Letters, is a priest of the diocese of Perpignan, France. Currently a member of the *Institut de cinéma Jean Vigo* in Perpignan, he teaches film – courses on cinema, the sacred and faith – in the *Faculté de Théologie* of the *Institut Catholique de Toulouse* and works at the *Centre Nationale l'Enseignement*

Religieux in Paris. Father Marty contributes to a number of journals and collaborates on the production of the Catholic television program "*Le Jour de Seigneur*," regularly giving homilies for televised Masses. The author of diverse works, he has published principally in the area of film. His books include *Ingmar Bergman: Une poétique du désir* and the forthcoming *André Delvaux: De l'inquiétante étrangeté à l'itinéraire initiatique*, in collaboration with Henri Agel.

John R. May is Alumni Professor of English and Religious Studies at Louisiana State University. In addition to books on apocalyptic themes in American fiction and on Flannery O'Connor, he is the coauthor of *Film Odyssey: The Art of Film as Search for Meaning* and *The Parables of Lina Wertmuller*, the coeditor of *Religion in Film*, and editor of *The Bent World: Essays on Religion and Culture* and *Image and Likeness: Religious Visions in American Film Classics*. He is completing a book of reflections on the worldview of the Apostles' Creed in literature and film, tentatively titled *Nourishing Faith through Fiction*.

José Tavares De Barros has degrees in philosophy and classical letters. His Master's thesis was on Christian Metz, and for his doctorate in comparative literature, his dissertation was on the intersemiotic relations between literature and cinema. After two years of intensive film study in Milan under the guidance of Nazzareno Taddei, S.J., he began his academic career at the Federal University of Minas Gerais, becoming a full professor of film theory, criticism and editing. The editor of some thirty short films and four feature films, Dr. Tavares was twice elected president of OCIC-Latin America. Presently film and video critic for *Jornal de Opinião*, a weekly publication of the Archdiocese of Belo Horizonte, he has edited two collections of essays for Ediciones Paulinas of Bogota, *La imagen nuestra de cada día* and *La realidad imaginada*.

Marjeet Verbeek has a doctorate in practical theology, with a specialization in mass communication studies, from the Catholic Theological University in Amsterdam, the Netherlands. During her theological studies, she was involved in researching the docudrama *Een Spannend Bestaan* ("An Exciting Existence"), produced and broadcast by the Ecumenical Broadcasting Organization (IKON) of the Netherlands. This television program was her final thesis. From 1986 until 1992, Dr. Verbeek worked at the Catholic Mediacentre in Driebergen, giving lectures and courses on audiovisual media, and publishing articles and study-books on ways of dealing with film and television in the family, religious communities, schools and parishes, as well as in theology. Although still active in this field, since 1992 she has done freelance work and is currently researching a television program on "art and religion" for the Catholic Broadcasting Organization (KRO) in The Netherlands.

François Vokouma is a native of Burkina Faso. After receiving his baccalaureate degree from De La Salle College, run by the Christian Brothers, he studied at the University Institute of Technology in Belfort, France. Returning to Burkina Faso in 1976, he obtained a *Licence* in Audiovisual Sciences from the African Institute for Cinematographic Training and Education (INAFEC). Later, he earned a *Maîtrise* in cinema from the University of Nancy II in France, specializing in audiovisual techniques. He has since served as a university assistant at INAFEC, then at INSE, the Institute for the Sciences of Education, both in Burkina Faso. From 1988 to 1993, he was director general of SONACIB, Burkina's National Society for Cinema Development and Distribution. Since 1977, he has been a founding member of the Panafrican Festival of Film and Television of Ouagadougou (FESPACO), participating in film festivals from Cannes to Los Angeles and Moscow.

Robert A. White, Jesuit director of the Center for Interdisciplinary Studies in Communication at the Gregorian University in Rome, is professor of media theory and social ethics of communication, and editor of the book series "Communication and Human Values" for Sage Publications. Since 1981 he has been coordinator with Peter Henrici, S.J. (now Bishop of Zurich), of the International Conferences on Theology and Communication held at Cavalletti. He is currently general editor for Sheed & Ward of their series "Communication, Culture and Theology," in which this volume appears. The cochair of the publications committee of the International Association for Media and Communication Research, Father White has written extensively on the mass media and the religious imagination, communication ethics, and communication and theological formation, contributing to *Communication Research Trends, The Church and Communication, Communication et Nouvelles Technologies,* among other journals and collections of essays.

Reinhold Zwick has studied Catholic theology and German language and literature. He received his doctorate in theology from the University of Regensburg, Germany, and is currently professor of Old and New Testament Exegesis at the Katholische Fachhochschule Freiburg. His book *Montage im Markusevangelium* deals with the narrative structure of Mark's Gospel from a media-transcendent angle, including filmic structuring. Dr. Zwick has published several articles on the dialogue of theology and film studies and is a member of the Catholic Film Commission of Germany. His current book project deals with the genre of the Jesus film and will provide a detailed analysis of works by Pier Paolo Pasolini, George Stevens, Roberto Rossellini and Franco Zeffirelli, among others.

Index